Register for Free Membership to

solut ions@syngress.com

Host Integrity Monitoring

Using Osiris and Samhain

Brian Wotring

Bruce Potter   Technical Editor

FOREWORD BY
MARCUS J. RANUM

KEY	SERIAL NUMBER
001	HJIRTCV764
002	PO9873D5FG
003	829KM8NJH2
004	HGTTYY87YT
005	CVPLQ6WQ23
006	VBP965T5T5
007	HJJJ863WD3E
008	2987GVTWMK
009	629MP5SDJT
010	IMWQ295T6T

PUBLISHED BY
Syngress Publishing, Inc.
800 Hingham Street
Rockland, MA 02370

Host Integrity Monitoring Using Osiris and Samhain

Printed in the United States of America
1 2 3 4 5 6 7 8 9 0
ISBN: 1-597490-18-0

Publisher: Andrew Williams
Acquisitions Editor: Gary Byrne
Technical Editor: Bruce Potter
Cover Designer: Michael Kavish

Page Layout and Art: Patricia Lupien
Copy Editor: Judy Eby
Indexer: Nara Wood

Distributed by O'Reilly Media, Inc. in the United States and Canada.

For information on rights, translations, and bulk sales, contact Matt Pedersen, Director of Sales and Rights, at Syngress Publishing; email matt@syngress.com or fax to 781-681-3585.

Syngress Acknowledgments

Syngress would like to acknowledge the following people for their kindness and support in making this book possible.

Syngress books are now distributed in the United States and Canada by O'Reilly Media, Inc. The enthusiasm and work ethic at O'Reilly are incredible, and we would like to thank everyone there for their time and efforts to bring Syngress books to market: Tim O'Reilly, Laura Baldwin, Mark Brokering, Mike Leonard, Donna Selenko, Bonnie Sheehan, Cindy Davis, Grant Kikkert, Opol Matsutaro, Steve Hazelwood, Mark Wilson, Rick Brown, Tim Hinton, Kyle Hart, Sara Winge, C. J. Rayhill, Peter Pardo, Leslie Crandell, Regina Aggio, Pascal Honscher, Preston Paull, Susan Thompson, Bruce Stewart, Laura Schmier, Sue Willing, Mark Jacobsen, Betsy Waliszewski, Kathryn Barrett, John Chodacki, Rob Bullington, Aileen Berg, and Wendy Patterson.

The incredibly hardworking team at Elsevier Science, including Jonathan Bunkell, Ian Seager, Duncan Enright, David Burton, Rosanna Ramacciotti, Robert Fairbrother, Miguel Sanchez, Klaus Beran, Emma Wyatt, Chris Hossack, Krista Leppiko, Marcel Koppes, Judy Chappell, Radek Janousek, and Chris Reinders for making certain that our vision remains worldwide in scope.

David Buckland, Marie Chieng, Lucy Chong, Leslie Lim, Audrey Gan, Pang Ai Hua, Joseph Chan, and Siti Zuraidah Ahmad of STP Distributors for the enthusiasm with which they receive our books.

David Scott, Tricia Wilden, Marilla Burgess, Annette Scott, Andrew Swaffer, Stephen O'Donoghue, Bec Lowe, Mark Langley, and Anyo Geddes of Woodslane for distributing our books throughout Australia, New Zealand, Papua New Guinea, Fiji, Tonga, Solomon Islands, and the Cook Islands.

Rainer Wichmann, Samhain creator, for sharing his expertise.

Author

Brian Wotring is the CTO of Host Integrity, Inc. a company that specializes in providing software to help monitor the integrity of desktop and server environments. Brian studied computer science and mathematics at the University of Alaska and the University of Louisiana.

Brian founded and maintains knowngoods.org, an online database of known good file signatures for a number of operating systems. He also is the developer of ctool, an application that provides limited integrity verification for prebound Mac OS X executables. Brian is currently responsible for the continued development of Osiris, an open source host integrity monitoring system.

As a long-standing member of The Shmoo Group of security and privacy professionals, Brian has an interest in secure programming practices, data integrity solutions, and software usability. Along with Bruce Potter and Preston Norvell, Brian coauthored the book, *Mac OS X Security*. Brian has presented at CodeCon and at the Black Hat Briefings security conferences.

Technical Editor

Bruce Potter is a Senior Associate at Booz Allen Hamilton. Prior to working at Booz Allen Hamilton, Bruce served as a software security consultant for Cigital in Dulles, VA. Bruce is the founder of the Shmoo Group of security professionals. His areas of expertise include wireless security, large-scale network architectures, smartcards, and promotion of secure software engineering practices. Bruce coauthored the books *802.11 Security* and *Mac OS X Security*. He was trained in computer science at the University of Alaska, Fairbanks.

Technical Reviewer

Rainer Wichmann is system administrator and research scientist at the University of Hamburg. He has studied physics and astronomy at the University of Heidelberg and received his Ph.D. in astronomy from there. He is responsible for the development of the Samhain host integrity monitoring system, and he has authored various other small applications in the fields of astronomy and computer security. He has written several computer security articles published by Samhain Labs. Rainer reviewed Chapter 7 covering Samhain.

Foreword Contributor

Marcus Ranum has been building computer security systems since the late 1980s, when he was an early innovator in designing Internet firewall systems and products. Since that time he has been involved in every aspect of the computer security field: writing, teaching, designing and developing products, consulting, and managing and founding successful product companies. He lives in Morrisdale, PA, with his wife, Katrina, and a small herd of horses, dogs, and cats.

Author Acknowledgments

First and foremost, I would like to thank my beautiful wife, Kaleigh, and my perfect son, Ezekiel. This book would never have happened without your patience and support. Thanks to Bruce Potter for providing solid technical editing for all of these chapters. Your practical perspective on security has made this book even better. Thanks to Holt Sorenson, who has always impressed me with his knowledge and authority on this subject, and for reviewing various related works of mine over the last couple of years. Thanks to Dave Hooley for reviewing some of my initial work on this book. Thanks to Rainer Wichmann for writing Samhain, and for reviewing the Samhain chapter. Thanks to Andrew Williams and Gary Byrne from Syngress for all of your help throughout this process.

I would like to express my gratitude to all of the people who have contributed to the development of Osiris over the years. Thanks to Preston Norvell and Bruce Potter for conceiving the idea and making it a reality. Thanks to Paul Holman for providing invaluable contributions to the original design, specifically with respect to security and usability.

Additional thanks to John Viega, Ben Laurie, Rodney Thayer, Tina Bird, Crispin Cowan, Jon Callas, Brian Caswell, Spike Illaqua, Len Sassaman, Adam Shand, Peter Johanson, Duane Dunston, Karen Wieprecht, Luke West, Peter Frey, Lance Ahern, Tim Laughlin, Jeremy Verne, Robert Tarrall, Orrie Gartner, Brian Daugherty, Scott Hallock, Zach DiUbaldo, Jeremy Gebben, David Thiel, Jason Frisvold, John A. Sullivan, Andrew Steingruebl, Aaron Racine, Yuri D'elia, Richard Johnson, Alan Sparks, Andrew Norsworthy, and Indra's Net in Boulder.

Brian Wotring
brian@hostintegrity.com

x

Contents

Foreword

Are you comfortable with the idea of being ignorant and complacent? I bet you're not—very few people are! Yet, somehow, in the last 10 years of computer networking, we've built massive networks of systems that we literally do not understand. They are like huge, uncharted forests, with system/network administrators who are afraid to wander into the far reaches out of fear that something may grab them in the darkness. From a standpoint of security, virtually all the networks I've seen in the last five years are out of control—if you ask a system administrator "what applications do you have running on your network?" you can expect little more than a blank stare in response. Ask system administrators "do you know which files on your servers change on a regular basis?" and many of them will reply, "I'd just be happy if I knew *where* my servers *are*."

Let's start with some history. Back in the mainframe days of computing, administrators used to follow a mysterious process called "change control." Basically, it's the idea that you should follow a process to *understand* and *manage* the updates, upgrades, and alterations to your system. Mainframe administrators consider change control absolutely crucial to keeping the system up and running reliably. On the other hand, users view change control as an impediment to getting things done. They think that following the change control process is too slow and that it's basically a trick the system analysts use to protect their position of importance.

But the desktop revolution changed all that: suddenly people who could afford a relatively inexpensive computer could do whatever they wanted with it, when they wanted, without asking or telling anyone. It's impossible to overstate the importance of the desktop revolution to computing because it simultaneously liberated computing by driving costs down and stimulated the development of hundreds of thousands of user-oriented applications. It also murdered the art of system administration.

So, welcome to this book. This book is about one of the crucial (and often ignored) aspects of system and security management: host integrity protection. Fundamentally, the idea of host integrity protection is all about understanding the changes that happen to your system—friendly or hostile, deliberate or accidental—and understanding the impact of those changes. In other words, it's change control in a hostile environment. Best of all, this book is written by Brian Wotring, a man who has been there and done that—someone who has designed and deployed host integrity monitoring systems, used them, and relied on their results. It's hard to overstate the value of such experience; people like Brian, who has worked on a problem with his own hands, are the best-qualified people to teach about it because they understand what's real and what's merely theoretical. And they can explain the difference. Books like the one you're holding are the survival kits for the future of computing. They're full of the important clues that you're going to need if you want to be one of the survivors instead of the statistics.

—*Marcus J. Ranum*
mjr@ranum.com

Preface

In February 2004, portions of Microsoft's source code for Windows NT and Windows 2000 were posted to Internet Relay Chat (IRC) chat rooms and eventually all over the Internet. In March 2004, Cisco took a similar blow when a Russian Web site reported that roughly 800MB of Cisco's IOS source code had been stolen. In the following days, an analysis of the stolen material revealed that it was taken from one of Cisco's Sun servers; thus, it is reasonable to conclude that it was taken from within Cisco's corporate network. In August 2003, the primary File Transfer Protocol (FTP) servers for the GNU project were compromised and all of the source code packages they served were at risk.

What is interesting about all three of these incidents is that the initial compromise was not discovered for months, and in some cases it was an outside source that brought attention to the fact. This is not a good thing. Cisco's IOS platform is the most widely deployed networking platform to date, Microsoft owns the home desktop market, and GNU software is increasingly being deployed in many small business and enterprise environments. Monitoring the integrity of host environments used in the development and distribution of such critical software should not be considered optional. Furthermore, detecting a compromised host should not take months.

About This Book

This book provides you with the information necessary to understand the what, why, and how of host integrity monitoring. My goal was to provide a book that walks people through the entire process of establishing host integrity monitoring, including the fundamentals, understanding threats, planning, deployment, administration, and response. Too often people skip to the deployment part and just throw software at a problem. Effective host integrity involves more than just installing a security application; it is an ongoing process that involves understanding your host environments, understanding threats, and developing a well-thought-out plan for deployment, administration, and incident response.

The first half of this book focuses on what you should know about host integrity. This information is foundation building and is applicable to any product or environment. The second half focuses on the deployment and administration of Osiris and Samhain, two of the most popular and widely deployed open source host integrity monitoring systems (HIMS). Both have enjoyed recognition and integration into commercial software products. Osiris is the cornerstone of a host-based integrity-monitoring product sold by Host Integrity, Inc., and has been featured in many books. Advanced implementations of Beltane are available for commercial use, and Samhain was featured in *Linux Magazine* and numerous online publications. Both of these products have been deployed in small business, government, educational, and commercial environments.

This book is not a complete reference for any particular host environment. Operating systems are constantly changing; therefore, this chapter focuses more on the core elements of commonly deployed desktop and server environments, including FreeBSD (and the like), Mac OS X, Linux, Solaris, and Windows 2000, XP, and Advanced Server 2003. However, much of the emphasis is on the principles of host integrity that are common to all systems.

After reading this book, you will have a solid understanding of what is involved in planning and deploying an effective host integrity monitoring system. You will learn the importance of monitoring various elements of the host environment, how to plan for deployment, and how to interpret and respond to integrity violations. You will also learn the ins and outs of deploying Osiris and Samhain.

Target Audience

This book was written with intermediate to advanced security and system administrators in mind. The information is relevant for networks of all sizes, from home networks to large-scale desktop and server environments. This book assumes that you have a basic understanding of system administration and that you purchased this book because you want to learn more about the fundamentals of host integrity and how to properly deploy and maintain a HIMS.

This book is also valuable for system and security administrators that are already using a failed host-based monitoring scheme and are looking for a simpler, more effective means of monitoring the integrity of their host environments. As a security administrator, it is important to understand the details surrounding the proper deployment and usage of host integrity monitoring tools in order to be effective in maintaining the security of managed hosts.

Finally, this book will appeal to anyone who wants to learn about monitoring host integrity, what it does and does not include, and how open source software can be used to establish an effective HIMS. This includes computer security professionals, analysts, and consultants who must stay abreast of host-based security for their clients.

Organization and Content

This book consists of nine chapters and three appendices. It does not have to be read in sequence, but read Chapter 1 first, as it provides a realistic perspective on host integrity monitoring, what it includes, and why it is necessary, and presents information that is built on throughout the rest of the book.

Chapter 1, "Host Integrity," reveals everything that is involved in maintaining the integrity of your hosts. Host integrity monitoring is introduced and some arguments for and against it are explored.

Chapter 2, "Understanding the Terrain," explores many areas of the host environment with respect to establishing effective host integrity monitoring. Topics include users, groups, files and file systems, the kernel, libraries, runtime issues, network stacks, and nonvolatile memory.

Chapter 3, "Understanding Threats," examines some of the most common threats to the integrity of a host environment. It looks at malicious applications, internal threats, rootkits, and circumvention of integrity monitoring systems. It also looks at some of the most popular and successful worms, and examines the effects they have on their environment.

Chapter 4, "Planning," is dedicated to walking you through the process of planning the deployment of a HIMS. It looks at network topology, system architectures, requirements and security policies, and general considerations related to management.

Chapter 5, "Host Integrity Monitoring with Open Source Tools," introduces Osiris and Samhain. It briefly looks at their background and history, how each of these systems works, and their respective strengths and weaknesses.

Chapter 6, "Osiris," provides in-depth practical information about how to properly deploy, configure, and administer the Osiris HIMS.

Chapter 7, "Samhain," provides in-depth practical information about how to properly deploy, configure, and administer the Samhain HIMS.

Chapter 8, "Log Monitoring and Response," deals with life after deployment. Solutions for logging, reporting, and noise reduction are provided. In addition, it discusses some practical considerations to aid in the incident response process.

Chapter 9, "Advanced Strategies," outlines some progressive techniques that can be used to strengthen and fine-tune your host integrity monitoring deployment. It looks at audits for SUID/SGID and rogue executables, fire drills, and methods for dealing with prebinding and prelinking.

Appendix A, "Monitoring Linksys Devices," provides detailed information about how to monitor some popular Linksys routers using Osiris.

Appendix B, "Extending Osiris and Samhain with Modules," looks at the modular interfaces to Osiris and Samhain for specialized deployment requirements.

Appendix C, "Additional Resources," provides a list of resources that are helpful in complementing the content presented in this book.

Support and Contact Information

A Web site (http://www.syngress.com/solutions) has been established specifically for this book. This site contains all of the source code examples and scripts used throughout the practical chapters in this book.

For further information regarding this book, Osiris, Samhain, or host integrity monitoring, feel free to send me an e-mail at **brian@hostintegrity.com**.

## Chapter 1

Host Integrity

Solutions in this chapter:

- **Introduction to Host Integrity**
- **Introducing Host Integrity Monitoring**
- **Arguments against Integrity Monitoring**
- **Arguments for Integrity Monitoring**

- ☑ **Summary**
- ☑ **Solutions Fast Track**
- ☑ **Frequently Asked Questions**

Introduction to Host Integrity

Right now, you are settling down to read this book, and I am reading your e-mail. Not really, but how can you know for sure? If you are like most people, you have taken a number of steps to protect your hosts. Firewalls serve to deflect attacks, but complete protection is not a reality. Most software is poorly written, and there is a great deal of software standing between you and your e-mail. So, again, if an attack against your e-mail server were successful, how soon would you know? More importantly, how would you know what was compromised in the attack?

A great deal of energy is directed at perimeter security, and for good reason. Network monitoring can detect that an attack has occurred, but not whether that attack was successful. Attacks do not always originate from outside the network. Efforts are made to secure hosts, but compromises are a reality. Most countries have militaries to defend their borders and various levels of law enforcement to maintain order on the inside. Banks put alarms on their doors, and they place cameras and armed guards inside to keep watch over valuables. In addition to monitoring the perimeter, you also need to ensure the integrity of your hosts by monitoring their environment. Most corporations are well aware of the need for network security, but many are still learning of the importance of implementing host-based integrity solutions.

What Is Integrity?

In the world of computer security, when we discuss the integrity of a network or host, we mean adherence to an established security policy. Integrity is subjective and has no useful meaning without specifying which states or activities are acceptable.

This book discusses integrity at the host level. What is considered a valid state can vary significantly from host to host. For example, the integrity of a production build server may require that specific libraries and compiler tools not be tampered with. The integrity of a Web server may require that Hypertext Markup Language (HTML) and server configuration files not be altered. User logins might be a regular occurrence on an Internet service provider's dial-up server, but suspect on the provider's corporate Web server. Again, the thing to remember about integrity is that it is not an absolute. As an administrator or security officer, you establish what integrity means for each of your managed hosts.

Integrity can be threatened in many ways. Authorized users may attempt to elevate privileges using local exploits. A malicious attacker may scan your network looking for hosts that are vulnerable to remote exploits, or an administrator may install substandard software that leaves the host open to attack. Aside from substandard software, many security problems stem from the misconfiguration of software.

As a result, there are many different types of tools that administrators and security officers use to manage the integrity of their hosts. Each of these tools deals with certain types of threats better than others; therefore, the deployment of multiple tools is best. Truly effective host integrity requires many layers of security. The process of protecting at multiple layers is called *security in depth*.

Host Intrusion Detection

What constitutes a Host Intrusion Detection System (HIDS) is often the subject of debate. I have seen a simple file integrity checker labeled as a HIDS. In other cases, I have seen products that monitor incoming network traffic, logs, and configuration files labeled as a HIDS. In any case, a HIDS analyzes and reports on data that originates from the host environment as opposed to the network. The goal is to detect and report on changes that are suspicious or symptomatic of an intrusion. Traditionally, a HIDS analyzes log files, but it can also monitor events such as file access requests, user login/logout events, and buffer overflow attempts.

One advantage of a HIDS is that you can customize what is considered suspicious on a per-host basis. However, a truly effective HIDS will correlate events that occur on many hosts, factoring in time and input from a known bad signature database. A Hybrid Intrusion Detection System (IDS) is even more sophisticated than a HIDS; a hybrid IDS merges the management of both network- and host-based IDSes. Many security professionals consider this approach better than distinct host- and network-based intrusion detection deployments because, in theory, it is easier to correlate events that occur on both landscapes.

The two most common reasons for a HIDS deployment are to complement Network Intrusion Detection Systems (NIDS) and to keep tabs on any insider attacks or abuse. A HIDS is usually a passive participant in the world of host integrity, meaning that it detects and reports. A HIDS does not alter the host environment or attempt to engage suspicious behavior. For that, you must look at intrusion prevention.

Host Intrusion Prevention

A Host Intrusion Prevention System (HIPS) is newer than a HIDS, with the main difference being that a HIPS can take action toward mitigating a detected threat. For example, a HIPS deployment may detect the host being port-scanned and block all traffic from the host issuing the scan. A HIPS often monitors memory, kernel, and network state, log files, and process execution. A HIPS also protects against buffer overflows.

The advantage of intrusion prevention is that you do not have to wait for a security officer to respond before preventive measures are taken to maintain host integrity. This approach may prove helpful, especially because recent studies show how vulnerable systems can be compromised in minutes. A HIPS is often both signature and anomaly based. Unlike signature-based systems that can defend against only known bad signatures, an anomaly-based HIPS attempts to distinguish normal from abnormal behavior. This capability helps when a threat either has no known signature, or the signature database has not yet been updated.

The disadvantages of a HIPS is that the response taken may render the host useless or possibly impact the availability of a critical resource. It is one thing for an IDS to issue a false positive, but a false positive with some kind of reflexive action could be worse.

Like a HIDS, the functionality of a HIPS can vary significantly with each product. A good example of a successful and effective HIPS is Immunix, an intrusion prevention system (IPS) for Linux. Basically, Immunix takes access control that is normally applied at the user level and applies it to applications. Administrators can set up profiles that specify exactly what certain executables can and cannot do. Since a great deal of attacks involve the abuse of software, this method of intrusion prevention can be very effective. In this case, attacks can be stopped before they occur.

File Integrity Checking

File integrity checkers are programs designed specifically to watch for changes to files and to report on those changes. The basic concept is that periodic snapshots of certain files are taken and compared with the previous snapshot. The first version of Tripwire, written by Gene Kim and Gene Spafford, was a file integrity checker. Like most file integrity checkers, this version of Tripwire is limited because it is generally not client or server based. The problem with this is that all of the data is stored on the hosts themselves and at risk to tampering. Another problem with file integrity checkers is that they are notorious for being cumbersome to administer because of their deployment architecture and the amount of false positives that they tend to generate.

Security Administration

Security administration involves anything from patching and updating vulnerable software, to conducting penetration testing and fixing any of the vulnerabilities discovered in a host environment. Staying abreast of critical software security fixes and patches goes a long way toward maintaining the integrity of a system. Intrusion detection and prevention software applications can do only so much. The older the software updates, the easier it is for someone to unleash havoc on your systems. This is true of both internal and external threats.

Change Management

Change management has less to do with intrusions and more to do with auditing and policy enforcement. Change management attempts not only to pinpoint unwanted changes but also to note which user made the change and why. Another difference is that change management products often have the ability to roll back undesired changes to the last known good state. The commercial version of Tripwire is an example of a commercial change management solution. An open source example of this is Radmind (*http://www.radmind.org*).

The integrity of a host or set of hosts is not always about breaching firewalls, buffer overflows, or privilege escalation; it is also about enforcing your security policy. In the event that something bad happens, having a detailed audit trail of activity surrounding the event can prove very helpful in pinpointing the problem, responding to it, and preventing future violations.

Network Security

What does network security have to do with host integrity? The answer is security in depth. Network intrusion detection, inline IPS, intelligent network configurations, and firewalls all do their part to shield hosts from malicious traffic. Network security plays an important role because it is the first line of defense at keeping the bad guys out.

Ideally, all threats would be caught by perimeter or network defenses. Unfortunately, this is not always the case. As I write this, three new Internet Explorer (IE) vulnerabilities for XP SP2 have been published. Network security cannot always prevent you from unintentionally inviting threats onto your desktop, but sometimes it can help prevent threats from spreading to other hosts. In addition, host integrity monitoring (HIM) can serve as a valuable audit mechanism for your perimeter security. In some cases, it will be possible to detect how an attacker was able to compromise a host. You can sometimes use that information to strengthen your perimeter security so that it does not happen again.

Introducing Host Integrity Monitoring

Now that we have looked at host integrity in general, let's focus specifically on HIM—that is, what it is, how it works, and how it fits into the world of host integrity.

What Is Host Integrity Monitoring?

HIM is the recurring assessment of a host's environment based on a known good state or policy. A host can be a home user's PC, a corporate e-mail or Web server, a production build system, or a computer in an Internet café. A host can also be a router or a switch.

As shown in Figure 1.1, host's environment can be broken down into three categories: files, configurations, and runtime. Files are the most obvious and include the content and attributes associated with individual files as well as the file systems themselves. The configurations of an environment are higher-level elements such as users and groups, access control, configurations for services, and basically anything that dictates the initial state of the system. The runtime involves the dynamics of a running system such as the state of a network stack (e.g., open ports), user login/logout activities, kernel state (e.g., extensions, services, drivers), system resources such as memory, and the running process table.

Figure 1.1 Functional Overview of HIM

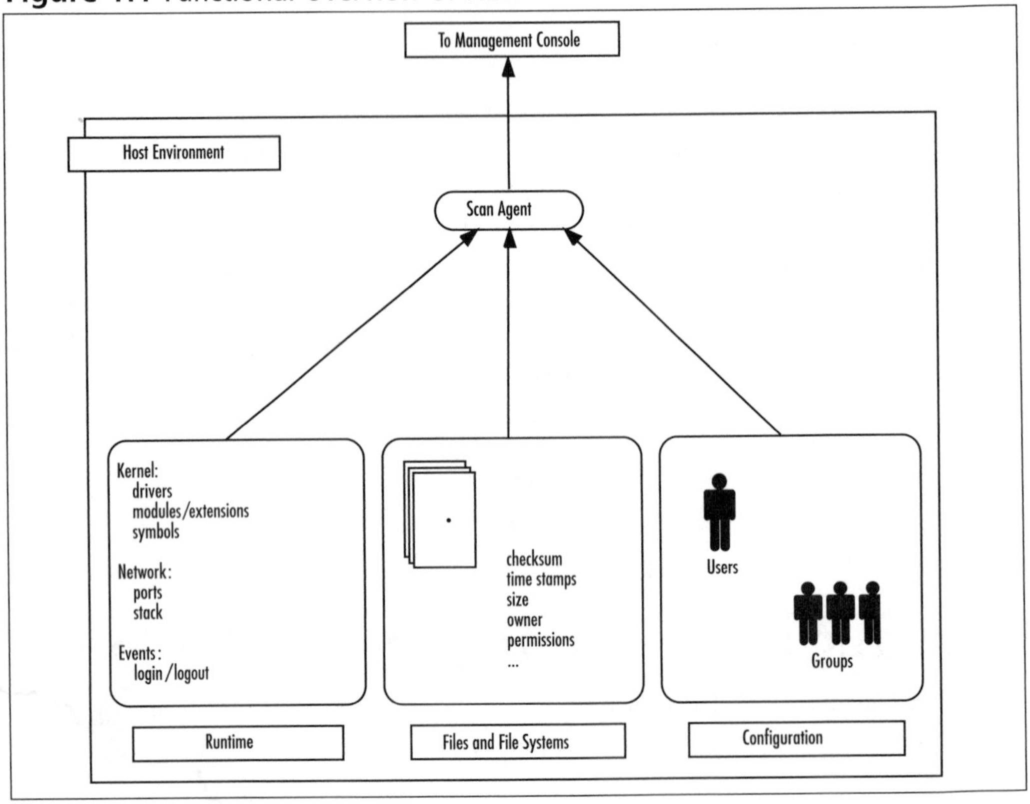

The overall goal is to detect and report on changes in the environment. However, things get tricky when we try to establish which of the detected changes are good, and which are not. Enter the concept of *integrity*. It may be that a change seems perfectly reasonable on one host, but suspect on another. For example, adding an entry to the */etc/passwd* file might be a regular occurrence on an Internet service provider's dial-up server, but not on its corporate Web server. Or it may be that an added entry is fine as long as the newly added UID is non-zero.

The main distinction between HIM and host intrusion detection is that the purpose of a HIDS is to detect an attack or an intrusion, whereas HIM is concerned with any changes to the environment that violate security policies. There are many disparate products that are referred to as host-based intrusion detection systems; you may be able to pigeonhole some into reporting all kinds of change, but in general this is not the case. However, intrusions are often the most concerned with changes to a host environment, so HIM applications usually pay a lot of attention to detecting changes related to an attack or intrusion.

HIM can also be used to ensure that the environment of a host or set of hosts has not been compromised. Often, this is the only way a violation of corporate policy is detected. Now that we know what a HIM system is, let's take a closer look at some of its most important attributes.

How Do HIM Systems Work?

A HIM system comprises software agents and at least one management console. The details of how these two components interact may vary, but in general, the agents gather information about the host environment, and the console performs analysis and reporting on that data. Because you are dealing exclusively with data that originates from the host environment, it is necessary to install an agent onto each host that is being monitored. This is often referred to as an *agent-based deployment scenario*.

Initially, each monitored host is scanned to create a *baseline*. The baseline is considered to be the trusted data set. This trusted data set contains information about the host environment, including file attributes, users, groups, kernel files, kernel modules and extensions, network ports, and login/logout events—basically anything about a host that is worth monitoring. The baseline is usually stored in some type of database.

Tools & Traps…

Baseline Integrity

It is strongly recommended that the baseline be established before the system is deployed or placed onto a network. Collecting baseline information from a pristine system allows you to start monitoring from a known good state. (See Chapter 4, "Planning.")

Monitoring can be either *inline* or *polling*. An inline HIM system is resident in the kernel and is able to monitor changes and events as they occur. A polling HIM system takes periodic snapshots of the host environment. Most HIM systems are polling. The advantage of a polling HIM system is that it can be easily ported to many systems, and does not necessarily involve running in the kernel. The disadvantage is that changes that occur between polling may go undetected. The advantage of an inline HIM system is that it is in a better position to monitor lower-level events such as binding to a privileged network port, system calls, and other kernel-level events. The disadvantage is that specialized development is necessary for each platform that the agent runs on. The two HIM systems discussed in this book, Osiris and Samhain, are polling HIM systems.

Polling a HIM system involves regularly scanning a host and comparing the results of the scan against the baseline. The security officer is then notified (e.g., e-mail, logs, paging) of the detected changes. As time goes on, the list of deltas between the current environment and the baseline grows. Each HIM system has its own way of updating the baseline.

Now that you have a basic understanding of the function of HIM systems, let's take a closer look at some key characteristics, including the scanning process, management, and common feedback vectors.

Scanning the Environment

Scan agents are used to periodically gather specific information about the host environment. Like a HIDS, they are passive; that is, they do not alter the environment. Scanning can be initiated by the agents themselves or by the console, depending on the design of the product. Agents that initiate a scan then must initiate a network connection to the console (non-trusted to trusted), as opposed to the console connecting to the agent (trusted to non-trusted). Depending on your network configuration and security policies, one of these scenarios may be preferable.

The polling frequency is determined by policy (why you are monitoring) and terrain (what you are monitoring). Like any security product, a HIM system has a trade-off with usability. Monitoring your executables every 10 seconds will most likely end up in a fight for resources and not be well received. The two most common (and important) questions that I have encountered when helping people deploy a HIM system are (1) What do I monitor? and (2) How often? The remaining chapters in this book will help you answer these two questions.

Scanning Files

Files make up a majority of a host's environment. They are used to store important data, and executed to operate on that data, which is why files and file systems are given so much attention. Secret or important information eventually ends up in some kind of file.

A HIM system monitors the attributes and content of files. The attribute list varies from system to system, and includes things such as the size, access permissions, and the last time the file was changed. A HIM system monitors the content of files the same way a file integrity checker does: with cryptographic checksums. Some HIM systems can monitor the actual content of certain critical system configuration files, but for most files, only the signature is maintained.

Files can also have hidden attributes or hidden data such as streams or forks, and some suffer from the efficiency of pre-binding or pre-linking. (See Chapter 2, "Understanding the Terrain.")

Scanning Configurations

HIM systems break away from file integrity checkers when they begin to monitor other elements of the host environment. This involves having an understanding of certain system files or stores, such as user and group databases. Sometimes this is in regular files (e.g., */etc/passwd*), and sometimes not, such as with NIS or NetInfo. Agents must know the specifics of how to acquire this information so that it can be included as part of the data collected during the scanning process. Other examples of agents scanning configurations include the kernel security level on Berkeley Software Distribution (BSD) systems, the service pack level on Windows, the Windows registry, and an Apache Web server configuration. Configuration scanning can be very helpful in detecting vulnerabilities in a host's configuration, whether intentional or not.

Scanning the Runtime

Scan agents that can collect information from the runtime environment provide a great deal of insight into the state and activities taking place on a host. Having a way to pin down a time window on certain changes can be very helpful in highlighting an attack vector, or filling in the gaps on a suspicious set of activities. Examples of runtime scanning include monitoring the state of the kernel and kernel extensions, user login and logout events, the content of system logs, system calls, the system process list, the use of network ports, and system resources (e.g., memory and disk usage).

Sometimes, monitoring the runtime is the first (or only) indication of a problem. The following is an example.

At a previous job, I came in one day to the following Osiris alert regarding one of our build machines:

```
[223][darwin][missing][mod_kmods][kern:com.apple.driver.AppleUSBKeyboard]
```

At first I thought this was an odd alert, but then realized that the keyboard for that system must be unplugged. As it turned out, someone had taken the keyboard from the system. In this case, the intention was not malicious in nature; no files were altered, and no system configuration changes were made. This could have been written off as a useless alert, but it was not. This was a trusted build machine and it was now apparent that anyone in the building had physical access to it. Runtime monitoring is extremely helpful.

Agent Security

Because scan agents operate in an environment that may be compromised, they often have mechanisms to mitigate attempts at tampering and subversion. Agents may have keys built into their executables and they may run self-checks as part of their normal initiation. Trusted communication with the console may be further established by maintaining pre-shared keys in memory so that start and stop events leave a mark. Or the agent process may be hidden from the normal methods of viewing the system process table, with the intent being to hide the fact that the host is being monitored.

Another useful feature is *privilege separation*. Agents almost always have to conduct privileged operations. Reading root-owned files and monitoring the list of kernel modules are good examples. It is not wise for the entire function of the agent process to run with root or admin privileges, especially when it is bound to a network port. Superuser privileges are only needed on occasion. Privilege separation is good for many applications of this nature, and goes a long way toward preventing an attacker from beating on the agent process itself, in an attempt to exploit a potential software defect or compromise the monitoring process.

Agents are software, and software can be smashed, but that does not mean that anti-tampering schemes like this are useless. I have been witness to more than one case where a HIM system was clearly in place and yet the attacker did not bother to disable or subvert it.

Centralized Management

Scanning agents send all of the data gathered from their environment to a management host for processing. This is important for two reasons: administration and data integrity.

Good for Administration

Having centralized management for monitored hosts is extremely valuable and may be necessary if you are monitoring hundreds or thousands of environments. From an administrative standpoint, centralized management saves time and helps prevent human error.

As an example, imagine that you are an administrator at a university, and required to monitor the integrity of 500 desktop environments using the open source version of Tripwire. This release of Tripwire is not centrally managed. Now, imagine you have to make changes to each host's local configuration file. As software is installed, many of these hosts will need baseline updates. Dealing with these tasks on a host-by-host basis is not only impractical, but also poor security administration. It will lead to poor configuration, gaps in monitoring, and ignored alerts.

Another administrative task made easier under centralized management is backups. If all configurations and scan data archives are stored in a single location, it is more likely that you will implement a sound backup procedure.

Good for Data Integrity

Centralized management allows for scan data and agent configurations for each host to be stored in a single secure location, and not on the less-trusted host environments. This goes a long way toward protection against tampering or loss. Scan agents run in environments that are not always trusted. In fact, the reason the agents exist in the first place is to detect a compromise of their environment. If a host is compromised or suffers a hardware failure, all of the data associated with that host could be lost or rendered unreliable. Backups can help with the loss problem, but again, this becomes an unnecessary administrative burden.

A good HIM system will keep the amount of data stored on a host to a minimum. Usually, this is not much more than an executable. Configuration files can be pushed to the host when needed, and scan data can be sent directly to the console, never having to be written to disk.

Because the management console is the keeper of sensitive data such as configurations and environment scans, it is absolutely critical that this host be locked down and protected at all costs, including both network and physical security. Although centralized management is beneficial, it can also be a single point of failure (see Chapter 4, "Planning").

Feedback

One of the most important aspects of any HIM system is the ability to provide feedback on detected changes. Logs are the most common way that feedback is given. Depending on the product, there are a variety of methods for alerting a security officer, which often vary depending on the urgency of the alert. Other alert vectors include e-mail, a pipe, an application, or even a page.

More important than having the correct feedback mechanisms, is making sure that feedback is being received. Logs are useless if they are not analyzed or monitored. To be truly effective, any alerts generated by the HIM system must be audited in a timely fashion (see Chapter 8, "Analysis and Response").

Arguments against Integrity Monitoring

This section explores some common arguments against deploying a HIM system. As with any security system, identifying and examining any weaknesses you can find is worthwhile, because then you can focus your efforts on finding ways to address those weaknesses.

The following arguments are not directed at any specific HIM system, but rather against HIM software in general.

Administrative Overhead

One of the more traditional arguments against HIM is that it requires a great deal of administrative overhead. This involves developing plans for deployment, configuration, response, and integration.

Unlike network monitoring, host-based monitoring requires some type of software agent to be installed on each host. This may involve a mass deployment effort, and a means to keep these software agents up to date for features and security. With large corporations, it is more likely that the information technology (IT) staff is familiar with this responsibility. If not, you may decide that it is only worthwhile to monitor a handful of critical hosts.

Another administrative issue with HIM is configuration. Again, unlike network monitoring, HIM software is configured on a per-host basis. The difference in use for any given host is limitless. As an administrator, you must examine each monitored host and understand what integrity means for that environment, to properly configure the monitoring system. This also means an investment in understanding the specifics of the HIM system software.

Integrity monitoring systems generate alerts just like an IDS system. As an administrator, you must be prepared to receive and respond to those alerts. The response will vary depending on the nature of the alert. Sometimes, this may require you to take the box offline for further analysis. Other times, it may require you only to restore a change to the environment. Like an IDS, a HIM system will also produce false positives. Again, since each host is often different, a false positive will require revisiting the requirements for that particular host and adjusting the configuration accordingly.

Finally, HIM systems have their own space in any security architecture. As a security administrator, you must understand the role of the HIM system and how it can be made to complement other tools in your security arsenal. Although it may be possible to integrate the management of the HIM system with the other management tools you are using, it is more than likely that deployment involves the use of yet another management interface.

There are a number of administrative burdens associated with security tools. You must make a conscious decision on whether you have the administrative resources to make HIM a worthwhile investment. It may be that you choose to deploy integrity monitoring for a thousand boxes on your network, or that you have the resources to monitor only a select few critical servers. In the end, it is all about maintaining the security of your environments. If you have to scale back in order to fulfill other more important security tasks, so be it.

Too Much Noise!

HIM systems report on all types of change. The goal in fine-tuning a HIM system is to prevent legitimate changes from generating alerts. Therefore, a false positive in a HIM system is essentially an alert regarding a legitimate change. If these false positives are too frequent, it may frustrate the administrator, and changes that would normally be given attention may go unseen. They get lost in the noise, so to speak.

Although this is something that can be classified as administrative overhead, I have singled it out because it is a legitimate gripe about HIM. Given the administrative overhead in deploying any agent-based integrity monitoring system, security administrators will most likely shelve these applications if they are too noisy. The academic version of Tripwire was often so cumbersome to use with respect to false positives that it was not uncommon for administrators to stop using it.

Return on Investment

Another question regarding HIM is whether or not the visibility it provides is worth the effort put into deployment and maintenance. To be effective, you must first define integrity and then understand the host environment enough to know how to maintain that integrity. Finally, the administrator must understand and deploy a software solution that satisfies the requirements. In the end, how do you know that all your work has paid off? This is not an easy question to answer.

Consider for a minute what would happen if you did not install monitoring software. Now imagine that a malicious attacker has compromised a system or that a disgruntled employee has taken aim at a production server. When would you be aware of these attacks? How much damage would be done in the meantime? How much different would the outcome be in these situations if you did or did not have integrity monitoring? There is no doubt that a properly deployed IMS will detect violations; the question is whether the detection is worth the administrative cost of deploying and maintaining the system, and whether it will detect the most important of violations. There are a lot of variables at work here. Determining cost-effectiveness is equally as complicated as with any IDS.

Questions to ask include the following: Is the detection system timely enough? What is the worst thing that can happen as a result of not staying on top of the integrity of these environments? What are the risks? Is it monetary loss? Is it a breach of privacy? Is it public humiliation? These risks are subjective and in turn are hard to quantify. As a result, it is difficult to assess whether the return on investment (ROI) for HIM is justifiable.

Another thing to consider with respect to ROI is how much administrative effort your environment requires. If you have thousands of hosts that are configured the same, it may be easy to deploy and maintain agent-based monitoring software. However, if you have many disparate configurations, the administrative costs of setup, deployment, fine-tuning, and response may be overwhelming.

Subversion

Another argument that surfaces from time to time is that HIM tools can be subverted. If an attacker knows that a host is being monitored, there are various ways they can compromise a system without the integrity monitoring software detecting it. An attacker can slip in under the radar or attack the integrity monitoring software directly. This section examines some ways in which HIM software can subverted.

Attacking the Agent

A simple means of attacking a host integrity system is to kill the monitoring agent process. The basic idea is that if the monitoring agent is not running, it cannot perform scans of the environment and thus cannot report on any detected changes. The problem with this approach is that it is probably not going to go unnoticed for very long. This may have worked 10 years ago, but most modern integrity monitoring systems produce an alert if a scheduled scan fails to occur for any reason. Also, the attacker would then have to clean up any log messages that occurred as a result of the process going away. These logs may be system logs or logs produced by the agent process as it is shutting down. Furthermore, if the host is set up to pipe logs to a logging host, tampering with the logs will be a more involved process.

Notes from the Underground…

Script Kiddies

A couple of years back, a friend of mine detected that one of his servers was compromised. Although the attackers were able to root the box, it was clear (after performing some analysis on the system) that they had no real idea what to do with their newly conquered prize. The commands that they were trying to execute clearly revealed they had no idea what they were doing. The integrity monitoring system picked up on it, and there was absolutely no way these attackers would have known how to subvert it. In this case, they probably did not even know that it was running.

Killing the agent process is probably not the greatest subversion technique, but what about replacing it with an imposter agent process? The basic idea is that attackers could compile their own agent applications that are similar in function but designed to serve the needs of the attacker. After the real agent is killed, the imposter agent is executed to take its place. Assuming that nothing tips off the administrator during the downtime, the main problem here is that the data that the agent normally reports back to the console acts as an authentication mechanism. That is, the attacker does not know what the agent last reported, so attempting to fool the console in this manner is difficult. It may be that the administrator decides to conduct a random scan of certain elements not normally monitored (see Chapter 9, "Advanced Strategies").

Clearly, attacking the agent process is not the best way to subvert a HIM system. However, the thing to remember about subversion techniques like this is that the attack will likely be detected, but it may not be detected until it is too late. Remember, most integrity monitoring agents do not report in real time. If the goal is to set up a backdoor or to own the host for some long-term purpose, the problem is relatively minor. However, if the attacker is able to compromise a host and make off with sensitive data, the fact that your monitoring system detects the compromise within an hour does little good. This is where the whole concept of security-in-depth becomes important. A log analysis application or a HIPS may prove more helpful in this example.

Playing Hide and Seek

Common in many rootkits, are programs that can be used to subvert monitoring software by setting back timestamps on executables or log files. The process is rather simple. An attacker would replace any executables with Trojans. Just before the monitoring software is run, the original executables would be restored and the necessary timestamps set back to trick the monitoring agent into thinking nothing has changed. The problem here is that the attacker must make sure that any files tampered with are restored whenever the agent conducts a scan. If the agent's scans are periodic, it is a more cumbersome issue and the attack may be successful. Some HIM systems purposely conduct scans on an irregular basis for this very reason.

Hiding Files

There are many reasons that an attacker may want to store files on a host without them being detected. They may be providing a safe house for Trojan executables, or providing unauthorized backdoor access to sensitive information. On both Windows and UNIX systems, it is possible to store data on the file system without it being seen by the normal operating system commands (such as *dir* or *ls*) or by a monitoring agent. The attacker knows where these files are and is able to access them, but the administrator and the HIM system are unaware that they exist.

Applications such as The Coroner's Toolkit (TCT) allow you to scan entire disk images for traces of hidden files. However, this type of analysis must be conducted offline, so any regular analysis such as this is not realistic. Your only real shot at detecting something like this is if the attacker messes up during the process and triggers something that prompts your attention.

Kernel Rootkits: The Ultimate Subversion

The most effective way to subvert any software is to conduct an attack at the heart of the operating system—the kernel. Kernel rootkits have existed for years and are familiar on Windows, Solaris, BSD, and Linux. The idea is basically the same for all: intercept and bend the function of system calls to hide anything and everything. Because kernel rootkits run in the kernel, they can control everything, including the hardware. There are many different kinds of rootkits, and using one to subvert a HIM system is very effective, though not necessarily as easy as some of the afore-mentioned subversion methods.

A kernel rootkit does not have to disrupt the function of a monitoring agent or modify system files. The HIM system can be left intact and go about its normal exe-cution. The basic idea is that the kernel is modified to intercept specific system calls that are then redirected to perform whatever the attacker wishes. Even if you have trusted executables on read-only media, they cannot be trusted once the kernel has been compromised. An intelligent attacker can do anything at this point, and detec-tion is no longer in the realm of practical. The only way to detect something like this is to perform an offline analysis of the system or make use of specialized hard-ware (see Chapter 3, "Understanding Threats").

HIM agents are software, and software can always be smashed. Always. Whatever measures are taken to detect attacks can be outdone by the attacker. Basically, it is a never-ending battle of wits. One ever-present disadvantage for the attacker is that they never know for sure whether they have sounded any alarms during the course of an attack. Attacks can be simulated, but the environment that is eventually attacked is never the same as the simulation.

From a security perspective, it is extremely useful to know where software falls short so that you can take action toward mitigating threats that attempt to exploit those shortcomings. In fact, it is good practice to constantly be on the lookout for holes in your HIM systems. In the same way that building managers conduct exer-cises in fire alarm systems, you should simulate integrity violations so that you can verify the system, stay on top of gaps in your defenses, and be prepared to deal with real violations (see Chapter 9, "Advanced Strategies"). In Chapter 3, we take a closer look at some additional threats directed specifically toward HIM systems.

Arguments for Integrity Monitoring

Now that we have examined some arguments against HIM, let's look at some important benefits. The arguments in favor of host-based monitoring are similar to those for network monitoring. Although there is some intersection, the two actually complement each other quite well. In fact, most experts will tell you that a hybrid approach involving the analysis of both host- and network-based events is the most effective.

Auditing

An advantage of HIM is that it allows you to maintain records of change activity for later analysis. With each scan, all information gathered can be archived and secured against tampering. This is good for a number of reasons. It may be that you want to enforce something specific in your security policy and that you want to conduct periodic reviews of the data. Let's look at a few reasons why you might want to audit a change history for managed hosts.

You want to make sure that your administrators are not abusing their privileges. As part of their job, system administrators often require elevated privileges to perform software upgrades, add new accounts, or deal with the configuration and set up of system services. If an administrator installs a backdoor account, sets up a public MP3 server on company resources, or reads the CEO's e-mail, he or she should be fired.

NOTE

This is a good reason why security officers should be in charge of handling the HIM system, and not system administrators.

Administrators sometimes make mistakes. They sometimes fat-finger the sudo command or type a command in the wrong shell window. Having a record of what has happened and when can prove very helpful in tracking down a mistake.

In larger corporations, it is not uncommon for the IT staff to test, approve, and bless specific versions of software applications to be considered the corporate standard. This process reduces the technical support burden and helps ensure a smoother operation of technical resources. Having a record of an unauthorized software upgrade can help prevent a violation in corporate policy and wasted resources.

Detecting Internal Attacks

Detecting internal attacks is the strongest argument for deploying some type of HIM system. Network monitoring is most helpful in shielding private networks from outside attacks. Host-based security is primarily directed at thwarting insider attacks, and HIM is no exception. This is true for two reasons: origination and proximity. More often than not, attacks originate from within a network. Because host-based security applications run on the hosts themselves, they are better equipped to detect the activity.

The media in the United States have done a wonderful job of convincing the public that most computer-related crimes have to do with malicious hackers breaking through firewalls to steal money and install viruses. As is often the case, they are distorting the truth in order to sell ad space. Malicious attacks regularly occur, but most attacks originate from within the network by authorized users. This may take the form of a disgruntled employee, an abusive administrator, or a user trying to gain access to privileged information. Most of the theft reported by retailers comes from employees, not shoplifters. It should not be surprising that employees with access to computer systems would be any different.

The second reason that HIM systems are best at detecting internal attacks is because of their proximity to the activity. If an attacker already has authorized access to a host, the noise surrounding the attack is often not on the wire, but the environment being attacked may be littered with symptoms. Symptoms of an attack can be found in log files, system resources, and altered files.

When I was in college, the computer science department had just deployed a new lab filled with relatively fast Sun boxes. The lab was intended for computer science students, but other students had access to it as well. It did not take long for other students to figure out that this new small lab had much faster systems than the main labs on campus, and soon it became impossible for the computer science students to walk in and find an available terminal. The most frustrating thing about this was that most of these students seemed to be busy chatting on Internet Relay Chat (IRC) and downloading music. Being the practical computer science student that I was, I dealt with the problem by developing a program that would bring these Sun boxes to their knees within seconds. This was not a technical feat by any means, but it sure was useful. Before going to the lab, I would log in to an unsuspecting chatterer's terminal from the old lab and run the malicious program. By the time I got to the lab, the "busy" student was long gone, having given up waiting for the system to respond. I would power-cycle the system, and then have a computer to use.

The point here is that network security is useless at detecting this type of abuse. From the perspective of the network, nothing out of the ordinary was going on. Of course, the administrator could log in and detect that the system was being abused or that the uptime had changed, but how would the administrator know to check in the first place?

Detecting insider abuse and attacks is the most important reason for deploying a HIM system. Without a HIM, there is no way to realistically manage the integrity of a host environment. Furthermore, they provide a way to help with damage assessment to determine what was compromised and how to prevent future compromises.

Detecting Intrusions

An intrusion is basically an unauthorized entering. For our purposes, we mean detecting successful attacks that originated from outside your private network. Firewalls are useful in defending against these types of attacks. NIDs such as Snort are excellent at detecting malicious or suspicious activity pounding on the doors of your network. However, how do you know for certain whether a detected attack was successful?

Again, host security should complement network security. A network IDS such as Snort can be configured to watch for specific types of attacks. The next logical step is to configure HIM to continue that watch in the host environment. Without a HIM solution or a HIDS, you have to conduct an offline analysis of the system. If the host in question is your corporate Web server, this is probably not going to be well received every time you detect an attack.

Although HIM systems are often the first to pick up on internal attacks, sometimes they can also be the first to pick up on intrusions. I have been witness to multiple cases where an intrusion was first detected by the HIM system, not the network IDS.

Forensics

The last argument in support of HIM is forensics. When a host is compromised, it is often subjected to a thorough analysis. The reasons for this may vary, but the common ones include finding vulnerabilities and learning from them, discovering what was compromised, and establishing an audit trail for use in building legal recourse.

It is not uncommon for attackers to cover their tracks, which they do mainly to avoid detection and to exclude other attackers from taking their prize. Having detailed information about a host's environment before, during, and after an attack can help prevent future attacks by highlighting compromised elements of the system over time.

Although much can be learned from a forensic examination, having an archive of data about the environment of a host can also be helpful when the examiner is trying to discover the "when," "where," and "how" of the initial intrusion. This is a lot like a fireman examining a burned-out building trying to find out what started the fire and where it originated. Now, imagine that the firefighters had time-stamped pictures of every room in the house before and while the fire was burning. I think they would find that helpful. HIM systems can provide a great deal of visibility for forensic examiners to construct an audit trail and piece together what actually occurred on a host or set of hosts.

To be considered reliable in a legal sense, care must be given to the handling of forensic and archived scan data. Storage usually involves the physically secure storage of read-only media and a detailed custody chain. For the details of what constitutes legally viable evidence, I suggest talking to a lawyer.

Summary

This chapter provided a solid introduction to the world of host integrity, with an emphasis on HIM systems. We examined how integrity is a subjective term, and looked at the types of tools that security professionals and administrators use to verify and maintain the integrity of managed hosts. Finally, we looked at some arguments for and against HIM. Reasonable arguments against a HIM system include administrative overhead and certain subversion techniques. The strongest arguments in support of a HIM system are detecting internal attacks and damage assessment. By now, it is likely that you appreciate the important role that host-based integrity monitoring tools can play in your security architecture.

Solutions Fast Track

Introduction to Host Integrity

- ☑ Integrity is a subjective term that becomes meaningful only after acceptable change or activities have been determined.

- ☑ A host can be anything from a home PC to a corporate Web server. To maintain integrity of managed hosts, their environments must be monitored.

- ☑ There are many host-based tools in the arsenal of the security professional, including intrusion detection and log analysis, intrusion prevention, and security administration.

Introducing Host Integrity Monitoring

- ☑ HIM systems work by monitoring and reporting on changes to a host environment, including files, configurations, and runtime.

- ☑ HIM systems can provide visibility of host environments and are used to detect unwanted change, internal attacks, and intrusions.

- ☑ A HIM system will detect all kinds of change, not just malicious change. You can use integrity monitoring to maintain an audit trail of any type of change specified in your corporate security policy.

Arguments against Integrity Monitoring

☑ HIM involves agent-based software deployments. Software is susceptible to tampering, and HIM agents are no exception.

☑ Host-based integrity software has a reputation for being too noisy. As a result, there exists the risk that legitimate events go undetected, or the administrator ignores the system altogether.

☑ Since integrity can vary from host to host, the administrative burden associated with configuring a HIM system can be considered more trouble than it is worth.

Arguments for Integrity Monitoring

☑ Monitoring the integrity of a host environment is sometimes the first indication of unwanted or malicious activity.

☑ HIM complements existing security measures by filling in gaps left behind by both network- and other host-based security products.

☑ HIM provides periodic snapshots of the state of a host environment that can be used in forensic analysis in the event that a host is compromised.

Frequently Asked Questions

The following Frequently Asked Questions, answered by the authors of this book, are designed to both measure your understanding of the concepts presented in this chapter and to assist you with real-life implementation of these concepts. To have your questions about this chapter answered by the author, browse to **www.syngress.com/solutions** and click on the **"Ask the Author"** form. You will also gain access to thousands of other FAQs at ITFAQnet.com.

Q: What is the difference between host intrusion detection and HIM?

A: Many different types of applications are labeled as host-based intrusion detection. In general, the distinction is that with a HIDS the end goal is the detection of malicious activity in a host environment, whereas a HIM system aims to provide visibility into all kinds of change. Detecting malicious change or activity is a big part of a HIM system, but that is not the entire motivation behind its deployment.

Q: Will I still need to maintain internal network defenses if I use a HIM system?

A: If you still want to protect your networks from policy violation or abuse, then yes. Although a HIM system can be the first line of defense in combating internal attacks, it is passive. Internal firewalls and other network defenses are still needed to detect and mitigate internal threats from spreading.

Q: Is it useful to deploy a HIM system on a home network?

A: Yes. With the increasing popularity of broadband, home users are leaving their personal computers connected to the Internet more than not. It is not uncommon for laptops to find themselves jumping to and from wireless hotspots. A HIM system can be just as effective at detecting unwanted change on a personal computer as it can on the enterprise.

Q: Can a HIM system tell me which user made a change to a file or configuration?

A: Some can, some cannot. It is harder for integrity monitoring systems that poll the environment to determine this. Information as to which users modified an environment is something more commonly found in change management systems.

Q: My network IDS boats real-time processing of events. Should my HIM system be real time as well?

A: Not necessarily. There is a belief that real-time processing of host-based events is good because it is natural at the network level. This is simply not the case. Host-based integrity monitoring usually involves a great many more nodes compared with network monitoring. If you receive host-based alerts in real time, are you going to respond to them in real time? Usually the answer is no. The best way to stop attacks in their tracks is to prevent them from happening in the first place. The intrusion prevention product made by Immunix is a good example of this.

Chapter 2

Understanding
the Terrain

Solutions in this chapter:

- **Users and Groups**
- **Files and File Systems**
- **The Kernel**
- **Libraries and Frameworks**
- **Runtime**
- **Network**
- **Nonvolatile Memory**

☑ **Summary**

☑ **Solutions Fast Track**

☑ **Frequently Asked Questions**

Introduction

You must understand a host's environment to effectively monitor its integrity for two reasons: *planning* and *response*.

A solid understanding of a host's environment will facilitate the translation of security requirements into a practical configuration, thereby providing a foundation for effective planning. Imagine that one of your goals is to protect the data associated with a Web server. First, you must know where the data files are kept, who has access to them, which file permissions will compromise the security of the data, which access methods the Web server provides, and which changes indicate a compromise in security. Being able to answer these questions requires an understanding of the host environment, file permissions, access control, and so on.

The second reason for understanding the environment is your response. As an administrator or a security officer, you must understand the meaning of any alert and any significance that those changes will have on the integrity of the system. Is the change a false positive? Does it indicate a serious threat to the integrity of your host? Understanding the nature of a detected change can help you initiate the incident response procedures defined in your security policy and, in turn, effectively manage the integrity of your hosts.

This chapter examines some of the important elements of modern host environments, including users and groups, files and file systems, kernels, libraries, runtime security issues, networks, and nonvolatile memory. The goal is to provide information about the most commonly monitored parts of the system, not a complete reference of any of these topics.

Users and Groups

Users and groups constitute the backbone of the security model for most operating systems. Users are granted a certain level of privilege that dictates access to the system, access to files, and the ability to execute or perform certain operations. User accounts can be tied to a person or used for a service (known as a *logical user*). Users can be organized into groups to apply policy to a set of users for a particular operation, or to provide access to a resource.

This section looks at the various ways users and groups are handled on UNIX, Linux, and Windows. An improper configuration or change in the user and group settings can leave a host wide open to attack.

Users and Groups on UNIX

Traditionally, users and groups on UNIX systems are defined in *flat* files. Users' accounts are listed in the */etc/passwd* file and groups are listed in the */etc/group* file. In both files, each user or group entry is listed on a single line with the attributes separated by colons.

The */etc/passwd* file stores information about local user accounts. Not all of these accounts are associated with a person; many are system accounts used for services (e.g., Secure Shell [SSH]). Following the principle of least privilege, most of these service accounts do not have a login shell. The following example lists a password file from a FreeBSD system:

```
root:*:0:0:Charlie &:/root:/bin/csh
toor:*:0:0:Bob Root:/root:/bin/csh
daemon:*:1:1:Owner of many system processes:/root:/usr/sbin/nologin
operator:*:2:5:System &:/:/usr/sbin/nologin
bin:*:3:7:Binaries Commands and Source:/:/usr/sbin/nologin
tty:*:4:65533:Tty Sandbox:/:/usr/sbin/nologin
kmem:*:5:65533:KMem Sandbox:/:/usr/sbin/nologin
news:*:8:8:News Subsystem:/:/usr/sbin/nologin
man:*:9:9:Mister Man Pages:/usr/share/man:/usr/sbin/nologin
sshd:*:22:22:Secure Shell Daemon:/var/empty:/usr/sbin/nologin
www:*:80:80:World Wide Web Owner:/nonexistent:/usr/sbin/nologin
nobody:*:65534:65534:Unprivileged user:/nonexistent:/usr/sbin/nologin
brian:*:1001:0:User &:/home/brian:/usr/local/bin/bash
osiris:*:2223:2223:Osiris Host Integrity
Monitor:/usr/local/osiris:/sbin/nologin
```

Each unique user account is assigned a User ID (UID), which is an integer. The UID of zero is reserved for the root user, who has complete control over the system. The names assigned to users are not important; the UID uniquely identifies a user. Thus, any user with a zero UID is considered a root user.

The */etc/group* file contains a listing of all groups for a host and which users belong to each group. The following example shows a group file from FreeBSD:

```
wheel:*:0:root
daemon:*:1:
kmem:*:2:
sys:*:3:
tty:*:4:
operator:*:5:root
```

```
bin:*:7:
news:*:8:
man:*:9:
staff:*:20:
sshd:*:22:
guest:*:31:
network:*:69:
www:*:80:
nogroup:*:65533:
nobody:*:65534:
osiris:*:2223:
```

Each group is issued a Group ID (GID), which is also an integer. The zero GID is usually known as the *wheel group* or the *system group* and is reserved for privileged users.

The information kept in these two files is referenced by the system when enforcing file permissions and runtime privileges. Changes to these files can significantly undermine the security of a host. Again, this is the traditional UNIX user/group model. Although the cumbersome process of managing multiple hosts has led to the adoption of other means of defining users and groups on UNIX systems, monitoring these files is still important. In some cases (e.g., Mac OS X), these files are not used by default, but can be. If the system becomes mindful of these files, you must make sure that they have not been compromised.

It is not uncommon for an attacker to add user accounts as a means of establishing a backdoor into the system. Changes especially suspect include additions to the wheel group or adding another user with a zero UID. Even if your user and groups are defined elsewhere, the changes to user and group files can be the first indication of an attack.

Logging In

Local access to a host is very important and should be very secure. Once an attacker obtains local access, an abundance of opportunities for misuse and abuse become available. At this point, network defenses become powerless. Perimeter defenses serve to prevent attackers from exploiting software and obtaining unauthorized access; however, eventually a situation will exist where the perimeter can be breached.

The security surrounding passwords has caused the password file to evolve, with most systems now shadowing their passwords. Basically, this means that the encrypted passwords are not found in the */etc/passwd* file, but in a separate file with stricter file permissions. The name of the shadow file varies depending on the type of system, but the file is usually named */etc/master.password* or */etc/shadow*.

Initially, passwords were stored in the */etc/passwd* file as the second field of each user entry, which was obviously a security problem. To help secure passwords, they were encrypted and only the encrypted passwords were stored. Upon login, the password presented by the user was encrypted and compared against the entry in the *passwd* file. Because it was trivial to conduct brute-force attacks on these passwords, it became necessary to remove them from the file altogether. Today, most UNIX systems store encrypted passwords only in a shadow file, and introduce a salt into the encryption process as a means of mitigating dictionary attacks. The key is to realize that all password authenticating has been susceptible to compromise. Access to user accounts is not well protected, and therefore, monitoring the surrounding elements of user logins is critical in detecting unauthorized access.

A common authentication scheme used on UNIX systems is the pluggable authentication module (PAM). PAM is basically an interface to various authentication schemes that allow many disparate applications to offload their user authentication handling. PAM is modular, so administrators can, with relative ease, add a new authentication scheme to a host, as long as a PAM module has been implemented for it. Configuration files for PAM were originally stored in */etc/pam.conf*, but are now commonly found in the */etc/pam.d* directory with a file for each module. The following example shows a PAM module file for Secure Shell Daemon (SSHD) on FreeBSD:

```
# PAM configuration for the "sshd" service
#
auth            required        pam_nologin.so          no_warn
auth            sufficient      pam_opie.so             no_warn
no_fake_prompts
auth            requisite       pam_opieaccess.so       no_warn
allow_local
auth            required        pam_unix.so             no_warn
try_first_pass
account         required        pam_login_access.so
account         required        pam_unix.so
session         required        pam_permit.so
password        required        pam_unix.so             no_warn
try_first_pass
```

The four module types (*auth, account, session,* and *password*) deal with various aspects of the authentication scheme. The *auth* type handles verification. The *account* type is used to place restrictions on access. The *session* type is used to handle various tasks upon login/logout related to the service before and after access has been granted. The *password* module is responsible for updating authentication tokens.

Changes to a PAM configuration file can seriously impact the integrity of a system. administrators must make sure that their PAM configuration files are understood and secure. All PAM files should be monitored for any type of change.

Finally, user login activity is commonly stored in the log files */var/run/utmp*, */var/log/wtmp*, and */var/log/lastlog*. The *utmp* file is a binary file that contains records of the users currently logged in to the system, and is used by commands such as "who." The *wtmp* file is a binary log file with records of user login and logout activity, and of system restart/reboot. The *lastlog* file is a log file with records listing the time, terminal, and connecting host associated with each user's last login. All of these files should be owned and only writable by root and monitored for any changes to the access permissions.

SUDO and the SU Command

All UNIX and UNIX-like systems require administration; eventually, updates must be performed and services configured. administrators sometimes need privileged access to the system to perform these operations, which is accomplished by joining an administrative group and gaining access to the Super User DO (SUDO) and Super User (SU) commands. The main difference between SUDO and SU is auditing. SUDO is generally preferred because it logs the time, identifies the user, and provides fine-grained access control over what operations SUDO users can perform; the SU command lacks these auditing capabilities. Depending on the configuration, it may be possible to subvert additional auditing with the following command:

```
$ sudo bash
```

The SUDO configuration file is usually found in */etc/sudoers* or */usr/local/etc/sudoers*. It is common for this file to be readable only by the root or the wheel group, and writable only by the root. This file should be monitored for any kind of change. Another thing to note is that changes to groups often have an effect on SUDO privileges. It is not uncommon for SUDO to be restricted to users in the wheel group. Aside from the obvious effect, a user being added to the wheel group in this case is equivalent, giving that user root access to the host.

Advanced User Management

Maintaining password and group files for thousands of hosts is impractical. As a result, some solutions to this problem have evolved and are still in widespread use.

Some popular solutions include the Network Information Service (NIS) and NetInfo.

NIS was developed by Sun Microsystems in the 1980s. NIS manages users, groups, and hosts, essentially */etc/passwd*, *NIS/etc/group*, and */etc/hosts*. Instead of consulting local files for user authentication, an NIS server is used to verify authentication credentials. Improvements to NIS (including the encryption of the authentication process over a network) were made and released as NIS+. The good thing about NIS is that the user and group data for thousands of hosts can be stored in a central location. The bad news is that the user and group data for thousands of hosts can be stored in a single location. This information is stored by the NIS server in *dbm* files, usually somewhere under */var*, depending on the system (usually */var/yp*).

Although Mac OS X assumes a great deal of its UNIX underpinnings from FreeBSD, some legacy NeXTStep features still persist. One such feature is NetInfo, which essentially solves the same problem as NIS. By default, Mac OS X and Mac OS X Server do not use */etc/passwd* and */etc/group*; rather, they use a local NetInfo domain. administrators can configure Mac OS X to make use of an actual NetInfo domain, or the traditional */etc* files. The local NetInfo domain files are stored in */var/db/netinfo/local.nidb* and should be monitored. This file is owned by root, and should be readable and writable only by root.

All UNIX systems have important files related to logging in, authorization, access to services, and for raising privileges (e.g., SUDO). All of these files should be monitored by your HIMS. Both Osiris and Samhain have the ability to monitor these files.

Users and Groups on Windows

Although they serve the same purpose, users and groups are very different on Windows than on UNIX and UNIX-like systems. Managing a network of users and groups was initially handled by domain controllers and more recently with Active Directory. Active Directory is based on Lightweight Directory Access Protocol (LDAP) and is used to control all resources (including users and groups) that are part of a Windows network. (When we refer to Windows, we mean various versions of Windows XP, Windows 2000, and Windows 2003 Advanced Server.)

Every user and group on a Windows network is either local or considered part of a domain. This distinction is important because even though a Windows host can authenticate against an Active Directory controller to gain access to the network, local accounts are still very much alive and involved in specifying what users can and cannot do to the host.

Unlike UNIX systems, Windows uniquely identifies users and groups with a Security ID (SID). The SID is a binary structure, and can be represented by a string that looks like the following:

```
S-1-5-32-544
```

The format is: S-R-I-S... where S means the string is an SID, R is the revision, I is the authority, and S is one or more sub-authorities. A SID is similar in purpose to the UID on a UNIX system. The key difference is that the SID is a structure, not an integer, and it contains more information about the user, such as which domain the user belongs to. The SID structure is a key element in the complicated Windows security model. In the world of computer security, simplicity is your friend. As you will see in the next couple of sections, simplicity is not the appropriate word to use to describe the Windows security architecture.

Windows Users

Windows users are either local or part of a domain. The equivalent to the root on a Windows system is the administrator. The local administrator has complete control over a host, just like the root user on UNIX systems. A distinct characteristic of the administrator account is that it cannot be deleted or disabled; however, the local administrator can add local users, domain users, and domain groups to the local machine.

The guest user has limited access to the system and does not have a password. By default, the guest account is created but initially disabled. The guest user is a member of the guest group, which is given the least amount of privilege by default. However, the guest account does have the ability to shut down or restart the system.

A user's privileges on Windows are determined by the groups that user belongs to. For example, if you add user "Bob" to the administrator's group, then Bob is essentially an administrator user.

Windows Groups

Every Windows host has a handful of built-in groups, each with varying levels of privileges. By default, the administrators group has the most privileges, with at least one administrator user. The administrator group is similar to the wheel group on UNIX systems. The group with the least amount of privileges is the guest group.

Where Are Users and Groups Stored?

Before Active Directory, all information about users and groups was stored in the registry where the escalation of privileges (or group hopping) was not uncommon.

Monitoring the integrity of a Windows host under this system requires persistent monitoring of the registry, which contains important data that can indicate a compromise in the integrity of the host and is an important part of HIM on Windows systems.

With Active Directory, all user and group information is stored in the *%SystemRoot%\ntds\ntdis.dit* file. Host integrity monitoring systems that monitor users and groups on an Active Directory server will not interact with this file directly, but rather use a Windows application program interface (API) to get the information. However, this file itself should be monitored for changes in permissions or ownership.

User and group information for all local users on a Windows host are stored in the *%SystemRoot%\Windows\user.dat* file in the registry. Usually, backup files exist with similar names and are used in case one of the registry files becomes corrupted or is missing.

In summary, Windows users and groups are more complex than UNIX users and groups. As a result, there are many ways an attacker can subvert access control on Windows and elevate their privileges. Monitoring users and groups on Windows is absolutely necessary when monitoring the integrity of a Windows host.

Files and File Systems

Files make up the majority of a host environment and come to mind when considering the integrity of a host. The configurations, the certificates, the private keys, and the executables (that get loaded and affect the runtime) are all stored in files. On UNIX systems, everything, including memory and peripherals, is represented by the OS in the form of a file.

The security of any host depends on file permissions. Executables, shared libraries, and other system files are only writable by the root or administrator. A large part of the distinction between privileged and unprivileged users resides in the degree to which they interact with files. File permissions serve to limit the impact certain users or system services have on the overall function of the system. UNIX and Linux file permissions are relatively simple compared with Windows. Again, simplicity is a friend to security and a simple file permissions model, though limited in some respects, can be a blessing.

When a system is attacked or misused, at least one file in the process is usually altered. This is similar to throwing a stone into a calm body of water. The key is to know what ripples to look at and be able to understand the impact that certain changes in the file system have on the integrity of a host. This section looks at files and file systems in both UNIX and Windows environments.

What Is a File System?

To understand some of the common attributes of files and the impact of certain types of changes to a file system, it helps to understand their general makeup.

In basic terms, a file system is a collection of files. Disks are divided into partitions and each partition contains at least one file system. There are three basic components to most file systems: *superblocks*, *inodes*, and *data*. The superblock contains all of the data regarding the current state of the file system, including the number of blocks in the file system, the size of each block, and the number of inodes. The superblock is basically a map of the file system; without it, retrieving data from the file system would be very difficult. Most file systems maintain multiple backups of the superblock in case it becomes corrupted. When a file system is created, it is divided into sections (usually called *blocks*), each with a certain number of inodes. As files are created, they are each assigned an inode, which contains metadata associated with that file (e.g., permissions), as well as where all of the data for that file is physically stored on the disk.

There are many different types of file systems, and some are better suited for certain deployments than others. The most common local file system on UNIX platforms is the Unix File System (UFS), which is relatively basic but still widely use today. FreeBSD and NetBSD both use a version of UFS. Mac OS X has the option to install UFS, but by default uses an extension to Apple's Hierarchical File System (HFS) called HFS+. On Linux systems, you usually encounter ext2 or ext3 and sometimes Reiser FS, a journaling file system.

Windows XP, 2000, and 2003 Advanced Server use the NT File System (NTFS). NTFS is quite different from many of the aforementioned file systems, but the overall concept is basically the same. The first portion of an NTFS partition is used to store data about the volume and metadata (inodes) for all of the files.

Modern operating systems work with many different types of file systems. To shield the kernel from knowing the specifics of any particular file system, a software abstraction known as a virtual file system (VFS) is used. A VFS facilitates the reading of many different local file systems, as well as other types of file systems such as NFS or media-specific file systems such as the ISO9660 CD-ROM.

UNIX File Security

Everything in the UNIX world has a file representation, including devices and peripherals, sockets, pipes, and memory. This being the case, the overall security of a UNIX or UNIX-like system such as Linux is very dependent on file permissions and file security. File permissions on UNIX are relatively simple. Although you may encounter more complicated Access Control Lists (ACLs) with IRIX, Solaris, and some Linux deployments, most UNIX systems do not have them.

This section examines the structure of files on UNIX, specifically permissions links and misconceptions, and also takes a close look at the metadata associated with files on a UFS.

A Realistic View of Files

Files have names, metadata (such as permissions and an owner), and data. All of the elements associated with files are not stored in one place on a disk. The filename is stored as part of the directory, the metadata is stored in an inode, and the file data is stored across multiple logical blocks on the disk. The hardware driver further abstracts the physical disk locations of all of the data associated with that file. For the sake of usability, the operating systems will hide these details when you interact with files through a terminal or some type of graphical user interface (GUI).

File Inodes

Every file is assigned one inode when it is created. The purpose of an inode is to maintain information about the file (e.g., permissions) as well as which blocks on the file system make up the data portion of the file (see Figure 2.1).

Figure 2.1 The Structure of a Typical Inode

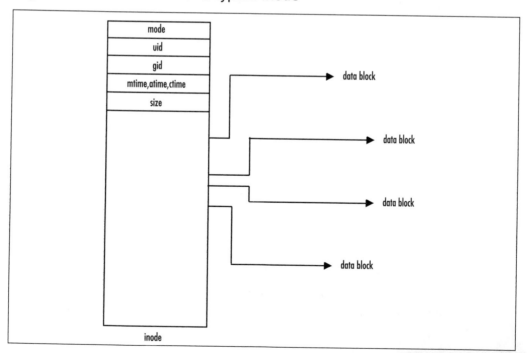

The file's mode consists of the file type and the permissions. The first 16 bits of the mode are usually reserved for the file type. The three time stamps are: modification, access, and change (discussed later in this chapter). The size is the number of bytes of data associated with a file. The UID and GID are the user and group owners of the file. Figure 2.1 is a simplification; these fields are found in most file systems. Each file system has different fields and designates its own layout for how these fields are organized in the inode structure.

Directories

The names given to files are stored in a directory, which is a file containing a list of file names and their inodes. Directories serve the obvious logical purpose, and also provide mapping between a file's inode and a file's name. Although every file is uniquely identified by its inode, they also have names for the sake of usability, similar to hostnames and Internet Protocol (IP) addresses.

Deleting, adding, or renaming a file is a modification of a directory and not the file itself (see Figure 2.2).

Figure 2.2 Relationship between File Inodes and Directories

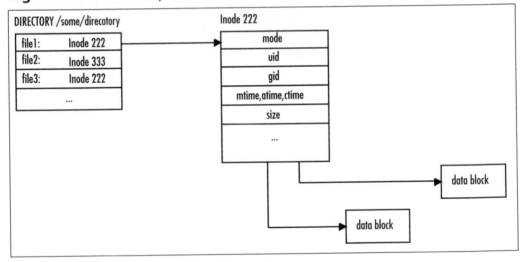

File Permissions

Every file on UNIX has an owner, a group, and a set of permissions called the *mode*. The mode actually contains information about the file type, as well as access control. The access control information defines who can access the file and what they can do with it. The mode is usually represented as a string reading from left to right (see Figure 2.3).

Figure 2.3 The UNIX File Permissions String

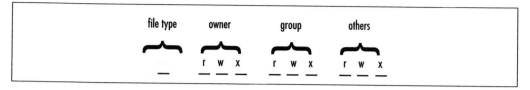

The file type is represented by a single character, "–" for regular files, "s" for sockets, "b" for block devices, "c" for character devices, "p" for FIFO or named pipes, and "l" for symbolic links. The next three sections of the mode specify access permissions and apply to the file owner, file group, and all other users. Table 2.1 describes the read, write, and execute privileges for files and directories.

Table 2.1 Read, Write, and Execute Privileges for Files and Directories

	Read Privileges	Write Privileges	Execute Privileges
File	Contents can be viewed.	File contents can be altered.	File can be loaded and executed.
Directory	Can list files contained in the directory.	Files can be added or removed from the directory.	Directory can be searched or entered (e.g., with the **cd** command).

Although this system of access control seems simple, there are some caveats to watch out for. A change in permissions, though seemingly benign, may violate your security policy. Following are some things to consider:

- Because a directory is basically a list of file names, read access for a directory means you can view a listing of the files in that directory, not the files themselves. Disabling read access to a directory does not prevent files in that directory from being read, modified, or deleted.

- Disabling write access to a directory does not prevent existing files from being modified; it only prevents files from being added, removed, or renamed.

- If write access to a directory is enabled, files can be added or deleted regardless of their permissions. (The only exception to this is described later in this chapter.)

- If a user owns a file and is also a member of the group that owns the file, the owner privileges apply to that user and the group privileges are ignored.

- Enabling execute privileges for a directory allows a user to see the details for files in that directory, regardless of their permissions. Disabling execute privileges for a directory prevents users from being able to see file details or write to files in the directory, regardless of the permissions for those files.

Special File Permissions

The mode specifies execute privileges for the owner, the group, and all other users. However, there are three additional types of file privileges that can be represented in the execute sections of the mode string. This includes the set user ID (SUID), the set group ID (SGID), and *sticky bits*.

An SUID file means that (when executed) it runs with the effective UID of the owner of the file. Directories can be set with SUID, but in most cases, it has no effect. On some systems, setting a directory to be SUID means that the user who owns the directory automatically owns any files created in that directory. A SUID file is represented in the owner-executable portion of the mode string. However, the SUID status is distinct from the owner execute privileges, so there are certain symbols that are used to designate which bits are set (see Table 2.2).

Table 2.2 UNIX File Execute Permissions

Symbol	Meaning
-	Execute bit not set; SUID bit not set
x	Execute bit set; SUID bit not set
S	Execute bit not set; SUID bit set
s	Execute bit set; SUID bit set

The *passwd* program is a good example of an SUID executable. The mode string for the *passwd* program on Mac OS X is:

```
-r-sr-xr-x  1 root  wheel  39992 17 Dec 07:17 /usr/bin/passwd
```

An SGID file is similar to a SUID file except that when executed, it runs with the effective GID of the group that owns the file. Likewise, the mode string is handled the same as with SUID except that it is represented in the group execute section of the string.

The third special case for file privileges is the sticky bit. The sticky bit is used for shared directories and means that even the owner of the directory cannot remove a file marked "sticky." The sticky bit is represented in the execute section of the file mode string.

NOTE

The sticky bit is represented in the execute section of the file mode string, because sticky originally meant that the application was kept in swap. This is no longer the case, but the convention for representing the sticky bit in the mode string remains.

(The details of the SUID and SGID applications are discussed later in the "Runtime" section of this chapter.)

Hidden File Flags

On Berkeley Software Distribution (BSD)-based systems, there are additional access control bits associated with each file. These file flags are sometimes referred to as *immutable flags* (see Table 2.3).

Table 2.3 BSD Special File Flags

Flag	Name
uchg	User immutable
schg	System immutable
uappnd	User append-only
sappend	System append-only

Normally, the mode string can be viewed with the *-la* options to the *ls* command; however, use the *o* option to view the immutable flags for a file. For example:

```
$ ls -lo /tmp/myuchgfile
-rw-r--r--  1 brian  wheel  uchg 0 25 Jan 22:11 /tmp/myuchgfile
```

When the user immutable flag (uchg) is set on a file, the owner cannot modify or delete it no matter what permissions that file has.

The system immutable flag (schg) is the same as the uchg, except the root user cannot modify or delete a file. Once the schg flag is set on a file, the root user cannot remove the flag. The only way to unset the flag or modify the file is to boot into single-user mode. The main point of a schg is to attempt to prevent files from being modified in case the root account has been compromised.

The uappnd flag and the system append flag (sappnd) only allow data to be appended to a file. Any existing data in the file cannot be altered. Like the immutable flags, the root user cannot remove the sappnd; to do so requires that the system be booted into single-user mode.

Immutable flags are used as a means of preventing unintentional or unauthorized access to system-critical files. The basic idea is that physical access to the box is required (single-user mode) in order for the files to be modified, deleted, or the flags removed. These flags are also tied to the BSD security level. (Kernel security levels are discussed in detail later in this chapter.)

File Links

Most UNIX systems have two types of links: *hard* and *soft* (usually called a *symbolic link*).

Hard links are directly referenced to files residing on the same file system. A file can have a number of hard links, but there is only one copy of the file contents on the file system. Any changes made to the hard link are also made to its corresponding file. A hard link is an entry in a directory structure for a file that exists somewhere on the same file system. Because of this, hard links can refer only to files on the same file system, not to directories.

Symbolic (soft) links are different from hard links in that a symbolic link is a separate file, which contains the path to another file. Since symbolic links are paths, they can point to the existing directory as well as to files and directories on other file systems. Because symbolic links are actually files, determining whether an operation is applied to the link file or the target file can be confusing. Most applications operate on the target file (called *traversing the link*). Some applications that operate on the link file (and do not traverse the link) are the *ls, rm, file*, and *mv* commands. The mode of a symbolic link denotes the file as a link file, symbolized by the *l* character. Because a symbolic link is a special type of file, it does not have permissions associated with it. The *ls* command displays a symbolic link's permissions; however, they are meaningless.

WARNING

Mac OS X is a UNIX-based system containing a third type of file link called an *alias*. Mac OS X is based on BSD, specifically FreeBSD. Consequently, Mac OS X has soft links, hard links, and aliases. The alias is a legacy concept originating from the original Mac OS environment, and is similar to a symbolic link because it is a file that can be modified or deleted without modifying the target file. However, unlike symbolic links, an alias is more resilient because it can be moved around while still pointing to the target file. An alias stores information about the target file in a special *file fork*. (File forks on HFS+ are discussed later in this chapter.) Aliases are higher-level file links, similar to shortcuts on Windows. As a result, some of the traditional file system applications on Mac OS X do not handle alias files well.

File Time Stamps

Every UNIX file has three distinct time stamps: modification, access, and change. These time stamps exist for every type of file except symbolic links. Although these seem straightforward, there are some pitfalls to consider when determining why a given time stamp has changed and the significance of that change.

The modification time (mtime) is the last time the file data was modified, which is what most users see when they view the details of files in a directory either through the GUI or a command such as *ls –l*. If a file's inode changes, it does not necessarily mean that the data has changed. Whenever a file's mtime is changed, the contents of that file have been altered or written to disk. The mtime of a file can be set using the **touch** command.

The access time (atime) is the time that a file was last accessed, and is updated whenever the file is opened or the inode is modified. Some operating systems provide a means for setting the access time, and some do not.

The change time (ctime) is the time that the metadata stored in the inode associated with the file was last changed. Like with the mtime, it is possible for the ctime of a file to change without actually altering the contents of the file. Common commands that will alter the ctime for a file include *chown*, *chmod*, *chgrp*, and *chflags*.

Most UNIX File Systems provide these three time stamps and, depending on the file system, the inode may contain even more time stamp information. For example, the Linux ext2 file system contains time stamps associated with inode creation and deletion.

Tying It All Together

File access control is critical to maintaining the integrity of UNIX hosts. Although the simplicity of traditional UNIX file permissions should be commended, there are elements that may seem odd until you understand some of the basics of file system design. A single change to file permissions, intentional or not, can place the entire host environment at risk of compromise. Make sure you understand the privileges afforded by file permissions, and any oddities on the file systems you are using.

SUID and SGID flags alter the runtime permissions of a process. Like regular file permissions, one change will render a system vulnerable to attack or misuse. The SUID and SGID permissions also affect the runtime privileges of a process, not just access to files. Any change involving SUID and SGID should immediately be brought to an administrator's attention. (The significance of the SUID and SGID bits are discussed later in this chapter.)

Although symbolic links are convenient, malicious users can use them to subvert file access control. There are many poorly written software applications that blindly open files without paying attention to the fact that the file is a symbolic link. Some software applications make this distinction, but most do not. Pay close attention to any newly created symbolic links that point to system-critical files or root-owned files. Since a symbolic link is a path, it can point to any file, even those that are not readable by the user who created the link. Symlink attacks can also be a serious threat to the integrity of a host, the basic concept being that poor judgment on the part of the software can lead to a compromise in privileged information, unauthorized escalation in privileges, and denial of service (DOS) attacks.

Finally, file time stamps must be monitored (usually just the modification and ctimes time stamps). Aside from scheduled upgrades, libraries and executables should not change without the knowledge of an administrator or security officer.

Windows File Security

The following section discusses the NT File System (NTFS). Previous file systems for Windows (FAT16/FAT32/VFAT) have no security features; therefore, anyone maintaining the file system security on Windows must use NTFS.

NTFS is a recoverable file system found on true 32-bit Windows operating systems' such as Windows NT, Windows 2000, Windows XP, and Windows 2003 Advanced Server. Transactions involving the file system are logged in multiple places before being committed, which make it easy to recover or roll back the file system in the event of a failure or unexpected shutdown. Although there are similarities between the overall structure of the file system and the file systems mentioned earlier, NTFS is more complicated. That being the case, we do not detail how NTFS is structured. Instead, we examine the elements of NTFS files that interest integrity monitoring, including access control, various file attributes, and the registry.

NTFS File Structure

With the NTFS, files are a collection of attributes and the file contents are an attribute of that file. The design of NTFS is conducive to the practice of extending the list of attributes associated with files (discussed in more detail later in this chapter).

Every NTFS file has the following set of attributes: name, standard information, data, and security descriptor. File names on NTFS are based on the Unicode (16-bit) character set. The standard information attribute of a file includes the modification, change, and access time stamps, as well as some legacy attributes carried over from file allocation table (FAT) file systems (e.g., system, hidden, read-only). A file's security descriptor contains ownership and access control information similar to an inode, but slightly more complicated.

Directories are a mapping from the file name to references of that file. The difference with NTFS is that directories are an index as opposed to a regular file. Indexing allows the directory to organize its contents for faster searching. Also, certain attributes of a file (including the standard attributes) are resident on the equivalent of a superblock on NTFS—the master file table (MFT). This allows for quick listing of contained files and their time stamps (a common operation on a directory).

Included in part of the design of the NTFS was the ability to dynamically alter the file system without changing the underlying implementation. An example of this is *reparse points*. An NTFS reparse point has the ability to associate a set of data and some functionality with a file. Establishing a reparse point involves providing a unique tag for the reparse point and providing the file system with a set of code called the *filter* that will act on that data when the file is accessed. Basically, when any request is made for a file containing a reparse point, the tag is used to look up the filter and the data associated with the reparse point is then handed off to the filter for processing. Reparse points are application-specific, meaning applications decide on the functionality and format of the data. Microsoft uses reparse points to handle special cases such as symbolic links (shortcuts) and junctions (links to a directory). Tags associated with a reparse point for a file are stored in that file's attributes.

Another unique aspect of files on an NTFS volume is their ability to store multiple data streams (discussed in detail later in this later chapter).

NTFS ACLs

The NTFS complicates administration by implementing a complex system of access control. Every object in Windows (including NTFS files) has an attribute known as a *security descriptor*, which contains information about the owner of the object and the ACL. The ACL specifies which users and groups may operate on a file and what they can do to it.

There are two types of ACLs on Windows: a Discretionary Access Control List (DACL) and a System Access Control List (SACL). The SACL contains auditing information and specifies which operations on the file must be audited by the system. Only the system administrator can modify a SACL. File permissions are stored in a DACL. (For the remainder of this section we refer to a file's DACL as an ACL.)

An ACL contains a sequence of entries known as Access Control Entries (ACE). An ACL can have any number of ACEs. Each entry contains a reference to a user or a group, a set of permissions, and an entry type. A SID denotes the user or group. The permissions include attributes such as read, write, and so on. The type specifies whether the specified permissions are allowed or denied (see Figure 2.4).

Figure 2.4 Altering Windows ACLs

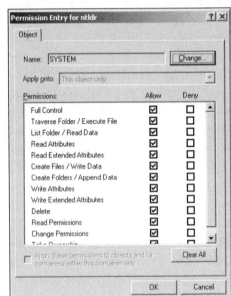

Not every file has an ACL attached to it, which leaves it without security. Files without an ACL allow every user and group to have full control over that file. If a file has an ACL but no entries in that ACL, access to the file is implicitly denied. When a file is created, the system attempts to inherit the ACL from the parent folder. If that fails, a default ACL is provided by the system's object manager and, if that fails, the user account may have a default ACL associated with it. It is possible for all of these attempts to fail and for the file to be created without an ACL object. Again, this leaves the file without security.

ACE

Every ACE specifies a type (allowed or denied), an SID, and a set of permissions. The permissions in an ACE include:

- Generic read
- Generic write
- Generic execute
- Generic all access
- Ability to modify the SACL
- Ability to delete
- Ability to read the security descriptor
- Ability to synchronize
- Ability to write the DACL
- Ability to change ownership

When access to a file is requested, the system steps through the ACE list until the access request is either granted or denied. One problem is that the allowed permissions specified by a list of ACEs vary, depending on their order. A file's ACE list can consist of inherited and object-specific ACEs and two ACEs can directly contradict each other. Enter the *permissions resolution* problem. Windows attempts to mitigate these problems by establishing an order or grouping that ACEs should be kept in. The following list is from the Microsoft Developer Network online documentation describing the preferred order of ACE in an ACL, which can be found at: **http://msdn.microsoft.com/library/default.asp?url=/library/enus/secauth z/security/order_of_aces_in_a_dacl.asp.**

1. All explicit ACEs are placed in a group before any inherited ACEs.
2. Within the group of explicit ACEs, access-denied ACEs are placed before access-allowed ACEs.

3. Inherited ACEs are placed in the order in which they are inherited. ACEs inherited from the child object's parent come first, then ACEs inherited from the grandparent, and so on up the tree of objects.

4. For each level of inherited ACEs, access-denied ACEs are placed before access-allowed ACEs.

Obviously, these rules are not simple. To make matters worse, the rule set is not always enforced by the system. Applications that directly modify a file's ACL are not forced to comply with the aforementioned precedence suggestions.

ACEs can be inherited and inherited dynamically. When a file is created, it can inherit permissions from the directory it is created in. In addition, an ACE can be created specifically for that file; thus, an ACE is considered either inherited or direct. Furthermore, inherited ACEs are dynamic in that they are linked to the parent ACE so that when the parent's ACE is updated, the change propagates down to all of the inheriting ACE objects. Each ACE has a header that can be flagged *inherited* or *not inherited*. In addition, every file can be set to not inherit permissions. An ACE that is directly applied to a file takes precedence over all inherited ACEs in an ACL.

File access control on Windows is not simple. Administrators and IT departments usually favor the fine-grained system of access control provided by Windows; however, this is another example of feature sets taking precedence over security. You can learn all of the details and become an expert, but the reality is that complicated systems are generally not understood as well as less complicated systems. Less understanding leads to holes in security policies that go unnoticed until they are taken advantage of.

The Windows Registry

One of the big differences between the UNIX and Windows systems with respect to file integrity, is the registry. The registry was an attempt by Microsoft to shed itself from inconsistent formats for metadata associated with applications and system-level services. The problem is that it is now an underground hierarchical system of data that is somewhat out of control. Registry keys have ACLs, just like files, which is good because it is a familiar concept for administrators. However, it can also be considered dangerous because of how complex Windows ACLs are. The registry, like files, runs the risk of being misconfigured with respect to access control.

The registry is a hierarchical system of information that is stored in two files: *ntuser.dat* and *System.dat*. These files are not edited directly, but through specialized applications that allow you to edit, import, and export the data. The structure of the registry consists of five top-level keys called *hives*:

- HKEY_CLASSES_ROOT

- HKEY_CURRENT_USER

- HKEY_LOCAL_MACHINE

- HKEY_USERS

- HKEY_CURRENT_CONFIG

The CLASSES_ROOT hive exists primarily to provide support for older Windows applications, and contains information about file extensions and their associations with specific applications. This information is currently stored in the LOCAL_MACHINE and CURRENT_USER hives. The CURRENT_USER hive is the currently logged in user's profile that resides in the USERS hive. The LOCAL_MACHINE hive is the main hive, which contains the bulk of the information about installed software, security settings, and various bits of system information. The USERS hive stores profiles for all local users. The CURRENT_CONFIG is used for information related to the system's hardware configuration.

Not all of these hives are stored in the same physical files. Beginning with Windows XP, a new format for registry files was created (called the "latest" format). Windows NT and Windows 2000 use the "standard" format (see Table 2.4).

Table 2.4 File Locations for Windows Registry Hives

Registry Hive	File Location
HKEY_CURRENT_USER	ntuser.dat
HKEY_LOCAL_MACHINE	system.sav,software.sav, security.sav,SAM,Sam.log,Sam.sav
HKEY_USERS	DEFAULT
HKEY_CURRENT_CONFIG	SYSTEM,System.sav, System.dat,System.log,System.alt

Some of these files may not exist, depending on the version of Windows and the format being used for the files (either latest or standard). All of these files reside either in the system root drive, user-specific folders, or in %SystemRoot%\system32\config.

Monitoring the registry is very important, because changes to the registry can undermine the integrity of the system. In fact, it is common for malicious applications to launch themselves at startup by adding themselves to the *run* section in the registry. There are many sections in the registry that can be altered so that executables are run upon startup, including those in the LOCAL_MACHINE and CLASSES_ROOT hives. In fact, the blaster worm made use of a registry setting to launch itself. Registry hacking is so common that antivirus and anti-spyware applications routinely monitor the registry for specific changes that could indicate malicious activity.

Forks and Streams

File permissions and access control mechanisms are very important; however, some file systems have problems that many administrators are not aware of. Steps can be taken to hide data or executables on the file system; however, some file systems provide legitimate storage mechanisms that are usually ignored by the tools commonly used to view files and their attributes. This section examines two specific examples of how this can effect common files systems. First, we look at the resource forks that can exist with the HFS+ file system, and then we look at alternate data streams on NTFS.

HFS+ Resource Forks

By default, Mac OS X installs the HFS+ file system. This file system has some legacy attributes of the Mac OS world, specifically resource forks. Files on HFS+ consist of two forks, a data fork and a resource fork. Resource forks are used by applications to store bitmaps, UI resources (e.g., icons audio files), and other pieces of information specific to the application. Modern Mac OS X applications do not use the resource forks, but some older carbonized applications still do. One example of such an application is the version of Acrobat Reader that shipped with the first versions of Mac OS X. Since Mac OS X, Apple has begun the process of suggesting that application developers store these resources in the data fork. One problem is that the BSD tools are ignorant of the resource fork; command line operations involving files would deal with only the data fork, and data stored in the resource fork would get lost.

To reference the resource fork of a file, append */rsrc* onto the end of any filename. For example, create an empty file in the */tmp* file and add data to the resource fork.

```
$ mkdir /tmp/example
$ touch /tmp/example/myfile
$ ls -la /tmp/example
total 0
drwxr-xr-x    3 brian    wheel    102 29 Jan 19:36 .
drwxrwxrwt   13 root     wheel    442 29 Jan 19:36 ..
-rw-r--r--    1 brian    wheel      0 29 Jan 19:36 myfile
```

Now, add some data to the file's resource fork and show that the file size (of the data fork) is still zero.

```
$ cat /etc/hosts > /tmp/example/myfile/rsrc
$ ls -la /tmp/example
total 8
drwxr-xr-x    3 brian    wheel    102 29 Jan 19:36 .
drwxrwxrwt   13 root     wheel    442 29 Jan 19:36 ..
-rw-r--r--    1 brian    wheel      0 29 Jan 19:36 myfile
```

Now let us look at the file size for the resource fork and note that it is not zero:

```
$ ls -la /tmp/example/myfile/rsrc
-rw-r--r--    1 brian    wheel    375 29 Jan 19:36 /tmp/example/myfile/rsrc
```

As far as most command-line applications are concerned, the data in the resource fork is not there. If you copy the file around, list the size, or compute its Message Digest 5 (MD5) checksum, the resource fork is ignored. If the data in a resource fork on Mac OS X is modified, the only attributes that change are the mtime and the ctime. Therefore, even if your monitoring solution is not able to monitor resource forks, it is still possible to detect that a file's resource fork has been modified. Monitoring resource forks directly will give you more information about the nature of the change. Osiris has the ability to monitor all aspects of resource forks for files on Mac OS X that contain them.

NTFS Alternate Data Streams

Like HFS+, NTFS also has more than one data segment associated with a file, which are called Alternate Data Streams. As mentioned earlier, an NTFS file consists of attributes; the file's data is also an attribute. Most files on NTFS have only one data attribute; however, unlike HFS+ where there are two data streams, NTFS can have many data streams, because each stream is another attribute of the file. There are many reasons that NTFS supports multiple data streams, one of them being to support Macintosh files (resource forks). However, the ability to support multiple data segments in a file has created the perfect hiding place for attackers wanting to hide data on the file system.

To specify a specific data stream in an NTFS file, separate the filename and the name of the stream with a colon. Using an example similar to the preceding one, you can create a new data stream in a file and add some example data, as follows:

```
C:\temp>echo random_text > myfile:mystream
C:\temp>dir
 Volume in drive C is SYSTEM
 Volume Serial Number is BCF7-6665
 Directory of C:\temp
```

```
01/29/2005   08:02 PM     <DIR>              .
01/29/2005   08:02 PM     <DIR>              ..
01/29/2005   08:02 PM                     0 myfile
              1 File(s)                    0 bytes
              2 Dir(s)     2,580,427,776 bytes free
C:\temp>dir  myfile:mystream
 Volume in drive C is SYSTEM
 Volume Serial Number is BCF7-6665
 Directory of C:\temp
File Not Found
C:\temp>
```

Note that the *dir* command is not aware of the data stream. If the file were opened with Notepad, the data would be visible. Unlike with HFS+, alternate data streams can be added to directories. To specify the stream for the current directory, leave out a filename. For example:

```
C:\temp>echo  random_text  > :mystream
```

Again, the *dir* command would not reveal this newly created stream. Alternate data streams for files do not have permissions for themselves. The permissions that apply to the file are the same when an alternate data stream is accessed. The copy commands in Explorer, as well as with the *copy* command, maintain alternate data streams as long the files remain on an NTFS file system. If an alternate data stream for a file is altered, the mtime is also altered.

It is possible to put something into NTFS file streams that could easily reside undetected under normal use. Executables or scripts can be hidden inside images and other types of files, and the administrator probably would not know they exist. No known malicious programs have been known to use alternate data streams, but that is not for a lack of demonstration. Proof-of-concept viruses have been written to bring attention to the fact that this characteristic of NTFS files could be abused.

The Kernel

The kernel is the core of the OS. In general, the kernel is a piece of software designed to provide controlled access to the underlying hardware. Modern kernels serve mainly to control process and thread management, memory management, file systems, network management, and interprocess communication. Most users do not interact directly with the kernel, but every process makes use of the kernel in some way. Access to the services provided by the kernel is done through software interfaces known as *system calls*.

There are a few different kinds of kernels, but most systems have either *microkernel* or a *monolithic* kernel. A microkernel breaks down kernel services into modules that run in (unprivileged) user space, whereas the monolithic kernel implements all abstractions provided by the kernel in (privileged) kernel space. The advantage of a microkernel is that a software defect in one service does not necessarily take down the entire system. The advantage with the monolithic kernel is that the abstractions are tightly coupled and therefore more efficient. The original UNIX, BSD variants, and Linux are all monolithic kernels. Mac OS X, MACH, and AIX are popular systems that have microkernels. Supporters of each are happy to argue about the differences and advantages, but the reality with either model is that the kernel controls the hardware. If you own the kernel, you can basically do whatever you want.

Every good host integrity monitoring system monitors the kernel in some way. Rootkits that install themselves into the kernel can be used to subvert monitoring tools, buffer overflow prevention, or hide changes to other parts of the system (e.g., files, processes). There are entire books written about the implementation details of specific kernels. This section is concerned with the general structure of kernel extensions (KEXTs), drivers, modules, and runtime security levels.

Extending the Kernel

Most kernels provide a means of expanding their functionality in some way. Even with monolithic kernels, it is necessary to provide a means to do this, because no kernel should attempt to support every type of service or oddball hardware component.

Linux

An extension to the kernel on Linux is known as a Loadable Kernel Module (LKM). Kernel modules on Linux are used to implement device drivers, system calls, network drivers or shims (e.g., virtual private network [VPN]), file systems, and executable interpreters. LKMs have been around since Version 1.2 of the Linux Kernel (the mid 1990s). The location of the kernel module files has changed over time, and is generally somewhere such as */modules* or */lib/modules*. To list the currently loaded modules in the Linux kernel, use the *lsmod* command:

```
$ lsmod
Module                  Size  Used by     Not tainted
ipt_pkttype              472   4 (autoclean)
ipt_TOS                 1048  12 (autoclean)
ipt_MASQUERADE          1496   0 (autoclean)
ipt_REJECT              3256   4 (autoclean)
ipt_LOG                 3480  12 (autoclean)
```

```
ipt_state               568   23 (autoclean)
ip_nat_irc             2704    0 (unused)
ip_nat_tftp            2096    0 (unused)
ip_nat_ftp             3472    0 (unused)
ip_conntrack_ftp       4496    1 [ip_nat_ftp]
ipt_multiport           696    2 (autoclean)
ipt_conntrack          1208    0 (autoclean)
iptable_filter         1740    1 (autoclean)
iptable_mangle         2168    1 (autoclean)
iptable_nat           18360    3 (autoclean) [ipt_MASQUERADE ip_nat_irc
e100                  59796    1
```

To insert a Linux kernel module into the running kernel, use the *insmod* command. To remove a running kernel module, use the *rmmod* command.

FreeBSD

FreeBSD originally provided kernel extensions through the Linux LKM interface. However, starting with FreeBSD 3.0, FreeBSD provided a replacement for that known as Kernel Loadable Modules (KLD). Kernel loadable modules can be used to implement drivers, generic kernel code, or additional system calls.

Kernel modules are stored in */modules* or */boot/modules* and can automatically be loaded by adding them to the configuration files under */etc/rc.conf*, or by using the *kldload* command. The files that usually reside in the modules directory and that end in *.ko* are called *link files*. A link file is not necessarily a module; it may contain a single module, or it may contain many modules. For example, to view a list of currently loaded link files, use the *kldstat* command:

```
-bash-2.05b$ kldstat
Id Refs Address    Size    Name
 1    3 0xc0400000 322824  kernel
 2   14 0xc0723000 537f0   acpi.ko
```

This command lists the files that have been dynamically linked into the kernel, *not* the individual modules. This is an important distinction. To view the loaded modules, use the verbose flag. For example, to view the modules contained within the *acpi* link file:

```
-bash-2.05b$ kldstat -v -n acpi.ko
Id Refs Address    Size    Name
 2   14 0xc0723000 537f0   acpi.ko
        Contains modules:
```

```
Id Name
 1 nexus/acpi
 2 acpi/acpi_button
 3 acpi/acpi_isab
 4 pcib/acpi_pci
 5 acpi/acpi_pcib
 6 pci/acpi_pcib
 7 acpi/acpi_sysresource
 8 acpi/acpi_timer
 9 acpi/acpi_tz
10 acpi/acpi_acad
11 acpi/acpi_cmbat
12 acpi/cpu
13 acpi/acpi_ec
14 acpi/acpi_lid
```

Solaris

Solaris also supports the concept of dynamic LKMs. Many kernel components (including drivers and system calls) on Solaris are implemented as modules. A typical Solaris installation has more than 100 loaded kernel modules. Also, Solaris has had multiple reported vulnerabilities involving unauthorized insertion of LKMs. To load and unload kernel modules on Solaris, use the *modload* and *modunload* commands. To view a list of currently loaded kernel modules on Solaris, use the *modinfo* command:

```
$ modinfo
Id Loadaddr   Size Info Rev Module Name
 6 1014c000   431b   1    1  specfs (filesystem for specfs)
 8 10151bf8   331c   1    1  TS (time sharing sched class)
 9 101547d0    8d4   -    1  TS_DPTBL (Time sharing dispatch table)
10 10154858  28f63   2    1  ufs (filesystem for ufs)
11 1017b74b    1f7   -    1  fssnap_if (File System Snapshot Interface)
12 1017b89b  12238 226    1  rpcmod (RPC syscall)
12 1017b89b  12238 226    1  rpcmod (32-bit RPC syscall)
12 1017b89b  12238   1    1  rpcmod (rpc interface str mod)
13 1018b17b  666b0   0    1  ip (IP Streams module)
13 1018b17b  666b0   3    1  ip (IP Streams device)
14 101e7d5b   1952   1    1  rootnex (sun4u root nexus 1.90)
15 101e92b8    210  57    1  options (options driver)
```

```
17 101e99ac    18d8   12    1   sad (Streams Administrative driver's)
18 101eb00c     67b    2    1   pseudo (nexus driver for 'pseudo')
19 101eb515   176d0   32    1   sd (SCSI Disk Driver 1.340)
. . .
```

Mac OS X

There are two methods for dynamically adding functionality to the kernel on Mac OS X systems,: KEXTs and IOKit drivers. A KEXT can be used to implement support for a file system or to enhance the network stack. IOKit drivers are generally reserved for interacting with hardware or providing device-driver functionality. IOKit drivers are based on a well-designed C++ framework, whereas the KEXT implementations are written in C and are more in line with the way kernel modules are implemented on other platforms.

KEXTs are traditionally stored in */System/Library/Extensions* on Mac OS X. To load and unload KEXTs or IOKit drivers, use the *kextload* and *kextunload* commands. To view a list of all currently running KEXTs or IOKit drivers, use the *kextstat* command:

```
$ kextstat
Index Refs Address     Size     Wired    Name (Version) <Linked Against>
    1    1 0x0         0x0      0x0       com.apple.kernel (7.7.0)
    2    1 0x0         0x0      0x0       com.apple.kpi.bsd (7.7.0)
    3    1 0x0         0x0      0x0       com.apple.kpi.iokit (7.7.0)
    4    1 0x0         0x0      0x0       com.apple.kpi.libkern (7.7.0)
    5    1 0x0         0x0      0x0       com.apple.kpi.mach (7.7.0)
    6    1 0x0         0x0      0x0       com.apple.iokit.IONVRAMFamily
  (7.7.0)
    7    1 0x0         0x0      0x0       com.apple.driver.AppleNMI
  (7.7.0)
    8   63 0x0         0x0      0x0       com.apple.kernel.6.0 (6.9.9)
    9    1 0x0         0x0      0x0       com.apple.kernel.bsd (6.9.9)
   10    1 0x0         0x0      0x0       com.apple.kernel.iokit (6.9.9)
   11    1 0x0         0x0      0x0       com.apple.kernel.libkern
  (6.9.9)
   12    1 0x0         0x0      0x0       com.apple.kernel.mach (6.9.9)
   . . .
```

Windows

Microsoft Windows allows extensions to the kernel through the implementation of kernel mode drivers. A Windows driver can control everything from a specific hardware component to file systems, network interfaces, or virtual devices such as VPN network adapters. Every driver exports a common set of functionality that Windows uses to interact with the device, whether virtual or physical. The Windows driver module is layered, and some drivers are made up of components in multiple layers. This section is concerned only with Windows 2000, Windows XP, and Windows Advanced Server 2003 drivers. The driver models for older versions of Windows (including NT) are much different and have their own particular complexities.

There are three types of kernel mode drivers: *high, intermediate,* and *low.* The highest drivers sit closest to and interpret data from the application layer, and depend on the functionality of other lower-level drivers that deal with the hardware. Intermediate drivers also depend on low-level device drivers and include *function drivers* and *filter drivers.* A function driver is what you normally think of when thinking about a driver for a device. Function drivers exist to provide a functional interface (support) for a hardware device. Filter drivers serve to modify the features provided by a device by modifying input/output (I/O) requests for the device. The lowest type of device driver for Windows deals specifically with managing the I/O bus that devices use.

Extending the kernel functionality on Windows is complicated. To make things even more difficult , Windows does not provide a native way to list all of the currently loaded drivers. Drivers interact with different areas of the system; you can view loaded drivers through GUI tools, but not in any one specific location. The Windows 2000 Resource Kit provides a command called *drivers.exe* that functions similar to *lsmod* on Linux, and lists the names and attributes of currently loaded drivers:

```
C:\ drivers.exe
```

ModuleName	Code	Data	Bss	Paged	Init	LinkDate
ntoskrnl.exe	429184	96896	0	775360	138880	Tue Dec 07 16:41:11 1999
hal.dll	33600	5536	0	31680	15680	Sat Oct 30 16:48:14 1999
BOOTVID.DLL	5664	2464	0	0	320	Wed Nov 03 18:24:33 1999
pci.sys	12704	1536	0	31264	4608	Wed Oct 27 17:11:08 1999
isapnp.sys	14368	832	0	22944	2048	Sat Oct 02 14:00:35 1999

compbatt.sys	2496	0	0	2880	1216	Fri Oct 22 16:32:49 1999
BATTC.SYS	800	0	0	2976	704	Sun Oct 10 17:45:37 1999
intelide.sys	1760	32	0	0	128	Thu Oct 28 17:20:03 1999
PCIIDEX.SYS	4544	480	0	10944	1632	Wed Oct 27 17:02:19 1999
pcmcia.sys	32800	8864	0	23680	6240	Fri Oct 29 17:20:08 1999
ftdisk.sys	4640	32	0	95072	3392	Mon Nov 22 12:36:23 1999

...

To control the quality and security of loaded drivers, Microsoft digitally signs drivers that pass a suite of tests. These tests inspect the driver for reliability and compatibility with the system and Microsoft standards. For systems that support driver signing (Windows 2000, Windows XP, Windows Server 2003), driver signing checking can be set to ignore, warn, or block drivers that fail the driver signing checks. The default is to warn and prompt the user whether to load the driver or not. This warning can be ignored (or subverted through registry changes), but given the complexity of the Windows driver model, the whole driver-signing process is not a bad idea.

BSD Kernel Security Levels

All of the operating systems that descend from BSD4.4, including FreeBSD, NetBSD, OpenBSD, and Mac OS X, support the concept of kernel security levels. The basic idea is that the kernel attempts to establish levels of runtime security by limiting certain operations. The levels range from −1 to 2 (or 3, depending on the system) with the higher levels being more restrictive. The goal is to prevent unauthorized or unintentional change from occurring. Even the root user is not allowed to make certain changes under the higher security levels.

During the boot sequence, the **init** process sets the security level. The root user can raise the security level, but only the init process can lower it. Table 2.5 lists the security levels and their meanings.

Table 2.5 BSD Kernel Security Levels

Level	Significance
-1	Permanently Insecure Mode: Setting to –1 means that the system will always run at security level 0 in multiuser mode.
0	Insecure Mode: Immutable and append flags can be turned on or off.
1	Secure Mode: Immutable and append flags cannot be turned on or off. Memory devices (*/dev/mem* and */dev/kmem*) are read-only. FreeBSD only: kernel modules may not be loaded.
2	Very Secure Mode: Immutable and append flags cannot be turned off. Certain file system restrictions exist, such as not being able to run newfs or unmount file systems. The system clock can only be advanced, not set back. FreeBSD: The system clock cannot be modified by more than one second.
3	Ultimate Security (FreeBSD only): Same as level 2 except that IP packet filter rules cannot be modified. This includes ipfw, ipfirewall, and pfctl.

One of the problems with this type of security is that there are often operations performed during the boot process that are restricted by the higher security levels. Consequently, the kernel security level is set late in the boot process, and therefore, full protection cannot be relied on during the initial boot sequence.

Another problem is that the security level can only be raised, not lowered, and certain types of administrative tasks may require that the system be taken offline.

The kernel security level can be lowered by init, by booting into single-user mode, or by adjusting a file that dictates what level init should set the level to upon booting. With Mac OS X, running at level 0 requires a rebuild of the kernel; to run at level 1 or 2 requires adjusting the */etc/rc* file. For FreeBSD and NetBSD, the kernel security level can be set in the */etc/rc.local* file. OpenBSD stores the security level in the */etc/rc.securelevel* file.

Libraries and Frameworks

Most systems allow for the creation of two different kinds of libraries: *static* and *shared* (or *dynamic*). Static libraries are essentially a collection of compiled code that developers can link into their programs. Thus, static libraries are relevant only during compilation, not during runtime.

Shared libraries allow multiple applications to use a common set of code without having to incorporate that code into multiple executables. Each program linked against a static library contains the used code from that library. With a shared library, each application contains a reference to the library. Only one copy of the shared library is loaded into memory, where all applications can use it. Static library files usually have file suffix *.a* (*archive*) and shared library files have file suffix *.so* (*shared object*). On Windows, shared libraries are known as *dynamic link libraries* (*.dll*).

If a library has both static and shared versions, most systems will produce executables that use the shared library. However, developers can specify explicitly that they want the library to be statically linked to the executable. The exception is with Mac OS X (discussed later in this chapter).

Problems with Shared Libraries

There are downsides to all shared libraries, but the two that concern us most regard the integrity of the applications that use them.

First, there is the integrity of the library files themselves. With a statically compiled executable, the only dependency is with the runtime environment. Executables that use shared libraries not only depend on the integrity of the runtime environment, but also on the integrity of the shared library files they use, every time they are executed. It is possible for an attacker to replace a shared library with one that performs malicious acts to the system. Furthermore, it is possible for an attacker to replace a shared library that continues to perform its normal function, but also does malicious things, making it difficult to detect .

The second problem has to do with the location of the shared library files. Table 2.6 shows some common places where shared libraries are kept.

Table 2.6 Common Locations for Library Files

OS	Library Directories
*BSD	*/lib, /usr/lib, /usr/local/ib*
Mac OS X	*/usr/lib, /usr/local/lib, /System/Library/Frameworks, /Library/Frameworks*
Linux	*/lib, /usr/lib, /usr/local/lib*
Solaris	*/lib, /usr/lib, /usr/local/lib, /opt/...*
Windows	*%WindowsRoot%, %SystemRoot%*

Shared libraries can reside anywhere on a file system. When an application that requires a shared library is executed, the system attempts to find the required library. Every system has its own procedure for how the dynamic loader locates the necessary library files; some use environment variables. A couple of problems exist under these circumstances. Upgrades may leave a previous (possibly vulnerable) library in the search path first. An attacker may place a malicious library ahead in the search path, or may modify the search path and order directly. Monitoring the integrity of shared library files is very important; almost all modern systems use them. The problem is that you do not necessarily know where to look. The locations listed in Table 2.6 are common for shared libraries, but they can exist anywhere. It is not uncommon for applications to have their own *lib* directories. This is important because applications can be running with dependencies on dynamic libraries that exist anywhere on the file system, and you may or may not be monitoring the integrity of those libraries (see Chapter 4, "Planning").

Dynamic Libraries on Mac OS X

Frameworks are a unique concept of Mac OS X. A framework is basically a directory tree that contains a dynamic (shared) library. Bundled as part of the framework are header files, documentation, and icons or other images. Frameworks are versioned; in other words, multiple iterations of the framework exist in the same directory tree. When an executable is linked with a framework, the path to that framework is embedded into the executable. Because a framework is essentially a dynamic library, only one copy of the framework is loaded into memory at any one time. Multiple applications use the same loaded framework. Just as with other operating systems, there are standard locations, but a framework can exist anywhere on the file system. When an application must make use of a framework and that framework cannot be located, the following paths are searched:

- *$(HOME)/Library/Frameworks*

- */Library/Frameworks*

- */Network/Library/Frameworks*

- */System/Library/Frameworks*

Dynamic libraries on Mac OS X do not necessarily have to be in the form of a framework, but most of them are. Dynamic libraries on Mac OS X have file name suffix *dylib* (dynamic library). Some examples of stand-alone dynamic library files can be found in */usr/lib* and */usr/local/lib*.

Another interesting piece of information about Mac OS X is that all executables are linked against at least one dynamic library—the System Framework (*/System/Library/Frameworks/System.framework*). This is not necessarily peculiar; by default, many systems will link executables against a dynamic version of the C runtime. What is peculiar about Mac OS X is that it is not possible to produce a completely statically linked executable. Most other development environments allow developers to statically link an executable at compile time. This is not possible with Mac OS X.

Technically, it is possible to produce a completely static executable on Mac OS X; however, it requires importing a static C runtime library from the Darwin Source tree. Apple does not support complete static linking with its shipped development environment, and highly recommends against doing so. The other exception to this is with KEXTs, which are also statically linked.

To view the list of the dynamic libraries that an executable is linked against, use the *otool* application:

```
$ otool -L /bin/ls
/bin/ls:
        /usr/lib/libncurses.5.dylib (compatibility version 5.0.0, current
version 5.0.0)
        /usr/lib/libSystem.B.dylib (compatibility version 1.0.0, current
version 71.0.0)
```

The *otool* command is somewhat similar to the *ldd* command on Linux and FreeBSD.

Another oddity of Mac OS X with respect to shared libraries is the concept of *prebinding*. Prebinding involves determining the addresses of all of the symbols in other libraries referenced by an executable or a library, and storing those addresses in the executable or library file. The goal is to prevent this from having to be done by the dynamic linker each time an application is run, and to reduce launch times for applications. Prebinding is a complex tree of dependencies. Applications depend on libraries, and libraries in turn depend on other libraries. The built-in Mac OS X installer and software update applications refer to updating prebinding information such as "optimizing."

The main problem with prebinding is that with every library update, any executables that use that library must have their prebinding information updated. Depending on what information needs to be updated, the mtime, ctime, checksum, and possibly the inode for files change every time prebinding for an executable is updated. The system performs a check when an application is launched and updates the prebinding information if needed. This makes monitoring the integrity of executable files on Mac OS X very difficult and, for all practical purposes, impossible. To complicate things further, the system checks for stale prebinding when applications are launched; therefore, time stamps and checksums will change at irregular intervals, which produces a great deal of noise for host integrity monitoring systems.

An application does not have to be prebound; however, all of the system executables that ship with Mac OS X are prebound. In addition, all applications built using Apple's development environment (xcode) are built as prebound executables by default. To check if an executable or a library is prebound, use the *otool* command with the *h* and *v* options. For example:

```
$ otool -hv /bin/ls
/bin/ls:
Mach header
      magic cputype cpusubtype   filetype ncmds sizeofcmds    flags
   MH_MAGIC      PPC       ALL    EXECUTE    15       1912   NOUNDEFS
DYLDLINK PREBOUND TWOLEVEL
```

One way to mitigate the noise problem of prebinding is to isolate when it will occur. This can be done by renaming the system utilities that update prebinding (*redo_prebinding, update_prebinding*). The problem with this approach is that you will suffer a performance impact as more and more prebinding information becomes stale. To deal with the performance problems, you can schedule prebinding updates to minimize the window of change. The problem with this approach is that there is a race condition between the time the prebinding is updated and the time the new states are established. A more obvious problem with this approach is that it requires more administrative overhead, and this is an administrative decision. Turning off prebinding completely will ensure that more reliable monitoring can be conducted.

Another way to deal with prebinding updates is with the *ctool* command (*http://www.hostintegrity.com/tools/ctool*). The ctool application computes MD5 and SHA-1 checksums of the portions of the files that are not affected by prebinding. The idea is that no matter what kind of prebinding information is updated, the checksum will not change. The downside to this approach is that it will not detect malicious changes to prebinding information (known exploits that take advantage of this do not currently exist). Another downside is that ctool is a stand-alone application that is not easily integrated into a monitoring system. Tools like ctool are more useful when conducting a close examination or spot-checking a handful of files. The ctool will detect if an executable is completely replaced. Otherwise, you have no way of knowing if the whole executable is different, or if only the prebinding information is different.

Finally, the */usr/bin/redo_prebinding* command (installed with the developer tools) has an **undo** feature where it will zero out the prebinding information in a prebound executable. However, it does not appear to be the most reliable command. In the past, I have had to run the command multiple times to arrive at a checksum that could be used for comparison with other systems. To use the *redo_prebinding* command, use the *-z* and *-u* arguments. For example, to undo prebinding on */bin/ls* do:

```
$ cp /bin/ls /tmp

$ cd /tmp
$ redo_prebinding -u -z /tmp/ls
$ openssl md5 /tmp/ls
MD5(/tmp/ls)= 601a9c34aaae8f8fd52786eebc95eb2a
$ redo_prebinding -u -z /tmp/ls
$ openssl md5 /tmp/ls
MD5(/tmp/ls)= a5abdd473d4ae550d73991c2fa02b8b8
$ redo_prebinding -u -z /tmp/ls
$ openssl md5 /tmp/ls
MD5(/tmp/ls)= a5abdd473d4ae550d73991c2fa02b8b8
```

In this case, the undo operation had to be performed twice. There may be a good reason for this, but the main page for this command does not offer any clues.

Mac OS X is not alone in this approach. The Gentoo distribution of Linux provides a similar feature for speeding up the load times of executables (called *prelinking*). However, Gentoo provides the ability to undo the prelink information with the **undo** option to the *prelink* command. This feature facilitates monitoring the integrity of prelinked files.

Runtime

When a host is powered up, the process table comes alive with activity. File access control, runtime privileges, and various other elements of the host environment interact to make up the runtime integrity of the host. The system and user processes affect the kernel and network states. This section takes a closer look at some of the more consequential elements of the runtime, including runtime privileges and access tokens, RPCs, and processes in general.

SUID and SGID Privileges

Every running process on UNIX and Linux systems has at least three UID values associated with it: *real*, effective, and *saved*. There are also real, effective, and saved GID values.

NOTE

Older UNIX systems did not have the concept of a saved UID; however, almost all systems you encounter today do. The saved UID was introduced with the 4.4 release of BSD.

The real UID is the UID of the user that started the process. This value never changes, or at least it should not. The effective UID can change, and is used to determine privileges at any point in time when it is necessary to know whether a process can perform a certain operation (e.g., opening a file). The saved UID is the initial value of the effective UID. The existence of the saved UID allows the effective UID to change and then be restored.

With most executables, the real, effective, and saved UID values are all the same and do not change. If user Bob starts a process, the real, effective, and saved UID are all Bob's UID. The SUID permissions bit changes all of this. If Bob executes an SUID root application, the real UID is Bob's UID, the saved UID is zero, and the initial effective UID is also zero. The SGID bit has the same effect, except that it affects the real, saved, and effective GID values.

Although some SUID applications are not owned by root, most are. The point is to allow users limited abilities to do things that require root privileges. A classic example of this is the "passwd" program that requires write privileges to the password file.

On some systems (e.g., Linux), it is not possible to make a shell script SUID, and for good reason. On other systems such as Mac OS X, it is possible to make a shell script SUID root. (For security reasons, starting with release 10.3.9 of Mac OS X, it is no longer possible to create SUID shell scripts. However, previous versions of Mac OS X still allow for them.) SUID shell scripts should never exist. Monitoring for shell scripts that are SUID is a very good idea, because shell scripts can be manipulated very easily. Shell scripts usually invoke many other commands and often do not use full paths. Other considerations with shell scripts include runtime race conditions and homebrewed use of temporary files,, which generally lend themselves to patched-together error-prone logic made to perform administrative tasks.

Any executable can be installed as SUID root. There are essentially three ways that applications handle this special privilege. First, they ignore it and allow themselves to run with root privileges for the entire duration of execution. Second, the application can lower its privileges and raise them only when root privileges are needed. Finally, the application may perform privileged operations upon start-up and permanently lower its privileges for the remainder of the process execution. This option is ideal because the amount of time the process has root privileges is limited. If privileges are raised and lowered as needed, an attacker who has compromised the process will always be able to restore the effective UID to the root privileges in the saved UID.

Another option available to SUID applications is to implement a form of privilege separation. This works by spawning a child process that permanently drops its privileges and performs the bulk of the functionality of the application. The privileged parent process exists solely to perform privileged operations; the privileged process is limited in functionality and less likely to be exploited. Obviously, this complicates things with respect to signal handling, interprocess communication, and some overhead involved in offloading privileged operations. However, the reduced risk is generally considered worth the trade-off in development and runtime overhead.

As an administrator, you should be aware of all SUID root applications on a system. It is not easy to determine how responsible an SUID or SGID application is with its privileges. Applications that implement privilege separation may not do so correctly and could possibly jeopardize the system more with the added complexity. The best way to manage SUID and SGID applications is to not have any of them; however, this is not a realistic goal because the base installation of most systems contain at least a handful of SUID and SGID applications. As an administrator, it is up to you to decide which of these applications are necessary. In any case, third-party SUID root applications should be highly suspect.

WARNING

As a professional software engineer, I have seen my fair share of software applications installed as SUID root that were very problematic. In one case, an application was installed as SUID root when it never needed the privileges in the first place. As a result many systems contained a poorly written piece of software that ran as root, for no good reason. In another case, I encountered a project that consisted of more than 5MB of poorly written buggy code. This executable would launch other executables, open network ports, and communicate with kernel modules. One day the developers discovered that this application was parsing configuration files multiple times a second, and none of them knew why. This application was installed as a SUID root and deployed onto thousands of hosts. Not surprisingly, buffer overflow vulnerabilities were eventually disclosed, much to the embarrassment of the company and risk to the users.

Poorly written software installed as the SUID root can jeopardize the integrity of a host or a network of hosts. Monitoring for the appearance of SUID root applications is critical. A reasonable assurance that an SUID or SGID application is not a threat to the integrity of a host can be acquired by knowing all of the ways that such an application can be used, abused, and misused, which is practically impossible to determine. Therefore, minimizing the number of SUID/SGID files on your systems, auditing the ones that exist, and monitoring them for changes is your best course of action with respect to powerful file permissions (see Chapter 9, "Advanced Strategies").

Windows Access Tokens

Runtime privileges, like file permissions, are more complicated on Windows. Every running process on a Windows system contains an access token. Access tokens provide information about the identity and privileges associated with a user account. Windows runtime security involves many elements such as SIDs, security descriptors (ACLs), security principles, and generic access permissions. All of these are managed using access tokens.

Upon login or authentication, a primary access token is created. This access token includes the user's SID, the group SIDs for all groups that the user is a member of, default access control information, impersonation level (explained later in this chapter), and other privilege specifications. After authentication, any process launched on behalf of the user maintains a copy of this access token. Modifications to user accounts on Windows or any of the groups or privileges associated with the user do not take effect until the next time that user authenticates.

Whenever a process requests access to the system or attempts to perform a privileged operation, the system consults that process's access token to determine if the operation should or should not be allowed. In the same way that UNIX and Linux systems have effective and real UID values, Windows processes and threads have a similar concept with access tokens. In the Windows world, there are primary access tokens and impersonation access tokens. The primary access token is associated with the user who is responsible for the process, or thread, whereas the impersonation access token is a deviation from the primary token, though not quite the same in purpose as the effective UID on UNIX.

The main goal of impersonation access tokens is to allow services to assume a user's privileges when providing access to a resource; these are usually client/server interactions. When a request is made of a service, the client provides an impersonation level that designates to what degree the service can impersonate the client. The service then assumes the identity of the client for the duration of the request by using an impersonation access token.

RPC and DCOM

Search on Google for Remote Procedure Call (RPC) and Distributed Component Object Model (DCOM), and you will most likely see a list of vulnerability bulletins and security alerts involving known exploits, viruses, and worms on Windows. RPC is a more general term that describes the process of allowing an application to invoke a procedure within another process on another host. Microsoft Windows implements support and implementation of RPC. Windows provides built-in RPC support that is enabled by default, and developers can incorporate RPC into their own applications. RPC is basically an abstraction of interprocess communication that takes place over a network. The RPC runtime takes care of hiding the fact that there is a network standing between the processes. Windows RPC makes use of Hypertext Transfer Protocol (HTTP) as the transport protocol.

The DCOM is an extension to the Component Object Model (COM). DCOM is a protocol that uses Windows RPC. The relatively scalable, language-independent DCOM provides for network efficiency for RPC-related functionality. DCOM is associated with many recent Windows RPC exploits. Any Windows host that has RPC over HTTP enabled will also accept DCOM requests. It is possible to disable DCOM, but it requires a registry tweak. A more effective approach is to simply disable RPC.

If you look at the Services program on Windows, you will notice two RPC-related services. One is the RPC locater service and the other is the general RPC service that listens on port 135 (see Figure 2.5).

Figure 2.5 Windows RPC Services

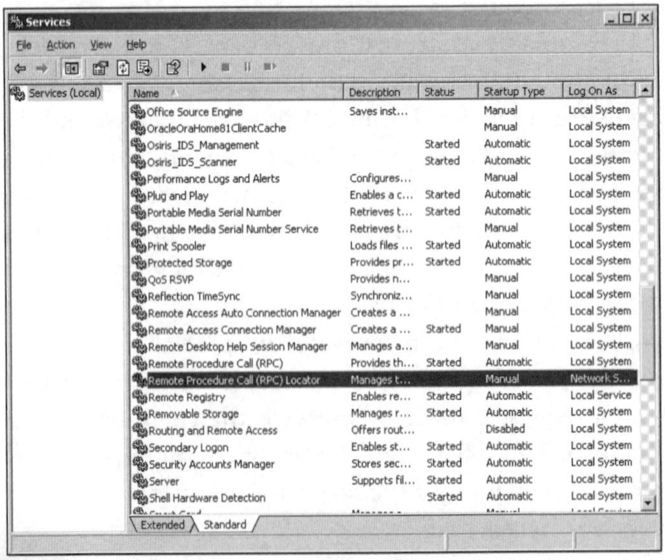

The RPC service is used for many applications. For example, Exchange and Active Directory are big users of RPC, but many other Windows services also depend on it. Disabling RPC can have a significant impact on functionality. For this reason, the RPC service cannot be stopped through the services panel. Disabling RPC can be done, but requires uninstalling it through the Windows control panel. Although workarounds for RPC-related vulnerabilities have been to disable RPC in the past, the practical solution is to download and patch the system.

The RPC Locater Service is responsible for maintaining a listing of available RPC services and servers. The locater is generally only run on servers or domain controllers. This service does not run (set to manual) by default. Both the RPC service and the locater service have a history of vulnerabilities that have led to the development of some malicious remote exploits. Exploits taking advantage of RPC can demonstrate themselves in a number of ways. A HIMS will often pick up on, but not necessarily highlight, the fact that it is related to RPC. For example, there have been many worms that have taken advantage of RPC vulnerabilities that are most often found through the existence of new files, modified system executables, and suspect registry modifications.

Processes

On a typical default installation of RedHat 9, there are more than 60 processes running, with more than half of them running as root. On Mac OS X, the results are similar. On most of the Linux systems I have access to, the process count is close to 200 at any given time. Users and administrators place a great deal of faith in these nebulous blocks of executable code. There is an implicit trust in the processes that ship with the baseline distributions of popular operating systems, but that does not mean that these processes cannot have a negative impact on the integrity of the run-time environment. Even with systems such as FreeBSD where the source for the entire system is available, most administrators trust that someone else is reviewing the code and that any noteworthy security risk will come across the bugtraq mailing list. The point is that most administrators do not spend their time with binary analysis or proofreading source code.

When a system shows signs of being overloaded, unresponsive, or suspicious in any way, a common response is to look at which processes are running and how much system resources they are each consuming. Resource consumption can be any combination of CPU, memory, or I/O. The *ps* command can reveal a great deal of information about running processes, including CPU and memory usage. On Windows, the "task manager" reveals most of the relevant information, including CPU and memory usage. For advanced process analysis, the Resource Kit provides the pstat application to reveal detailed per-process memory and CPU utilization. Most UNIX systems also support *lsof*, a very useful utility that will display a list of all opened files and their associated PID and user. The *lsof* command is a very useful utility for analyzing the file activities of suspicious executables. Finally, most systems also provide a means of tracing the system calls requested by an application. On Linux and BSD systems, there is the *strace* command, for Mac OS X there is *ktrace*, and for Solaris there is *truss*.

One of the roles of the kernel is process management. However, this usually involves things such as CPU scheduling, responding to system calls, and maintaining the integrity of the memory space of each process. As far as keeping processes inline, the kernel allows most processes (even those executed by unprivileged users) to consume massive amounts of system resources. An application that does nothing but consume I/O, memory, or CPU cycles can bring a system to its knees. Therefore, monitoring the system process table and various elements of process behavior is an important part of monitoring a host's integrity.

Networking

What does networking have to do with the integrity of a host? Plenty. In many cases, it is easy to distinguish between security at the network level and security at the host level. However, the data on a network originated from a host of some kind. Although network monitoring can detect attacks, pinpoint vectors for worms, or detect unauthorized activity, in some cases, it makes more sense to monitor the origin of this activity by monitoring your host's networking environments.

Interfaces

After gaining control of a system, an attacker sometimes places a network interface into *promiscuous* mode in order to sniff the network for other sensitive information. Although network security monitoring can detect a promiscuous interface, it is also something that a host integrity monitoring system can easily detect. Most UNIX systems reveal promiscuous status in the interface viewed with the *ifconfig* command. For example, on FreeBSD:

```
$ ifconfig bfe0
bfe0: flags=8943<UP,BROADCAST,RUNNING,PROMISC,SIMPLEX,MULTICAST> mtu 1500
        options=8<VLAN_MTU>
        inet6 fe80::20f:1fff:fe4a:e945%bfe0 prefixlen 64 scopeid 0x1
        inet 10.10.0.1 netmask 0xffffff00 broadcast 255.255.255.255
        ether 00:0f:1f:4a:e9:45
```

```
media: Ethernet autoselect (100baseTX <full-duplex>)
status: active
```

It is possible to mitigate this problem through system configuration. On FreeBSD, it is possible to disable an interface from being put into promiscuous mode by removing Berkeley Packet Filter (BPF) support in the filter. This requires a kernel recompile as the default kernel comes with BPF support. However, this is not always an option because some applications (e.g., Snort) require this support. In that case, it makes sense to monitor your network interfaces so that you are aware of which interfaces are promiscuous and when.

Ports

Open network ports are sometimes the first indication of a problem for a host. Worms or trojans may open network ports as a means of propagation or to relay information back to a home base of some kind. An attacker may open a network port as part of a backdoor for access to the system later. Or a new piece of software may have been installed without authorization. In any case, it is very important to stay aware of your host's listening network ports. Network monitoring tools such as Nessus and Nmap can be used to analyze a host's open network ports. However, these tools are more suited for random scans. Scanning all of your hosts for open ports every few minutes is not practical and will probably trigger false positives on your network-monitoring infrastructure. It makes more sense for this to be done by a host integrity monitoring system.

The *netstat* command is common on most systems and can be used to list network ports that are currently in the LISTEN state, waiting to receive connections:

```
$ netstat -na | grep LISTEN
tcp4      0      0  127.0.0.1.631        *.*          LISTEN
tcp46     0      0  *.22                 *.*          LISTEN
tcp4      0      0  *.3306               *.*          LISTEN
```

The following example was taken from Mac OS X. In this case, there is one port (631) accepting only local connections. This is the CUPS printing support. The other two allow remote connections (SSH, MySQL). However, these are only the TCP ports; you can also get a listing of open UDP ports:

```
$ netstat -na -p udp
Active Internet connections (including servers)
Proto Recv-Q Send-Q  Local Address           Foreign Address          (state)
udp4      0      0    127.0.0.1.52671         127.0.0.1.52671
udp4      0      0    *.5353                  *.*
udp4      0      0    *.*                     *.*
udp4      0      0    127.0.0.1.49162         127.0.0.1.1023
udp4      0      0    *.*                     *.*
udp4      0      0    *.631                   *.*
udp4      0      0    10.10.1.190.123         *.*
udp4      0      0    127.0.0.1.123           *.*
udp4      0      0    *.123                   *.*
udp4      0      0    127.0.0.1.49159         127.0.0.1.1022
udp4      0      0    127.0.0.1.49158         127.0.0.1.1022
udp4      0      0    127.0.0.1.1022          *.*
udp4      0      0    127.0.0.1.1023          *.*
udp4      0      0    *.68                    *.*
udp4      0      0    127.0.0.1.1033          *.*
udp4      0      0    *.514                   *.*
udp6      0      0    *.514                   *.*
```

Obviously, ports accepting remote connections expose the host more, but all should be monitored. Firewalls can prevent open ports from being reachable, but can also be subverted. Also, local users or malicious applications can attack an open local network port in an attempt to disrupt a service or escalate privileges. Monitoring hosts for changes in their list of open network ports is very important.

Nonvolatile Memory

Ten years ago, conducting an integrity assessment of a system involved performing checksums of certain binaries. Rootkits were not nearly as involved as they are today. If a system was compromised, attackers might hide their tracks by planting evil versions of *ls* or *ps*, but not all methods for getting information about files or processes. In today's world, integrity assurance is a much more difficult task. Rootkits have evolved significantly; attackers and security administrators are constantly fighting to stay ahead of each other in a world that is increasingly becoming obsessed with the importance of security at both network and host environments. As older threat models are being dealt with, attackers are resorting to newer, less protected fronts in order to compromise a host. One of the fronts destined to attract more attention will be with the exploitation of nonvolatile memory.

Nonvolatile memory is a hardware component like FLASH and EEPROM. Devices including Ethernet controllers, graphics, and video boards, and the basic input/output system (BIOS) or CMOS contain writable memory elements that retain their state even when not powered. The concept of malicious code being written to the BIOS is not new, and BIOS manufacturers have since resorted to taking steps toward virus protection, but it has not proved to be very successful. With advances in technology for components such as Ethernet, graphics cards, disk controllers, and others, writable nonvolatile memory is finding itself in more elements of a system, and with greater capacity. If a system is compromised, most people believe that erasing the disk and rebuilding the system from trusted media will result in a known good trusted initial state. However, if the malicious source is actually stored in nonvolatile memory of some kind, rebuilding may not help at all. With nonvolatile memory gaining a bigger footprint on systems, this is becoming more of a risk to the integrity of hosts.

The problem is that attack scenarios involving nonvolatile memory are specific to hardware and certain system configurations. This can significantly limit the ease at which malicious software can propagate. For the same reasons, it is difficult to implement support for monitoring all of these disparate hardware sources of nonvolatile memory. In any case, the problem exists; it is not impossible for a worm to exploit something like an Ethernet controller and spread many similar hardware configurations throughout a network. Think about the security of mobile devices such as phones and personal digital assistants (PDAs). By and large, security relied on the proprietary nature of their environments; however, we are starting to see antivirus software for mobile devices.

Summary

This chapter covered many facets of a typical host environment, including common UNIX, Linux, and Windows operating systems. Although these environments vary, it is helpful to understand the general landscape of a host, and that host integrity involves monitoring more than just files.

Users and groups provide the backbone of access control, whether for the relatively simplistic UNIX model or with the more byzantine access control mechanisms found on Windows. Although the kernel serves to abstract and facilitate safe use of hardware, it is exposed through the ability to dynamically load code and other APIs that make it vulnerable to abuse. Libraries and frameworks are an important and critical aspect to the runtime security of a host. Processes run with varied privileges and interact with other processes consuming various amounts of system resources. The network stack provides a gateway to the network, allowing incoming and outgoing data that must be controlled. Finally, areas of the host environment that are not often included in integrity monitoring, such as nonvolatile memory, are future battlegrounds in the overall fight to maintain host integrity. Monitoring the integrity of a host involves keeping a watchful eye on all areas of the host environment.

Solutions Fast Track

Users and Groups

☑ Users and groups provide the basis by which access control and privilege is enforced for file system activity and processes.

☑ Escalation of privilege is a common goal for attackers and malicious users. Effective host integrity monitoring on any platform includes monitoring changes to user and group configurations.

Files and File Systems

☑ Files make up a large part of host integrity monitoring because most system interaction involves operating on files in some way.

☑ The integrity of a host is dependent on the file system security, especially for system executables and libraries.

☑ Understanding the basic structure of file systems and file attributes will help you understand the significance of a detected change, and how to respond to that change.

The Kernel

☑ Most kernels support dynamic loading of code; this feature is often the target of attack.

☑ The kernel has complete control over the system. An attacker that has compromised the kernel can make it very difficult to detect that an intrusion has occurred, and can destroy the integrity of the environment by altering the behavior of system calls.

☑ Monitor as many aspects of the kernel as possible, including kernel object files, the kernel file itself, symbol tables, and the list of currently running KEXTs.

Libraries and Frameworks

☑ Dynamic libraries are an ongoing integrity concern because the integrity of the library files is an issue each time a dependent application is run.

☑ Dynamic libraries are often neglected because they are separate from the executables and can exist anywhere on the file system. All dynamic library files should be treated like executables and strictly monitored for any changes.

☑ Prebinding and prelinking present a serious problem for file integrity monitoring because they change files without any practical way of verifying the nature of the change. Applications such as ctool and prelink on Linux are helpful, but not ideal solutions.

Runtime

☑ SUID and SGID applications allow processes to run with specific privileges, regardless of which user started the process. These access permissions must not be taken lightly. Host integrity monitoring should include regular audits for SUID root executables.

☑ Operating systems allow unprivileged processes to consume massive amounts of resources. A host integrity monitoring deployment must watch for processes that are consuming more than acceptable amounts of system resources.

☑ Complicated access control and runtime privilege schemes are a threat to the integrity of a host. Administration is difficult, and the ramifications of changes are not often realized. Monitoring the integrity of the runtime environment is an essential part of host integrity monitoring.

Network

☑ A compromised host is sometimes used as a launching pad for other attacks. Monitoring your host's network facilities can sometimes be the first indication that you are being attacked or misused, or that malicious activity is attempting to spread to other hosts.

☑ Buggy software attached to the listening end of a network port can create a vector for worms to spread from host to host. Monitoring open network ports is essential in detecting when a host has left itself open to attack.

Nonvolatile Memory

☑ Nonvolatile memory will likely become more and more popular in the area of host integrity.

☑ Attacks involving nonvolatile memory are more complex, but also becoming more of a reality. Mass deployments of like hardware configurations are ripe targets for worms or viruses that hide themselves in nonvolatile memory of some kind.

Frequently Asked Questions

The following Frequently Asked Questions, answered by the authors of this book, are designed to both measure your understanding of the concepts presented in this chapter and to assist you with real-life implementation of these concepts. To have your questions about this chapter answered by the author, browse to **www.syngress.com/solutions** and click on the **"Ask the Author"** form. You will also gain access to thousands of other FAQs at ITFAQnet.com.

Q: Other than changes to the root or administrator user, why is it so important to monitor changes to other users or groups?

A: Changing user and group information usually involves administrator privileges. If a change to the user or the group configuration of a host was not done by an administrator, this is a problem. Monitoring for unauthorized changes can detect compromised accounts, as well as unauthorized or unintentional change. Whether or not a change was authorized, the resulting impact of a user or group change is not always apparent. Users added to groups open new file system privileges and may provide them with additional runtime privileges.

Q: Do I need to understand how file systems and files are implemented?

A: No; it is not necessary. What is important is being familiar with the attributes of files so that when you see a change, you understand the significance of that change.

Q: Does disabling the ability to load kernel modules prevent the kernel from being tampered with?

A: No. While kernel modules and extensions are often attacked, there are other ways of compromising the kernel. First, the kernel file itself can be altered or replaced with one that is built to do the bidding of the attacker. Second, the running kernel memory itself can be altered and compromised. Thus, it is important to monitor as many facets of the kernel as possible, including runtime characteristics and the supporting files.

Q: Does performing a regular analysis on the checksum of a file detect all changes to that file's contents?

A: No. Changes to resource forks and alternate data streams are often not picked up even by moderately sophisticated integrity monitoring tools.

Q: I protect my hosts with firewalls. Why is it necessary to monitor for open network ports?

A: External firewalls exist mainly to protect software services that cannot be trusted to withstand an attack. Firewalls are themselves software that can fail or be subverted. It does not make sense to build a wall around your host while network services are allowed to run, because eventually, the wall will crumble. Instead, configure your host as if you do not have a firewall, locking down services and exposing only ports that you need. Monitor this configuration for any change. The firewall serves as an added layer of protection.

## Chapter 3

Understanding Threats

Solutions in this chapter:

- **Malicious Software**
- **Internal Threats**
- **Rootkits**
- **A Tour of Successful Worms**
- **Circumventing Host Integrity Monitoring**

☑ **Summary**

☑ **Solutions Fast Track**

☑ **Frequently Asked Questions**

Introduction

Threats to hosts are everywhere. They include software such as remote exploits, viruses, and poorly written software applications. A threat can also be a malignant administrator, a malicious user, or even uncontrolled physical access. This chapter focuses on the threats that host integrity monitoring looks for, specifically insider threats and rootkits. We also look at some successful worms and their effect on the hosts they infected. Finally, we look at threats to host integrity monitoring (HIM) tools and discuss ways to mitigate them.

Before you can establish a plan for monitoring the integrity of your hosts, you must understand their environment and the threats to that environment. This process includes defining what the threat is and its potential impact on the environment. Once you understand the impact, you can define symptoms that will indicate if a threat has been realized. Those symptoms are used to establish a plan for monitoring the environment.

An example of this is the training required to become a doctor. Even though most doctors eventually specialize, their medical training still requires them to understand basic anatomy. This background proves helpful when detecting things that are out of the ordinary. In addition, doctors study the nature and effects of diseases to learn how they behave and to be able to detect them. Like all analogies, this one eventually breaks down, but effective host integrity monitoring requires an understanding of the host environment, how it can be attacked, and how those attacks can be detected.

Malicious Software

Malicious software is classified and comes in many different forms. These classifications are not perfect and there are always exceptions; however, they help relay information about the nature and behavior of the software in question, including viruses, worms, Trojans, and spyware.

Viruses

A computer virus is software that attaches itself to other software with the intent of spreading to other systems. The secondary purpose of a virus is to consume resources, destroy data or other software, and inflict damage to the underlying hardware.

A computer virus is self-replicating, traveling from computer to computer through human interaction (opening e-mail attachments, downloading and installing software from unknown sources, sharing infected files). Viruses generally do not spread on their own; they take advantage of common human interaction. Melissa is a good example of a successful virus. Melissa took advantage of Microsoft Word macros and spread by mailing itself to the first 50 e-mail addresses in the Microsoft Outlook address book. People often open attachments and unintentionally run viruses because they recognize the sender of the file.

Viruses have infected computer systems for many years. Many people consider purchasing antivirus software a necessary part of the cost of owning a personal computer. The reality is that many viruses can be thwarted by responsible use; using antivirus software is not always the best way to deal with the problem. Unfortunately, some people are easily convinced that they need a yearly subscription for antivirus software.

Worms

A software worm is self-replicating and moves from computer to computer autonomously. The distinguishing factor between a virus and a worm is that a worm can spread on its own accord; no human interaction is needed. This can be more problematic than a virus because a worm can spread rapidly. Even if you detect that a system is infected, the worm may have already been used as a stepping-stone to infect other machines. A successful vector for a worm is determined by access and the nature of the vulnerability. Worms can also adversely affect patch management. In some cases, it may not be possible to patch vulnerable hosts before they are infected. For example, the SQL Slammer worm doubled its infected host count every 8.5 seconds, and hit 90 percent infection of vulnerable hosts in 10 minutes. After this worm took off, patching was not possible. Furthermore, a HIMS in this situation would be completely useless to you. Also, vulnerabilities may be made public before the vendor provides a fix. Sometimes there are workarounds, but they can be challenging when thousands of hosts are involved.

Although the first Internet worm surfaced in the late 1980s, they did not garner much attention until recent years. The widespread adoption of broadband Internet connections has resulted in more vulnerable computers being connected to the Internet for longer periods of time. This development, combined with the continual discovery of software vulnerabilities, has resulted in network landscapes ripe for spreading software worms. Some examples of popular worms include Blaster, Linux Slapper, Code Red, SQL Slammer, and Nimbda (discussed later in this chapter).

Trojans

Trojan software is software that looks legitimate, but is actually used as a vehicle for conducting malicious activity on a host. There are many vectors for Trojan software. A Trojan can be sent in an e-mail disguised as an attractive piece of software, or, ironically, as a security update. An attacker may compromise a vendor's Web site and plant Trojan copies of its software. Users who cannot verify the source of the software then become victims. Because Trojans mask themselves as legitimate software, they are not easy to detect. A good example of this is the GNU File Transfer Protocol (FTP) server compromise (*http://www.linuxsecurity.com/content/view/114468/65/*).

A classic use for Trojans is with rootkits. When an attacker compromises a system, it is not uncommon for them to replace certain system executables with versions containing Trojans in order to leave backdoors, hide specific information about the environment from administrators, or hide the intrusion itself.

Some examples of popular backdoor Trojans include Back Oriface and NetBus. These two Trojans install servers that allow unrestricted remote access to certain versions of Microsoft Windows. The Phel.A Trojan affects more recent versions of Windows, specifically XP SP2. This Trojan modifies the registry so that it is executed every time the system is booted.

Spyware

Another software-based threat is spyware, which is software that collects information about the host environment or the actions of users (without their consent), and then sends the information to a central location. There are many different types of spyware. Some attempt to steal passwords or financial information. Some collect statistics-related usage such as purchasing habits, which Web sites are visited, and search engine activity. Most spyware is hidden so that the users do not know it exists on their systems; however, there are many Web browser add-on modules that claim to provide some sort of benefit. Regardless of the function, the attribute that ties all of this software together is collecting information without the consent of the user.

In recent years, many companies have tried to find a solution for this threat. Even Microsoft has released software to deal specifically with spyware (*http://www.microsoft.com/athome/security/spyware/software*). Many antivirus companies claim that their technical support lines are ringing off the hook with issues related to spyware. These types of threats have existed for years; however, now there is a means for them to see widespread infection.

General Considerations

Software can also be unintentionally malicious. Although not common, there have been cases where someone developed a virus or a worm but did not intend it to be destructive. Sometimes proof-of-concept viruses and worms are written to bring attention to a vulnerability. In other cases, someone may be developing software for educational purposes and accidentally release it. A doctoral student at Cornell University wrote the first Internet worm in 1988. The first worms were designed to make computer systems and networks more productive.

> **NOTE**
>
> The most important thing to remember is that the real problem is flawed software. Viruses are not a problem, because people do not have the latest trendy antivirus program or up-to-date virus signatures. Internet worms are not a problem because people leave their computers connected to a DSL modem overnight. The real problem is that most software is flawed. Software applications may satisfy a list of functional requirements, but they often unintentionally allow themselves to be abused and leave hosts vulnerable to attack. The primary line of defense for a host should not be a firewall, network security appliances, antispyware, or antivirus software. These are all tools that may prove helpful, but they should not constitute the backbone of your host's security defenses.

Operating systems and software applications and services should provide adequate security for hosts, and firewalls should be considered icing on the cake for secure host environments. In my experience as a software engineer, the development of secure software is not a goal for most commercial software vendors, even those with security-related products. Until this situation changes, you will see vulnerabilities in software systems being exploited every day. In the meantime, it helps to know how some of these malicious software applications work. (We look at a few effects of some software worms later in this chapter.)

Internal Threats

Internal threats are not a new concept. Employees abuse insider privilege, store clerks help themselves to cash from the register, CIA agents sell national secrets to other governments, and so on. It is no surprise that people with internal access to computer systems abuse their access privileges.

Firewalls and other perimeter defenses are powerless to detect internal attacks or misuse. So much effort is directed at keeping the bad guys out, that many systems are left vulnerable to inside attacks. I have seen studies that concluded that internal attacks are more prevalent than external attacks. I have also seen studies that claim the opposite or that they are equally as frequent. Whatever the case, most systems are designed to defend from the outside more than from the inside. The problem with this is there are different factors involved with threats that originate from the inside.

An attacker may know the established protocol for incident response, and whether network- or host-based monitoring or auditing is being conducted and how to subvert it. Insiders often know of weaknesses or vulnerabilities, defense mechanisms, software versions, patch levels, and information about where sensitive information is being stored. Furthermore, a malicious insider may have designed network or security architecture or been an administrator or security officer. They may have physical access to systems. The insider threat is indeed a problem. To understand how to detect insider abuse, we look at some of the ways that internal attacks are realized.

Local Access

Local access implies that you have circumvented perimeter security, legitimately or not. It means that you have shell access in some form or that you are sitting in front of the console and have access to accounts on a host or network of hosts. Local access is a big deal. Many security professionals consider unauthorized local access to a host the final stretch in rooting a box. That is, once an attacker has taken advantage of a non-root remote exploit to gain access to a system, it is simply a matter of time before he is able to elevate his privileges; there always seems to be a way. The abuse of local access can be seen in different forms.

The humdrum of unprivileged local access can be remedied through a number of local exploits. Locally based exploits that allow non-root users the ability to elevate their privileges, are constantly being discovered. For example, *cve.mitre.org* reports more than a dozen Solaris vulnerabilities in 2004 alone, involving locally based exploits being used to gain unauthorized access. One of the more interesting of these is the Solaris root exploit using the passwd program (*http://www.ciac.org/ciac/bulletins/o-088.shtml*). Sun Microsystems claims there are no symptoms that would indicate that the exploit has been executed. However, if you are monitoring processes on your Solaris system and see a shell process being executed by the root, I would argue that it is a symptom. Local exploits are not going away; however, steps can be made to detect when an attacker is pounding on the door attempting to gain access.

Bad software is another risk that fuels the threat of local access. In the same way that lousy software paves the way for remote exploits, it also allows for locally based exploits. The difference is that many times there is no firewall to deny access to open ports. Some applications listen exclusively on the loopback adapter, which means local users have the ability to hurl data at those open ports. Software often makes the bad assumption that local users always have the best of intentions. Finally, software is often not installed correctly with respect to permissions, file and group ownership, or special permissions such as Set User ID (SUID) root. Local users attempting to abuse software can show a variety of symptoms. First, you may see the appearance of core files generated by system utilities. Core dump files from SUID root applications are highly suspect. Furthermore, you may see time stamps for configuration files changing that cannot be traced back to an administrative task. Another indication of software abuse is increased resources associated with scripts or software that is being made to run a marathon of cycles in hopes that it will falter.

The default installations of most operating systems do not have strict compliance with the principle of least privilege, specifically about file permissions. Unprivileged users can often view system logs, the contents of configuration files such as the syslog, and the contents of */etc/passwd*. A strict interpretation of least privilege means that unprivileged local users should not have access to this information. In the event that an account is compromised, an attacker can gain a great deal of information about the system, its configuration, and other users. All of this can be used to mount a successful attack. There is no reason that unprivileged users have to execute or read access to all of the executables in */sbin* or */usr/local/sbin*, or the like. Although most systems do not allow non-root users the ability to write to system executables, they often allow them to read or execute them.

Universities, Internet service providers, and other organizations that have systems with thousands of users run the risk of having compromised accounts. When I was in school, getting credentials for a university account was easier than finding your way around campus. Aside from all of the aforementioned symptoms, compromised accounts can sometimes be detected by monitoring the login and logout events associated with users. Specifically, you can check for an unrealistic amount of login sessions or logins to systems at suspicious times.

Finally, local access enables users to consume more system resources than you might expect. Most operating systems prevent themselves from falling over, but most do not stop users from doing anything short of that. On most systems you can write applications that will continually allocate memory, or make use of an input/output (I/O) device and bring all other facilities to a slow crawl. Serious abuses of this are easy to discover by monitoring the network, I/O, memory, and other resources. This can sometimes lead to the detection of other unauthorized activities or compromise such as a backdoor or a file sharing service.

Administrative Negligence

An often-overlooked internal threat is administrative negligence. If an administrator or security officer does not keep abreast of new security information, they cannot apply it to their jobs. If they are careless with their administrative tasks, they can leave hosts open to attack.

Poorly written software can have a big impact on the integrity of a host environment. Administrators are not aware sometimes that a certain software application can leave a host open to local or remote exploits. Fortunately, the installation of new software is easy to detect. When your host integrity monitoring system (HIMS) continually monitors the system for new executables, it is unlikely that another administrator (or software) will install new applications without your knowledge.

Along with poorly written software is the configuration of software. An administrator may not learn how to properly configure a software deployment and trust the integrity of the host to the vendor's default configuration. The configuration of remote access services such as Secure Shell (SSH), database servers, and Web servers can determine the fate of a host. Configuration issues are harder to monitor directly. However, once you have established a known good configuration, you can monitor the content changes to certain configuration files so that any changes do not go unnoticed.

Auditing and logging are critical for maintaining the security of a host. The establishment of proper logging mechanisms can be used to detect local and remote attacks. It is also useful when conducting damage assessment or forensics. Logging systems that are attacked or simply never set up, are a threat to the integrity of the host. Monitoring logging services (such as syslogd), as well as their configuration, is a good practice.

Administrative Abuse

Administrative abuse is the ultimate in local threats, because system administrators not only have local access to the system but they also have privileged access as a requirement for some of their duties. System administrators often know how systems are designed, where auditing trails are, and how they can cover their tracks.

Ideally, security administrators are not in charge of security for a host or network. Instead, they have privileged access, but their actions are fully logged and audited. If another person or department is in charge of security, it is much harder for a malicious administrator to subvert security measures. Mitigating the threat of an administrator abusing their privileges can be done by involving multiple administrators in the reporting of host integrity monitoring reports or any other security-related alerts for that matter.

Rootkits

A rootkit is a collection of modified system applications or kernel code that is used to create a backdoor to a system without being detected. Rootkits can be deployed onto a system via a worm, or an attacker can use a local vulnerability. Traditionally, rootkits were modified system utilities such as **ps**, **ls**, **find**, **netstat**, and others, which would perform their function, but be built to serve the needs of the attacker; for example, hiding a system process or files, collecting passwords, or opening a backdoor. Although effective at one time, modern host integrity monitoring systems will notice these right away. When talking about rootkits today, what we mean is kernel rootkits.

The idea is the same with a kernel rootkit; alter the system and create an undetected backdoor. The difference with a kernel rootkit is that the altered code involves a Trojan or patched kernel code. A kernel rootkit is loaded as a driver or a kernel extension and usually takes advantage of *call hooking*. Because kernel rootkits involve compromising the kernel, they can basically do anything, including avoiding detection by other software.

Kernel rootkits require a full compromise of the system to be installed. That is, an attacker must have obtained root or administrative privileges to install the rootkit. Unfortunately, remote administrative level exploits of Microsoft Windows is not unheard of. It is not surprising that many kernel rootkits are developed for Windows. This is another case in point for the power of local access. Locally based exploits provide a means for malicious users to install kernel rootkits. Although there has been a great deal of discussion about this topic (e.g., Microsoft, RSA 2005), kernel rootkits for Windows have existed for years; they are not a new phenomenon and are becoming more refined.

NOTE

An interesting thing to note about kernel rootkits is that they are mostly based on call hooking. This involves redirecting the normal execution of code to code placed by an attacker, which can happen within an application, a library, or OS syscalls. An attacker will often call the original code to simulate what would be the normal result of the call, which is a common way to avoid detection. An example would be to return the contents of a directory; only the list would exclude the attacker's file(s).

Rootkits can do various things, such as provide backdoor access to a host, capture network traffic, or steal sensitive information by logging keystrokes. A kernel rootkit that installs itself without being detected and does not bring attention to itself, presents a very serious problem. At this point, the only recommended way to detect this kind of attack involves offline analysis. Other indications may involve the events surrounding the initial compromise, a mistake in covering the installation of the rootkit, or some other detected hiccup or change in system behavior.

A Tour of Successful Worms

This section takes a close look at the impact some of the more popular software worms have had on their infected hosts. For each worm, we provide basic information about how it gains access to the host and what it does to the environment. The goal of this section is to see firsthand the effects of software worms and learn from the footprint left on the host terrain. Worms come and go, and although these worms were not released yesterday, you can see how they impact their environment and use that information to develop a plan of what to monitor in the host environment.

Worm #1: W32 Blaster

Name: W32/Blaster
Affected systems: Windows NT, Windows 2000, Windows XP, Windows 2003 AS
CVE: CAN-2003-0352

Description

The Blaster worm exploits vulnerabilities in the Remote Procedure Call (RPC) Distributed Component Object Model (DCOM) implementation of certain versions of Microsoft Windows. In addition to performing all of the attributes of a worm such as locating and infecting other hosts, this worm also attempts to conduct a denial-of-service (DOS) attack on the Microsoft Windows update Web server (*http://www.windowsupdate.com*).

Footprint

- Sets the registry key:

```
HKLM\SOFTWARE\Microsoft Windows\CurrentVersion\Run  "windows auto
update"="msblast.exe"
```

- Sends traffic on port 135 to attempt to infect other hosts.
- Opens a backdoor by listening on Transmission Control Protocol (TCP) port 4444 to accept remote commands.
- Opens User Datagram Protocol (UDP) port 69 to send *msblast.exe* to other hosts.

Analysis

The interesting thing to note here is that you may not see any changes to the file system; the closest thing is the registry key change. This worm will not be detected by port 135, because most Windows systems require that port. UDP 69 is also not likely to trigger alerts. TCP port 4444 being open and in the LISTEN state will likely be the alerting factor with this worm.

Worm #2: Linux Slapper

Name: Linux Slapper
Affected Systems: Linux
CVE: CAN-2002-0656

Description

This worm attempts to exploit one of the vulnerabilities of OpenSSL to obtain a root shell on the target host. This worm looks for Apache Web servers running Hypertext Transfer Protocol over Secure Socket Layer (HTTPS) and attempts to exploit the vulnerability and execute */bin/sh*. Vulnerable versions of OpenSSL include all released versions up to and including version 0.9.6d. Although other products suffer from this vulnerability, the Slapper worm uses a Linux shell code exploit and thus, is limited to Intel-based Linux systems. The purpose is to allow remote root access and use it in a distributed DOS (DDOS) attack.

Footprint

- A single process called ".bugtraq" is running.
- Opens UDP port 2002.
- The following files exist:
    - /tmp/.uubugtraq
    - /tmp/.bugtraq.c
    - /tmp/.bugtraq

Analysis

In this case, files are stored in */tmp*, which is not a common place to monitor. Seeing small *.c* files in */tmp* may or may not be uncommon. Monitoring for a process called ".bugtraq" is also not likely to be found by an integrity monitoring system. The opening of UDP port 2002 would be detected.

Worm #3: BugBear

Name: W32 BugBear
Affected Systems: Windows 95, Windows98, Windows ME, Windows 2000, and Windows XP
CVE: CVE-2001-0154

Description

This worm is busy. It can be spread through the automatic opening of e-mail attachments, or it can spread by locating open network shares and copying itself into the start-up locations of remote hosts. This worm infects executables, logs keystrokes, opens backdoor access to the system, and attempts to kill executables used by antivirus and firewall products. The list of applications that are infected are hard-coded, as are the list of e-mail addresses to send logged keystrokes. Some variants of this worm target financial institutions. This worm is sometimes called a virus because it involves e-mail interaction; however, it can spread on its own, so technically it is a worm.

Footprint

- Worm executable copied to start-up folder with a varying name.
- Over 20 executables are possibly altered in the content.
- Firewall or antivirus process may be terminated.
- New dynamic link library (DLL) file in %SystemRoot that is 5,632 bytes.
- New .*dll* and .*dat* files in %WindowsRoot% and %SystemRoot%.
- Open TCP port 1080.

Analysis

The easiest place for this worm is the listening network port on TCP 1080. Additionally, this worm installs files under the system directory for keystroke logging. Although you can monitor startup folders or the process table to check that a firewall or antivirus program has been disabled, watching for new files is easiest.

Worm #4: SQL Slammer

Name: SQL Slammer
Affected Systems: Windows systems running Structured Query Language (SQL)
Server or the Microsoft Desktop Engine 2000 (MSDE)
CVE: CAN-2002-0649

Description

This worm does not obtain root privileges; it just spreads itself. However, the
damage caused in network downtime and availability of resources was huge, especially considering how bad it was at locating and infecting other machines. This
worm attacks a host by connecting to UDP port 1434 and exploiting a buffer overflow with the SQL service. It then randomly computes Internet Protocol (IP)
addresses and attempts to propagate.

Footprint

- Increased network resources and DOS to the SQL server.

Analysis

The use of UDP allowed this worm spread quickly. Not only that, but the code
basically attacked as many vulnerable hosts as it could find. The other frustrating
factor with this worm is that it does not leave a trail on the file system. Instead, it is
only contained in memory (most virus checkers at the time never stood a chance).
The best way to detect this worm is by monitoring process utilization on the host.
However, given the rapid speed of this worm, prevention is the only effective coun-
termeasure. Another interesting thing about this worm is that the vulnerability was
known, and Microsoft had released patches. The worm would have been a failure
had system administrators patched their servers.

Worm #5: Nimbda

Name: W32 Nimbda
Affected Systems: Windows (IIS, Outlook, Outlook Express, Internet Explorer)
CVE: CVE-2001-0154

Description

This worm can arrive as an e-mail attachment that takes advantage of a Multipurpose Internet Mail Extensions (MIME) exploit, or it can infect via Internet Explorer if the browser is being used to view a compromised Internet Information Server (IIS) Web server. It also spreads by locating IIS servers vulnerable to the Unicode Web traversal exploit (FIXME) and opening a network port on UDP 69. Upon infection, the IIS server index files are modified to redirect clients to an *.eml* file in an attempt to infect clients through their browser.

Footprint

- Modifies *system.ini* file and adds the following:

```
Shell = explorer.exe load.exe -dontrunold
```

- Registers a new service.
- Worm executable stored in *%SystemRoot%\load.exe*
- Modifies the registry key:

```
HKLM\SOFTWARE\Microsoft\Windows\CurrentVersion\Network\LanMan\[C$ -> Z$]
```

- Trojans the Windows DLL: *Riched20.dll* and copies this file to many different locations.

Analysis

The easiest target here is the detection of the *Riched20.dll* file being compromised from the system directory and possibly appearing in many places on the file system. The next thing to monitor for is the addition of a new service; however, it is possible that Nimda will not create a service. Monitoring for a new file called *load.exe* under the system root directory is also easy.

Conclusion

Software worms are similar to music superstars. Many are considered very successful, yet most are not rooted in any real talent. We have examined only a few successful software worms, but from this we can see that detection is not that difficult as long as you are monitoring the right areas of the host environment. In cases like the SQL Slammer worm, detection would not have helped the problem much, but for the rest, detection does not involve complicated rules or configurations. The appearance of new *.dll* or *.exe* files under system directories should always generate an alert. Likewise, the appearance of TCP ports accepting outside connections should also warrant investigation. UDP ports are not as easily detectable because of the difference in UDP and TCP protocols; UDP is connectionless whereas TCP has specific states and it is easier to detect an open and listening TCP port than an open UDP port.

In all of these cases, it is obvious that we are not dealing with the most sophisticated programmers. If you read the detailed descriptions for these and other famous viruses or worms, you will find some very entertaining failures. For example, the VBS/SST virus (aka Anna Kournikova) attempts to replicate itself on the system and ends up creating an empty file, it is clearly not the most tested of code. Further analysis of the propagation techniques for these malicious bits of code will reveal that they are somewhat lacking in their propagation logic. The Nimbda worms are an exception to this; their logic is somewhat intelligent for locating and infecting other hosts.

Circumventing Host Integrity Monitoring

Chances are that the most severe threats to your host involve all of the things previously mentioned in this chapter, and not the subversion of your host integrity monitoring system; however, it is possible. Generally, the way this works is that someone analyzes the monitoring tool of the day (this has been done for Tripwire many times) and then figures out ways to defeat it and publish the findings. The next step is to integrate this into a rootkit or bundle it as part of an exploit. This section explores ways that people can subvert monitoring, and the attempts by application developers to mitigate this threat.

The Never-Ending War

As long as the solutions to monitor the integrity of hosts are entirely built in software, they will be defeated. Software can never be fully trusted to implement a completely reliable integrity monitoring system. The only way to end this war is to have the host integrity monitoring system use some type of separate hardware key storage mechanism. This may not sound like a good idea, but we run services all of the time and rely on software to protect things such as passwords, certificates, private keys, and so on.

In the last decade, we have seen a handful of papers and presentations showing how to defeat integrity monitoring systems. The problem is that most of this information is no longer an issue; attacks and subversion techniques and integrity monitoring systems are more advanced. The current threat of subversion lies within the kernel.

Former Battlefields

There was a time when simple file integrity verification would buy a great deal of integrity assurance. Those days are clearly over. The following techniques should be considered standard procedure as far as a HIMS is concerned.

Time-Stamp Modification

A time-stamp modification attack occasionally appears in a 2600 article. The idea is that an attacker has installed a backdoor or modified a system-critical file and needs a way to cover his tracks so that his attack is not picked up by a file integrity check. This involves saving the time-stamp information for a file or files, changing those files, and restoring their time stamps back to their original values. The mtime of the file is set back with a touch command or something similar. Resetting the file's inode time (ctime) can be easily accomplished with methods that involve altering the system clock. The problem is that most host integrity monitoring systems will detect a change in the checksum; therefore, this subversion technique is flawed.

Process Killing

If the monitoring system runs as a daemon or a service, it can be eradicated so that the agent does not continue to monitor the host environment. If it does not run as a service, the executable or configuration files can be altered so that the application does not run. This is equivalent to disabling a surveillance camera with spray paint. This is no longer an intelligent way to subvert a modern host integrity monitoring system. Centralized management allows for the console to expect agents to check in and provide information about their environment. If an agent fails to do this, an alert is usually generated.

Falsifying Scan Data

Technically, it is possible for an attacker to hijack an agent and replay the same information to the console so that alerts are not generated. The problem with this is that most agents do not maintain information on the last scan locally; it is sent to some type of console. Therefore, an attacker would not only have to hijack the agent executable, but also monitor at least one scan and save that information for replay. This also assumes that the agent is configured to scan the same information each time. A tactic used by administrators is to rotate scan configurations. To be successful, the attacker must save the entire state of the current system to properly spoof the scan results. Thus, the data returned by the scan agent is often a secondary means for the console to authenticate the agent.

Hide and Seek

Another attack technique is to analyze the scan period of the agent and restore the environment for the duration of the scan. The problem with this is that it assumes the scans are periodic. If they are not, this technique fails.

The Modern Battlefield

All of the techniques in the previous section were valid for very simple file integrity checking systems such as the academic version of Tripwire, but not with modern host integrity monitoring systems. Not only are those attacks ineffective, they are hard to maintain and can fail in too many ways to keep track of. To truly subvert a host integrity monitoring system, you must attack it by owning the kernel.

Most host integrity monitoring systems trust the kernel, which presents a problem for systems that do not have a means of verifying kernel integrity. The problem is that kernel rootkits can fool agents by hiding the fact that various elements of the system have been altered. A good example of this is when a kernel rootkit is designed to hide files containing Trojans by altering the way the system calls to *open()* and *exec()* work. Imagine that an attacker wants to plant Trojans but does not have the changes detected by a monitoring agent. First, the attacker will maintain the original executable and plant a Trojan copy on the file system. When any application issues a call to open the executable, the rootkit directs the application to the original version; however, any calls to execute that file will be directed toward the Trojan. The agent is thus tricked into computing a checksum for a different file than what is actually being executed. In a similar manner, calls to *stat()* that return inode information can also be redirected or spoofed. Finally, the rootkit can take steps to hide the fact that the file containing the Trojan exists. This technique can be used to hide files, processes, drivers, and kernel extensions from being detected by the agent.

Mitigation Techniques

Most host integrity monitoring systems assume that they will eventually be a target, and, therefore, have some type of defensive strategies built into their design. Although they are not foolproof, they can serve to deflect many attacks or subversion attempts.

Session Keys

Scan agents that are persistent or run as a daemon can exchange and establish a shared key, which is kept resident in memory only. Whenever the agent communicates with the console they exchange keys, which serves two purposes. First, it can act as part of the authentication process based on the last known contact. Second, it can be used to determine if the agent process has been restarted. Since the key is only kept in memory, it will be lost upon process termination. The assumption is that memory has not been compromised. An attacker that has obtained the session key can spoof the authentication and the uptime.

Executable Keys

The agent executable file may be signed or have a key built into it. If another component of the system has knowledge of this key, it can be used to perform limited verification of the data produced by an agent. The basic idea is that an attacker cannot easily Trojan the agent executable. The problem is that reverse engineering the executable will reveal the key. Steps can be taken so that only the root can read the executable, however, an attacker who has the ability to overwrite the agent executable has the ability to read and extract the key. Sometimes the key is distributed across the executable, but again, this is more of a hindrance to the person performing the reverse engineering than a foolproof method of preventing access to the key.

Log and Database Signing

Log messages and scan databases can be digitally signed, which is helpful for two reasons. First, it makes it more difficult for an attacker to spoof log and database data. Second, it is useful for forensics. Having archives of monitoring data can be helpful, but the authenticity of that data must be preserved. Having digitally signed logs and databases is one step in the process of establishing trusted monitoring data that is used for forensic examinations or as evidence in legal contexts.

Invisibility

If a process does not appear to be running on the system, it probably will not be found. This also holds true for the scan agent. Scan agents should not have much presence on the file system; hiding a running process may fool an attacker into thinking that the agent is not installed or is not running. Steganographic steps can be taken to hide the agent executable and any configuration file(s) into an unrelated file such as a JPEG or an audio file.

The fact that most of these features exist in modern host integrity monitoring systems is testament to the fact that they are real threats. Although none of these techniques are perfect, they go a long way toward mitigating the threat of an attacker subverting an established host integrity monitoring process.

Summary

There are many disparate threats to host environments. Some examples of common threats are viruses, worms, Trojans, and spyware. Internal threats are varied and range from unprivileged local access to administrative abuse of privileges. The developers of kernel-level rootkits are orchestrating very complicated and effective schemes for compromising a system and remaining undetected—a far cry from the rootkits of the past. Malicious software worms spread faster than systems can be patched; however, they can be detected because most leave some type of imprint. You have to know which elements of the environment to monitor. The circumvention of host integrity monitoring efforts is possible, but the development of most systems reveals that this problem has been considered and that mitigation techniques have been implemented to protect the integrity of the monitoring process.

Solutions Fast Track

Malicious Software

- ☑ Malicious software comes in many forms, but some common labels are viruses, worms, Trojans, and spyware.

- ☑ Computer viruses are like biological viruses in that they require human interaction to perform their function, as opposed to a worm that propagates on its own.

- ☑ Trojan executables hide themselves inside or are masked as legitimate software applications, but really serve to perform malicious activities.

Internal Threats

- ☑ Local access is a very big deal. Intelligent attackers intent on obtaining root privileges will likely do so if they have local access. Fortunately, detecting the abuse is usually possible; even the best of exploits leave some kind of evidence.

- ☑ Local attacks often involve the abuse of poorly written software. These attempts can be detected by monitoring for unexpected changes to configuration files, use of system resources, and core dump files.

☑ Administrative abuse is not easy to detect because system administrators often have the privileges to cover their tracks and know how to do so.

Rootkits

☑ Rootkits alter and Trojan a system, but require the existence of either a local or remote root exploit to be installed.

☑ Kernel-level rootkits are a serious threat to host integrity, because they can effectively avoid detection by today's security defenses and are often well written, as opposed to viruses or worms.

A Tour of Successful Worms

☑ Most of the worms seen in the last few years are easily detected by monitoring system files and network ports.

☑ Although worms are still not very well written pieces of code, they seem to be able to take advantage of poorly written software and badly configured systems.

Circumventing Host Integrity Monitoring

☑ Although circumvention is possible, most host integrity monitoring systems have a way of detecting compromise through executable keys, session keys, and signed reports and logs.

☑ The data collected by a host integrity monitoring system is itself part of the authentication of the scan agent and testament to the integrity of the monitored host.

Frequently Asked Questions

The following Frequently Asked Questions, answered by the authors of this book, are designed to both measure your understanding of the concepts presented in this chapter and to assist you with real-life implementation of these concepts. To have your questions about this chapter answered by the author, browse to **www.syngress.com/solutions** and click on the **"Ask the Author"** form. You will also gain access to thousands of other FAQs at ITFAQnet.com.

Q: What does disabling loadable kernel modules do to prevent locally based root exploits?

A: Many local root exploits take advantage of kernel modules. However, disabling loadable kernel modules (LKMs) is not a foolproof way to prevent modifications to the kernel. An attacker can modify kernel memory directly or modify the kernel file itself. Disabling the loading of kernel modules may stop some specific attacks, but not all.

Q: What are some of the ways that rootkits can be detected?

A: The best way to deal with rootkits is to prevent them from happening. However, there are a few different approaches you can take for a suspicious host. First, applications such as Osiris and Samhain may indicate a compromise by revealing changes in the environment using known good records of previous state. Offline analysis of the file system may reveal the existence of a rootkit. There are also applications such as *chkrootkit* that can be used to detect the presence of known rootkits. The www.rootkit.com Web site has a great deal of information and source code for rootkits and related techniques.

Q: What is the role of host integrity monitoring with respect to viruses, worms, and spyware?

A: There are many tools available to monitor hosts for threats like viruses, worms, Trojans, and spyware. None of them is complete and all of them have their strengths and weaknesses. Antivirus software is generally signature-based and is useless for newly discovered worms. The more recent anomaly based intrusion prevention software is best at detecting potential new threats out to do malicious things to the environment. Host integrity monitoring can catch many threats that are less obvious, and also fill in where antivirus and intrusion prevention solutions have failed.

Q: What are some ways that host integrity monitoring can be used to mitigate the damage done by poorly written software?

A: Establish a dedicated testing environment to analyze the effects of the software. Host integrity monitoring software reveals changes in the environment after the software has been installed or is running. This can reveal many things, including new network ports, SUID root executables and other file permissions, new processes or kernel modules, changes to users or groups, and all of the files that were installed. Use past vulnerabilities in the software as a starting point for where to look for signs that the software may be putting your host(s) at risk.

## Chapter 4

Planning

Solutions in this chapter:

- **Understanding the Big Picture**
- **Understanding Roles: The Bank Analogy**
- **Planning Principles**
- **Requirements**
- **Planning a Management Console**

- ☑ **Summary**
- ☑ **Solutions Fast Track**
- ☑ **Frequently Asked Questions**

Introduction

One of the most important steps in deploying a host integrity monitoring system (HIMS) is to plan ahead. Every deployment scenario is different; however, all are driven by the demands and constraints of the security policy and the objectives for deploying a HIMS. The goal of planning a host integrity monitoring deployment is to increase the visibility of the integrity of your hosts without placing excessive demands on your administrative resources. If your deployment suffers from too much noise, it will be a wasted effort. More importantly, if it distracts from other critical security issues, it will be a failure. Proper planning can make a big difference in how you plan to use your integrity monitoring software, which features you decide to leverage, and which hosts you monitor.

This chapter provides practical information for planning every step of your deployment process, including the initial setup and build environments, agent deployment, establishing your management console, and administration.

Understanding the Big Picture

In many respects, host integrity monitoring is no different than any other tool used by security administrators: if not deployed correctly, it can be a real headache. The key to proper deployment is understanding that host integrity monitoring is just a "drop in the bucket" as far as overall security is concerned. The best deployments are the simplest ones, because they are the easiest to understand. If your deployment is so complicated that you must send your security administrators for additional training, you are off to a bad start. The "big picture" is maintaining the security and integrity of your network and hosts. Software vendors instigate the problem by providing complicated interfaces and facilitating complicated deployment scenarios. Whenever possible, deploy only what you need to maintain the security of your enterprise. Do not be lured into using complicated software features if you do not need them (this applies to both Osiris and Samhain). Both of these products have features that seem impressive but may not be the best choice for your deployment. Later in this chapter, we present some fundamental principles to keep in mind throughout your planning process.

Understanding Roles: The Bank Analogy

One of the initial steps in planning a host integrity monitoring deployment is to understand the role that it will play in the security architecture (i.e., the "big picture"). One common analogy is bank security, which has numerous layers, many of which are similar to the layered security of a host. This analogy highlights the importance of host integrity monitoring, and will help you plan which role host integrity monitoring will play in your existing security measures.

Table 4.1 lists common bank security measures and their corresponding host-based security approaches.

Table 4.1 Common Bank Security Measures

Bank Security	Host Security
Limited entry/exit points (thick doors with locks)	Network security (firewalls)
Guards with guns	Host Intrusion Prevention System (HIPS)
Alarm system, tellers (with silent alarms), motion detection, infrared triggers	Host Intrusion Detection System (HIDS)
Security procedures: access control, internal auditing, employee background checks	Security administration/change management
Cameras	HIMS

This table shows that each measure is necessary for establishing a complete host security solution. The intersection of coverage of these areas will vary depending on the tools used. Each of these tools address a specific layer of security.

Notes from the Underground…

Which Approach Is Better?

I once had a brief encounter with a vice president of engineering who manages software security products for a large corporation. The topic of integrity monitoring came up, and this person dismissed it as an outdated approach to host security compared with "modern" technologies such as HIPS. The problem with this way of thinking is that it can lead to gaps in your host security structure.

Continued

Believing that one approach to host security is better than another is irresponsible. It is no different than believing that regular vehicle inspections are antiquated compared with the more modern airbag. Each handles different threats related to vehicle safety; however, neither is better than the other.

Network security is ideal for blocking malicious and unauthorized network traffic from penetrating a host. Although useful for fending off attackers, it is useless once an attacker breaches the perimeter. Once a thief enters a bank, the fact that the bank has thick steel walls and doors with locks is insignificant. Detecting and preventing a compromise in security now rests with the other security measures that are in place.

Host intrusion prevention is best applied towards the active and dynamic defense of a host from non-specific threats. When a host is deployed, it should be locked down and steps taken to prevent it from being abused or compromised. The HIPS is similar in that it attempts to enforce the security policy by filling in the gaps in the lockdown process and in undiscovered vulnerabilities. With respect to host security, the HIPS implements policy enforcement by acting as overseer to the interactions between applications and privileged kernel space. If anything violates the policy, the HIPS will take action to stop or mitigate the event. Likewise, banks have armed guards to prevent robberies. For example, a robber inside a bank pulls out a gun and attempts to open the vault. In this scenario, the guards may be able to foil the robbery attempt; however, if they do not see what is happening or are rendered ineffective, the security of the bank rests with the additional security measures. An alternative analogy would be to give tellers guns so that they have a means to fight back.

Host intrusion detection is implemented by monitoring logs and system events. A good example of what a HIDS detects and reports on is multiple remote login attempts that generate failed passwords. Considering the bank analogy, we find many items that trigger compromise in a bank, including an alarm system, motion detectors, infrared cameras, and a silent alarm button under the teller's desk. All of these things can pinpoint the area of compromise, but cannot monitor the specifics of a situation. The motion detector may provide the time and location of a bank robbery, but it will not provide a detailed description of what was stolen, what the robbers looked like, or how many there were. The HIDS serves as a major deterrent to attackers. Likewise, if thieves know that a bank has motion detectors and silent alarms, they will be less likely to attempt a break-in.

Security administration and change management help establish a protocol for how authorized operations take place, and highlights deviations from those procedures. Locking down a host is an effective way to protect its integrity. Because there are so many software solutions addressing security issues, the basic system security administration is not getting enough attention. Regarding the bank analogy, there are internal procedures and policies that can prevent a number of compromises, including employee background checks, internal audits, multiple checks and balances for authorizing high-dollar transactions, and implementing least-privilege policies for passwords and keys.

Finally, host integrity monitoring allows you to gain visibility into the specifics of what has occurred in a host environment. This is similar to placing cameras inside a bank; although the cameras may not be the first indication of a compromise, they may be the only way of knowing what happened during a robbery (i.e., how many robbers were involved, what they looked like, how they got in, and what was stolen). However, the cameras may not be aimed at the right places or they may have been replaced with old footage; consequently, the attackers go unnoticed. Host integrity monitoring completes the security arsenal by providing detailed information about changes that have occurred on hosts. It can detect a compromise and, most importantly, it helps conduct damage assessment, therefore, aiding forensic examinations and preventing future compromises.

The bank analogy is not perfect, but it does illustrate that even though these layers intersect others in certain areas, they are each distinct and an important component of host integrity.

Planning Principles

Keep the following three principles in mind throughout your planning process. These principles are useful for any type of security-related software deployment and are also helpful in keeping you on track when designing and deploying a host integrity monitoring solution.

Make Everything Simple

This is the most important of the three planning principles. At every step of planning and deployment, consider whether or not you are introducing unnecessary complexity into the system. The effects of not maintaining simplicity can render your deployment a failure and possibly do more harm than good. With the documentation fresh in your mind, you will easily recognize that certain configurations translate to a more administrative burden in the long term. This includes everything from large decisions such as which features to use, to simple decisions such as naming conventions. It is pretty straightforward: the simpler your plan, the easier it will be to understand and use the deployment. The rest of this book points out the complicated aspects of Osiris and Samhain that you want to avoid if possible.

Keep Functionality to a Minimum

Following in the footsteps of simplicity, configure your host integrity monitoring software to do only what is necessary (i.e., the less going on, the less that can go wrong). For example, if you have a HIDS in place to monitor login and logout events and application or kernel events, you should focus specifically on changes to files and the file system. Osiris and Samhain both have the ability to monitor different elements of a host environment; however, you do not have to use all of them. Do not fill your host integrity monitoring deployment too full; the more hosts it monitors, the more you have to deal with on an administrative level. Table 4.1 shows that host integrity monitoring fulfills a need that no other layers of security can provide: maintaining a database of changes to the host environment over time (i.e., find out what needs the most attention and stick to it).

Document Your Requirements

The remainder of this chapter explores the necessary steps needed to set up a HIMS. Through each step of this process, you must determine how this information applies to your requirements, constraints, and security policy. Reading and soaking up information is not sufficient; you must document how this information applies to your network, host environments, and administrative resources. Not only will this facilitate the deployment process, but it will also help prevent you from neglecting or forgetting important aspects of your system.

Requirements

This section covers the major issues to consider when establishing a requirements document for your host integrity monitoring deployment. You could simply read this chapter and absorb the information; however, it is strongly recommended that you translate this information into written form. It does not have to be complicated, just one document stating how each of the following issues apply to your situation. This will help you maintain simplicity, share your goals with other administrators and management, and translate your plan into practical information. Your document should contain a heading for each of the following topics:

- Goals
- Build and Test Environments
- Network Topology
- Host Count

- Operating Systems and Architecture Types

- Monitoring Requirements

- Scheduling and Scan Frequency

- Notifications

- Logging

- Incident Response

- Forensics

List as many requirements and notes for each topic as possible, keeping them clear and concise. List the requirements and the non-requirements. Non-requirements are useful because they allow you to document what you are doing and why. The goal is to have a collection of information that describes exactly how you will fix these problems so that you can make design decisions and solve deployment problems before you begin writing your requirements document.

Goals

The most important step in identifying your integrity monitoring goals is planning. Your motivation for establishing a HIMS will affect all aspects of the deployment process. This is important because it not only sets the stage for the remainder of the planning and design process, but also provides you with expectations and allows you to define criteria for success. Without this, you have no way of knowing whether your efforts were effective.

There have been situations where security administrators were told to deploy a HIMS either because management deemed it important or because it was required by a security policy. In some cases, the motivation was not clear; it was simply considered "a good thing to do." In this case, you must inquire as to what the motivation is, or establish one. Try to determine what you are attempting to accomplish with your deployment and document it. Some examples include:

- Detecting internal attacks, or attempting to gain privileged access to the system.

- Detecting intrusions or rootkits by analyzing changes to specific files or the kernel.

- Monitoring upgrades to system executables and libraries.

- Monitoring changes to users or group settings.

Start by listing the general goals, and then attempt to narrow them down. Finally, put them in order by priority.

Build and Test Environments

If possible, establish a dedicated system for both build and testing. Although not a necessity, it is strongly recommended. Not all systems that you deploy on will have compilers. If you have to build the software from source, do so in a single trusted location. For anything more than casual inspection, you will want a trusted platform for building and testing.

The most important reason for establishing a dedicated build environment is so you can easily update new, trusted releases of your scan agents, or establish a new console. Updates to software are inevitable; security fixes and feature enhancements arrive with each release. At some point, you will want (or need) to upgrade both your console and your agent software. In the case of security issues, having a trusted build environment specific to your deployment can be very helpful. Another reason is reliability. Building all like agents from the same platform ensures consistency in configuration and compilation and also facilitates testing. Finally, a dedicated build environment allows you to build trusted executables for your console and your scan agents. If you start with a compromised management console, the entire system is worthless. If you start with flawed agents, you have potentially compromised all of your hosts. Although it is technically possible for the source code and installer packages to be compromised or contain back doors, it is not likely. What is more realistic is that you will encounter the need to address a security issue or upgrade your agent software. A dedicated build environment allows you to easily deal with these issues.

Another important reason for establishing a dedicated testing system is so you can test configuration changes before applying them to your production system. You must do this periodically; systems and policies change, and sometimes monitoring configurations change. If you test a configuration change on a production system and it backfires, you are at risk of compromising the integrity of your monitoring system or disrupting normal services. Another reason for having a dedicated testing environment is to test your deployment; ideally, a test system is a mirror image of the production system. This way, you can experiment with configurations and test performance issues while becoming familiar with administration, before loading them onto your real hosts. You can also fine-tune your scan configurations on a test system without worrying about the consequences of an incorrect configuration. Once the settings are stable and working, you can translate them to your production system.

Establishing dedicated systems for building and testing is important; at the very least you should establish test systems. Software is not infallible. Test it with safety nets before going into production or you may find that you have to revise your deployment strategy. One thing to consider is ways to replicate these systems. For both build and test systems, it is helpful to ghost or image a build environment in the event that you have to recreate it. For test systems, you want to have a way to mirror as much of the production environment as possible. For build and test systems, you must have at least one system for every architecture type (e.g., if you are only monitoring Windows servers, you only need one build environment. However, if you have Windows, Linux, and Berkeley Software Distribution (BSD) systems, you must build a system for each unique operating system and architecture type). If you have an existing test environment, use it to establish a new test system for your HIMS.

Network Topology

The organization of your network affects how many management consoles you need and where they will be located. If all of the hosts you are monitoring are on the same network, you will probably only need a single management console. However, if you have hosts spread across multiple networks, you must establish a management console on each separate network. Some administrators attempt to modify their networks, punch holes in firewalls, and set up routing hacks just so they can administer all of their hosts from a single management console. Although this can be done, it is generally not a good idea. More than likely, the networks were separated for a reason (e.g., lab networks versus corporate networks). Questions you should ask yourself include:

- How many networks do I need for the hosts that have to be monitored?

- How many management consoles do I need?

- What are the concerns or limitations for the physical location of management consoles?

Host Count

If you are monitoring only a handful of hosts, a host count is not an issue. However, if you plan to monitor hundreds or thousands of hosts, there are three major considerations:

- Management Console Resources

- Deployment

- Administration

If you have a lot of hosts sending data to the management console, you must consider the amount of disk space and other hardware requirements that are necessary for managing so many scan agents. Your requirements will vary depending on how many hosts you have and how you configure them. More frequent scans means storing more data. A higher host count translates into an increased load on your network and on the management console processor that is analyzing the received scan data. On average (using the default configurations), a single scan consumes approximately 1MB of disk space (if using Osiris or Samhain); a CPU can sometimes top 50 percent.

The more hosts the bigger the deployment effort. Because integrity monitoring is an agent-based deployment model, you must plan for how you will initially deploy the agent software, and how you will perform updates on all of your hosts. If you are only monitoring a few hosts, you should do this on a host-by-host basis. However, for thousands of hosts, you need to devise a way to deploy the software or integrate the installation process into an existing mass deployment scheme that your enterprise already uses. Both Osiris and Samhain have ways of facilitating mass deployment; however, neither of them provides a complete solution.

Finally, you must consider the administrative effort required to manage the hosts that you will be monitoring. The biggest administrative issue you will encounter as you increase the number of monitored hosts is responding to events. Issues related to the initial setup and deployment are not uncommon. However, fine-tuning configurations for each of your systems and responding to detected changes can be overwhelming when monitoring hundreds or thousands of systems. The more varied your hosts are, the bigger this issue will be (e.g., the administrative effort involved in monitoring 100 disparate desktop systems is going to be far more involved than monitoring 100 test systems that have identical configurations.

Operating Systems and Architecture Types

When considering all of the hosts that you will be monitoring, you must also consider how many unique combinations of operating systems and architecture types are involved. There are two reasons for this:

- It will directly impact the amount of effort involved in building and deploying scan agent software. You have to establish a build system and possibly a test system for each different operating system. Likewise, if you have different architecture types, you must build and test systems for each of them (e.g., if you deploy Solaris on x86 and Sparc, you have to establish a build and test system for each).

- Each operating system involved will require unique scan configurations and involve different fine-tuning efforts. The more operating systems you have means more work establishing custom configurations. The worst-case scenario is that you will need to develop a different scan configuration for every monitored host. The best-case scenario is that you will only need to develop one configuration for each operating system. At the very least, note the number of distinct combinations of operating systems and architectures involved in your deployment.

Monitoring Requirements

Developing monitoring requirements is a critical part of the planning process. If neglected or done in haste, they can severely limit the effectiveness of an integrity-monitoring effort. To be reasonably assured of the integrity of critical components, you should determine which elements of the environment must be monitored. Once you have a list of requirements for each host, they can be translated into a practical configuration. The overall process for determining monitoring requirements for a host is as follows:

1. Determine the most critical components.
2. Determine the environmental elements required to constitute the integrity of each critical component.
3. Determine which critical element changes are violations.
4. Determine which critical element changes are not violations.

Again, you should document each of these steps for all like hosts. Once you complete these steps, it will be easier to translate the information into a practical configuration specific to your monitoring tools. This is very important; there have been situations where security administrators attempted to develop a configuration from the defaults and adapt it to their systems while on the fly. This often results in critical elements being left out of the configuration, and as a result, it is possible that a critical element was modified without being detected.

You do not have to document every single change; however, you should pinpoint the ones that are clear violations, which will help with incident response. The changes that are not violations will help establish and verify the correctness of filters either through the monitoring system itself or through log analysis.

Also, remember **not** to monitor everything; your monitoring will be more effective if you stick to the basics and the most critical elements of the system. Decide which components are important, and analyze the system elements that can be used to detect violations in those components.

Scheduling and Scan Frequency

Various factors, including forensics, resources, risk assessment, and scan configuration details, will influence your decision about how often to scan your hosts.

If you require a certain degree of granularity for forensic purposes, you must make sure that your hosts are being monitored with enough frequency to capture the desired amount of information. The concern here is that you may miss information that could prove helpful in a forensic examination. For example, if a host is being monitored once per day, you may only get the before-and-after effects of an incident. However, if you are monitoring events on the hour (or more frequently), you will see a more detailed view of the sequence of events. The reason for this is that multiple changes to the same parts of the system could occur between scans, and therefore not be included in the information trail.

Hardware and administrative resources are also influencing factors when establishing scan schedules. If you are archiving all of your scan data, you must consider that every scan will consume additional disk space. Another issue to consider is the load on the network and the management host.

Hosts have different levels of risk. Some run services such as mail or Domain Name System (DNS) and some have Web servers. Others store source code, production build systems, and key management systems. All of these examples have varying levels of risk based on their exposure and the content and services that reside on them.

Finally, scan configurations themselves influence scan frequency and scheduling. Scanning certain resources during peak usage times may have a negative impact; consequently, you may have to conduct scans when usage is low. Also, the types of information from the environment may dictate scan frequency. For example, Set User ID (SUID)/Set Group ID (SGID) audits are not something that you would do every 10 minutes. In addition to being impossible, conducting scans of that nature often has no added value. A counterexample is scanning for open network ports; querying a host every 10 minutes for that information may not be unrealistic in some cases.

Notifications

Notification can mean the difference between being alerted and not being alerted to a security incident. All scanning and log analysis is useless if the information does not go to the correct security administrator. Issues to consider with respect to notifications include:

- What information should be considered worthy of notification?
- Who should receive notification for each of the monitored hosts?
- How should the notifications be issued?

Some of the information regarding detected changes is logged, whereas other information is sent to a security administrator in addition to being logged. What constitutes the difference is related to the goals that you have established. For example, if you are mostly concerned with the integrity of a source code repository, you may want changes involving that part of the host sent directly to a list that the security administrator monitors. All other alerts may be analyzed and logged so that they do not draw attention from the most critical part of that host.

Decide who will be involved in the notification process; it may be one person or an entire group within an organization. You will sometimes find yourself monitoring hosts that are the responsibility of various other security groups; thus, it is important to decide how this information will be distributed. Also, for accountability reasons, you should enforce a policy dictating that no one single person be responsible for receiving information regarding certain hosts.

Finally, decide how you want the information to be transmitted. E-mail is the most common way of providing information regarding critical alerts. Both Osiris and Samhain support this and other notification vectors. Other means of notification include wearing a pager or being available on the Web.

Logging

Logging is another important planning consideration, because if important information about a detected change is not logged, it cannot be interpreted and thus it cannot invoke a response. There are many outlets for logging, including system logs, files, pipes to applications, console logging, and storage in relational databases.

The most important consideration regarding logging is access—how to facilitate the analysis and regular interpretation of log data. It does not make sense to send log information to a database if there is no practical means for security administrators to review that data.

Next, consider storage. Logs contain sensitive information. Decide which security measures you have to put into place to protect sensitive data. There is also integrity; think about how you will react if someone tampers with your log data. Also, consider backing up log data. The advantage of a management console providing a centralized store for logging data is that you can build a wall around and protect a single location. The downside is that it is also a single point of failure. It is important to decide on a solution for securely backing up log data.

Finally, plan to use some kind of log analysis tool. Logging enthusiasts encourage collecting as much log data as possible, which is generally a good thing. However, to organize log data in order of importance, you will have to use a log analysis system. (Chapter 8 details the use of Swatch to monitor logs for Osiris and Samhain.) If you have another solution for log analysis, consider what is involved in using it with your host integrity monitoring deployment.

Incident Response

There will come a time when you receive a notification or alert requiring a response. Every enterprise should have an incident response team and a set of procedures established to handle these events. This is important to consider when you are planning so that you can facilitate the correct transfer of information to the correct people. This is much like the scan configuration, logging, and forensics issues (e.g., an incident response team requires certain information such as timestamps and an IP address to effectively deal with an incident).

Tools and Traps...

Plan for Response

I once worked at a company where an employee inadvertently placed an open wireless access point onto the corporate network. Established network monitoring measures picked up on it and notified the appropriate incident response team.

To satisfy forensics and incident response team requirements, document what you need regarding detected changes. Take into account what you are monitoring and use for the starting point to gaining information; the information you want to collect and maintain may not always be obvious.

Forensics

One of the most important benefits of periodically monitoring host integrity is the ability to ascertain which elements of the system were modified. Having snapshots of a host environment for many periods of time can be invaluable to forensic examinations. When considering forensics, you must consider your requirements for the internal analysis of collected data, as well as the legal issues associated with using that data.

Both Osiris and Samhain can be configured to report changes; however, they do not save any logs or scan data associated with the detected change. Although this helps conserve disk space and reduce administrative overhead, it is of little forensic use. Generally, the more information you have the better. Save as much scan data and logs as possible. Again, the more frequent you scan, the more data you will have.

Consult a lawyer regarding any legal issues surrounding scan data and logs. The laws change constantly. Do not assume that a time stamp or a Pretty Good Privacy (PGP) signature is sufficient. You may need to maintain a log detailing the chain of custody, write-once functionality, and multiple storage locations. Consult legal counsel to determine the requirements for using your logs in a legal setting.

Two excellent resources for acquiring more in-depth information regarding forensics include *Computer Forensics: Incident Response Essentials* by Warren G. Kruse and Jay G. Heiser, and *Forensic Discovery* by Dan Farmer and Wietse Venema.

Planning a Management Console

The management console is the core of the HIMS. Thus, there are some important considerations to document as part of the planning process.

General Security Considerations

You must secure the host that will serve as your management console. Following are some of the most important general issues to consider when planning the deployment of your management console:

- Dedicate a host
- Location on the network (access)
- Choice of operating system
- Installed software and services
- Worst-case scenario plan

Even if you do not establish dedicated build and testing environments for your deployment, it is important that you dedicate a system specifically for use as a management console. There are a few reasons for this. First, you will not have to establish a way to protect the console data from other users, services, or applications. Downtime or administration of other services could impact or conflict with the runtime demands of the console. Second, you will almost always require all of the processing power, disk space, and input/output (I/O) available for handling interaction with scan agents. Finally, the more a host is responsible for, the more that can go wrong. Using a host specifically for the management console will enable you to manage the simplicity and security of the system.

Consider the network location of the console host. On one hand, you need to make sure that the console host is available to all of the hosts that are being monitored; ideally you want nothing else to have access to it. Consider the risks associated with the network location you decide to use for your console, specifically which hosts or networks have access to it. Document this in your plan so that when you secure the console host this information is available when configuring various elements of network security (e.g., firewalls, network monitoring, or Transmission Control Protocol [TCP] wrappers).

You will probably pick the operating system you will use for your management console. *The most important thing to remember is that the operating system you decide on should be the operating system that is known best by the administrative staff.* Everyone has his or her opinion about what system is "better," but it is pointless if none of the staff knows how to lockdown and administer the "better" system. If you know Windows 2003 Advanced Server inside and out, but have never used FreeBSD, it makes sense to deploy your console on a Windows environment. Subsequent considerations regarding the operating system include licensing, hardware compatibility and costs, and performance issues.

Install only the software necessary for the function of the management console or the HIMS in general (e.g., log analysis). In many cases, you must make a conscious effort to install only the minimal footprint or base of the operating system. Do not install software at every step, unless you can justify it regarding the function of the console. In some cases, you will not have a choice. For example, it is possible to bootstrap a Gentoo Linux system fairly easily. However, with Windows 2000, you may or may not have a choice regarding certain components. Remote Procedure Call (RPC) is a good example. In these cases, you must perform some post-installation lockdown and removal of services. No operating system will result in the ideal installation for your management console. Plan to configure, lockdown, and remove unnecessary services. Document which services you need to remove and why. This procedure is a good argument for creating an image or ghost of your management console so that you can easily resurrect or establish additional consoles with the same lockdown configuration.

Finally, consider the available options for protecting the console in the event it is compromised. For example, an encrypted file system can prove very helpful if the physical system is stolen. Consider and document everything that you must do to protect the compromise of data in the event that of unauthorized access.

Physical Access

All of the security precautions in the world will be useless if your management console host is physically accessible by someone other than the trusted administrators. Physical access is important for a couple of reasons. First, physical access means that someone can literally steal the console host, at which point all of the security patching, lockdown, and other precautions you have taken become useless. This is not unlike the security of a locked briefcase. Why bother picking the lock when you can just take the briefcase and smash the lock? Even if you are using encrypted file systems and are fortunate enough to have backups of your management console, there is still the downtime between the compromise and when your console is available again.

The second reason physical access is important is because an attacker can compromise the host by booting into single-user mode or booting off of a CD to gain access to the system. Consider all of your options for protecting the system in the event that there is unauthorized physical access. Few of these options are complete solutions, but they can help raise the bar in the event that someone attempts to gain unauthorized access to the system. There are some steps that you can take (such as Basic Input/Output System [BIOS] or firmware passwords) to prevent the most unsophisticated types of attacks.

Finally, you should monitor the integrity of the management console itself. With a scan agent installed on the monitoring host, you can detect reboots, changes to hardware configuration, and kernel modules that may indicate physical access. If you have configured your management console to periodically report a status, chances are that any kind of attack involving physical access will not go undetected.

Document your plans for protecting physical access to the console, including where you plan to physically store the system, which administrators have access to the system and what their roles are, any hardware configurations that you make, and steps that you take to audit access to the system.

User Access

The management console should only be accessible to security administrators who need to read logs or manage monitored hosts. Do not install the management console on your corporate mail server and expect passwords or file permissions to provide adequate security for the system. Guest accounts should be shut off; at the very least remote access should be limited to only those who need it. List all of the personnel who require an account on this system and what their role is. This will facilitate the general security administration for the host (e.g., which accounts will have SUDO access).

Note how you will be auditing the actions of user accounts on the management console host in your planning document. This is important for accountability, change management, and the detection of suspicious behavior.

Hardware Requirements

Two issues to consider regarding hardware are the requirements for your management console system(s), and is the hardware necessary to establish build and testing environments.

If monitoring more than 10 hosts, you must consider what your hardware requirements are. The biggest issue with running a management console is I/O. All monitored hosts send their scan data or logging information to the console over the network. The management console performs analysis, which often involves large files or large amounts of data. When you think about a management host receiving data from potentially hundreds of hosts at the same time and performing analysis on that data, this is not a job for your average personal computer. If you have thousands of hosts, you need more than a single management console. There is no magic number of hosts that a single management console can handle; the determining factors are how much scan data you are archiving and your scan frequency. You can easily monitor 500 hosts from a single console if you are only monitoring the integrity of their kernels and have distributed their schedules. However, you can easily consume the resources of a single management console with 20 hosts if you scan the complete file system every hour and archive all of the data (another reason to establish a test environment).

Ideally, you will have hardware dedicated to building and upgrading agents and for testing. The hardware necessary for building agents and console software does not have to be speedy. All that is necessary is that the system supports the operating system necessary for generating compatible executables for all of your deployment systems. For testing, you want to have hardware that is as close to the production systems as possible. These systems do not have to be self-aware; they do need to be able to produce builds. For the management console, you want something that can handle the I/O and disk requirements.

Summary

The importance of proper planning should not be underestimated. Document as much as possible before beginning your deployment, to reduce the number of problems you may encounter along the way. Do not worry about producing too much information during the planning process; you can always review and edit information so that it is clear and usable for future reference. Remember to consider all aspects of your deployment, including your goals, testing, network architecture, the number of hosts, the operating systems involved, scheduling, notifications and logging, incident response, and forensics.

Even if you do not utilize all of the information in this chapter, it is important that you document what does not apply and why. You cannot expect to tackle everything; however, developing a written plan will initiate the thought process, dialogues, peer reviews, and brainstorming about what is involved in deploying your management console(s).

Solutions Fast Track

Understanding the Big Picture

- ☑ Ease of use is the most important objective in deploying a HIMS.

- ☑ Avoid complicated configurations and administrative tasks; they will have a negative impact on the long-term maintenance of the system.

- ☑ The best deployment is the simplest deployment.

Understanding Roles: The Bank Analogy

- ☑ A HIMS is a necessary component for maintaining host integrity. Be aware of other host-based security measures and plan how a HIMS will complement the security of your hosts.

- ☑ A HIMS is analogous to the placement of security cameras within various parts of a bank to capture the state of the environment.

Planning Principles

☑ Make everything as simple as possible.

☑ Keep functionality to a minimum.

☑ Document your requirements and develop a written plan.

Requirements

☑ Develop a written plan that details your goals and plans for deploying a HIMS.

☑ Document requirements and non-requirements.

Planning a Management Console

☑ The management console is the heart of the HIMS; plan to dedicate a host (or set of hosts) to be used exclusively to manage scan agents.

☑ Choose an operating system that your administrative staff knows how to secure, administer, and maintain.

Frequently Asked Questions

The following Frequently Asked Questions, answered by the authors of this book, are designed to both measure your understanding of the concepts presented in this chapter and to assist you with real-life implementation of these concepts. To have your questions about this chapter answered by the author, browse to **www.syngress.com/solutions** and click on the **"Ask the Author"** form. You will also gain access to thousands of other FAQs at ITFAQnet.com.

Q: If I am monitoring only two or three systems, is it still better to deploy a single console to manage those hosts?

A: Osiris and Samhain are both designed to be deployed as a centrally managed system. Both of them also support being able to deploy in a stand-alone fashion where the console and agent are both installed on each monitored host. The obvious problem is that you have to administer each console. The bigger problem is that the trusted data resides on the monitored host. However, there are cases where this makes sense. For example, you may have network restrictions that make it more of a problem to deploy a single console. Or, you may not have the resources available to establish a dedicated console. Running Osiris or Samhain as stand-alone configurations is usually more effective, but not always.

Q: I already have a HIDS and a HIPS deployed for my hosts. Do I still need a HIMS?

A: The goal is to be able to effectively establish a means of detecting and reporting on critical changes. If you have enough intersection between your HIDS and HIPS, there is little point in adding additional administrative burden. However, chances are the HIPS and HIDS will not provide as complete and in-depth reporting on the details of detected changes to your host environment as a HIMS.

Q: How long should I plan to archive scan data?

A: As long as you possibly can. You can never have too much log data or too much scan data. Be realistic, but plan to maintain archives of as much of this data as you can.

Q: Can I use Osiris or Samhain as a change management system?

A: Yes, but they are far from the best change management solutions. Commercial and open source change management solutions offer more in-depth auditing of changes and allow administrators more interaction and control in the change auditing process. Osiris and Samhain attempt to minimize the interaction necessary by enabling you to isolate certain attributes to monitor, and by focusing on the critical elements of a host that are indicators of compromise. Tripwire is a good example of a commercial change management solution, and Radmind is a good example of an open source change management solution.

## Chapter 5

Host Integrity Monitoring with Open Source Tools

Solutions in this chapter:

- Osiris
- Samhain

☑ Summary
☑ Solutions Fast Track
☑ Frequently Asked Questions

Introduction

Osiris and Samhain are two of the most widely deployed open source host integrity monitoring systems today. This chapter examines how each of these systems work and their respective strengths and weaknesses. Osiris and Samhain are very different; therefore, one of them will be more suited to your requirements than the other.

Osiris

Preston Norvell and Bruce Potter released the first version of Osiris in the summer of 1999. This release consisted of two small Perl scripts designed to provide file integrity checking for Windows NT. The popularity of these scripts paved the way for the Osiris project, which released its first version (written in C) in the fall of 1999.

At the time, open source options for file integrity monitoring were limited. Tripwire was too cumbersome to use, and many administrators found it difficult, primarily because it was not centrally managed. Thus, the Osiris project was borne out of the desire to produce a host integrity monitoring application that would do the following:

- Provide easy-to-use, centralized management
- Monitor as much of the host environment as possible

At the time of this writing, Osiris Version 4.1 monitors files, network ports, users, groups, kernel modules, and more. Information about Osiris, including the latest releases, anonymous source access, support mailing lists, and documentation, can be found at http://hostintegrity.com/osiris.

How Osiris Works

Osiris consists of three distinct components: a command-line client, a management console, and a scan agent. A scan agent is deployed onto every host that is to be monitored. A single management console stores all of the scan data, scan agent configurations, and logs; manages scheduling; and handles notifications—it is the brains of the system. The command-line client communicates only with the management console, and only the management console communicates with scan agents (see Figure 5.1).

Figure 5.1 Components That Make Up the Osiris Host Integrity Monitoring System

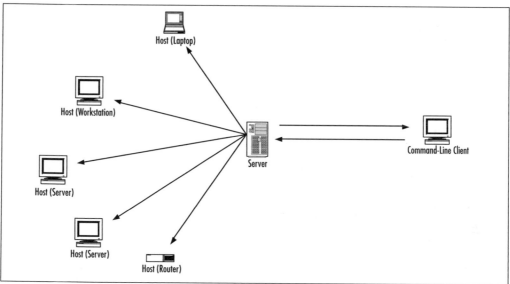

The console regularly tells the agents to scan. The scan agents respond by collecting information from their environment and sending it back to the console. The console stores this information in a database file, compares it against data from a previous scan, and reports on the differences.

The significance of the three components of the architecture that makes up Osiris is best explained by learning how they are used in a typical deployment. The management console and the scan agent software running on each monitored host constitute the majority of the functions of Osiris. As an administrator, you generally do not use these two components; however, there will be times when you must log in to the console using the command-line interface (CLI). The CLI is commonly used to configure and add additional scan agents to the console, fine-tune scan configurations, and take steps to reduce false positives. When an incident occurs, you may log in to the console to obtain access to logs or data associated with previous scans (see Figure 5.2).

Figure 5.2 Interactions of Osiris Components When Obtaining Status Information from Agent

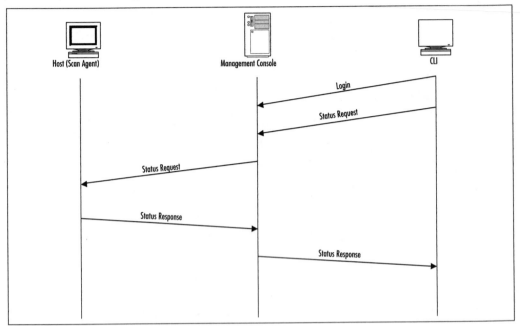

Authentication of Components

All of the Osiris components communicate over a Secure Sockets Layer (SSL) tunnel. The scan agent sends sensitive data to the console, which must be authenticated. Likewise, the console must trust the scan agent. Osiris accomplishes this by using session keys and X509 certificates.

The management console maintains a certificate and a private key. Upon initial contact with an agent, the console presents it with a session key. With every subsequent connection to that agent, the scan agent is required to present that session key as a form of authentication.

The scan agent maintains the root certificate for the console. Upon contact, the scan agent validates the certificate presented by the console using the root certificate.

The command-line client works similar to the scan agent in that it maintains the root certificate, but the pre-shared key is actually a password. The console maintains a password database and requires the client to present a password to gain access.

Thus, scan agent and CLI authentication is a pre-shared key, whereas console authentication is basic SSL certificate validation. The scan agent authenticating the console is similar to the way a Web client validates the authenticity of a Web server.

By default, Osiris generates a self-signed certificate; however, you can generate one, signed by a trusted certificate authority (CA), as shown in Figure 5.3.

> **NOTE**
>
> The use of SSL by all Osiris components exists to protect the integrity and privacy of all communications during transport. Keep in mind that all of the scan data and log messages are not signed or encrypted when they are stored on the management console.

Figure 5.3 Osiris Uses SSL and Digital Certificates to Secure All Communication between Components

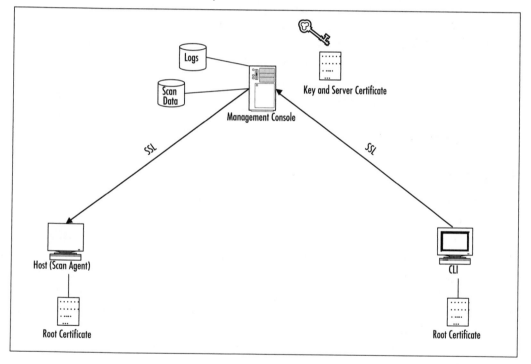

Scan Data

When a scan agent scans the environment, it packs things into records and sends them to the console. The scan agents never store their scan configuration or scan data on disk. In fact, the only thing kept on monitored hosts is the root certificate and the scan agent executable.

When the console receives scan data, it stores it in a Berkeley database file. The structure of this file is platform independent and can be moved offline for further examination or storage for forensic and auditing purposes. This is true of the entire directory where the console stores logs, configurations, and databases. The amount of scan data can vary significantly, but the average for each scan is roughly 1MB.

There are three different ways to configure the management console to maintain scan data, which can be configured on a per-host basis: the console can save every scan database, only the databases that contain changes, or only the latest created scan database. The reason for this is that some administrators may want to keep archives of every scan and every log for forensic purposes. The problem with keeping archives, however, is that they consume disk space, and not everyone wants to keep all of the data. Therefore, you have the option of storing only the databases that indicate change. The console defaults to storing only the minimal information necessary to provide a report of what has changed since the last scan.

With every host integrity monitoring system (HIMS), there is a baseline concept, which is considered the last known good scan of the environment. Osiris can be configured to automatically set the trusted database to be created with this scan. This capability, combined with the minimal storage of scan data, allows for a fairly low maintenance monitoring system that sends reports on what is changing in the host environments.

Logging

The management console is responsible for all data analysis; therefore, all log data resides on the console host. After every scan, the console performs a comparison between all of the data in the newly created scan database and the trusted database for that host. Any differences result in a log message.

Osiris has a few different logging vectors. Scan logs generated by the console can be saved to a file, sent to the system log, or piped to an application. Just as with scan databases, logs associated with a scan can be configured in three different ways ranging from minimal to one for each scan.

Each log message has an ID to facilitate parsing by log analysis tools (see Figure 5.4).

Figure 5.4 Osiris Log Format Structure

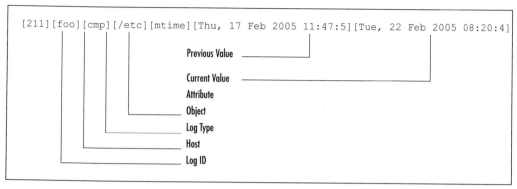

Filtering Noise

To deal with noise, Osiris has a filter engine that can be used to exclude certain detected changes from generating a log entry. This filter engine is essentially a list of regular expressions that are applied to each log message. Filters do not prevent data from being saved; they serve to prevent the creation of log messages. If necessary, you can always compare the two databases at a later date to see the complete list of changes.

Notifications

In addition to using Osiris to send log messages to an application or to the system log, administrators can configure Osiris to send them detected change reports via e-mail. This is configurable on a per-host basis. These e-mail notifications can be sent after every scan or only if changes are detected. Some administrators want to receive notification after each scan as an assurance that monitoring is taking place and that no changes were detected. In addition, Osiris can be configured to send e-mail notifications in case a scan agent is unresponsive or has lost its resident session key. This may happen if the scan agent process was restarted or if the host was rebooted. The following is an example of a typical e-mail notification report generated by the Osiris console:

```
From brian@example.com  Mon Feb 28 11:53:42 2005
To: brian@example.com
From: "Osiris Host Integrity System" <osirismd@example.com>
Date: Mon, 28 Feb 2005 11:53:43 -0700
Subject: [osiris log][host: powerbook][3 changes]


    compare time: Mon Feb 28 11:53:43 2005
```

```
              host: foo
       scan config: stat (cbbd7002)
          log file: no log file generated, see system log.
     base database: 2
  compare database: 3


[211][foo][cmp][/usr/local/bin][mtime][Mon, 28 Feb 2005 11:53:2][Mon, 28 Feb
2005 11:53:3]
[215][foo][cmp][/usr/local/bin][bytes][340][374]
[203][foo][new][/usr/local/bin/nmap]


Change Statistics:
----------------------------------


        checksums:  0
       SUID files:  0
  root-owned files:  1
 file permissions:  0
             new:  1
         missing:  0


total differences:  3
```

Strengths

The biggest accomplishment of the Osiris project is that it resulted in a host-based integrity-monitoring product that is easy to use. One of the risks with any security product is that it is too complicated, and administrators end up either not using it or not configuring it correctly. A typical *./configure;make;make install* routine can be used to build and install a working copy of Osiris on any host. Also, administrators do not need to edit configuration files directly; this is accomplished through a CLI to prevent misconfiguration. In addition, Osiris has intelligent defaults for host configurations and default scanning configurations for common operating systems.

The Osiris architecture allows for centralized management. One of the biggest problems with Tripwire and others like it is that they require you to either log in to each monitored host or create your own custom shell scripts (Secure Shell [SSH]) as part of the regular usage model. Centralized management not only eases the administrative burden associated with monitoring more than a handful of hosts but also allows you to establish a central secure location for sensitive data.

Osiris runs on all true 32-bit versions of Windows (Windows NT, Windows 2000, Windows XP, and Windows 2003 Advanced Server). It also runs on most UNIX and UNIX-like systems, including FreeBSD, NetBSD, OpenBSD, Mac OS X, Linux, IRIX, AIX, and Solaris. The management console can be established on any of these platforms. What is unique is that you can monitor Windows and UNIX-like hosts from a single location.

The Osiris scan agent has a modular interface; therefore, if you are not satisfied with the abilities of the scan agent, you can easily write and integrate your own modules to extend what is gathered from the host environment.

Finally, excluding all arguments for and against open source, Osiris is free and released under a Berkeley Software Distribution (BSD)-style license.

Weaknesses

The biggest downfall to Osiris is that, like any host-based security product, it requires software agents to be installed on every monitored host, which creates an administrative overhead. Scan agents have to be installed and maintained. In the case of security-related problems, updating all of the agents is a big job. IT departments often deal with this problem with respect to deploying software updates for other applications or with updates to the operating system itself. Additionally, if your agents are all configured differently, the ongoing administrative operations can be difficult.

Another weakness of Osiris is that managing thousands of hosts can be a challenge from a Unique Identifier (UI) perspective. The CLI does not lend itself well to deployments of this size. There is no concept of dealing with groups of hosts. Each host is treated independently.

Osiris log filtering is handled by regular expressions. Although this allows for great flexibility, the reality is that many administrators may not know how to translate what they want in a filter into a regular expression without some research. Or even worse, they could unintentionally prevent critical log entries from triggering alerts because of a mistake in writing a filter rule.

The scan agents are modular, and the console is not. This presents a problem if you want to alter how the console does some of its analysis of detected change. As you will see with Samhain, both the scan agent and the server can be modularized.

Samhain

Rainer Wichmann released the first version of Samhain on October 31, 1999. It was released on October 31, the date that the ancient Celts labeled as the end of summer. This initial release was a simple file integrity checker and, like the first version of Osiris, was not centrally managed.

The goal of Samhain was to produce a centrally managed host integrity monitoring system that would monitor many disparate aspects of the environment, not just the files. The idea was to think beyond Tripwire and provide an open source product that would enable people to monitor the integrity of their hosts. In December 1999, Samhain released Version 0.8, which implemented true centralized management of logging, configuration, and scan data. Although Osiris and Samhain shared very similar goals, they evolved independently of each other, as proved by the distinct differences in their design.

At the time of this writing, Samhain is at Version 2.0.4 and has the ability to monitor files, file system mount points, and login and logout events; to conduct Set User ID/Set Group ID (SUID/SGID) audits; and to monitor the integrity surrounding the kernel. All information about Samhain, including the latest releases, support mailing lists, and documentation, are on the official Web site located at http://www.la-samhna.de/samhain.

How Samhain Works

Samhain consists of three components: a console, a server, and a scan agent (often called the client). The agents are deployed onto every host that is to be monitored. A single server acts as a central location for logs, scan configurations, and scan data. The console is a Web-based control center written in Hypertext Preprocessor (PHP) that presents a UI that can be used to update databases or edit scan configurations. An optional component is a relational database server (e.g., PostgreSQL or MySQL) that can be used for log storage (see Figure 5.5).

Figure 5.5 Components That Make Up the Samhain Host Integrity Monitoring System

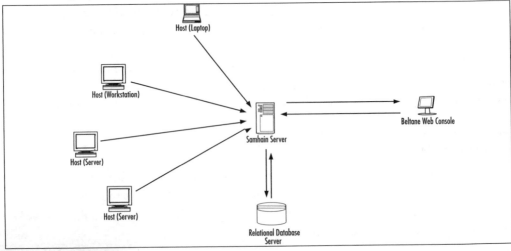

Each scan agent has a configuration that determines when and what to scan on the host environment. The agents compare the current environment against the trusted database established from a previous scan. Any differences generate logs, which are then sent back to the server. An agent's scan configuration and the trusted database can be stored on the server and are requested by the scan agent when needed. Optionally, logs can be stored in a relational database.

Notes from the Underground...

Push or Pull

Samhain follows a completely different model than Osiris with respect to the communication between the scan agents and the console. Specifically, Samhain agents initiate communication with the console, as opposed to Osiris where the console initiates connections to the scan agent. There are advantages and disadvantages to each model. The main benefit with the Samhain method is that the monitored hosts do not have to open a listening network port. The main benefit of Osiris is that administration is much easier because the deployed agents do not have to maintain the location of the management console. Furthermore, Samhain pulls the baseline database from the server down to the monitored host for comparison, whereas Osiris pushes the scan data to the console for analysis. The benefit of Samhain is that the console only needs read privileges for the baseline database. The benefit of Osiris is that the trusted data is never kept resident on the monitored host and thus is less susceptible to tampering.

Authentication of Components

The scan agent sends sensitive logging data back to the console, and the console provides the scan agent with the scan configuration and trusted database to be used for comparison. Thus, these components must authenticate each other. Additionally, all of this communication must be encrypted.

The Samhain scan agent and server authenticate each other using the Secure Remote Password (SRP) protocol. When the scan agent is compiled, a password is embedded into the executable. Additionally, a verifier is stored in that agent's configuration file. When the scan agent and the server connect, they each compute a key based on an initial data exchange. The scan agent and the server authenticate each other by verifying that they both computed the same key.

Samhain encrypts all traffic between the scan agent and the server using Advanced Encryption Standard (AES) for encryption. As a result of the authentication process, the scan agent and the server establish ephemeral keys. These keys are used to sign and encrypt communication between the two for the duration of that session. This is a very effective means of securing scan agent and server communication because an attacker would have to take apart the running Samhain scan agent process to get the current keys or take apart the executable to obtain the password used to authenticate to the server.

Scan Data

Samhain can be run as a stand-alone process in a manner similar to Tripwire; however, most deployments are centralized where the agents store their configuration and scan data on the server.

Upon start-up, a scan agent requests and downloads a signed copy of the trusted database. After a scan is completed, logs are generated that contain all of the information that is different between the current environment and the trusted database. These logs are sent back to the server for verification and storage.

To update the contents in the trusted database, the administrator uses the console to integrate data from the logs into the database file. Alternatively, the database file can be transferred to the monitored host, and Samhain can perform the update by integrating the state of the current environment into the database file. The database file then must be transferred back to the server.

Logging

There are many logging mechanisms available with Samhain. Logs can be sent to the server, a remote Structured Query Language (SQL) database such as PostgreSQL or MySQL, and a local log file redirected to an application, printed to standard output or the console, or sent to syslog.

Samhain agents have an embedded 64-bit key that is used to sign all log messages. Each log message has an attached signature computed by using the embedded key and the actual contents of the log message. Upon receipt of the log message, the server verifies the signature, signs it, and stores the log data or directs it to the correct logging facility.

Samhain defines many different severities and classes for log messages. This process is useful for analysis as well as throttling the amount of log data sent back to the server. The severity may be low, such as debug, or it may indicate a more severe message, such as an error or critical event. The log class is used to describe the payload of the log message, such as whether it is a rekey event, a keep-alive, or a policy violation. This is basically the same thing as the facilities and priorities used by syslog. To filter out certain log messages, the server can be configured to set thresholds for each facility. If an incoming log message does not meet that threshold, it is not logged (see Figure 5.6).

Figure 5.6 Samhain Log Format Structure

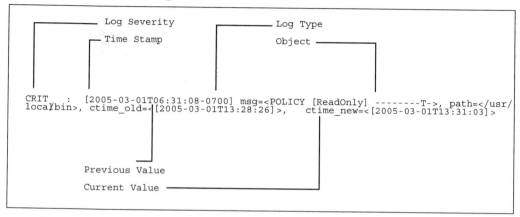

Notifications

Aside from all of the logging vectors supported by Samhain, logs can also be OpenPGP signed and e-mailed to an administrator. This can also be configured on a per-host basis. Samhain has Simple Mail Transfer Protocol (SMTP) code built into it so that it is not dependent on a Mail Transfer Agent (MTA). E-mail notifications can be sent to one or more recipients, and a limit can be specified to prevent too many e-mail notifications from being sent within a specified time window. The following is an example of a Samhain e-mail notification:

```
From: <daemon@example.com>
To: <brian@example.com>
Date: Tue, 01 Mar 2005 06:31:49 MST
Subject: [2005-03-01T06:31:48-0700] example.com


-----BEGIN MESSAGE-----
[2005-03-01T06:31:48-0700] example.com
CRIT   :   [2005-03-01T06:31:48-0700] msg=<POLICY [ReadOnly] ----H---TS>,
path=</usr/local/bin>, hardlinks_old=<10>, hardlinks_new=<11>,
size_old=<340>, size_new=<374>, ctime_old=<[2005-03-01T13:31:03]>,
ctime_new=<[2005-03-01T13:31:43]>, mtime_old=<[2005-03-01T13:31:03]>,
mtime_new=<[2005-03-01T13:31:43]>,
CRIT   :   [2005-03-01T06:31:48-0700] msg=<POLICY ADDED>,
path=</usr/local/bin/nmap>, mode_new=<-rwxr-xr-x>, imode_new=<33261>,
```

```
hardlinks_new=<1>, idevice_new=<0>, inode_new=<952675>, owner_new=<root>,
iowner_new=<0>, group_new=<wheel>, igroup_new=<0>, size_old=<0>,
size_new=<400340>, ctime_new=<[2005-03-01T13:31:43]>, atime_new=<[2005-03-
01T13:31:43]>, mtime_new=<[2005-03-01T13:31:43]>,
chksum_new=<75553746C7D7F779F7A02B8965648A7271CD026DC9A49B0F>

-----BEGIN SIGNATURE-----

CA4FD78E2209BEAA1595D5F29F5D4B1BA60F5652D6415FC6

000000 1109683908::example.com

-----END MESSAGE-----
```

Strengths

One of the biggest strengths of Samhain is its ability to monitor specific elements of a host environment on different time schedules. For example, you may want to conduct an SUID check once a day, but monitor the contents of *bin* every hour.

Another strong feature of Samhain is the vast array of logging vectors, especially the ability to log to a solid relational database such as PostgreSQL. Logging is critical; without logs, the integrity monitoring system would be almost useless. The many logging outlets provided by Samhain make integration into an existing log analysis infrastructure easier.

Samhain's design allows for a very powerful modular interface that lets you extend which elements of the environment are monitored. You not only add functionality to the scan agent but also customize how that data is analyzed and compared with subsequent scans. The configuration file syntax is also customizable so that you can pass any kind of parameters to custom modules.

Samhain has many strong antitampering features as part of its design. Executables have built-in keys to prevent an attacker from dropping a Trojan scan agent onto a host. The scan agent executable, log files, and database files can all be altered so that it is not obvious that they are related to Samhain. The executable name can be renamed upon installation so that it is not obvious that Samhain is installed. Furthermore, the Samhain process can be hidden from the process listing so that an attacker cannot see the scan agent daemon running. The scan configuration file can be steganographically hidden (i.e., attached to an image or postscript file) to avoid detection—an excellent feature.

Finally, Samhain has the ability to monitor the integrity of the kernel on Linux and FreeBSD systems. When these kernel checks are enabled, Samhain checks for the presence of rootkits by monitoring modifications to the system call table and the interrupt descriptor table.

Weaknesses

One of the biggest problems with Samhain is that it is not easy to configure and install. The configuration file is complicated with respect to logging, modules, and file monitoring. Samhain is very configurable, has a great deal of features, and has many antitampering defenses, but deploying it can be a huge undertaking.

Samhain modules, though very powerful, are not easy to develop. Developing even the most simple of modules requires modifying various parts of the code, including the build environment itself. The functions used to store data in the database are very file oriented, making writing modules to monitor other elements of the environment cumbersome.

The bulk of the kernel-monitoring facilities implemented by Samhain are only useful for Linux and FreeBSD. Likewise, some of the stealth features, such as hiding the scan agent process, are only supported for Linux systems.

Samhain is very UNIX and Linux centric. Although you can compile and run Samhain under the Cygwin environment, this is not supported, or even recommended, for security reasons. The Samhain code was designed to monitor UNIX and Linux environments, so if you have to monitor Windows environments, this may create an administrative burden.

Summary

Osiris and Samhain are the two most popular and widely deployed open source host integrity monitoring products. Each has an agent-based deployment model that provides detailed reports about changes to various aspects of a host's environment, including files, network ports, users, groups, kernel modules, kernel state, user login events, and more.

Neither one is better than the other; they both have their strengths and weaknesses. Although they both share the same goals, Osiris and Samhain have different feature sets; therefore, some environments are going to favor one over the other.

Solutions Fast Track

Osiris

- ☑ Osiris provides centralized host integrity monitoring for UNIX and Windows platforms.

- ☑ Osiris is easy to use and can be extended with modules; however, the modular interface is somewhat limited.

- ☑ Osiris relies on SSL to secure all communication between the agents, the console, and the command-line interface.

Samhain

- ☑ Samhain provides centralized host integrity monitoring for UNIX and Linux environments.

- ☑ Samhain has many antitampering defenses and can digitally sign log messages and database files.

- ☑ Samhain makes use of the Secure Remote Password protocol and AES encrypted Transmission Control Protocol (TCP) sessions for all communication between the agents and the console.

Frequently Asked Questions

The following Frequently Asked Questions, answered by the authors of this book, are designed to both measure your understanding of the concepts presented in this chapter and to assist you with real-life implementation of these concepts. To have your questions about this chapter answered by the author, browse to **www.syngress.com/solutions** and click on the **"Ask the Author"** form. You will also gain access to thousands of other FAQs at ITFAQnet.com.

Q: Can I use Osiris and Samhain to monitor the same host?

A: Yes. Osiris and Samhain will not get in each other's way; however, managing both applications means you have to monitor two different sets of logs for the same type of service.

Q: Can I set up multiple Osiris consoles or multiple Samhain servers?

A: Yes, you can. Sometimes network topology does not give you a choice. In both cases, the consoles are distinct and do not share data. The exception to this is with Samhain where both consoles can talk to the same SQL database.

Q: How many agents can an Osiris or Samhain management console handle?

A: Hundreds, possibly thousands. There are many variables at play. It depends on how often the agents are scanning, how much data each agent is collecting, and the hardware and system resources available to the management console.

Q: What are the license restrictions for Osiris and Samhain?

A: The Osiris source code is licensed under a BSD-style license. Samhain is licensed under the GNU Public License. Both are free to use in commercial and noncommercial environments.

Q: What is the difference between Osiris and Samhain with respect to the operating systems they support?

A: Samhain is somewhat UNIX centric and runs on Linux, BSD, Mac OS X, Solaris, AIX, HP-UX, UnixWare, and Alpha/True64. Osiris runs on BSD, Mac OS X, Solaris, Linux, AIX, IRIX, and Windows NT/2K/XP/2003. The major difference is that Osiris has native support for Windows, whereas Samhain requires POSIX emulation like Cygwin to run on Windows.

Chapter 6

Osiris

Solutions in this chapter:

- **Configuring and Building Osiris**
- **Additional Deployment Considerations**
- **Establishing a Management Console**
- **Command-Line Interface**
- **Scan Agents**
- **Administering Osiris**

☑ **Summary**

☑ **Solutions Fast Track**

☑ **Frequently Asked Questions**

Introduction

Osiris is one of the most widely deployed open source host integrity monitoring systems available today. In Chapter 5, we explored how Osiris works; this chapter covers all of the steps involved in deploying Osiris, including building from source, deployment, configuration, and administration.

It is always good practice to test software in a dedicated testing environment before incorporating it into your production system. This is useful for a few reasons. First, it allows you to gain familiarity with the software before you deploy it (mistakes can be made without much consequence). Second, it allows you to determine what functionality you need for your software agents (modules). It also allows you to fine-tune configurations so that you can begin production with fewer false positives. Finally, it is recommended that you maintain at least one test system to be used just for experimenting, testing policy changes, and simulating upgrades.

This chapter marks the start of the practical section of this book. It contains more information and detail about deploying Osiris than any other source. As of this writing, Osiris is at version 4.1.8. The goal here is to provide detailed, applicable information on how to deploy Osiris. Although the attempt is made to stick to the core elements, keep in mind that Osiris is under active development, so not all of the screenshots or output will exactly match future versions.

Configuring and Building Osiris

The first step in deploying Osiris is to create trusted software builds. The best way to do this is to verify the source, build it offline on a trusted host, and then burn the binary installers to read-only media. Having trusted binaries on read-only media is helpful because you can easily distribute the software to new hosts.

This section covers establishing a trusted build environment and creating installation packages to be used for deployment, including UNIX-like platforms and Windows. Although not necessary, it is helpful to dedicate a system specifically for building Osiris, which makes adding a module to the scan agent or deploying a newer version of the software easier. Ideally, the host used to create trusted builds is never connected to a network, and is secured physically.

This may seem overly cautious, but it is not. As a software engineer, I have seen many broken production build environments: build hosts on the corporate network, unpatched and unsecured; build hosts where all of the developers have access to the system; and build hosts where the root password is written on sticky notes on the side of the box. As a result, I have seen builds with Trojans and releases containing software viruses. When you consider that this software may be deployed on thousands of hosts, it is a serious concern. When you consider what is at stake, the small burden associated with maintaining an isolated build environment is a worthy investment.

Getting Osiris

The source code for Osiris can be downloaded from http://hostintegrity.com/osiris (distributed as a *gzipped tar file*). The Message Digest 5 (MD5) checksum and a Pretty Good Privacy (PGP) signature are posted for every Osiris release. The Osiris source can also be downloaded from an anonymous subversion mirror that contains tags for all of the releases and the latest (unstable) development code; however, the subversion repository is simply a mirror, and none of the code is signed. Other than for experimenting, you should always obtain the source code from the Osiris Web site, because it is the only source that can be verified.

All Osiris releases are signed with a PGP key with the following fingerprint:

```
FBBA B237 EF74 19F1 AC2F 8C0F 0DEC 799E 9674 763D
```

This PGP key is available on the Osiris Web site and on public PGP key servers. The first step to obtaining a verified copy of the source is to download the key using Gnu Privacy Guard (GnuPG) or PGP software. The most important thing is to make certain that you verify the software on a trusted environment, and that the fingerprint of the key is the same as the one we just showed. Next, download the Osiris source code and its corresponding PGP signature using either a Web browser or a command-line utility such as *curl* or *wget*:

```
$ curl hostintegrity.com/osiris/data/osiris-4.1.8.tar.gz -o osiris-
    4.1.8.tar.gz
$ curl hostintegrity.com/osiris/data/osiris-4.1.8.tar.gz.sig -o osiris-
    4.1.8.tar.gz.sig
```

Burn these two files to read-only media such as a CD-ROM or DVD, and verify the PGP signature. Assuming that the signatures match, you now have verified copies of the Osiris source that cannot be altered. If you are using any Osiris modules, follow the same procedure and place them on the same disc. This is useful because you can use this disc as a starting point to building trusted binaries of the software. The fact that the build host is not on a network is a non-issue; all that is required is that it has a CD-ROM or DVD drive.

Download the PGP key from www.hostintegrity.com/brian/brianwotring.asc or, if you are using GnuPG, download the key from one of the key servers by doing the following:

```
$ gpg --search-keys osiris@hostintegrity.com
gpg: searching for "osiris@hostintegrity.com" from hkp server
subkeys.pgp.net
```

```
(1)        Brian Wotring <brian@shmoo.com>
           Brian Wotring <brian@fortnocs.com>
           Brian Wotring <brian@metasecura.com>
           Brian Wotring <brian@hostintegrity.com>
           Brian Wotring <osiris@hostintegrity.com>


             1024 bit DSA key 9674763D, created: 1999-11-10
Keys 1-1 of 1 for "osiris@hostintegrity.com".  Enter number(s), N)ext, or
Q)uit > 1
gpg: requesting key 9674763D from hkp server subkeys.pgp.net
gpg: key 9674763D: public key "Brian Wotring <brian@shmoo.com>" imported
gpg: no ultimately trusted keys found
gpg: Total number processed: 1
gpg:                 imported: 1
```

What is important is that the specified key matches the fingerprint, which can be verified by doing the following:

```
gpg --fingerprint osiris@hostintegrity.com
pub    1024D/9674763D 1999-11-10
       Key fingerprint = FBBA B237 EF74 19F1 AC2F  8C0F 0DEC 799E 9674 763D
uid                    Brian Wotring <brian@shmoo.com>
uid                    Brian Wotring <brian@fortnocs.com>
uid                    Brian Wotring <brian@metasecura.com>
uid                    Brian Wotring <brian@hostintegrity.com>
uid                    [jpeg image of size 4891]
uid                    Brian Wotring <osiris@hostintegrity.com>
sub    2048g/D33C2213 1999-11-10
```

Once you have the correct key and have verified the signature, set its trust and verify that the signature file matches the downloaded source. Assuming that the source and signature are in your current directory, use the following commands to trust the signing key and verify the source:

```
$ gpg --edit-key osiris@hostintegrity.com
gpg (GnuPG) 1.4.1; Copyright (C) 2005 Free Software Foundation, Inc.
This program comes with ABSOLUTELY NO WARRANTY.
This is free software, and you are welcome to redistribute it
under certain conditions. See the file COPYING for details.


pub  1024D/9674763D  created: 1999-11-10  expires: never        usage: CSA
```

```
                                trust: full              validity: unknown
sub   2048g/D33C2213   created: 1999-11-10   expires: never        usage: E
[ unknown] (1). Brian Wotring <brian@shmoo.com>
[ unknown] (2)   Brian Wotring <brian@fortnocs.com>
[ unknown] (3)   Brian Wotring <brian@metasecura.com>
[ unknown] (4)   Brian Wotring <brian@hostintegrity.com>
[ unknown] (5)   [jpeg image of size 4891]
[ unknown] (6)   Brian Wotring <osiris@hostintegrity.com>


Command> trust

pub   1024D/9674763D   created: 1999-11-10   expires: never        usage: CSA
                                trust: full              validity: unknown
sub   2048g/D33C2213   created: 1999-11-10   expires: never        usage: E
[ unknown] (1). Brian Wotring <brian@shmoo.com>
[ unknown] (2)   Brian Wotring <brian@fortnocs.com>
[ unknown] (3)   Brian Wotring <brian@metasecura.com>
[ unknown] (4)   Brian Wotring <brian@hostintegrity.com>
[ unknown] (5)   [jpeg image of size 4891]
[ unknown] (6)   Brian Wotring <osiris@hostintegrity.com>


Please decide how far you trust this user to correctly verify other users'
keys
(by looking at passports, checking fingerprints from different sources,
etc.)


  1 = I don't know or won't say
  2 = I do NOT trust
  3 = I trust marginally
  4 = I trust fully
  5 = I trust ultimately
  m = back to the main menu


Your decision? 5
Do you really want to set this key to ultimate trust? (y/N) y


pub   1024D/9674763D   created: 1999-11-10   expires: never        usage: CSA
                                trust: ultimate          validity: unknown
sub   2048g/D33C2213   created: 1999-11-10   expires: never        usage: E
[ unknown] (1). Brian Wotring <brian@shmoo.com>
```

```
[ unknown] (2)   Brian Wotring <brian@fortnocs.com>
[ unknown] (3)   Brian Wotring <brian@metasecura.com>
[ unknown] (4)   Brian Wotring <brian@hostintegrity.com>
[ unknown] (5)   [jpeg image of size 4891]
[ unknown] (6)   Brian Wotring <osiris@hostintegrity.com>
Please note that the shown key validity is not necessarily correct
unless you restart the program.


Command> quit
dhcp-64-101-69-190:~/Desktop brian$ gpg --verify osiris-4.1.8.tar.gz.sig
gpg: Signature made Thu Mar 24 07:47:03 2005 MST using DSA key ID 9674763D
gpg: checking the trustdb
gpg: 3 marginal(s) needed, 1 complete(s) needed, PGP trust model
gpg: depth: 0  valid:   1  signed:   0  trust: 0-, 0q, 0n, 0m, 0f, 1u
gpg: Good signature from "Brian Wotring <brian@shmoo.com>"
gpg:               aka "Brian Wotring <brian@fortnocs.com>"
gpg:               aka "Brian Wotring <brian@metasecura.com>"
gpg:               aka "Brian Wotring <brian@hostintegrity.com>"
gpg:               aka "Brian Wotring <osiris@hostintegrity.com>"
```

Assuming that the signature is good, you now have a trusted source on read-only media and are ready to begin setting up your build environments and building Osiris from a trusted source.

NOTE

Software signing applies to all PGP- and GnuPG-signed software. Make every effort to verify the authenticity of the software that you download. I recommend that you use the "ultimate" trust setting for the key to avoid confusion with trust warnings during the verification process. Feel free to use a lesser trust setting, and do not always trust keys that you download from the Internet.

Establishing Build Environments

You must establish at least one build environment for every platform you want Osiris scan agents on. For UNIX-like systems, this is relatively easy; for Windows, it is more involved, which is why binaries for Windows are available with every Osiris release. However, this is only for convenience. The Windows binaries are the default configuration options and contain only the stock modules. If you are planning to monitor Windows hosts, it is recommended that you establish a Windows build environment.

UNIX Build Environment

The Osiris source uses two major software projects: OpenSSL and Berkeley database (DB). The functionality of Osiris is highly dependent on Berkeley DB; therefore, the source for a trusted and tested version of Berkeley DB is included with Osiris. Osiris will not use Berkeley DB on your system. The present version of Berkeley DB (v.4.2.52) included with Osiris, has been tested extensively and works well with Osiris. OpenSSL is an external dependency. The software requirements for building Osiris on UNIX-like systems are:

- American National Standards Institute (ANSI) C compiler (*gcc* recommended)

- OpenSSL (v.0.9.7e or greater recommended: www.openssl.org)

In addition, some utilities such as tar and GNU Zip (gzip) are used to create install files. Although gcc is not required, it is recommended. For platforms that do not normally contain gcc (such as Solaris, AIX, IRIX, and so on), gcc ports are available. Although the Osiris source code has been stripped of any gcc dependencies, modules may or may not have gcc dependencies. You will likely save yourself some trouble by compiling Osiris using gcc.

Windows Build Environment

This section lists the steps required to create a Windows build environment using Windows XP. This environment can be used to build a console or scan agents, which can be deployed on Windows 2000, Windows XP (Home or Professional), and Windows 2003 Advanced Server. The software requirements for building Osiris on Windows are:

- MinGW v.3.1.0 or greater (www.mingw.org)

- MSYS v.1.0.10 or greater (www.mingw.org)

- NSIS Installer v.2.0.5 or greater (nsis.sourceforge.net)

- Active Perl v.5.6.1 or greater (www.activestate.com)

- OpenSSL v.0.9.7e or greater recommended (www.openssl.org)

The preceding software requirements are all open source requirements; no commercial software is needed (other than Windows) to build Osiris. Minimalist GNU for Windows (MinGW) is a Windows development suite consisting of header files and libraries that can be used to produce native Windows executables that are not dependent on third-party libraries (such as *Cygwin*). MSYS provides an environment that can take advantage of the configure scripts and Makefiles traditionally used to build software on UNIX-like systems. MinGW and MSYS together, allow you to create native Windows executables without Visual Studio, and also allow all platforms to take advantage of the same build system. NSIS is a highly configurable, scriptable Windows installer system that provides a graphical installer familiar to Windows environments, and allows for silent installations that are useful in mass deployment scenarios. Perl is needed to configure and build OpenSSL. Other Perl distributions can be used for Windows, but Active Perl is easy to install.

You can download from the preceding project sites or from the Osiris Web site. The first step is to download the most current Osiris Windows development kit and its PGP signature:

- http://hostintegrity.com/osiris/data/windows-dev.zip
- http://hostintegrity.com/osiris/data/windows-dev.zip.sig

Burn these files to a CD and verify the PGP signature. Windows XP has native support for reading zip files, so this should be all that you need. If your build host is Windows 2000 or 2003 Advanced Server, you must download a zip utility. The software should be installed in the following order:

1. NSIS
2. Active State Perl
3. MinGW
4. MSYS
5. OpenSSL

Accept the defaults for NSIS, Active Perl, and MinGW, which put Perl in your path and leaves MinGW installed on *c:\mingw*. When installing MSYS, change the install path to *c:\msys* (see Figure 6.1), which will make it easier to work with.

Figure 6.1 Installing MSYS

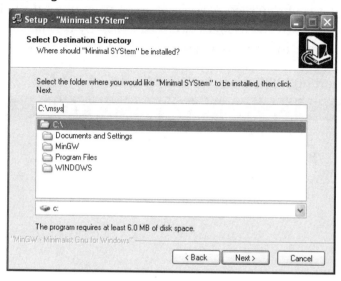

At the end of the MSYS installation, there is a post-install script that will prompt you for the location of MinGW. Answer **y** to the first two questions, and provide the path *C:/mingw* (see Figure 6.2). Note that the path is a forward slash, not the traditional path separator for Windows.

Figure 6.2 MSYS Post-install Script

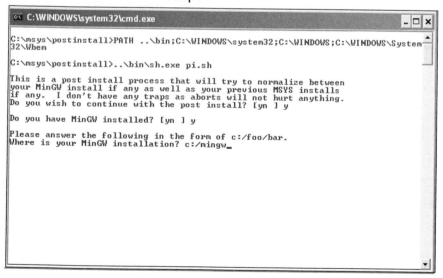

Next, compile and install OpenSSL. Copy the OpenSSL source into your *MSYS home* directory (located in *C:\msys\home* by default). Next, start MSYS from the Start menu; you should see an *rxvt* terminal (see Figure 6.3). By default, you will be in your *MSYS home* directory and should see the OpenSSL source file.

Figure 6.3 Starting MSYS from the Start Menu

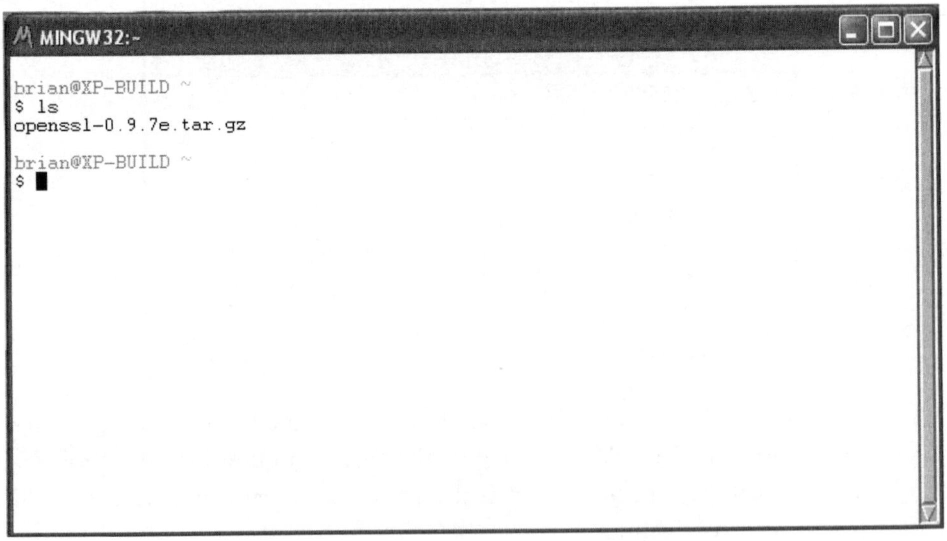

To build OpenSSL, first unpack the source:

```
$ tar xvfz openssl-0.9.7e.tar.gz
```

Next, configure it for MinGW and build the toolkit:

```
$ cd openssl-0.9.7e
$ ./configure mingw
$ make
```

Finally, install OpenSSL so that the Osiris build system can use it:

```
$ make install
```

At this point, the build environment for Windows is complete. All you need to do is place the Osiris source in your *MSYS home* directory. From this point on, there is no difference in the way you configure and build the Osiris executables between the Windows and UNIX-like systems.

Configuration Options

The configure script used to prepare the source tree for building, has a number of options that can be used to custom-build Osiris. If you do not specify any options, reasonable defaults will be used. To see what these defaults will be, run configure:

```
$ ./configure
```

This command configures the source, and prints the default values at the end of the configuration process as well as the modules that will be linked into the scan agent (if built). The default values look like this:

```
==> Configuration Complete.
==> Osiris has been configured with the following options:


                  Host: powerpc-apple-darwin7.8.0
              Compiler: gcc
        Compiler flags: -Wall -g -O2
     Preprocessor flags:
           Linker flags:
             Libraries: -lpthread  -lssl -lcrypto -lresolv
   Privilege Separation: yes
          SSL Location: (system)
 Osiris Root Directory: /usr/local/osiris
           Osiris user: osiris
    Osiris MD Directory: /usr/local/osiris
          Osiris MD user: osiris
   Osiris MD config dir: /usr/local/osiris


=======================================
 Found Scan Agent Modules:

     ==> mod_groups
     ==> mod_kmods
     ==> mod_ports
     ==> mod_users
=======================================
```

The source code for the local copy of Berkeley DB is also configured. All configure options are passed only to the Osiris source code. The Berkeley DB code is configured to build only the static copy of the library, and is not installed on the system.

The following are available configure options and their significance:

```
--with-ssl-dir=<PATH>
```

All three components of Osiris, including the command-line interface (CLI), the management console, and the scan agent, are linked against the OpenSSL library. This option allows you to specify where that copy of OpenSSL is on the file system. By default, the build system attempts to find an installation of OpenSSL and uses the first one it encounters. This option is useful in cases where you do not have OpenSSL installed, or you do not want to install it on the build system. You can build OpenSSL and have just Osiris linked against that build. For example, if you download and build OpenSSL in */usr/local/src/openssl-0.9.7e/*, you can link against that build by doing:

```
$ ./configure --with-ssl-dir=/usr/local/src/openssl-0.9.7e
```

Some systems (such as IRIX) may already have OpenSSL installed, but built with a different compiler or settings that make it incompatible with gcc. If this is the case, you should download and compile a local build of OpenSSL and use it to build Osiris:

```
--with-root-dir=<PATH>
```

Both the scan agent and the management console have a directory on the file system where they store certificates and host data. By default, this directory is */usr/local/osiris* on UNIX-like systems and *%WindowsRoot%\osiris* on Windows. This configure option allows you to change where the Osiris repository is established upon installation. There are several reasons not to use the default location:

- Different operating systems have different conventions for storing various types of data.

- Your administrative policy places constraints on where you can store data of this nature.

- Disk space; depending on how many hosts you are monitoring or how much scan data you are storing, you may want to dedicate a disk specifically for Osiris scan data and logs:

```
--with-osiris-user=<USERNAME>
```

As part of the installation process, a user and a group are created specifically for Osiris; the default name for this user and group is "osiris." The console and scan agent processes all run as this unprivileged user, and all files used by Osiris are owned by the Osiris user and group. This configuration option allows you to specify the user and group used by Osiris. If the user and group specified do not exist, they are created. The console service and scan agent service on Windows run as administrator; therefore, this configure option has no effect on Windows systems:

```
--with-md-dir=<DIR>
```

This configure option is the same as the **--with-root-dir** option, except that it is specific to the management console. Again, if you have partition constraints or you want to specify exactly where the console stores all logs, configurations, and scan databases, this is the option to use. The default location is */usr/local/osiris*:

```
--with-md-conf-dir=<DIR>
```

Following is another console-specific option that is used to specify the directory where the Osiris management console configuration file (*osirismd.conf*) is stored. By default, the configuration file is stored in the Osiris root directory (*/usr/local/osiris*):

```
--with-md-user=<USERNAME>
```

Use this option to specify a user and group specifically for the management console. By default, the scan agent and management console use the same user and group:

```
--enable-fancy-cli=YES|NO
```

For example, to enable the *fancy-cli* feature and specify an alternative default path (*/var/local/osiris*), you would run configure as follows:

```
$ ./configure --enable-fancy-cli=yes --with-root-dir=/var/local/osiris
```

The Osiris command-line application can be configured to provide useful enhancements such as command completion and a command history buffer. Osiris will automatically use the GNU readline library if it is installed. If it is not installed or if you would rather use the built-in Osiris command-line enhancements, specify the *fancy-cli* argument to configure. Because the built-in command-line enhancements are not stable, they are turned off by default.

In most cases, the default configure options are sufficient. These options exist to make it easy for administrators to customize the deployment of the Osiris agents and console according to the particulars of their systems. Once the source has been configured, check the final output to make sure that any options you provided were interpreted correctly.

Adding Modules

The Osiris source contains four native modules at the time of this writing: *mod_users*, *mod_groups*, *mod_kmods*, and *mod_ports*. At one point, these modules were part of the scan agent code, but were removed when the modular interface was developed. Not all modules are this useful, but there are a few other modules that you may want to add. A collection of modules that has been reviewed and tested can be found on Osiris' Web site http://hostintegrity.com/osiris/modules.html.

All modules are kept in a directory called *modules* under the source code for the scan agent. Each module is in its own directory. To add a module to the build, all you have to do is unpack it in the *src/osirisd/modules* directory. You do not have to run the configure script again; the build system will automatically build the module into the scan agent executable.

Building Installer Packages

The final step is to build the Osiris executables and create the installer package. An installer package is a single file that can be distributed to your production (or test) systems that allows you to run a script (or an executable on Windows) or to install the agent or the console software, which makes it easy to distribute the software to multiple hosts. If you are installing many agents, you will want to create an installer package.

Many operating systems come with ways to download and install binaries or build and install from source using only a couple of commands. FreeBSD has ports and packages, Mac OS X has fink, Gentoo Linux has ebuilds, RedHat uses RPMs, and so on. Using a port or a package of some kind can prove helpful for deployment, but is not recommended: ports and packages make assumptions about configure and installation options, and your target systems may not have compilers on them. Binary packages strive to attain maximum compatibility, catering to the lowest common denominator as far as optimizations go. To control exactly how Osiris is built, you must build it from source.

Building UNIX Install Packages

For UNIX-like systems, there are two installer packages: one for the agent and one for the management console. After the source has been configured, you can build the agent and create an installer with the following command:

```
$ make agent
```

This command builds only the necessary files for the scan agent, creates an installation script mindful of your configuration options, strips the binaries, and stores everything in a gzipped tar file. The installer file is located in the *src/install* directory, and the filename contains the Osiris version, operating system, and architecture type. When the package is created, you will see output that lists the installer file name and its contents:

```
------------------------------------------------------------------
building release tarball: src/install/osiris-agent-4.1.8-rc1-powerpc-Darwin-
7.8.0.tar
installer package contents:
total 1984
-rw-r--r--  1 brian   brian     5132 18 Mar 21:08 LICENSE
drwxr-xr-x  6 brian   brian      204 18 Mar 21:08 darwin
-rwxr-xr--  1 brian   brian    31081 18 Mar 21:08 install.sh
-rwxr-xr-x  1 brian   brian   843208 18 Mar 21:08 osiris
-rwxr-xr-x  1 brian   brian   125208 18 Mar 21:08 osirisd
-rw-r--r--  1 brian   brian       72 18 Mar 21:08 version.h
------------------------------------------------------------------

installer package created.
```

To build an installer package for the console, use the following command:

```
$ make console
```

This will create another gzipped tar file that contains all of the binaries necessary to install a management console. The location and naming convention for the installer file are similar to the agent installer. Once you have built packages for the agent and the console, burn them to read-only media. Remember, whatever platform and architecture you build a package on is the only kind of platform that package can be installed on (e.g., if you build the package on Mac OS X, you can only install it on Mac OS X systems. If you build it on Linux, it will be useful only for Linux systems, and so on). The Osiris build system does not have a means of building fat binaries for use on multiple platforms.

Building a Windows Installer

The agent and console are packaged as a single installer for Windows. First, you must build the Osiris components:

```
$ make
```

Before you build the Windows installer, you must strip the executables:

```
$ strip src/cli/osiris.exe
$ strip src/osirisd/osirisd.exe
$ strip src/osirismd/osirismd.exe
```

This will reduce their size by roughly one half, and keep the installer from being bloated. The *src/install/windows/osiris_install.nsi* file dictates how to build the Osiris installer. Right-click on this file and select menu option **Compile NSIS script**. You will see a dialogue listing the details of the creation process (see Figure 6.4). If successful, the installer file is named *osiris_install.exe*. Rename this to something meaningful and burn it to read-only media.

Figure 6.4 Details of the Osiris Creation Process

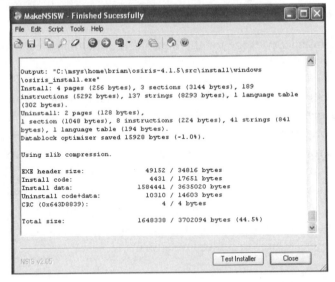

Additional Deployment Considerations

At this point, you should have trusted copies of installers on read-only media. However, before you begin deployment, there are additional issues that you should consider.

Read-Only Media

It is possible to deploy a scan agent to be run from read-only media, which is often suggested as the "secure" way to deploy host-based security agents. The idea is that an attacker cannot alter the agent executable or related files; thus, they can always be trusted. Not true. In previous chapters, you learned that there are many different ways to subvert software agents. They depend on the integrity of the runtime environment (kernel syscalls, memory, and so on); therefore, preventing the agent executables from tampering is only a partial solution. Furthermore, updates are cumbersome because you have to burn new media. Servers often do not have CD-ROM or DVD drives, or you may not want to dedicate the drive to be used specifically for Osiris. All things considered, this is not a good idea because it is not practical.

NOTE

I have seen deployments of software such as Osiris, where administrators were sold on the idea of deploying on read-only media because that was the "secure" way to do it. In the end, the administrative overhead became such a burden that the entire system became useless. At that point, you have to ask yourself which is better; a useful deployment that you know is not perfect or nothing at all?

Pre-provisioning Digital Certificates

Another deployment consideration is the pre-provision of digital certificates. The scan agent and the CLI both authenticate the management console using certificates. By default, the management console generates a self-signed certificate upon installation. The first time the CLI connects to the console, it saves the presented root certificate to be used to authenticate the console on subsequent connections (not unlike the way Secure Shell [SSH] saves host keys). Likewise, the scan agent automatically trusts and saves the first root certificate that connects to it.

The most obvious problem with the default behavior is that the scan agents are vulnerable; any host can connect to them and force the agent to save any root certificate. Another problem is that the system is using a self-signed certificate. In any case, it is recommended that you pre-provision certificates whenever possible. The main reasons this is not mandatory is because of usability and convenience.

Administrators who do not know how to generate key pairs and deploy root certificates do not have to; the system provides adequate security, especially for evaluation
purposes. At the same time, you have the ability to change it; it is recommended that
you do so.

There is no way to pre-provision the CLI, which is not much of a problem
because the user interface displays the presented certificate fingerprint and gives you
the option of whether to save it or not. The CLI is not installed on different
machines, so you only have to deal with this once. The certificate is saved in your
home directory; for UNIX-like machines, it is *~/.osiris/osiris_root.pem* and for
Windows systems, it is *%SystemRoot%\Documents and Settings\<username>\Application
Data\.osiris\osiris_root.pem*.

To install your own certificate on the console, you must replace two files: the
certificate and the key. The certificate is stored in
<OSIRIS_ROOT>/certs/osirismd.crt and the key for this certificate is stored in
<OSIRIS_ROOT>/private/osirismd.key. These two paths and filenames are not configurable. Whether or not you encrypt your key file is up to you. Keep in mind, if it
is encrypted, you will not be able to start the console until you manually enter a
password.

In order to pre-provision your agent installer, you must copy your root certificate into the Osiris source directory, specifically *src/install/osiris_root.pem*, and then
rebuild the agent installer. On UNIX-like systems, make sure you see *osiris_root.pem*
listed as one of the files added to the installer:

```
-rw-r--r--  1 brian   brian      5132 19 Mar 09:24 LICENSE
drwxr-xr-x  6 brian   brian       204 19 Mar 09:24 darwin
-rwxr-xr--  1 brian   brian     31081 19 Mar 09:24 install.sh
-rwxr-xr-x  1 brian   brian    843208 19 Mar 09:24 osiris
-rw-r--r--  1 brian   brian      1155 19 Mar 09:24 osiris_root.pem
-rwxr-xr-x  1 brian   brian    125208 19 Mar 09:24 osirisd
-rw-r--r--  1 brian   brian        72 19 Mar 09:24 version.h
```

On Windows, you have to scroll up on the installer creation log and look for the
line that begins with File: *osiris_root.pem* (see Figure 6.5).

Figure 6.5 Copying the Root Certificate into the Osiris Source Directory on Windows Systems

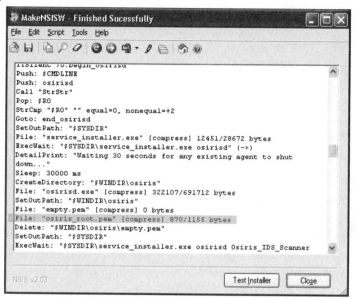

Operating System Specifics

You must build a separate agent installer for every type of operating system you want to monitor. Each operating system has its own peculiarities and restrictions for binary compatibility. Osiris does not have any kernel-resident code; therefore, it is relatively easy to build agent installers that are compatible with a variety of different operating system releases. The following is a list of helpful hints to consider when building installer agents:

- If you build on Windows XP, this installer will work on all of the Windows platforms supported by Osiris, including all versions of Windows 2000, Windows XP, and Windows 2003 Advanced Server.

- For Mac OS X, the general rule is to build on the lowest version that you need to support. For example, if your build host is running Mac OS X v.10.1.5, the built executables will run on v.10.1.5 and greater. However, if you build on v.10.4, you may encounter problems with library versions on older Mac OS X hosts. Since Osiris has no kernel run code, there are no issues related to kernel compatibilities to worry about.

- You will not encounter any problems with Linux as long as you compile the agent statically against all used libraries. If you are using gcc, set your

CFLAGS environment variable before you build the source. For example, assuming you are using a bash shell, you would set this by doing:

```
$ export CFLAGS="$CFLAGS -static"
$ ./configure [options]
$ make
```

- Berkeley Software Distribution (BSD) systems such as FreeBSD, NetBSD, and OpenBSD are the least problematic as far as binary compatibility is concerned. Obviously, you have to build separate installers for each supported architecture type.

- Osiris is tested on Solaris versions 2.8 and 2.9, and this should work fine for systems running version 2.5 or greater. For older SunOS-based systems, it is recommended that you compile separate agent installers. By default, the executables on Solaris are static and compiled as 32-bit applications. There is no significant advantage in altering the build so that it produces 64-bit executables.

Testing

The last thing you want to consider before deployment is testing. At this point, you have trusted installers on read-only media. It is a good idea to test these installers and the software itself. Only after you are satisfied with the installs and familiar with Osiris *should* you put it into production.

When testing the installer, you want to make sure that the **init** scripts work. Reboot your test system and make sure that the agent started correctly. Also, make sure that the default file permissions for the Osiris *root* directory, the root certificate, and any other installed files are set correctly. By default, these files are owned by the Osiris user and group. On UNIX-like systems, the permissions should look something like the following:

```
drwxr-xr-x      9 osiris    osiris       306 Mar 15 11:24  .
drwx------      3 osiris    osiris       102 Nov  2 20:08 ./certs
-rw-r--r--      1 osiris    osiris      1155 Nov  2 20:08
./certs/osirismd.crt
drwxr-xr-x     20 osiris    osiris       680 Mar 15 07:48 ./configs
-rw-------      1 osiris    osiris      8192 Feb 21 13:52 ./filter.db
drwx------      4 osiris    osiris       136 Mar 11 06:58 ./hosts
-rw-------      1 osiris    osiris      1155 Mar 15 11:22 ./osiris_root.pem
-rw-------      1 osiris    osiris       225 Mar 15 11:24 ./osirismd.conf
```

```
drwx------     4 osiris     osiris       136 Nov   2 20:08 ./private
-rw-------     1 osiris     osiris      8192 Nov   2 20:08 ./private/auth.db
-rw-------     1 osiris     osiris      1679 Nov   2 20:08
./private/osirismd.key
```

The **init** scripts are located in different locations for each platform. Table 6.1 shows the locations for the **init** scripts on common systems. This is useful information if you are testing or troubleshooting.

Table 6.1 Locations of Init Scripts on Common Operating Systems

Platform	Init Scripts Location
Mac OS X	*/System/Library/StartupItems/Osiris/Osiris*
Solaris	*/etc/init.d/osirisd, /etc/init.d/osirismd*
Linux	*/etc/init.d/osirisd, /etc/init.d/osirismd*
BSD systems	*/usr/local/etc/rc.d/osirisd,* */usr/local/etc/rc.d/osirismd*
IRIX	*/etc/init.d/osirisd, /etc/init.d/osirismd*
AIX	*/etc/rc.osirisd, /etc/rc.osirismd*

Establishing a Management Console

This examines everything that you need to know to establish a management console. Specifically, we examine the anatomy of the management console, look at its components and features, and discuss how the management console can be configured. Then, we walk through a typical installation. Finally, we configure and do some post-installation tasks.

By now, you should have decided which operating system you will use for your console. In addition, you should have installed the base operating system and locked it down. (For more information see Chapter 4.) The host that you are using as a management console is the most important part of the Osiris system; a compromised management host will render the entire integrity monitoring system useless. Make sure that this host is fully patched and locked down before installing the console software.

Management Console Components

The management console consists of the *osirismd* executable and a directory of files that are used to store logs, configurations, certificates and passwords, scan data, and more. This section looks at some of the major components that make up the Osiris directory.

Directory Structure

By default, all of the data related to the management console is stored under a single directory (*/usr/local/osiris* on UNIX systems and *%WindowsRoot%\osiris* on Windows) (see Figure 6.6).

Figure 6.6 Directory Structure for the Osiris Management Console

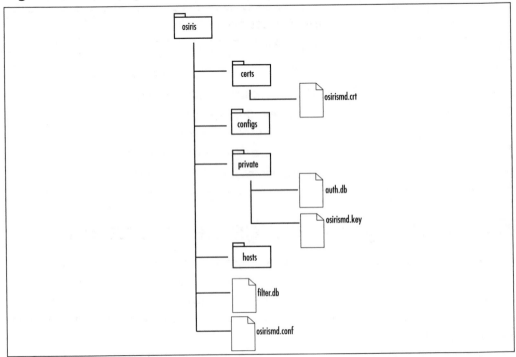

Every host that is monitored by the console has its own directory under the **hosts** directory (see Figure 6.7).

Figure 6.7 Host Directories

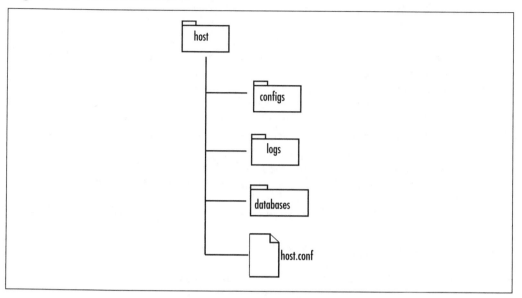

Because this directory contains all of the information about each host, including scan data and logs, you might want to consider a separate disk partition for your *osiris* directory. This will help with disk space, and allow greater flexibility with respect to the analysis and portability of your installation.

Notes from the Underground…

Remember Your Backups

All of the files in the *Osiris* directory are platform-independent; therefore, all of the data related to the console can be kept under a single directory. Thus, it is easy to make backups of your console. For example, on UNIX you can take a quick snapshot of the management console by doing the following as root:

```
# tar cvfz /tmp/console-backup.tar.gz /usr/local/osiris
```

This will create a backup of the console data in the */tmp* directory. You can then copy this to another host or burn it to read-only media. Furthermore, you can set up a *cron* job to do this on a regular basis.

On Windows XP systems, you can accomplish something similar by choosing "File->New->Compressed (zipped) Folder" from any Explorer Window.

Continued

After copying the files from *%WindowsRoot%\osiris* into the newly created zip folder, you can burn this file to read-only media or copy it to another host. How you choose to back up this directory is up to you; everyone's backup procedures are different. The important thing to remember is that you should back this data up and take steps to secure it. The information collected by the console is sensitive. Whenever I create backups for the systems that I monitor, I encrypt the backup file(s) before I burn them to read-only media.

Another useful thing about keeping backup files and the platform-independent characteristic of the *osiris* directory is that you can easily migrate your management console to another operating system. For example, if you want to migrate from Windows to FreeBSD, all you have to do is install the console on your FreeBSD system, unpack your console backup file, and restart the osirismd daemon. This ability is due largely in part to the use of Berkeley DB files as stores for the scan data.

User Authentication Database: *auth.db*

When you login to the management console using the CLI, you must authenticate by providing a password. The management console stores passwords in the *private/auth.db* file, which is a Berkeley DB file. The passwords are not encrypted. In fact, the file does not contain passwords; instead, it contains the MD5 checksums of the passwords. Upon login, the console computes the MD5 of the provided password and matches that to the one found in the database. This file is protected by file permissions and is readable and writable only by the Osiris user. (For more information about console users, see "Administering Osiris" later in this chapter.)

Comparison Filter Database: *filter.db*

In an attempt to help reduce noise, the management console can maintain a database of filters, which is a list of regular expressions. Each log message generated by the management console is subjected to this list of filters before being written to the various logging vectors. Filters are stored in the *filter.db* file in the root of the main *Osiris* directory. For efficiency reasons, this file is a Berkeley DB file; therefore, you must use the CLI to edit or view the filter list.

Management Console Processes

On UNIX, the management console is a daemon and consists of a single executable called *osirismd*. By default, this executable is stored in */usr/local/sbin*. The osirismd application is Set User ID (SUID) and owned by the Osiris user and group. The permissions should look something like the following:

```
$ ls -la /usr/local/sbin/osirismd
-rwsr-xr-x  1 osiris   osiris   856832 19 Mar 14:13 /usr/local/sbin/osirismd
```

This executable is large for a typical daemon, because it is statically linked against both the OpenSSL libraries and the Berkeley DB library. When osirismd starts up, it spawns two processes: a *master daemon process* and a *scheduling process*. The master daemon process is responsible for accepting and handling new requests. The scheduling process is responsible for monitoring the schedules of hosts and telling them when they must scan. The osirismd process is not multithreaded on UNIX systems, so it spawns a new process for each request, including CLI sessions and handling incoming scan streams from monitored hosts. Thus, at any point in time, you will see two or more osirismd instances.

On Windows, the management console consists of a single executable called *osirismd.exe*, which is stored in *%SystemRoot%\osirismd.exe*. The osirismd service is launched on startup and runs with administrator privileges. Unlike on UNIX systems, the osirismd application is multithreaded and starts out with two threads: one to handle requests and one scheduling thread. New threads are created to handle CLI sessions and any scheduled scan sessions (see Figure 6.8).

Figure 6.8 Configuring osirismd Elements through the Windows Service Control Panel

Alternatively, you can start and stop the osirismd service at any time by using the *net* command. For example:

```
C:\>net stop osirismd
The Osiris_IDS_Management service is stopping.
The Osiris_IDS_Management service was stopped successfully.
C:\>net start osirismd
The Osiris_IDS_Management service is starting.
The Osiris_IDS_Management service was started successfully.
```

Command-Line Arguments

Generally, the console is configured through the CLI and, ultimately, through a flat configuration file (*osirismd.conf*). However, the osirismd process does accept some command-line arguments. To see a listing of these arguments, do the following at a shell or command prompt:

```
$ osirismd -help

Osiris Management Console - Version 4.1.8-release
usage: osirismd [-r <directory>] [-f <file>] [-h]


 -r directory    : specify alternate directory for certs and hosts.
 -f file         : specify alternate configuration file.
 -h              : this usage statement.
```

On Windows, use the following code:

```
C:\>osirismd.exe --help

Osiris Management Console - Version 4.1.8-release
usage: osirismd [-r <directory>] [-f <file>] [-d] [-h] | [-u|-i]


 -r directory    : specify alternate directory for certs and hosts.
 -f file         : specify alternate configuration file.
 -h              : this usage statement.
 -i              : install as a windows service on local machine.
 -u              : uninstall windows service from local machine.
 -d              : run this application as a normal daemon, not a service.
```

The **-r** and **-f** options allow you to specify alternate locations for the Osiris *root* directory and the *osirismd.conf* file, respectively. The osirismd process accepts some additional arguments that can be helpful. The **-i** and **-u** options allow you to install and uninstall the osirismd service on the command line. The **-d** option can be used to run osirismd from a command prompt as opposed to a service, which can be helpful when trying to debug a problem with the console. Stop the service and start it up on a command prompt with the **-d** option; you will see the log messages printed to the window (see Figure 6.9).

Figure 6.9 A Command Prompt with Log Messages for osirismd *-d*

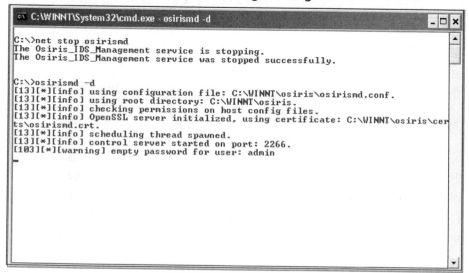

```
C:\>net stop osirismd
The Osiris_IDS_Management service is stopping.
The Osiris_IDS_Management service was stopped successfully.

C:\>osirismd -d
[13][*][info] using configuration file: C:\WINNT\osiris\osirismd.conf.
[13][*][info] using root directory: C:\WINNT\osiris.
[13][*][info] checking permissions on host config files.
[13][*][info] OpenSSL server initialized, using certificate: C:\WINNT\osiris\cer
ts\osirismd.crt.
[13][*][info] scheduling thread spawned.
[13][*][info] control server started on port: 2266.
[103][*][warning] empty password for user: admin
```

Installing the Management Console on UNIX

The first step to installing the management console is to move the installer *tar.gz* file to a reasonable location and unpack it. In this case, we use a Linux host:

```
$ cd /usr/local/src
$ tar xvfz osiris-console-4.1.8-linux.tar.gz
```

Installing the management console is fairly straightforward. The installer is a simple shell script (*install.sh*) that asks you a few questions and installs the executables. Specifically, *install.sh* will:

1. Prompt to continue the installation.

2. Display installation defaults.

3. Create local "osiris" user if it does not exist.

4. Create local "osiris" group if it does not exist.

5. Prompt to install local scan agent.

6. Prompt to install management console.

7. Prompt to install CLI.

8. Copy executables and default scan configuration files.

9. Copy init scripts for installed daemons.

10. Set reasonable permissions on installed files.

As root, run the *install.sh* script and select **yes** to continue installation:

```
$ cd osiris-console-4.1.8-release
# ./install.sh
Continue with installation? (y/n) [y]   y
```

You will see the installation script create an Osiris user and group:

```
==> creating user and group (osiris, osiris).
==> group 'osiris' added.
==> user 'osiris' added.
==> using existing Osiris management console user.
```

When prompted for what to install, answer **yes** to all three components. It is always a good idea to install a scan agent on the console. You will need the CLI to perform the initial installation.

```
Install osiris agent? (y/n) [y]   Y
Install management console? (y/n) [y]   Y
Install CLI? (y/n) [y]   Y
```

When prompted for a location for the executables, accept the default. The installer will install the start-up scripts and set permissions for the executables:

```
Installation directory for binaries: [/usr/local/sbin]
==> installed osiris CLI: /usr/local/sbin/osiris
Osiris scan agent root directory doesn't exist, creating.
==> installed scan agent: /usr/local/sbin/osirisd
==> installed management console /usr/local/sbin/osirismd
==> installed default scan configs.
==> installing rc startup for daemon(s).
Linux Distribution: gentoo
==> Skipping osirisd symlink creation.
  * osirisd added to runlevel default
```

```
 * Caching service dependencies...
 * rc-update complete.
==> Skipping osirismd symlink creation.
 * osirismd added to runlevel default
 * Caching service dependencies...
 * rc-update complete.
 ==> change owner and  permissions on /usr/local/sbin/osiris
-rwxr-xr-x  1 root wheel 765508 Mar 19 09:12 /usr/local/sbin/osiris
==> change owner and permissions on /usr/local/sbin/osirisd
-rwxr-xr-x  1 root wheel 110020 Mar 19 09:12 /usr/local/sbin/osirisd
==> change owner permissions on /usr/local/sbin/osirismd
-rwsr-xr-x  1 osiris osiris 788096 Mar 19 09:12 /usr/local/sbin/osirismd
```

Do *not* start the console and the scan agent when asked:

```
Start management console now? (y/n) [y]   n
 --> to start management console, run: /usr/local/sbin/osirismd
Start scan agent now? (y/n) [y]   n
 --> to start the scan agent, do sudo /usr/local/sbin/osirisd


Documentation is included with this source and available online at:
    http://hostintegrity.com/osiris/docs


(c) 2005 - Brian Wotring
```

At this point, Osiris is installed. Before starting the daemons, you must copy in your root certificate and private key. Copy your certificate file to */usr/local/osiris/certs/osirismd.crt* and your key file to */usr/local/osiris/private/osirismd.key*. If you want to have the console generate a self-signed certificate , you do not have to do anything.

Next, start the daemons. This will vary depending on your operating system. For BSD systems, this is usually accomplished by running the following commands as root:

```
# /usr/local/etc/rc.d/osirisd start
# /usr/local/etc/rc.d/osirismd start
```

For Solaris- and Linux-based systems, you can start the daemons with the following command:

```
# /etc/init.d/osirisd start
# /etc/init.d/osirismd start
```

For Mac OS X, use the following command:

```
# /System/Library/StartupItems/Osiris/Osiris start
```

Now verify that the daemons are running by using the *ps* command. You should see two instances of the management console daemon (osirismd) and two instances of the scan agent (osirisd). For example, on Linux:

```
$ ps -ef | grep osiris
root      17984  0.0  1.2  3028  772 pts/0     S     09:29   0:00
/usr/local/sbin/osirisd
osiris    17986  0.0  2.1  3220 1304 pts/0     S     09:29   0:00
/usr/local/sbin/osirisd
osiris    18035  0.0  2.6  3696 1612 ?         S     09:29   0:00
/usr/local/sbin/osirismd
osiris    18037  0.0  2.6  3700 1616 ?         S     09:29   0:00
/usr/local/sbin/osirismd
```

All osirismd processes should be running as the Osiris user. For the scan agent, you should see one running as root and one running as the Osiris user. The root run scan agent process exists solely to perform privileged operations for the scan agent; the root run process does not listen on any network ports.

Installing a Management Console on Windows

Installing a management console on Windows is easy; simply run the installer program by double-clicking on it. The first prompt you will encounter is the "End User License Agreement." Click the button that reads **I Agree**. The next prompt asks you which components to install. Since you are installing the management console, make sure that all three components are selected (see Figure 6.10).

Figure 6.10 Installing the Management Console on Windows

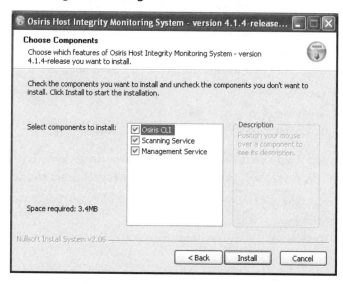

Installation takes at least one minute because the installer attempts to locate and gracefully shut down any existing Osiris services. When the installation is complete, you will see the phrase "Setup was completed successfully" at the top left of the dialogue box (see Figure 6.11). Click the **Close** button.

Figure 6.11 Completing the Installation of Osiris on Windows

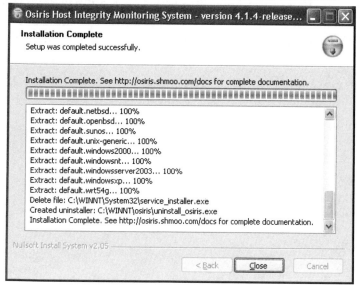

After the installation is complete, the scan agent and the console are installed and running. Unfortunately, there is no option to **not** start the services upon installation. Therefore, to add your own certificate to the management console, you must stop the service, copy in your own certificate, and restart the service. To stop the Osiris console service, open a command prompt and type the following:

```
C:\>net stop osirismd
The Osiris_IDS_Management service is stopping.
The Osiris_IDS_Management service was stopped successfully.
```

Next, copy your own certificate file to *%WindowsRoot%\osiris\certs\osirismd.crt* and the key file to *%WindowsRoot%\osiris\private\osirismd.key*. Restart the service:

```
C:\>net start osirismd
The Osiris_IDS_Management service is starting.
The Osiris_IDS_Management service was started successfully.
```

Understanding Configuration Settings

Now that the management console is installed and running, you must define some additional configuration parameters. However, before you do that, you should go over all of the configuration options so that you know what is available and what each of them does.

The configuration for the management console is stored in the *osirismd.conf* file, which is kept in the root of the *Osiris* directory. This is a flat file that is relatively easy to understand. When osirismd starts up, it looks for this file; if it is not there, it creates one with reasonable defaults. Following is an example of the default *osirismd.conf* file:

```
syslog_facility = DAEMON
control_port = 2266
http_port = 0
http_host =
notify_email =
notify_smtp_host = 127.0.0.1
notify_smtp_port = 25
notify_app =
allow = 127.0.0.1
hosts_directory =
```

The following is a complete list of settings that are found in the *osirismd.conf* file as of Osiris v.4.1.8:

- **syslog_facility=<FACILITY>** Use the specified syslog facility to log all log messages. The management console will log everything to the system log on UNIX hosts and the event viewer on Windows. This setting is only applicable to UNIX systems. Although there is a common set of syslog facilities, some have facilities that others do not. Consult your syslog main page for available facilities. The default value for this setting is DAEMON. (Do not include the *LOG_* prefix that is commonly associated with syslog facilities.

- **control_port=<PORT>** This is the network port that osirismd listens on for connections from the CLI. The default value for this port is 2266.

- **http_port=<PORT>** The management console has the ability to listen on a port and accept Hyper Text Transfer Protocol over Secure Socket Layer (HTTPS) requests from a Web browser, to review and acknowledge detected changes for a host. This is a legacy feature that was initially developed for convenience purposes. The default value for this setting is zero (disabled).

- **http_host=<NAME>** All e-mail notifications sent out by the management console identify the management console by its current hostname; specifically, it uses what is returned by the system function (*gethostname()*). Depending on your system configuration, you may or may not find this acceptable. Whatever value is set here will be used to identify the management console, including the value of the "From:" header in e-mails. The default value for this setting is empty, meaning the result of *gethostname()* will be used.

- **notify_email=<EMAIL_ADDRESS>** This is the e-mail address where all notifications about the status of the console or hosts are sent. The default value for this setting is empty (disabled).

- **notify_smtp_host=<SMTP_SERVER>** This is the Simple Mail Transfer Protocol (SMTP) server that will be used to send all e-mail notifications. The default value for this setting is local host (127.0.0.1).

- **notify_smtp_port=<PORT>** This is the remote port that will be connected to the host specified in the *notify_smtp_host* field. The default value for this setting is 25.

■ *notify_app=<FULL_PATH>* This is the full path to a local executable where all log messages will be piped to. Upon start up, osirismd will launch the specified path and send all log messages to standard input on the launched application. Log messages are still sent to syslog or the event viewer, which is simply an additional outlet for log data. The default value for this setting is empty (disabled).

■ *allow=<IP> | <HOSTNAME>* The management console will refuse all connections to the port specified in the *control_port* except for those explicitly allowed in the configuration file under this setting. This is for security reasons. It is not recommended that you allow remote CLI connections to your management console, but if you do, this will allow you to limit which hosts the console will accept connections from. The syntax is one Internet Protocol (IP) address or hostname per line. You can use wild cards. For example, to specify two hosts, you could do:

```
allow=10.10.0.1
allow=10.10.0.2
```

Or, to allow an entire subnet, you could do:

```
allow=10.10.0.*
```

By default, osirismd will accept connections only from local host (127.0.0.1).

■ *hosts_directory=<FULL_PATH>* If you want to keep the hosts' directory outside of the main *Osiris* directory, you specify the location of that directory here. There are a few reasons for wanting to do this; one common reason is for disk space. The default value for this field is empty, meaning the host's directory is kept in the root of the *Osiris* directory (*/usr/local/osiris/hosts* on UNIX and *%WindowsRoot\osiris\hosts* on Windows).

Configuring the Management Console for the First Time

Now that you understand what the available settings are, you need to configure your newly installed console. The way to edit these settings is to use the Osiris CLI application. By default, the management console accepts connections only from the local machine, so you must be logged in to your management host or sitting in front of the console.

First, start Osiris without command-line arguments; it will connect to the local machine by default. Because this is the first time that you have connected to the management host, the CLI does not recognize the root certificate presented by the console. You will see a warning message that looks like the following:

```
$ osiris
Osiris Shell Interface - version 4.1.8-release
unable to load root certificate for management host:
(/Users/brian/.osiris/osiris_root.pem)
 >>> fetching root certificate from management host (localhost).


The authenticity of host 'localhost' can't be established.


  [ server certificate ]


 subject = /C=US/CN=Osiris Management Console/OU=Osiris Host Integrity
System
 issuer  = /C=US/CN=Osiris Management Console/OU=Osiris Host Integrity
System


            key size: 2048 bit
     MD5 fingerprint: 6D:6D:C6:60:94:C5:03:DA:9D:F8:79:4C:D3:98:56:C1


Verify the fingerprint specified above.
Are you sure you want to continue connecting (yes/no)?
```

When you see this prompt, respond **yes** to save the root certificate. When asked for a username, type **admin**. When asked for a password, press **ENTER**:

```
User: admin
Password:


connected to management console, code version (4.1.8-release).
hello.


WARNING: your password is empty, use the 'passwd' command
to set your password.


osiris-4.1.8-release:
```

At this point, you are logged into the management console. Upon successful authentication, the management console prints its software version and then displays a shell prompt. To set the admin password, type **passwd admin** at the prompt and give it a reasonable password. After the password has been set, you will be asked to log in again using your newly established password.

```
osiris-4.1.8-release: passwd admin
Password:
 >>> user: (admin) updated.
current login was edited, you must re-authenticate.
 >>> authenticating to (localhost)


Password:


connected to management console, code version (4.1.8-release).
hello.


osiris-4.1.8-release:
```

Next, you must edit the management console configuration settings. To do this, use the *edit-mhost* command. This prompts you for each setting and displays the current value in square brackets. To accept the default value, press **ENTER**. To clear a setting, enter a space and press **ENTER**. The following example shows how to set the e-mail address and add a host to the allow list:

```
osiris-4.1.8-release: edit-mhost


[ edit management host (localhost) ]


  > syslog facility [DAEMON]:
  > control port [2266]:
  > http control port [0]:
  > notify email (default for hosts) []: bob@example.com
  > notification smtp host [127.0.0.1]:
  > notification smtp port [25]:


  > authorized hosts:


   127.0.0.1


  Modify authorization list (y/n)? [n] y
```

```
    s) show current listing.
    a) add a new authorized host.
    r) remove authorized host.
    q) quit


    > a
    > authorized hostname/IP (*=wildcard): admin.example.com


    s) show current listing.
    a) add a new authorized host.
    r) remove authorized host.
    q) quit


    > q

[ management config (localhost) ]


syslog_facility = DAEMON
control_port = 2266
http_port = 0
http_host =
notify_email = bob@example.com
notify_app =
notify_smtp_host = 127.0.0.1
notify_smtp_port = 25
hosts_directory =
allow = 127.0.0.1
allow = admin.example.com


Is this correct (y/n)? y
 >>> management host configuration has been saved.
```

You can continue to use the *edit-mhost* command as many times as you want to configure the management console. All changes take effect in real time. If at any time you wish to see the current configuration, use the *mhost-config* command:

```
osiris-4.1.8-release: mhost-config

[ management config (localhost) ]
```

```
syslog_facility = DAEMON
control_port = 2266
http_port = 0
http_host =
notify_email = bob@example.com
notify_app =
notify_smtp_host = 127.0.0.1
notify_smtp_port = 25
hosts_directory =
allow = 127.0.0.1
allow = admin.example.com
```

There are two reasons why you should use the CLI to edit your management console configuration: it serves to protect you from introducing syntax errors, and it will restart the necessary components so that the changes will take effect in real time. If you edit the *osirismd.conf* file directly, the changes may or may not take effect immediately.

You may have noticed that there are actually two configuration settings that the CLI does not prompt for: *hosts_directory* and *notify_app*. The reason is that most administrators do not need to use them, and they would make the configuration process more complicated. These settings are documented; if you need to use them, edit the *osirismd.conf* file by hand and restart the osirismd process.

At this point, the initial configuration of your management console is complete. To close the command-line session to your console, use the *quit* command or type **q**:

```
osiris-4.1.8-release: q
```

Command-Line Interface

The Osiris command line is used for all interactions with the management console and indirectly with your monitored hosts. Although used briefly in the last section when initializing the console, in this section you are going to explore it in more detail. It is very useful to gain familiarity with the Osiris CLI, since it is the part of Osiris that you will use the most. CLI is used throughout the remainder of this book.

Command-Line Basics

The Osiris CLI is a connection-based client. The name of the application is Osiris on UNIX systems and osiris.exe on Windows. The CLI provides a shell-like interface to the console. All aspects of the Osiris system can be controlled through this interface. The CLI talks exclusively to the console, never to the agents, and all communications are done over a Secure Sockets Layer (SSL) tunnel, even if you are using the CLI on the console host. At this point, you have installed the CLI on the management host, but you can also install *just* the CLI on a workstation, or whatever you find to be most convenient. If you do not specify any command-line arguments, the console attempts to connect to a console running on the local system. As of this writing, the CLI accepts the command-line arguments:

```
$ osiris --help

Osiris Shell Interface - version 4.1.8-release


    usage: osiris [options] <management-host>


    -f <file>   specify a root cert file to authenticate management host.
    -p <port>   specify remote port for management host.
    -h          print this usage statement.
    -v          print version.
```

The **-f** option allows you to use a specific root certificate file to authenticate the console. The client does not manage multiple root certificates, so if you manage consoles with different root certificates, this option can be helpful. The **-p** option allows you to specify an alternate remote port to connect the console on. If not specified, the client will assume the default console port of 2266.

Authentication and Certificates

The first time you connect to the management console, the CLI does not have any way to verify the remote host. The CLI will print the fingerprint of the presented certificate and ask you if you want to trust it:

```
The authenticity of host 'localhost' can't be established.

  [ server certificate ]

subject = /C=US/CN=Osiris Management Console/OU=Osiris Host Integrity
      System
issuer  = /C=US/CN=Osiris Management Console/OU=Osiris Host Integrity
      System

          key size: 2048 bit
    MD5 fingerprint: 6D:6D:C6:60:94:C5:03:DA:9D:F8:79:4C:D3:98:56:C1
```

```
Verify the fingerprint specified above.
Are you sure you want to continue connecting (yes/no)?
```

If you are not connecting from a remote host, you can safely accept the certificate by entering **yes**. However, if you have explicitly allowed and are connecting from a remote host, you should verify the fingerprint. Once you accept this root certificate, it is automatically saved in your home directory. On UNIX systems, this is ~/.osiris/osiris_root.pem and %SystemRoot%\Documents And Settings\<username>\Application Data\.osiris\osiris_root.pem. Every time you make a connection to the console, the CLI will read this certificate file and use it to verify the certificate presented by the console. If the certificate validation fails, you will receive a message that looks like the following:

```
WARNING: certificate authentication failure: self signed certificate.
[ presented certificate ]

 issuer = /C=US/CN=Osiris Management Console/OU=Osiris Host Integrity
        System
 subject = /C=US/CN=Osiris Management Console/OU=Osiris Host Integrity
        System
untrusted MD5 fingerprint: 6D:6D:C6:60:94:C5:03:DA:9D:F8:79:4C:D3:98:56:C1.


If you trust this certificate, delete the saved root certificate and start
this application again.
```

The only way this will fail is if the certificate is no longer valid or if it does not match the certificate presented by the console. Sometimes, certificate validation fails because your system clock is set to an unreasonable value outside the validity period for the certificate. Or, you may have replaced the certificate on the console and need to purge the old root certificate stored by your client.

Once you have successfully logged in, you can display the details of the SSL session between the CLI and the console using the *ssl* command:

```
osiris-4.1.8-release: ssl


connected to (localhost)

    protocols allowed: TLSv1/SSLv3
            cipher list: AES256-SHA


 [ server certificate ]
```

```
subject = /C=US/CN=Osiris Management Console/OU=Osiris Host Integrity
    System
issuer  = /C=US/CN=Osiris Management Console/OU=Osiris Host Integrity
    System


public key size: 2048 bit
MD5 fingerprint: 6D:6D:C6:60:94:C5:03:DA:9D:F8:79:4C:D3:98:56:C1
```

Online Help

The CLI contains online help that you can use to list commands; you can also obtain the syntax and a brief description of any of these commands. To see the listing of available commands enter **help** at the prompt:

```
osiris-4.1.8-release: help


[ Management Commands ]
    mhost               host              new-user          edit-filters
    edit-mhost          edit-host         edit-user         print-filters
    print-mhost-config  list-hosts        list-users
    test-notify         new-host          delete-user       test-filter


[ Host commands ]
    status              list-configs      start-scan        list-db
    watch-host          new-config        stop-scan         base-db
    disable-host        push-config       print-log         set-base-db
    host-details        edit-config       list-logs         print-db
    print-host-config   print-config                        print-db-errors
    rm-host             rm-config                            print-db-header
    init                drop-config                         rm-db
    config              verify-config                       unset-base-db


[ Misc commands ]
    help                version           quit              ssl


  For help with a specific command, try: help <command>


osiris-4.1.8-release:
```

The command list is organized by commands: those that apply to the console and those that apply to monitored hosts. Many of these commands are intuitive, but some are not; therefore, we will go over them here. Using the *help* command, you can see the syntax and description for each command. For example, to see details for the *rm-db* command:

```
osiris-4.1.8-release: help rm-db

    usage: remove-db <db-name>

    Cause the management host to remove the specified database file from the
    currently selected host's database store.
    aliases: rm-db, delete-db, del-db
```

Scan Agents

Scan agents must be deployed onto every host that you want to monitor. The agent is a lightweight daemon that periodically collects information from the host environment and securely transmits that data back to the console. This section covers everything you need to know about Osiris scan agents, including an overview of the agent itself and its installation, configuration, and administration.

Scan Agent Overview

On UNIX systems, the scan agent is a daemon called *osirisd* and is installed in */usr/local/sbin* by default. This daemon implements a form of privilege separation. Upon start-up, there are two osirisd processes: one running with root privileges and one running with non-root privileges (usually the Osiris user). The non-root process handles all of the work; the root process is mostly idle. When the agent needs to access a file or element of the environment that requires root privileges, it asks the root process to do the work and return a file handle or the requested data. The root run process never opens any network ports and is only capable of performing a limited number of tasks. When the agent is asked to perform a scan, it forks another process to handle collecting and sending the information.

On Windows, the scan agent is a service that is run as Administrator. This service is always installed in *%SystemRoot%\osirisd.exe* and, by default, is started automatically upon boot. The scan agent on Windows is multithreaded so that all scans spawn a new threat.

The scan agent consists of a single executable and a root certificate file. On UNIX systems, the default location for the root certificate file is

/usr/local/osiris/osiris_root.pem; on Windows, the agent stores the root certificate in *%WindowsRoot%\osiris\osiris_root.pem*. To see a list of the command-line arguments, do the following at a shell or a command-line prompt where the agent is installed:

```
$ osirisd --help
Osiris Scan Agent - Version 4.1.8-release


usage: osirisd [-r <path>] [-p <port>] [-n <level>] [-q] [-h]


  -n <level>   use specified nice level.
  -p <port>    specify an alternate listen port (default:2265)
  -q           quiet mode, agent produces no log messages.
  -r           specify alternate root directory containing root cert.
  -h           print this usage statement.
```

On Windows, the supported arguments are as follows:

```
C:\>osirisd.exe --help


Osiris Scan Agent - Version 4.1.8-release


usage: osirisd [-i|-u] [-p <port>] [-h] [-d] [-q]


  -i           install as a windows service on local machine.
  -u           uninstall windows service from local machine.
  -d           run this application as a daemon, not a service.
  -p <port>    specify an alternate listen port (default:2265)
  -q           quiet mode, agent produces no log messages.
  -r           specify alternate root directory containing root cert.
  -h           print this usage statement.
```

The **-r** option allows you to specify the location of a root certificate file to be used to authenticate the management console. The **-p** option allows you to specify a listen port in case the default is not acceptable. The **-q** option prevents the scan agent from producing any local logs; this option is useful in cases where you do not want the activity of the daemon to be logged to the event viewer. The scan agent never logs information about scanning the environment, only about the daemon itself. On Windows, there are a couple of different options for installing and unin-stalling the scan agent service. These are the same options that are available for the management console. Windows also has an additional option (**-d**), which starts the scan agent in debug mode (see Figure 6.12). This can be a quick way to debug some problems. Basically, everything that would be sent to the logs is printed to standard output.

Figure 6.12 Starting the Osiris Scan Agent on Windows in Debug Mode

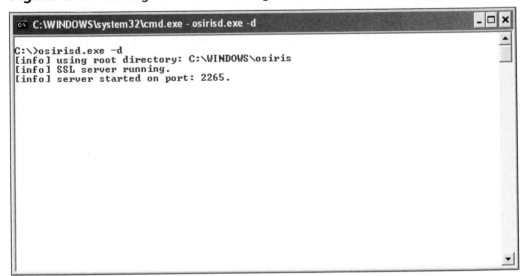

The scan agent process collects data from the host environment and passes that data back to the console. The agent does not scan on its own; it is merely a shell and responds only to the requests of the console. When the internal scheduler of the console decides it is time for a host to be scanned, it pushes a scan configuration file to the agent. The scan agent maintains a copy of that configuration in memory; it does not store it on disk. The agent then collects all kinds of data from the environment based upon the configuration. The scan data is sent directly back to the console; it is never written to disk on the monitored host.

Installing the Scan Agent

One of the biggest problems with the Osiris scan agent and all agent-based systems is that you must install the software onto every host you wish to monitor. If you have hundreds of hosts, this can be a cumbersome ordeal. Many operating systems such as FreeBSD and versions of Linux have source ports, or binary packages, available for Osiris. It is recommended that you build your own agent installer packages instead of using pre-built packages or ports. Building your own installers makes more sense because if you use a port, you are left with whatever configuration or set of modules the author of the port or package has included. If you are going to make the effort to set up a solid management host and deploy Osiris on many scan agents, you should have agents that do exactly what you want.

Another thing to consider with respect to agent installation is the ability to perform a non-interactive installation. If you plan on deploying more than a handful of agents, you want to make sure that the installer package installs the agent exactly as you want it to for that system (i.e., without prompts). Later in this chapter we look at some solutions for mass deployment that will allow you to build your own custom installer packages or automate using the default Osiris agent installer.

Installing on UNIX

In the beginning of this chapter, we discussed how to build agent installer packages. You must build an installer package for every operating system and architecture type you will be deploying. For UNIX systems, the installer package is a gzipped tar file. Installing the agent software involves unpacking the *tar.gz* file and running the installation script.

First, copy the installer *tar.gz* file to a reasonable location and unpack it. In this example, we install the agent onto a Gentoo Linux system:

```
$ osiris-agent-4.1.8-linux.tar.gz /usr/local/src/
$ cd /usr/local/src/
$ tar xvfz osiris-agent-4.1.8-linux.tar.gz
```

As with the management console installer, the installer is a simple shell script (*install.sh*) that will ask you a few questions and install the executables. Specifically, *install.sh* will:

1. Prompt to continue the installation.
2. Display installation defaults.
3. Create a local "osiris" user if it does not exist.
4. Create a local "osiris" group if it does not exist.
5. Prompt to install the local scan agent.
6. Prompt to install the CLI.
7. Copy the osirisd executable.
8. Create init script for osirisd.
9. Set reasonable permissions for osirisd.

As root, run the *install.sh* script and answer **yes** to continue installation:

```
$ cd osiris-agent-4.1.8-release
```

```
# ./install.sh
Continue with installation? (y/n) [y]   y
```

You will see the installation script create an Osiris user and group:

```
==> creating user and group (osiris, osiris).
==> group 'osiris' added.
==> user 'osiris' added.
==> using existing Osiris management console user.
```

When prompted for what to install, type 'y' to the agent.

```
Install osiris agent? (y/n) [y]   y
```

When prompted for a location for the osirisd executable, accept the default. The installer will set the suggested file permissions for osirisd and install an init script so that the daemon will be started upon boot.

```
Installation directory for binaries: [/usr/local/sbin]
Osiris scan agent root directory does not exist, creating.
==> installed scan agent: /usr/local/sbin/osirisd
==> installing rc startup for daemon(s).
Linux Distribution: gentoo
==> Skipping osirisd symlink creation.
 * osirisd added to runlevel default
 * Caching service dependencies...
 * rc-update complete.
==> change owner and permissions on /usr/local/sbin/osirisd
-rwxr-xr-x  1 root wheel 110020 Mar 19 09:12 /usr/local/sbin/osirisd
```

Finally, when asked about starting the scan agent, type **y**:

```
Start scan agent now? (y/n) [y]   y
```

At this point, the scan agent is installed. Now, verify that the daemon is running by using the *ps* command. You should see two instances of the osirisd process: one running as root and the other running as the Osiris user. For example, on Linux:

```
$ ps -ef | grep osirisd
root      17984  0.0  1.2  3028  772 pts/0    S    09:29  0:00
/usr/local/sbin/osirisd
osiris    17986  0.0  2.1  3220 1304 pts/0    S    09:29  0:00
/usr/local/sbin/osirisd
```

In addition, you should see syslog messages indicating that the scan agent has started. On most UNIX systems, you will see the scan agent log messages being written to the main syslog file. For example:

```
$ tail /var/log/messages | grep osirisd
Mar 23 21:22:57 localhost osirisd[5534]: [info] using root directory:
/usr/local/osiris
Mar 23 21:22:57 localhost osirisd[5534]: [info] SSL server running.
Mar 23 21:22:57 localhost osirisd[5534]: [info] server started on port:
2265.
```

You can also verify that the agent is alive and listening on port 2265 using the *netstat* command:

```
$ netstat -na | grep 2265
tcp4        0        0  *.2265                    *.*
LISTEN
```

Installing on Windows

Installing the scan agent on Windows involves using the same installer package as you used to install the console. Run the installer program by double-clicking on it. Accept the End User License Agreement by clicking the button that reads **I agree**. When prompted for which components to install, make sure that only the one labeled Scanning Service is selected, then click **Install** (see Figure 6.13).

Figure 6.13 Installing the Scan Agent on Windows

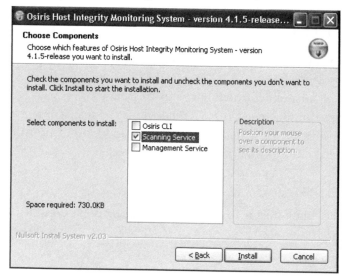

This will install only the scan agent and any pre-provisioned root certificate. The installation takes less than a minute. When the installation is complete, you will see the phrase "Setup was completed successfully" at the top left of the dialogue (see Figure 6.14). Click the **Close** button.

Figure 6.14 Completing the Installation of the Scan Agent on Windows

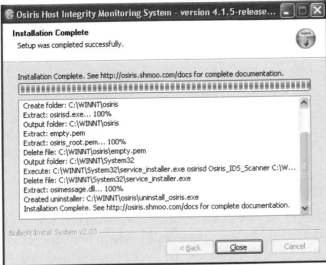

At this point, the scan agent is running and will only accept connections from your management console (or any console that presents a certificate signed by the root certificate the agent is using).

Configuration

This section covers everything you need to know about adding a host to the Osiris management console so that it can be monitored. This includes basic configuration settings, establishing a baseline, scheduling, and creating custom scan configurations. We start by configuring the agent that is installed on the management console host. However, the information presented here applies to any kind of host that you want to place under the control of the management console.

Adding a Host

The first step to adding a host is to login to the management console:

```
$ osiris
Osiris Shell Interface - version 4.1.8-release
 >>> authenticating to (localhost)
```

```
User: admin
Password:


connected to management console, code version (4.1.8-release).
hello.


osiris-4.1.8-release:
```

Next, the *new host* command is used to start the process of adding a new host. This command will ask a series of configuration questions and then populate the *Osiris* directory with a configuration for this host.

The first prompt asks for the name that will be used to identify the host. You can enter anything you want here, but keep in mind that this will be used to identify the host in logs as well as e-mail notifications. The name cannot contain any spaces. Since you are adding the host that resides on the console, use the name *local*; however, you can use whatever makes sense to you.

```
osiris-4.1.8-release: new-host


[ new host ]


  > name this host []:  local
```

The hostname is the actual hostname or IP address of the host. Since this is a local agent, we use 127.0.0.1 as the IP address. Using a hostname versus the IP address is up to you. If you find yourself reassigning IP addresses to your hosts, hostnames may be more practical. Depending on your environment either may be the better choice.

```
  > hostname/IP address []: 127.0.0.1
```

The description is optional, and meant to be a one-line description of the host to help identify hosts when interacting with the Osiris CLI. The description is not used outside of the CLI:

```
  > description []: agent installed on management console.
```

The agent port is the network port that the agent is listening on. If you have deployed your agents so that they are listening on a port different from the default, this is where you configure that port. In this case, we installed the agent on the management console using the default port.

```
  > agent port [2265]:
```

After every scan, the console produces a log file containing the results of the scan. This log file is stored under that host's *logs* directory. Because this can consume disk space, the default is to **not** create log files for every scan. If you want the console to generate a separate log file for each scan, answer **yes** to this question.

```
> enable log files for this host? (yes/no) [no]:
```

The next few questions deal with the storage of scan data for the host. For the agent stored on the console, accept the default options for prompts. The defaults are helpful, because they ensure that the databases directory for the host will not grow without bound:

```
Scan Databases:

    => keep archives of scan databases?  Enabling this option means that
       the
       database generated with each scan is saved, even if there are no
       changes
       detected.  Because of disk space, this option is not recommended
       unless your security policy requires it. (yes/no) [no]:

    => auto-accept changes?  Enabling this option means that detected
       changes are reported only once, and the baseline database is
       automatically set when changes are detected. (yes/no) [yes]:

    => purge database store?  Enabling this option means that none
       of the scan databases are saved.  That is, whenever the baseline
       database is set, the previous one is deleted. (yes/no): [yes]:
```

The next series of questions deal with e-mail notifications. Enter **yes** to enable the e-mail notifications for this host:

```
Notifications:

    => enable email notification for this host? (yes/no) [no]: yes
```

The next option is the scheduled scan failure notification. When the scheduler tells a host to scan, if it fails for any reason, an e-mail is sent that discloses the details surrounding the failure. Enter **yes** for this option.

```
    => send notification on scheduled scans failures? (yes/no) [no]: yes
```

When enabled, the next option sends an e-mail notification after every scan, regardless of whether or not there were any detected changes. Some administrators enable this option for a positive confirmation that the host was scanned (i.e., silence could mean that there were no changes or that there was a fatal error). Enabling this option rules out the error case and provides assurance of a scan. Unless you absolutely want this, it is usually best to accept the default (**no**), which is to send notifications only when changes have been detected:

```
=> send scan notification, even when no changes detected  (yes/no) [no]:
```

The next notification option is to send e-mail when the agent does not present a session key. The session key is kept resident in memory by the agent and used as a means of authentication. If the agent loses this key, it means that it was restarted. This often indicates the monitored host was rebooted, but not necessarily; it could be that the daemon or service was simply restarted. In any case, it is almost always a good idea to enable this option, as it may be the first indication that some unauthorized activity is occurring on the monitored host. Enter **yes** for this prompt:

```
=> send notification when agent has lost session key  (yes/no) [no]: yes
```

The last notification option is an e-mail address for all of the aforementioned notification settings. By default, hosts make use of the e-mail address specified in the management console configuration. However, at times you may find it useful to direct notifications about a host to another administrator or mailing list. Since you are configuring the agent that resides on the console, accept the default and use the one specified in the management configuration:

```
=> notification email (default uses mhost address) []:
```

The next few prompts deal with scheduling. The console periodically tells the monitored host to start a scan. Scheduling is very basic, consisting of a start date and a period specified in minutes. The first prompt asks about configuring a schedule for this host. Enter **yes**:

```
Scheduling:


 > configure scan scheduling information? (yes/no) [no]: yes
```

Next, establish the schedule starting point. By default, the date is the current time minus a minute (i.e., so that the scheduler will not try to scan this host before they are done configuring it). The only reason to worry about the schedule start point is if you are going to scan the host on a daily or weekly basis and want to specify the time that the scan occurs. For example, you may want to schedule it in the early morning when the load on the system is low. For the console, choose a reasonable scan time of once per hour so that the start point does not matter. Accept the default schedule start time:

```
[ scheduling information for local ]

    Scheduling information consists of a start time and a frequency value.
    The frequency is a specified number of minutes between each scan,
    starting from the start time.  The default is the current time.
    Specify the start time in the following format: mm/dd/yyyy HH:MM


    enter the start date and time
    using 'mm/dd/yyyy HH:MM' format: [Sat Mar 26 11:07:53 2005]
```

Next, specify how often you want the host to be scanned (in minutes). You may find that the load restricts how often you can run scans. On UNIX systems, the scan agent can be given a "nice" value so that it does not consume too many resources. Otherwise, it is not uncommon for the input/output (I/O) to consume over 50 percent of the CPU. The default scan period is 1440 minutes (once per day). For this prompt, enter 60 so that the host will be scanned every hour:

```
    enter scan frequency in minutes: [1440] 60
```

The final configuration question is whether or not to enable the host, which means that it will fall under the control of the scheduler. The scheduler ignores any disabled host . This is useful when you want to suspend the scheduled scans for a host, but not delete it. For example, if you take a host offline for some time and do not want to be bombarded with schedule failure notifications, disable it and then enable it once the host is back online. You are setting this host up for the first time, so you do not want to enable it just yet. Enter **no** to this prompt:

```
    > enable this host? (yes/no) [yes]: no
```

At this point, you have configured a new host to be added to the management console. All of the configuration settings are displayed for final approval. Enter **y** to add this host to the console:

```
host                    => local
hostname/IP address     => 127.0.0.1
description             => agent installed on management console.
agent port              => 2265
```

```
host type                => generic
log enabled              => no
archive scans            => no
auto accept              => yes
purge databases          => yes
notifications enabled    => yes
notifications always     => no
notify on rekey          => yes
notify on scan fail      => yes
notify email             => (management config)
scans starting on        => Sat Mar 26 11:07:53 2005
scan frequency           => hourly (every 60 minutes).
enabled                  => no


Is this correct (y/n)? y
 >>> new host (local) has been created.
```

Every time you create a new host and add it to the management console, you are prompted to initialize it. This gives you the option to specify a scan configuration (or use a default) and then perform an initial scan on the host to establish a baseline database. Enter **yes** to this prompt and, when asked for confirmation, enter **yes** again:

```
Initialize this host? (yes/no): yes


Initializing a host will push over a configuration, start
a scan, and set the created database to be the
trusted database.


Are you sure you want to initialize this host (yes/no): yes
```

The console then contacts the agent and determines the operating system and version so that it can suggest a default scan configuration to use. You are then asked if you want to use this default scan configuration, which are specific to a certain operating system. This can be valuable if you are overwhelmed by having to figure out how to create a custom configuration and what to include as part of your scans. Enter **yes**

```
OS Name: Darwin
OS Version: 7.8.0
```

```
use the default configuration for this OS? (yes/no): yes
```

The console then pushes the default scan configuration to the agent and tells the agent to start the scan. At this point, there are no databases for this host, so the database created as a result of the scan automatically becomes the baseline database. Also, because there was no baseline database, there is no report generated after this scan, because there is nothing known about the previous state of this host. At this point, you should see that the host was scanned and be at prompt:

```
>>> configuration (default.darwin) has been pushed.
>>> scanning process was started on host: local
osiris-4.1.8-release:
```

The scan agent installed on the management console is now fully configured. The only thing left to do is enable it so that the console's scheduler regularly tells this agent to scan. Do this with the *enable* command. It takes a single argument—the name of the host:

```
osiris-4.1.8-release: enable local
>>> host local is now enabled.
```

At this point, you have successfully added and configured the agent running on the management console host. This agent has a baseline database and is scanned regularly. The procedure for adding more hosts is exactly the same. If you have a lot of hosts that you wish to add to your management console and configure in the same manner, you probably do not want to add each one manually.

At any time, you can edit the configuration of any host using the *edit-host* command. This command takes a single argument: the name of the host to edit (use the *hosts* command to obtain a list of hosts). The prompts are almost the same as the ones you will encounter with the *new-host* command. The only difference is that you cannot change the name of the host, and you are not asked to initialize it at the end of the configuration sequence.

You can establish a new baseline for a host with the *init* command. This command pushes a configuration to the host, runs a scan, and sets the baseline database to be the just-created database. Ideally, you would create a baseline for the host offline, before it is ever connected to a network, but that is not always possible.

Talking to Agents with the Command Line

The Osiris CLI provides useful commands for interacting with your agents. You can obtain information about their current state, settings, scan databases, scan configurations, and logs. Additionally, you can control their behavior, including starting and stopping scans, enabling or disabling the agent, loading a new scan configuration, or purging their current scan configuration from memory. When you first login to the management console, you can list your available hosts using the *hosts* command. The following list includes the names of the hosts (in alphabetical order) that the management console is aware of and whether or not they are enabled:

```
osiris-4.1.8-release: hosts


[ name ]                 [ description ]              [ enabled ]


local                    local scan agent.            no
test1                    test system.                 yes
test2                    test system.                 yes
test3                    test system.                 yes
test4                    test system.                 yes


total: 5


osiris-4.1.8-release:
```

The prompt in the preceding example is not in any specific context. What this means is that any commands that are entered are not directed toward any specific host. Use the *host* command to enter a host context. For example, to deal specifically with the local agent installed on our management console:

```
osiris-4.1.8-release: host local
local is alive.
osiris-4.1.8-release[local]:
```

Notice how the prompt has changed to display the name of the specified host. This command connects to the agent to make sure it is up and running. Once in a host context, all host-related commands are applied to that host unless otherwise specified. To check the status of a host, use the *status* command:

```
osiris-4.1.8-release[local]: status


[ current status of host: local ]


    current time: Mon Mar 28 07:32:42 2005
       up since: Sat Mar 26 09:30:12 2005


last config push: Mon Mar 28 06:50:56 2005
```

```
configuration id: dae4b2e8

     agent status: idle.
    config status: current config is valid.
   osiris version: 4.1.8-release
               OS: Darwin 7.8.0


osiris-4.1.8-release[local]:
```

The *status* command displays a report on the current state of the agent. The *last config push* line is usually the last time the agent scanned, because the scheduler always pushes a configuration to the host before a scheduled scan.

Use the *details* command to display the settings for a host. This command accepts the name of the host as an argument; however, this is not necessary if you are in a host context:

```
osiris-4.1.8-release[local]: details

[ host details for: (local) ]

    enabled          : no
    hostname/IP      : 127.0.0.1
    configs          : 0
    databases        : 1
    host type        : generic
    log files        : no
    archive scans    : no
    auto accept      : yes
    purge databases  : yes
    notify enabled   : no
    notify always    : no
    notify on rekey  : no
    notify scan fail : no
    notify email     : (management config)
    scans start      : Mon Mar 28 06:49:35 2005
    scan period      : every 1440 minutes
    base DB          : 1
    agent port       : 2265
    description      : local scan agent.
```

To see the actual contents of the *host.conf* file, use the *print-host-config* command:

```
osiris-4.1.8-release[local]: print-host-config

[ host config (local) ]

host = 127.0.0.1
description = local scan agent.
type = generic
enabled = no
notify_enabled = no
notify_flags = 0
notify_email =
session_key = 51869C2A8C837DF337B7F209BF02023868276AF0
base_db = 1
log_to_file = no
schedule_start = 1112017775
schedule_period = 1440
db_flags = 6
port = 2265
config =
```

Use the *databases* command to print a listing of every scan database for a host. The baseline database is marked with an asterisk:

```
osiris-4.1.8-release[local]: databases
This may take a while...

  [ name ]                        [ created ]

  * 2                             Tue Mar 29 06:47:21
    3                             Tue Mar 29 06:47:39

total: 2
(*) denotes the base database for this host.
```

To see just the baseline database, print out the details of the host or use the *baseline* command. To manually set which database you want to use for a baseline, use

the *set-baseline* command. This command accepts a single argument—the name of
the database. For example:

```
osiris-4.1.8-release[local]: set-baseline 3
 >>> database: 3 is now the baseline for host: local
```

There are a handful of commands related to viewing the contents of a database,
the most common being *print-db-header* and *print-db*. The *print-db-header* command
displays the metadata associated with a database, including the configuration file
used, time stamps, and the results of the scan. You must be in a host context for this
command, and you must provide the name of a database:

```
osiris-4.1.8-release[local]: print-db-header 3


    DATABASE:   3


    status: complete
    errors: 0
   records: 1015
     config: default.darwin (c3dcf455)


    SCAN RESULTS:


            record type: UNIX1


       files encountered: 1015
          files scanned: 1015


    symlinks encountered: 25
       symlinks followed: 0


         files unreadable: 0
   directories unreadable: 0
      symlinks unreadable: 0


              scan started: Mon Mar 28 13:01:38 2005
              scan finished: Mon Mar 28 13:01:57 2005
```

The *print-db* command displays the actual contents of the database. Because
databases can be large, this command may take some time to download the specified
database. This command is not something you will use on a regular basis, but it is

helpful when you are fine-tuning your scan configuration and want to ensure that the agent is monitoring the correct elements of the environment. When you print a database, the CLI enters a new context that is specific to that database. You are then presented with a menu of options:

```
osiris-4.1.8-release[local]: print-db 3
This may take a while...


100% [=======================================>] 913408 bytes

    h) show database header.
    r) list file records.
    d) list file record details.
    m) list module records.
    x) list errors.
    q) quit
```

You can print the database header, errors, all of the files, all of the information about a scanned file, and all of the information gathered from the modules. For example, suppose you want to verify that this database contains the file */bin/ls*. You can print the details gathered about this file by doing the following:

```
[local:database: 3]: d
      file path: /bin/ls


-------- begin scan record -------

file: /bin/ls
record type: UNIX1
checksum: 7e35987a1b03b968ad39cb8138ad664f464915ee
checksum algorithm: sha
permissions: -r-xr-xr-x
user: root
group: wheel
device: 1039
inode: 70675
mode: 33133
links: 1
uid: 0
gid: 0
mtime: Thu Nov  4 18:24:59 2004
```

```
atime: Tue Mar 15 07:55:02 2005
ctime: Thu Dec  2 10:30:17 2004
device_type: 0
bytes: 22784
blocks: 48
block_size: 16384
```

To leave the database context, enter **q**. To leave any host context, enter **q** again:

```
[local:database: 3]: q
osiris-4.1.8-release[local]: q
osiris-4.1.8-release:
```

Alternatively, you can switch to another host context with the *host* command.

Using the *print-db* command is useful when you are initially tuning a scan configuration; however, it is not the best way to view the contents of a database. This functionality exists as a quick way to peer into a database for small amounts of information. To look at all of the data in a database, or to export it for statistical, forensic, or any kind of analysis, use the *printdb* command-line tool that is bundled with Osiris (discussed in detail in the "Administration" section of this chapter).

Use the *scan* command to manually start a scan. This tells the host to begin scanning with its current configuration. If there is no configuration, the CLI prints an error message that indicates that the host does not have a configuration. Use the *push-config* command to send a configuration to the agent. If the host has a configuration, it will begin scanning and automatically compare the scan against the baseline database:

```
osiris-4.1.8-release[local]: scan
 >>> scanning process was started on host: local
```

These are only a few of the host-related commands available from the Osiris CLI. Some commands were singled out because administrators use them frequently as part of the initial setup and administration of Osiris. All of the commands available from the CLI are documented and fairly straightforward.

Scan Databases

Whenever you add or edit a host configuration, you are asked a series of questions about how you want the console to maintain scan databases for that host. The main reason that these questions exist is because of the disk space involved in maintaining scan databases. Each time a host is scanned, the data is streamed back to the console and stored in a database file. The amount of disk space this takes up depends on how much information is scanned, and how often you scan your hosts. The default scan configurations generally produce database files that are between 500K and 2MB each, depending on the host. Imagine you have hundreds of hosts that are monitored once every hour or every thirty minutes; without a doubt this is something you must consider.

The advantage of saving every scan stream is twofold. First, you have a snapshot of the monitored host from every time that host was scanned. Much of the information is redundant; however, your security policy may require that you maintain this data as opposed to the deduction of what the state was based on the content of the logs. The second advantage of maintaining all of the scan data is that the contents of the database are not affected by filtering. That is, you cannot trust the contents of the logs to provide you with a complete list of detected changes for a host. For example, imagine that you need to know the permissions of a file at a certain time period. If you have all of the databases, you can find the database for that time period and view its contents to obtain permissions for the file in question. However, if all you have are the logs for that time period, you have no way of knowing if the permissions are the same as the previous scan, or whether they changed but were not logged because of a filter.

In most cases, you will not want to save every scan database; it is not practical for most deployments. You have already learned that taking the minimalist approach to scan databases leaves you with only the data in the logs, which is not complete because of log filtering. To deal with this problem, Osiris allows you to configure hosts such that only the databases that contain differences between the last databases are saved. That is, if a scan detects no new changes, the created database is not saved. Keep in mind that the size of the *databases* directory for a host can still grow without bound, but it only grows when changes are detected. Therefore, if you tune your configurations correctly, you will not be constantly dealing with disk space issues. The default for a host configuration is to ***not*** grow at all, saving only the baseline database.

Understanding the significance of each of the host configuration options related to scan data is very important. Not only can it mean more administrative overhead with respect to disk space, but you must also understand which scan data is being saved and which is not. To properly configure your hosts, you must know exactly what these options do.

Database Files

All scan data is stored in a Berkeley DB file and saved in the host's *databases* directory. The database filenames are numbers (starting with 1). When a database is saved, the name is always one number greater than the highest numbered database file in the *databases* directory. This scheme makes it easy to see the order in which databases were created. If a host does not have a baseline database, the first saved database file is automatically tagged as that host's baseline. What this means is that the *host.conf* file contains the name of the baseline database; the database file itself is never modified.

Archiving

When archiving is enabled, every scan produces a new database, which occurs whether or not changes are detected. For example, after a host has been initialized, it will have a single database named "1" that is the baseline database. Regardless of the configuration, the next scan will produce a database named "2." If you have archiving enabled, the next scan database created will be "3," then "4," and so on. If you do not have archiving enabled, the last database created will continue to be overwritten and compared to the baseline.

Auto-accept

The auto-accept host configuration option allows you to automatically reset the baseline database after changes have been detected. This option prevents you from being pestered by the same list of changes. Some administrators want to be bothered until they investigate a change and set the baseline themselves. However, most do not; therefore, auto-accepting the changes means you only hear about the same detected changes once. This makes sense, because there is little advantage in continually being notified about a change that has already occurred. In fact, it is better to be informed only once about a specific change, for a couple of reasons. First, having to set the baseline database manually can be a serious burden for many hosts. For hundreds of hosts, this is simply not practical. Second, if you do not set the baseline in a timely manner, the change reports can grow so large that you run the risk of not noticing critical changes.

The second reason for enabling auto-accept has to do with the archiving option. If you are **not** archiving your databases, you run the risk of overwriting the last scan database until the baseline is set. This option combined with not archiving allows you to preserve all changes and maintain some control over the size of the *databases* directory by saving only the databases that reflect change, not the duplicates.

Purging

When the baseline is set, the previous database is deleted if the purging option is enabled. The main reason this option exists is to prevent the *database* directory from growing without bound. When scans are archived, it is obvious why this can have an impact on available disk space. However, even with the non-archiving auto-accept configuration defined above, the *database* directory can still grow over time. The database purging option provides administrators with the ability to store only two databases for a host: the baseline and the last scanned database. To adopt this minimalist configuration, disable archiving, enable auto-accept, and turn the feature on. Using the purging option in conjunction with archiving makes no sense; the Osiris interface will notify you if you configured a host in this manner.

Putting It All Together

Using the three aforementioned options to specify how hosts under Osiris deal with scan data, is confusing. Presenting this information in a chart can sometimes be helpful. Table 6.2 includes some common configurations for a host and their significance.

Table 6.2 Common Configurations for a Host

	Archive	Auto-Accept	Purge	Significance
Most common	N	Y	N	Saves all unique databases; baseline updated automatically.
Minimalist	N	Y	Y	Saves no databases; has no disk increase; baseline updated automatically.
Maximum	Y	Y	N	Saves all scan data; baseline updated automatically; consumes great deal of disk space.
Paranoid	N	N	N	Saves databases only when baseline is updated manually; does not delete anything.

Session Keys

One of the configuration options for scan agents is to send out an e-mail notification when the agent claims to have lost its session key. This is a very useful feature, and it is recommended that it always be enabled.

To authenticate the agent, the console provides each scan agent with a unique session key. The agent does not actually save this key to disk, but retains it in memory. The console in turn, stores a hash of the assigned key in the *host.conf* file. Every time the agent and the console communicate, the agent presents the console with its session key. The console hashes it and verifies it with what is stored in the *host.conf* file. If it matches, communication continues; however, if it does not match, the console refuses to communicate with that agent. The third possibility is that the agent has lost its key. This usually happens because the agent process was restarted or the host was rebooted. In that case, the agent presents a null key to the console and the console responds by assigning that agent a new key and issuing an alert. Optionally, you can have the console send out e-mail when this happens. As an administrator, you should be aware of any reboots or tampering with the Osiris agent process.

Advanced Scan Configuration

Osiris comes bundled with default scan configuration files for common platforms. These configurations exist so that Osiris can be useful out of the box (i.e., new users can install Osiris and begin monitoring their hosts without having to edit any configuration files). The problem with this is that they are very generic; you will almost always want to customize what elements of the environment are monitored on your hosts. This section covers everything you need to know about writing custom Osiris scan configurations.

Scan Configuration Syntax

Osiris scan configuration files are flat files with a relatively simple syntax. If you are familiar with Apache configuration files, you will notice similarities. Configuration files consist of global options, a block containing a list of modules to execute, and a series of directory blocks related to file scanning (see Figure 6.15).

Figure 6.15 The Components for the Default Linux Scan Configuration File

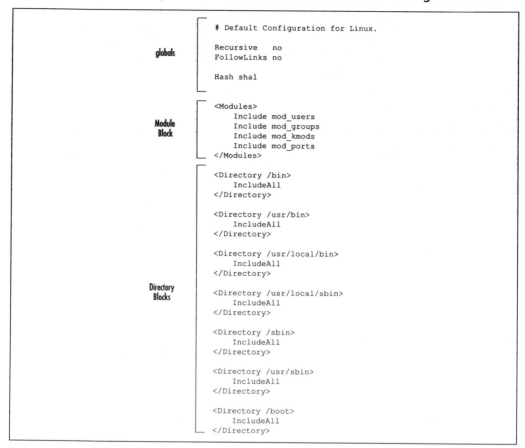

```
                           # Default Configuration for Linux.

        globals            Recursive   no
                           FollowLinks no

                           Hash sha1

                           <Modules>
        Module                  Include mod_users
        Block                   Include mod_groups
                                Include mod_kmods
                                Include mod_ports
                           </Modules>

                           <Directory /bin>
                                IncludeAll
                           </Directory>

                           <Directory /usr/bin>
                                IncludeAll
                           </Directory>

                           <Directory /usr/local/bin>
                                IncludeAll
                           </Directory>

        Directory          <Directory /usr/local/sbin>
        Blocks                  IncludeAll
                           </Directory>

                           <Directory /sbin>
                                IncludeAll
                           </Directory>

                           <Directory /usr/sbin>
                                IncludeAll
                           </Directory>

                           <Directory /boot>
                                IncludeAll
                           </Directory>
```

Every line in the scan configuration file consists of a *directive*; which are case-insensitive, except when specifying literals such as the names of files or directories. Spacing and tab characters are not important; however, directives cannot span multiple lines. You can place comments in the file by making the first visible character of a line the "#" sign.

The modules block defines which modules the agent should attempt to execute. This block consists of a list of *Include* directives, one for each module to execute. If the configuration references a module that is not compiled into the agent, the agent produces a log message to that effect. The modules *start tag* does not take any arguments. For example, to have the scan agent execute only the *mod_users* and *mod_groups* module, you would define your module block as follows:

```
<Modules>
    Include mod_users
```

```
     Include mod_groups
</Modules>
```

Directory blocks are used to define what and how the agent should scan the files contained in the specified directory. The directory *start tag* takes a single argument—a full path to a directory. A directory block consists of options and rules. The options specify the "how" and the rules specify the "what." The following is a list of the currently supported options:

- **Recursive <*boolean*>** When the boolean is set, the agent recursively scans all subdirectories in the current directory; otherwise, only a top-level scan of the files is performed. The default value for this is set.

- **FollowLinks <*boolean*>** When the boolean is set, the agent traverses all symbolic links when scanning; otherwise, all symbolic link targets are skipped. The only exception to this is when the symbolic link points to a directory and the **recursive** option is not yet set. The default value for this option is "not set."

- **Hash <*algorithm*>** Use the specified algorithm to compute all file checksums in the current directory. The default is MD5.

The values for a boolean must be one of the following: **yes**, **y**, **1**, **yup**, **no**, **n**, **0**, **nope**. The valid values for algorithms must be **MD5**, **sha1**, or **ripemd**; character case does not matter. To apply options to a specific directory, place them in a directory block. To set the default values for these options, place them outside of any directory block. If a directory block does not contain an option, the global value will be used. If the option is not set globally, the default value will be used.

The list of valid rules for a directory block include:

- **IncludeAll** Include all files.

- **ExcludeAll** Exclude all files.

- **Include** <*filter*> Include all files that match the specified filter.

- **Exclude** <*filter*> Exclude all files that match the specified filter.

- **NoEntry** <*dir*> Do not scan the specified subdirectory. The specified directory is assumed to be relative to the directory block this rule resides in. This directive does not accept regular expressions.

The agent interprets rules in the order they appear in the directory block. When the agent encounters a file, it proceeds to traverse the rules for that directory block until it finds one that matches, or it reaches the end of the rules. As soon as a match is found, all other rules are ignored and the agent moves on to the next file. If a directory block contains no rules, all files are included. A common mistake is to add rules to an empty block to filter out certain files. You must remember to add an "IncludeAll" rule at the end of the block. Otherwise, all files will be ignored, because the agent will only execute the rules that are in the block. For example, the following block has no rules and will include all files:

```
<Directory /bin>
</Directory>
```

Now, suppose you wanted to exclude the file */bin/ls*. You could do something like:

```
<Directory /bin>
    Exclude file( "^/bin/ls$" )
</Directory>
```

Now that this block has one or more rules in it, the default no longer applies, and because only an exclude rule exists, no files are actually monitored in this directory. The correct way to do this is as follows:

```
<Directory /bin>
    Exclude file ("^/bin/ls$")
    IncludeAll
</Directory>
```

Osiris defines a number of filters that can be used to help specify exactly which files you want to monitor. Use these filters as arguments to the *Include* or *Exclude* rules. You probably will not use most of the filters; however, there are some very useful ones. The following is a list of all of the supported rule filters:

- **sticky** Any directory or file with the sticky permissions bit set.
- **suid** Any file with the SUID permissions bit set.
- **sgid** Any file with the Set Group ID (SGID) permissions bit set.
- **uid***(x)* Any file that is owned by a user with the specified User ID (UID).
- **gid***(x)* Any file containing the group owner with the specified group ID (GID).
- **user***(x)* Any file that is owned by the specified username.
- **group***(x)* Any file that is group-owned by the specified group name.
- **sid***(s)* Any file that is owned by the specified Security ID (Windows only).
- **executable** Any file that matches a common executable format for the system the agent is currently running on.

- **Perl** Any file that appears to be a Perl script based on the presence of the path to the Perl executable within the first 30 bytes of the file.

- **python** Any file that appears to be a python script based on the presence of the path to the python executable within the first 30 bytes of the file.

- **script** Any file that appears to be a shell script of some kind based on the presence of the string *#!* or *BEGIN* appearing within the first few bytes of the file.

- **file**(*<regex>*) Any filename matching the specified regular expression.

- **suffix**(*x*) Any filename matching the dot-suffix *.x*.

- **md5**(*x*) Any file with the specified MD5 checksum.

- **sha1**(*x*) Any file with the specified Secure Hashing Algorithm 1 (SHA-1) checksum.

- **ripemd**(*x*) Any file with the specified Race Integrity Primitives Evaluation Message Digest (RIPEMD-160) checksum.

- **permissions**(*x*) Any file with a permissions string matching the specified string. Use * as the wildcard character.

- **header**(*x*) Any file that begins with the specified hexadecimal string.

- **tar** Any file that appears to be a TAR archive file.

- **gzip** Any file that appears to be a GNU gzipped file.

- **zip** Any file that appears to be a zip file.

- **pgp** Any file that appears to be a PGP-related file including public keyring, secret keyring, encrypted data, American Standard Code for Information Interchange (ASCII)-armored data, public key block, encrypted message, signed message, or signature file.

- **rpm** Any file that appears to be a Red Hat Package Manager (RPM) file.

More than likely, only a few of the filters above will be of use to you. The most commonly used are the *file*, *suid*, and *suffix* filters.

Examples

An effective method for learning the Osiris scan configuration syntax is by looking at some common examples. The following configuration snippets are examples that frequently appear on the Osiris users' mailing list. Some of these examples use regular expressions.

Excluding a Directory

It often becomes necessary to monitor a directory and all of its subdirectories, except for one or two. For example, suppose you want to recursively monitor the contents of */usr/share*, but not */usr/share/x* or */usr/share/y*. To do that you must use the *NoEntry* rule as follows:

```
<Directory /usr/share>
    Recursive yes
    …
    NoEntry x
    NoEntry y
    IncludeAll
</Directory>
```

The *IncludeAll* rule is necessary because the scan agent interprets rules by iterating through them until a match is found. If no match is found, the file is ignored. In this case, the first two rules are *NoEntry* rules. The last rule is a catchall rule that includes everything else. The *NoEntry* rule only accepts literal directory names; regular expressions are not permitted.

Excluding a Specific File

To exclude a specific file from a scan, use the *Exclude* rule with the file filter. For example, suppose you want to monitor the contents of */etc*, but you want to exclude the */etc/resolv.conf* file. To do that you would use something like the following:

```
<Directory /etc>
    …
    Exclude file("^/etc/resolv\.conf$")
    IncludeAll
</Directory>
```

The file filter uses regular expressions that match the full path of the file. In this case, the *^/etc/resolv\.conf$* expression is used. The "^" and "$" characters are "special characters" (anchors) for regular expressions that signal the beginning and end of the string, which ensures an exact match. The "." is a special character that must be escaped using the "\" character. Again, there is a catchall rule to include everything except the *resolv.conf* file.

Excluding Dot Files

Configuration files (also called *dot files*) are known to change; therefore, you may want to ignore them. An example is when monitoring the contents of the */root* directory excluding any *dot* files. To do this you would use the directory block:

```
<Directory /root>
    Recursive yes

    …

    Exclude file("^\.")
    IncludeAll
</Directory>
```

Excluding Log Files

On UNIX systems, many log files end with the suffix *.log*. You can exclude these files using the suffix filter:

```
Exclude suffix("log")
```

You can also use a more generic approach with the file filter and a regular expression:

```
Exclude file("\.log$")
```

The advantage of the second approach is that you can replace the "." with any other character, whereas the suffix filter only applies to filenames in the *ame.log* form.

Recursion and Subdirectories

At times, you may want to scan a directory recursively, but not other directories under that directory. To do this, define specific directory blocks for those subdirectories. When the agent encounters a directory, it first looks for a block specific to that directory. For example, if you want to recursively scan the contents of */etc* but not */etc/init.d*, you would define a specific block for */etc/init.d* to turn off the recursive option:

```
<Directory /etc>
    Recursive yes

    …

</Directory>

…

<Directory /etc/init.d>
    Recursive no
    IncludeAll
</Directory>
```

This causes all files in the */etc* directory to be monitored, whereas only the top-level files under */etc/init.d* are monitored.

Shared versus Local Scan Configurations

The management console stores configurations in the *configs* directory under the Osiris *root* directory. On UNIX, this is */usr/local/osiris/configs* and on Windows, it is *%WindowsRoot%\osiris\configs*. These configurations are known as *shared* configurations because any host can use them. Additionally, each host has a *configs* directory for scan configurations to be used exclusively for that host. The idea is that anytime you need to customize a configuration for a particular host, you make it a local configuration thus storing that configuration in the local *configuration* directory for that host. This keeps the shared configuration store from becoming cluttered.

Your like hosts should use the same scan configuration files as much as possible. The main benefit is that you can change a single configuration file and have multiple hosts automatically take advantage of that change. For example, imagine you have a network of Linux servers, and you upgrade them or add a new service to them that requires you to begin monitoring a new directory. If they are all using the same scan configuration, you can edit that configuration and make the appropriate change. However, if they are all using local configurations, you must update every host's configuration file. In the same way that shared configurations are useful, they can also be problematic. Remember that whatever change you make to a shared configuration will impact all of the hosts using that configuration.

Creating a Custom Scan Configuration

To create a new scan configuration file, use the *new-config* command in the Osiris CLI. This command requires a single argument—the name of the configuration. For example:

```
osiris-4.1.8-release: new-config darwin
```

If the CLI is in a host context, the created configuration will be a local configuration for that host; otherwise, it will be saved as a shared configuration. This command will spawn a text editor as defined by your *$EDITOR* environment variable. Edit the configuration as necessary. If prompted to save the file, choose to do so. Before the configuration file is saved, it is automatically analyzed for syntactical errors. For example, specifying Message Digest 4 (MD4) as a hash algorithm will cause the following error:

```
line 3: ==> Hash md4
unrecognized hash algorithm: md4

fix errors before saving? (y/n)
```

At this point, you have the option to fix the mistake. Choose **y** to open the editor, fix the error, and resave the configuration. When stored, you should see a message that looks something like:

```
>>> the configuration: darwin has been saved as a shared configuration file.
osiris-4.1.8-release:
```

Alternatively, you can start with one of the default scan configurations and extend it. To do that, make a copy of the configuration you want to modify using the *copy-config* command:

```
osiris-4.1.8-release: copy-config default.darwin darwin
 >>> configuration: (default.darwin) has been copied to (darwin).
osiris-4.1.8-release:
```

This creates a copy of the specified configuration and saves it in the context you are currently in. If you are in a host context, the copied configuration will be local to that host; otherwise, it will be a shared configuration. You can then edit the copy instead of starting from scratch. This can be helpful when first learning about scan configuration files.

To cause a host to start using your newly created scan configuration, use the *init* command. When asked to use a default configuration, enter **no**. You are then prompted for a configuration to use. For example, to initialize a host called "local" and have it start using a newly created configuration called "darwin," do the following:

```
osiris-4.1.8-release: init local

Initializing a host will push over a configuration, start
a scan, and set the created database to be the
trusted database.

Are you sure you want to initialize this host (yes/no): yes

OS Name: Darwin
OS Version: 7.8.0

use the default configuration for this OS? (yes/no): no

[shared configs]

  [ name ]                    [ id ]
```

```
        default.aix              6d2857b0
        default.bsdos            99a38a8c
        default.darwin           dae4b2e8
        default.freebsd          c3dcf455
        default.irix             ed6c0108
        default.linux            c8ce9c09
        default.netbsd           0cf39a70
        default.openbsd          91a7a6a1
        default.sunos            5c4aef88
        default.unix-generic     e088d50b
        default.windows2000      951cbd4e
        default.windowsnt        69a22176
        default.windowsserve     63f6bd00
        default.windowsxp        974cd899
        default.wrt54g           cd2c17fa
        darwin                   a0b8217f

total: 16

-no local configurations-

Specify a configuration: darwin
 >>> configuration (darwin) has been pushed.
 >>> scanning process was started on host: local
```

When this scan is complete, the resultant database will be tagged as the baseline and the host will be using the newly created scan configuration file. You can verify the syntax of a configuration file at any time, using the *verify-config* command:

```
osiris-4.1.8-release: verify-config darwin
the configuration: darwin is valid.
```

One thing to consider with respect to custom scan configurations is that they affect how much data is being stored for each host. Keep in mind your host's scan data configuration while making changes to a configuration. Also, think of how many hosts are using that configuration. A single change to one configuration file could significantly increase disk usage on the management console.

Mass Deployment

There are two main problems with the mass deployment of agent-based solutions such as Osiris. First, there is the issue of actually getting the agent software installed onto the remote hosts. If you have hundreds of hosts, this is not something you want to do manually. Second, setting up a configuration and adding each of the hosts to the management console is a problem.(Developing a well-designed user interface for the management of many hosts is also a challenge.

Osiris does not provide any direct solutions for these two problems. Organizations with multiple hosts probably already have a means of performing administrative tasks to a massive network of hosts. Another mass deployment method and application interface would bloat the system. Instead, Osiris provides indirect ways to facilitate mass deployment. To deal with the installation of software, both the UNIX and Windows installers have the ability to be deployed in a non-interactive mode. Administrators can set up the install packages the way they want them, and then install them with a single command. To help facilitate the integration of hundreds of hosts into the management interface, the management console's directory store was developed in such a way that it would be trivial to script it; that is, it is not in an odd or proprietary format.

Noninteractive Installations

To run the scan agent installer on UNIX systems without any prompts, provide command-line argument "silent." This assumes all of the defaults and runs the entire installation process:

```
# ./install.sh silent
```

When the script is completed, the agent will be installed and running. If you wish to customize any of the default values, you have to edit the *install.sh* file. All of the default settings are defined at the top of the *install.sh* file. Some parameters you might want to customize include the Osiris *root* directory, the user and group to be created/used by Osiris, and the location where osirisd will be installed.

Notes from the Underground...

Mass Deploying Osiris

Last year, Duane Dunston of NCDC posted an article to *LinuxSecurity.com* providing a step-by-step tutorial on how to use SSH and a Perl script to mass deploy Osiris scan agents. You may already have a solution for this, but if not, this may prove helpful. Although it is written with Linux in mind, with little to no modifications you can use this for any UNIX-like system as long as it has an accessible SSH server running. The URL for the article is: *www.sukkha.info/tap/osiris.html*.

To run the Windows installer without any interaction, you must use the silent switch (**/S**) followed by the names of the components you want to install. To specify the silent switch, you must run the installer on a command prompt or through some type of remote administration tool. The names of the components are "cli," "osirisd," and "osirsimd." In most cases, you will only be interested in this for agent deployments. To install only the agent on Windows hosts, without interaction or prompting, execute the following command:

```
C:\>osiris-4.1.8-win32.exe /S osirisd
```

The silent switch is a capital "S." To install all three components, execute the following command:

```
C:\>osiris-4.1.8-win32.exe /S cli osirisd osirismd
```

Depending on the version of the installer program, this command may return right away, but the installer will run in the background and install the specified components.

Adding Multiple Hosts to the Console

The source code for Osiris contains a *tools* directory with some helpful tools. One of them is a Perl script (*mass_add.pl*) that enables you to create host directories pre-configured for already-deployed agents. The benefit is that you do not have to add them to the management console manually. The inputs to this script are the IP addresses for the hosts you are adding and how you want those hosts configured. The output is a directory tree that you then copy into the root of your *Osiris* directory. There is no need to initialize these hosts; this script will generate the scan configuration and scheduling information. This script was written in Perl because Perl is one of the requirements for OpenSSL; therefore, it is assumed that at least one of the hosts available to you has Perl installed. This script depends on the NetAddr::IP module. Finally, this script is only useful for many hosts of similar configuration. If you have many different configurations, IP ranges, or operating systems, it may be faster to add them to the management console through the CLI.

The mass deployment script works by accepting a start and end IP address in Classless Inter-Domain Routing (CIDR) notation. For example, you may want to add hosts in range 192.168.1.100/24 through 192.168.1.200/24. In addition to contiguous addresses, the hosts must also share all of the same configuration settings, including the scan configuration file and the scheduling period. The *mass_add.pl* file is located in *src/tools/mass_add.pl* in the Osiris source. This script requires no arguments. For example, to create a hosts directory for agents in address range 192.168.1.100/24 through 192.168.1.200/24:

```
$ ./mass_add.pl
Enter config name to use for this set of hosts: default.linux
Enter IP address range: 192.168.1.100/24 - 192.168.1.200/24
Enable these hosts? (y/n): y
Enable email notification? (y/n): y
Notify on scan failures? (y/n): y
Notify always? (y/n): n
Notify on rekeys? (y/n): y
Enable logging to files? (y/n): n
Schedule period in minutes (1440=daily):
Archive Scan Databases? (y/n): n
Auto-Accept changes? (y/n): y
Purge Old Databases? (y/n): y
Agent listen port (suggested 2265):
>>> Building hosts for range (192.168.1.100/24) to (192.168.1.200/24)
    >>> created 192.168.1.100
    >>> created 192.168.1.101
    >>> created 192.168.1.102
    >>> created 192.168.1.103
    >>> created 192.168.1.104
    >>> created 192.168.1.105

    ...

>>> hosts archive created.
```

```
To deploy these hosts, copy the contents of hosts/*
to your osiris root directory.  This is usually /usr/local/osiris
on UNIX and %WindowsRoot%\osiris on Windows.

Once copied, do the following to setup permissions correctly:

    chown -R osiris hosts
    chgrp -R osiris hosts
```

The end result is a directory named *hosts* in the current directory, containing a directory for each host in the specified range. Assuming agents are installed on all of these hosts, all you have to do is copy these host directories into the Osiris *root* directory to begin monitoring these systems. Assuming you are on a UNIX system, first move the host directories as root:

```
# mv ./hosts/* /usr/local/osiris/hosts
```

Next, you have to set the permissions on these files so that the management console process owns them and has the ability to write to them:

```
# chmod -R go-rwx /usr/local/osiris/hosts/
# chown -R osiris /usr/local/osiris/hosts/
# chgrp -R osiris /usr/local/osiris/hosts/
```

The final step is to stop and restart the management console service, which is necessary for the management console scheduler to recognize the newly added hosts. How this is done varies with every platform. At this point, you do not have to initialize any of the hosts; they will start being monitored according to their schedules.

Administering Osiris

One of the biggest pitfalls with software security solutions (including Osiris) is that adequate administration is often ignored or the system is misconfigured. After you have deployed Osiris and established a management console, it is critical that you understand some administrative issues so that your deployment is a benefit to your security administration. The following sections deal specifically with logging, notifications (e.g., e-mail), scheduling, filters, users, and the management of the scan data. The goal is to make sure that your deployment does not become more of a problem than it is worth.

Logging

Logging is the most important behavioral aspect of Osiris (or any system like it). Whenever the management console performs analysis on scan data, the results are directed to the logs. The only downside to logs is that they must be read. This is a fundamental part of administrating a host integrity monitoring system that exists specifically to make sure that Osiris logs are presented to the appropriate person in a readable manner (see Chapter 9, "Analysis and Response").

The Osiris management console is the source of all logging data and has three vectors for log data: system logs, files, and pipes to external applications. All logging information is directed to the system log (usually syslog or the Event Viewer); which includes information about the workings of the management console itself, as well as all of the information about detected changes on monitored hosts. In addition to system logs, each host has a directory specifically for log files. After each scan, a host generates a report about detected changes and stores it in a log file. Finally, the management console has the ability to feed logs to an external application. This can be an executable or some kind of script. This works by redirecting log data to the standard input of the application.

Every Osiris log message has a code and a human readable text message. The code allows you to easily use log analysis tools to look for specific messages by not having to rely on the exact matching of the text message. All of the logging codes for Osiris are listed on the Osiris Web site at http://hostintegrity.com/osiris/logs.html. For example, the logging code for the detection of a file size difference is "215." An example log message using this code is as follows:

```
[215][local][cmp][/usr/sbin/winbindd][bytes][1565028][1580212]
```

Logs are each on a single line and made up of a series of fields defined by "[]." Note that the logging code is the first field.

The thing to remember about Osiris logs is that the information sent to the system log or piped to an application is the only complete outlet for information from the management console. Log files for hosts are strictly scan reports. E-mail notifications are also only scan reports. As an administrator, you must establish an analysis mechanism for Osiris logs (see Chapter 9).

Notifications

Osiris has the ability to send e-mail notifications about detected changes. If you are using some type of external log analysis system, it probably has the ability to notify you. In that case, you can easily turn off the notification features in the management console. The main reason that Osiris has its own notification system is to make deployment easier on the Administrator; no third-party applications are necessary. The biggest downside to Osiris notifications is that the information is not complete. If you want to be notified about any information related to the console itself, you have to use another application that specifically monitors the console logs. Although you can use a combination of the Osiris notifications and a log analysis tool, I do not recommend it. If for any reason you do not have the ability to set up a log analysis solution, the built-in Osiris notifications can prove helpful. However, if you are going to analyze the console logs, there is nothing in the Osiris notifications that cannot be gathered from analyzing the logs; thus, it is suggested that you do not mix the two.

Osiris notifications report on three different types of events:

- Scan Results
- Scan Agent Session Re-keys
- Scheduled Scan Failures

Scan results include all of the detected changes in the standard Osiris logging format, as well as a brief summary of the change. This is what makes the notification more of a report than simply a dump of the applicable logs. After every scan, the console compares the recently created database against the baseline database. During this comparison, some basic statistics are gathered and written to a temporary file (*log.temp*) along with all of the log entries. Specifically, it is stored in the logs directory for the appropriate host. At that point, depending on the notification settings, the contents of this file is mailed out as a scan report. If file logging is enabled for that host, the temporary log file is renamed and kept in the logs directory. Otherwise, the temporary log file is overwritten with the next scan. The following is an example of the information you can expect to find in an Osiris-generated scan report:

```
compare time: Wed Mar 30 07:46:00 2005
         host: local
   scan config: default.darwin (971e7550)
      log file: no log file generated, see system log.
  base database: 4
compare database: 5
```

```
[211][local][cmp][/bin/cp][mtime][Thu May 13 00:50:57 2004][Wed Mar 30
07:45:58 2005]

[211][local][cmp][/bin/ls][mtime][Thu Mar 24 09:47:19 2005][Wed Mar 30
07:45:58 2005]

[211][local][cmp][/bin/mv][mtime][Thu May 13 00:50:58 2004][Wed Mar 30
07:45:58 2005]
```

```
Change Statistics:

-----------------------------------


            checksums: 0

           SUID files: 0

      root-owned files: 3

     file permissions: 0

                  new: 0

              missing: 0


total differences: 3
```

In Example 6.85, there are only three changes detected, which are related to the *mtime* values of three executables. At the top of the report is the time, the host, the configuration used in the last scan, the name of the log file (if logging to files is enabled), and the databases analyzed while generating this report. After the logs are some basic statistics to help give you an idea about the overall nature of the detected changes.

As an assurance that scheduled scans are taking place, you can configure Osiris to e-mail scan reports for hosts after every scan, even if there are no detected changes. If you are monitoring many hosts and/or your scan frequencies are high, this can be a lot of mail. An alternative to this is to turn on notifications for scheduled scan failures.

Regardless of whether or not you have notifications or file logging turned on, you can still see this report data because it is written to a temporary file. To see the latest scan report generated for a host, login to the console, enter a host context, and view the logs with the *logs* command:

```
osiris-4.1.8-release: host local
local is alive.
osiris-4.1.8-release[local]: logs
This may take a while...


  [ name ]                  [ date ]


   log.temp                 Wed Mar 30 07:46:00


total: 1
```

Unless the host has never been scanned after the baseline, you will always see the log file *log.temp*. This is the temporary file that is created after every scan. To see the contents of this file through the CLI, use the *print-log* command:

```
osiris-4.1.8-release[local]: print-log log.temp
```

The next kind of notification that the console is capable of providing is related to session keys. Whenever an agent claims to have lost its session key (from a reboot or a restart) Osiris can be configured to send a notification about it. The following is an example of an e-mail notification about a session rekey:

```
To: bob@example.com
From: "Osiris Host Integrity System" <osirismd@example.com>
Date: Sun Mar 20 11:52:07 2005
Subject: [osiris rekey][host: local] session rekey.


The host, "local" seems to have lost its resident session key.
This key is lost when the agent is restarted or the host is rebooted.


This host is configured to generate an alert upon detection of this event.
To change this, adjust the notification settings for this host.
```

The third type of notification that you can set up within Osiris is related to the scheduler. When the scheduler attempts to tell an agent to start scanning its environment, it is possible that the agent is not running, does not respond, or the host itself is no longer available. This is important information for administrators, because the scheduler can be configured to send out e-mail notifications in the event that a scheduled scan failed to occur for any reason. Here is what an example of such a notification looks like:

```
To: bob@example.com
From: "Osiris Host Integrity System" <osirismd@example.com>
Date: Fri Nov 19 12:57:23 2004
Subject: [host: local] failed to start the scheduled scan.


The scheduler was unable to initiate the following scan:


host: local
scheduled scan time: Fri Nov 19 12:57:23 2004


The scheduler produced the following error message:


Unable to connect to host.
```

This notification is sent only if the scan agent does not acknowledge the scheduler's initial request to start scanning. If the agent encounters an error of any kind, or if the scan stream halts for any reason, you will not receive the notification. I have encountered situations where it was a requirement that the administrator be given confirmation that scans took place and were complete. In that case, you will need to either turn on notifications for every scan report for your hosts, or analyze the console logs to watch for the scan complete log entry (Log ID 501).

Scheduling

The Osiris console has a relatively primitive scheduling mechanism. Hosts are scanned in regular intervals as specified in their configuration file (in minutes). When the scheduler detects that it is time for a host to be scanned, the console pushes the configuration found in the baseline database to the agent, and sends that agent a start scan message. As an administrator, there are some things that you must be aware of regarding the Osiris scheduler.

First, you can specify a start time. This exists only in the cases where you want to control what time of day the scan should take place. For example, if you are scanning a host once per day, you can set the start time to be 4 A.M. so that scans do not take place during peak usage hours. Likewise, if you plan to scan a host once per week, you could set the start date to be on a Saturday or a Sunday for the same reason. The start time is in relation to the clock on the console, not the agents.

The minimum frequency that a host can be scanned is one minute (e.g., if you are only scanning ports, kernel modules, or some other element of the environment where scans are quick). The thing to keep in mind with respect to schedule frequency is how long a scan will take. For example, it makes a little sense to schedule a host to scan every minute if the scan process itself takes the agent two minutes. If that happens, you may end up receiving notifications (if enabled) that the scheduler was unable to start the scan because the host was already scanning the environment. One way to avoid this is to look at the latest scan results and see how long the scan took. Make sure the schedule for that host or hosts is higher than that time. Scan results are stored in the scan database. To see how long the last scan took for a host, use the *databases* command to see the listing of databases and then use the *print-db-header* command on the last database:

```
osiris-4.1.8-release[local]: databases
This may take a while...
```

```
   [ name ]                          [ created ]
      2                              Tue Mar 29 06:47:21
      3                              Tue Mar 29 06:47:39
      4                              Wed Mar 30 07:45:47
   *  5                              Wed Mar 30 07:45:59
      6                              Wed Mar 30 08:25:45


total: 5
(*) denotes the base database for this host.


osiris-4.1.8-release[local]: print-db-header 6


   DATABASE:   6


   status: complete
   errors: 0
  records: 34
   config: default.darwin (971e7550)


   SCAN RESULTS:


            record type: UNIX1


        files encountered: 34
           files scanned: 34


     symlinks encountered: 0
        symlinks followed: 0


        files unreadable: 0
  directories unreadable: 0
     symlinks unreadable: 0


            scan started: Wed Mar 30 08:25:45 2005
           scan finished: Wed Mar 30 08:25:45 2005
```

In this case, the scan took only one second so we are able to set the frequency to any resolution. Keep in mind that although you may be able to scan a host once per minute, it probably will not be useful, especially if you have many hosts or are archiving all of your scan data. Whether or not your scan frequency is reasonable depends on what you are scanning for, how soon you require detection, and how well you are able to respond. It may be that scanning a host every minute or every few minutes has little impact on the performance of the system. Or, it may be that scanning a host once per day is not sufficient because all that does is narrow down the window of change to a day when you require that window to be within minutes. These are all issues that you must take into account when determining how to schedule scans for your monitored hosts. Remember, the strong point of Osiris is that it will provide details about what has changed in your host environment. Whether or not you are informed in an hour or within 12 hours is not often significant.

Finally, you can suspend scheduled scans using the *disable* command at any time. In the CLI, enabling and disabling a host means it is under the control of the scheduler, which can prove helpful when you take a host offline for a scheduled task and do not want to be bothered by error messages during the downtime:

```
osiris-4.1.8-release[local]: disable local
 >>> host local is now disabled.
osiris-4.1.8-release[local]: enable local
 >>> host local is now enabled.
```

Filters: Reducing False Positives

Filtering log messages is arguably the most important administrative responsibility of Osiris (or any solution like it). Again, if you are using your own log analysis solution external to Osiris, you will likely offload this functionality to your log analysis engine as opposed to having Osiris do it. However, many Osiris deployments take advantage of this feature, because with no additional setup you are able to single out only certain attributes of the environment to monitor, or to filter out elements that you do not care about. For example, you may not care about timestamps on a file but you may care a great deal about the ownership or permission information.

Osiris filters are applied to every log message before it is distributed to the various logging vectors. Thus the information directed to e-mail notifications, log files, system logs, and pipes to an application are all affected by filtering. The biggest pitfall with respect to filtering is that there is the potential to inadvertently block important log messages from being generated. The good thing about filters is that they are applied on the output of the database analysis process as opposed to the ingress stream of scan data. This means that at any point in time you can compare two databases manually to see the true reflection of change without filtering. Therefore, if you are attempting to remove noise from the system, when in doubt add a filter instead of adjusting the scan configuration. Another useful element of filtering mechanisms is that they are applied to *all* log messages, not just messages related to change reports. The advantage here is that you have the option to throttle the amount of diagnostic information about the console being sent to the system log (if that is problematic for you).

Osiris filters are a collection of regular expressions. These regular expressions are stored in a Berkeley DB file named *auth.db* in the Osiris *root* directory. To see a listing of filters use the *filters* command:

```
osiris-4.1.8-release: filters


exclude anything matching: "\[^/etc$\]*\[mtime|ctime\]"


1 comparison filters.
```

This prints all of the filters stored in the filter database. To edit the filter database, use the *edit-filters* command; which opens an editor and allows you to add to or edit the current filter list using a standard text editor. Filters are stored one per line (see Figure 6.16).

Figure 6.16 Editing a Filter List Using *vi*

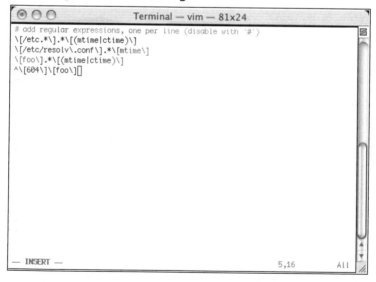

When you save the file and quit the editor, the filters are sent back to the console and stored in the filter database:

```
osiris-4.1.8-release: edit-filters
 >>> comparison filters have been saved.
osiris-4.1.8-release:
```

Filters are applied in the order that they are seen when you print them out with the *filters* command. As soon as a filter in the filter database matches, the rest are ignored. If the end of the list is reached and no matches have occurred, the log message is sent to all of the appropriate logging outlets.

To disable a filter, use the "#" character at the beginning of the filter to comment it out. This allows you to preserve the filter itself, but it will not be applied to log messages until you enable it again by removing the comment.

The biggest problem you will likely encounter with filters is being able to come up with regular expressions that do exactly what you intend them to do. It may be that your regular expressions catch more than you intended, or they may not work at all. Use the *test-filter* command to help debug your filters before you add them to the filter database. This command will ask for the source data and a regular expression and print the result applying that expression to your source data. To test your filters, paste a log message in as your source data and see if your regular expression matches. For example, using the filter added in the preceding example, we will paste a sample log message and see if it matches:

```
osiris-4.1.8-release: test-filter


   > enter sample data:
[215][local][cmp][/usr/sbin/winbindd][bytes][1565028][1580212]
   > enter regex: \[bytes\]


 >> pattern matches.
```

To try a failure case, we could change our regular expression slightly and verify that it does not match:

```
osiris-4.1.8-release: test-filter


   > enter sample data:
[215][local][cmp][/usr/sbin/winbindd][bytes][1565028][1580212]
   > enter regex: \[csum\]


   >> pattern does NOT match.
```

Although Osiris filters are very powerful, they can also be problematic if you do not have experience with regular expressions. The following examples are based on questions from the Osiris users mailing list and are geared towards scenarios you will likely encounter when developing rules to filter out certain types of log messages.

- **Block all mtime changes for the file** */etc/resolv.conf*:

   \[/etc/resolv\.conf\].*\[mtime\]

- **Block all mtime or ctime changes for** */etc/resolv.conf*:

   \[/etc/resolv\.conf\].*\[(mtime|ctime)\]

- **Block all mtime or ctime changes for files under the** */etc*
   directory:

   \[/etc.*\].*\[(mtime|ctime)\]

- **Block all mtime changes for files under** */etc* **and host foo:**

   \[foo\].*\[/etc.*\].*\[mtime\]

- **Block all mtime or ctime changes from host foo:**

   \[foo\].*\[(mtime|ctime)\]

- **Block all session rekey messages for host foo:**

   ^\[604\]\[foo\]

- <u>**Block**</u> **all console informative messages:**

   \[info\]

Remember that you need to escape periods and square brackets with a backslash character. The period matches almost any character, and the asterisk (*) repeats the previous item zero or more times. The "^" character matches the start of the string and the "$" character matches the end of the string. These are also known as anchors. A good online reference for regular expressions is www.regular-expressions.info. A good book for regular expressions is *Mastering Regular Expressions* by Jeffrey Friedl (O'Reilly and Associates).

Although you can filter out noise with filters, you can also filter out noise by adjusting your scan configuration; at some point, this is the better choice for handling noise. For example, if you are scanning */var/log* because you want to monitor a few files, you are probably going to encounter more files that change on a legitimate basis than those that do not. In this case, it makes sense to adjust your scan configuration for */var/log* so that you are only scanning specific files as opposed to scanning all of them and creating filters to block the legitimate changes. You can block all of the changes related to an entire directory by using a filter or a *NoEntry* directive; the result is essentially the same. Another thing to consider with filtering is that it does not stop the changes from being stored in the database, only the logs.

It is not obvious which way is the best route to take when dealing with noise, but generally, the rule is that filters are used only to tweak things; the majority of what is scanned should not be elements of the environment that you know are going to change regularly.

Multiple Management Consoles

The Osiris management console was not designed to work in conjunction with other console deployments. You can deploy multiple management consoles, which can be configured to not step on each other's toes, but there is little advantage.

One reason why you may want to deploy a second or third management console is because of the load on your console host. If you are managing thousands of hosts, it may be more practical to set up two or three consoles to distribute the overhead. Another reason has to do with your network topology. It may be that your network design restricts you from placing a console on the network where it can connect to all of the hosts you wish to monitor. Or, you may have hosts on completely separate networks. In any case, the problem with deploying more than one console is that you then have to manage more than one console. This includes the data associated with a console, as well as maintaining it (e.g., backups). Scan configurations, scan data, and logs are spread across multiple hosts and become more of a management burden.

I have also seen deployments with multiple consoles where the administrator was monitoring the same agent from different consoles. This has little value and is not recommended. Not only do you have the burden of managing more than one console, you now have to make sure that the consoles do not fight over the agents as far as scheduling is concerned. Never run multiple instances of a management console on the same host.

Database Files

All scan data that the console receives from the scan agents is stored in Berkeley DB files. As an administrator, you can choose whether to store all of the received scan data, at least some, or none at all. The advantage of storing at least some of this scan data is that you can go back and create a timeline of activity for a specific host.

Osiris databases take advantage of the Berkeley DB feature, which stores four separate databases within a single file. Every Osiris scan database file contains the following sub-databases:

- Headers
- Errors
- File Records
- Modules

The Headers database contains information about the scan, including the scan results and statistics. The Errors database contains any errors the scan agent produced while scanning the environment. The File Records database contains only file-related data The Modules database contains any information gathered by the executed modules.

WARNING

Scan database files contain sensitive information about your host environments. You should be very careful with these files if you are planning on removing them from your management console host for analysis. *Never* attempt to perform analysis on the actual databases files located in the Osiris *root* directory. Always make copies of those databases and perform any analysis on those copies. Also, the database files are not encrypted so be careful where you store these files when analyzing them.

The *tools* directory in the Osiris source contains an application named printdb, a small command-line application that allows you to view the contents of an Osiris database. The nice thing about Osiris database files is that they are platform independent. Thus, you can analyze their contents with printdb on your preferred platform or environment. To see the options available, run this command without any arguments:

```
$ ./printdb
osiris db command line utility (v0.2).
usage: printdb [-h] [-e] [-m] [-a] <database>

 -h  : print database header.
 -e  : print scan errors.
 -m  : print module records.
 -f  : print file records.
 -a  : print everything.
```

To print the headers for a database, use the *print-db* command with a single argument: the name of the database file. For example:

```
$ ./printdb 8

DATABASE: 8

    status: complete
```

```
        host: local
      config: default.darwin (6f973f54)


      errors: 4
 file records: 34
system records: 124


  SCAN RESULTS:


        record type: UNIX1


  files encountered: 36
     files scanned: 34


  symlinks encountered: 0
    symlinks followed: 0


     files unreadable: 0
directories unreadable: 4
   symlinks unreadable: 0


        scan started: Thu Mar 31 06:56:47 2005
        scan finished: Thu Mar 31 06:56:47 2005
```

In this case, you can see that this database is from the host called local and was created with the configuration default.darwin on March 31. The scan agent encountered four errors while scanning the environment. To see these errors, use the **-e** option to see only the errors:

```
$ ./printdb -e 8
[101] [Thu Mar 31 06:56:47 2005] [ error conducting lstat on file "/foo" ]
[100] [Thu Mar 31 06:56:47 2005] [ unable to open directory "/foo" ]
[101] [Thu Mar 31 06:56:47 2005] [ error conducting lstat on file "/bar" ]
[100] [Thu Mar 31 06:56:47 2005] [ unable to open directory "/bar" ]
```

In this case, the agent was not able to open some of directories, probably because they do not exist. To see all of the records in the database, use the **-a** option, which will print everything in the database, including the headers, file data, modules, and errors.

To view only a single file record, use *grep* to show only the output related to the file(s) you are interested in. For example, to view the details for the file */bin/ls* in the directory, do the following:

```
$ ./printdb -a 8 | grep -A 19 "/bin/ls"
file: /bin/ls
record type: UNIX1
checksum: 1b9ad9baabb63854faccfe5f43f0970b
checksum algorithm: md5
permissions: -r-xr-xr-x
user: root
group: wheel
device: 234881026
inode: 860280
mode: 33133
links: 1
uid: 0
gid: 0
mtime: Wed Mar 30 07:45:58 2005
atime: Thu Mar 31 06:52:43 2005
ctime: Wed Mar 30 07:45:58 2005
device_type: 0
bytes: 32464
blocks: 64
block_size: 4096
```

In this case, the record type was for UNIX files; therefore, we grepped for 19 lines. For other record types (such as Windows records) you will have to tweak the arguments to grep to get them to print the correct number of lines.

If your database file has modules in it, you can print out all of the data in the modules database using the **-m** option:

```
$ ./printdb -m 8 | less


[ MODULES ]


[group:admin][admin:*:80:root,brian]
[group:appserveradm][appserveradm:*:81:brian]
[group:appserverusr][appserverusr:*:79:brian]
[group:bin][bin:*:7:]
[group:brian][brian:*:501:]
...
```

Each module item is printed on a single line. One way to isolate the contents of a specific module item is to use grep with a regular expression. For example, assuming you had *mod_users* and *mod_groups* enabled when this database was created, you can view the group *bin* or the user *root* by doing the following:

```
$ ./printdb -m 8 | grep "^\[group:bin\]"
[group:bin][bin:*:7:]
$ ./printdb -m 8 | grep "^\[user:root\]"
[user:root][root:*:0:0:System Administrator:/var/root:/bin/sh]
```

Users

Near the beginning of this chapter when we established a management console, we set the password for the admin user. By default, this is the only user that exists when the management console is installed. Although you can add additional users to your console, remember that they are all created equal; there is no concept of privileged and non-privileged users. Why create additional users? Two reasons: *revocation* and *logging*.

If you have more than one security administrator using your management console, it makes sense to assign a user to each, which will make it easy to prevent that administrator from logging in if necessary. Of course, since all users are essentially root users, they can add backdoor accounts, lock other administrators out, or set the admin password. If you are worried about such things with your administrators, you should give them accounts on your console.

The second, most important reason that you should use multiple users on the console is for logging purposes. Every action performed through a CLI session is recorded in the system logs, along with the username. This makes it easy to see which administrator did what. For example, when the admin user logs in:

```
Mar 31 07:47:50 localhost osirismd[285]: [16][*][info] authorized connection
    from: 127.0.0.1 (localhost).
Mar 31 07:47:50 localhost osirismd[1131]: [101][*][info] authenticated user:
    admin
Mar 31 07:47:51 localhost osirismd[1131]: [400][*][info] received hello from
    management application.
```

Then, suppose the admin user sets the base database for the host local to "8." This action is recorded in the logs as follows:

```
Mar 31 07:49:38 localhost osirismd[1131]: [302][local][info] [admin] trusted
    database set to: 8.
```

I do not promote using multiple users for your management console, but if you require multiple security administrators to interact with your console, it is a good practice to set up individual user accounts so that each administrator's activities are logged.

Storing Scan Data in Relational Databases

One feature that Osiris lacks is the ability to log to a relational database. Samhain has the ability to do this, and do it well. Many administrators like this feature because it allows you to easily store and search massive amounts of data collected from your hosts over time. It also opens up more possibilities for analyzing the collected data. Although Osiris lacks this ability natively, there are ways you can set up the console to send this data to a database with a little scripting.

The easiest way to get Osiris to scan data automatically sent to a relational database is to use the *notify_app* features of the console. This is a logging outlet that allows you to configure the console to pipe all log messages to the standard input of an executable. The *tools* directory in the Osiris source code contains a sample python script (*notify.py*), which shows how to read the log messages and write them to a file. This script is relatively small and looks something like the following:

```python
#!/usr/bin/python
import sys

f = open( 'osiris.log', 'a' )

while 1:
    try:
        line = sys.stdin.readline()

        # no more data.

        if not line:
            break

        f.write ("%s" % line )
        f.flush()

    except:
        print "error reading data."

f.close()
```

It would not take much effort to modify this script so that, instead of writing these logs to a file, they are instead sent to a PostgreSQL, MySQL, or some other relational database. To set this up, all you have to do is place your script or executable somewhere, adjust the management console configuration file (*osirismd.conf*), and set the *notify_app* line accordingly. You have to edit this configuration file by hand, as the CLI does not acknowledge that this configuration setting exists. After restarting your console, your application should be receiving *all* log messages, not just logs related to scans. For example, a typical configuration calling */usr/local/bin/osilog.py* is as follows:

```
syslog_facility = DAEMON
control_port = 2266
http_port = 0
http_host =
notify_email =
notify_app = /usr/local/bin/osilog.py
notify_smtp_host =
notify_smtp_port = 0
hosts_directory =
allow = 127.0.0.1
```

Summary

Osiris is one of the most widely deployed open source host integrity monitoring systems available today. Osiris can monitor everything from UNIX environments like AIX and Mac OS X, to Windows desktops systems and servers. Osiris can monitor files, network ports, users, groups, and various elements of the kernel and administrator services. One of the biggest advantages of Osiris is that it is quite simple to use. Usability and simplicity were critical goals in the design of the Osiris system. The less complicated your Osiris deployment is, the more likely you will be successful in monitoring the integrity of your environments. The more complicated your Osiris deployment is, the more likely you will end up ignoring it altogether.

In this chapter we have covered all of the steps involved in deploying a simple and effective Osiris deployment. Some of the more complicated features of Osiris were intentionally left out. To find more information about Osiris, I recommend consulting the most current online documentation.

Solutions Fast Track

Configuring and Building Osiris

☑ Burn the Osiris source to read-only media, and verify the PGP signature before building installer packages.

☑ Establish dedicated building environments so that your installer packages can be trusted, and so that you can easily build trusted updates or make changes to your installers.

☑ Burn all installer packages to read-only media before your deploy them, so that you have a copy of what you have deployed that is free from tampering.

Additional Deployment Considerations

☑ Pre-provision all of your scan agents with root certificates so that way they trust only a specific management console out of the box.

☑ Always test your scan agents before you deploy them.

Establishing a Management Console

☑ The management console manages all of the information about monitored hosts; guard this host with your life.

☑ The management console should be a dedicated system that does not run any services except for what is needed for the function of the console.

☑ After installation, make certain you understand and configure the console according to your needs and requirements for logging, notifications, users, and access control.

Command-Line Interface

☑ The Osiris command-line interface is used to configure your console, and interact with your deployed scan agents.

☑ Ideally, the CLI should be run from only the console host; however, you can log in to your console from remote hosts if necessary.

Scan Agents

☑ Scan agents collect information from your host environments and securely report on that information to the console; the gathered information is never stored on the monitored host.

☑ Always install the scan agent from installers that you have built from a trusted source. Avoid using ports or packages whenever possible because they are tied to specific configurations and modules.

☑ Think of the default scan configuration files as a starting point. You will almost always need to extend these configurations to suit the monitoring needs of your hosts.

Administering Osiris

☑ The proper configuration and administration of Osiris can mean the difference between a useless burdensome deployment, and one that will allow you to realize change in your host environments.

☑ Log and store as much scan data as possible. If something bad happens, you want as much data as possible at your disposal so you can attempt to track down as much of the details as possible.

☑ Find the sweet spot of scheduling. As an administrator, you want to be careful to monitor the right stuff, at the right frequency. Scans that are too infrequent means less detail; too frequent means unnecessary overhead on your hosts.

Frequently Asked Questions

The following Frequently Asked Questions, answered by the authors of this book, are designed to both measure your understanding of the concepts presented in this chapter and to assist you with real-life implementation of these concepts. To have your questions about this chapter answered by the author, browse to **www.syngress.com/solutions** and click on the **"Ask the Author"** form. You will also gain access to thousands of other FAQs at ITFAQnet.com.

Q: Is it really necessary to go through the hassle of verifying the source and establishing dedicated build machines to build the agent and console installers?

A: Yes. It is necessary if you are serious about deploying a system that works, and that you can trust to provide reliable information about changes to your hosts. The verification step is necessary because, as seen in the last few years, source code repositories are not immune from attacks and just computing an MD5 means little. The source is PGP signed by the key listed in the beginning of this chapter. Dedicated build machines are necessary for a couple of reasons. First, it makes little sense to build your trusted source in an environment that you do not trust. There are certain elements to this whole process that you can control (e.g. build environments), and there are those that you cannot (quality of software). At the very least, take advantage of the steps you can control to better your chances of a successful deployment. The second reason dedicated build and test environments are useful is because they allow you to easily build upgrades or make small changes to your deployments.

Q: When I attempt to initialize or contact an agent, I encounter an error about session key negotiation failures. Why?

A: There are a couple of reasons that this may occur. The most common reason is that the host running the agent has a different concept of time than the console. The agent performs some certificate validation on the certificate presented by the console upon every connection. If the agent host has a messed-up system clock, certificate validation fails and (for security reasons) the agent immediately halts communication. As far as the console is concerned, the agent refused to give a session key; hence, the error.

Q: Why are some configuration options for the console and agents not acknowledged by the CLI?

A: If there is an option in one of these configuration files that the CLI does not allow you to configure, it is because that option was considered something that is not commonly used by most deployments. The main reason they are not in the CLI is because most users will not care, not understand what they are, or possibly configure them incorrectly. These options are documented. If you know what they are and how to use them, it should not be a problem to directly make a small edit to the configuration file.

Q: I made changes to a scan configuration file and scanned the host but the changes did not seem to take effect. Why?

A: When you scan a host manually with start-scan, all the command does is inform the agent to start scanning with its currently loaded configuration. If you make a change to a configuration file, you must push it to the agent(s) first using the *push-config* command, and then start the scan. This is only a problem if you are scanning manually using start-scan. If you make changes to a scan configuration file, the next scheduled scans that makes use of that configuration will assume the changes. This scheduler will always send the scan configuration file to the host before starting the scan, so that the host is always scanning based off of the current configuration.

Q: How do I disable all of my hosts at once? I have over 100 agents deployed and I want to suspend monitoring for maintenance.

A: There is no way to do this via the CLI. If you need to temporarily disable Osiris, shut down the console process. The way this is done will vary with each operating system. Since the agents never initiate communication with the console, this will not have any impact on the system.

Chapter 7

Samhain

Solutions in this chapter:

- **Features and Constraints**
- **Deploying Samhain Stand-Alone**
- **Deploying Samhain with Centralized Management**
- **Using Beltane: The Web-Based Console**

☑ **Summary**

☑ **Solutions Fast Track**

☑ **Frequently Asked Questions**

Introduction

Samhain is one of the most successful open source host integrity monitoring systems available today. This chapter examines all of the steps involved in a successful deployment of Samhain, including building and verifying the source, installation, and administration. The goal of this chapter is to show you how to effectively use Samhain to monitor the integrity of your hosts. Although all of the features and abilities available through Samhain are covered, this chapter focuses on the aspects of the system that will help you establish a simple yet effective integrity monitoring solution.

It is very important that you establish dedicated build and test environments. A dedicated build environment allows you to create trusted binaries of the software. If you are deploying the Samhain agent to many hosts, you must be sure that the executables are trusted and sound. Establishing a dedicated test environment is helpful for research and ongoing administration. Initially, a test environment can be used to gain familiarity with Samhain. Once you have deployed Samhain, your dedicated test environment can be used to test configuration changes, aid in the reduction of false positives, and test various administrative tasks before loading them into your production environment.

Samhain can be deployed in a solitary fashion (stand alone), and in a client/server mode. Deploying Samhain as stand-alone is useful when you have only a handful of hosts. The client/server mode is a centrally managed deployment for the enterprise or any situation where you have a large number of hosts that must be monitored. The first part of this chapter covers the basics of Samhain in a stand-alone deployment scenario. The second part of this chapter details deploying Samhain as a centrally managed system. If you are new to Samhain, it is recommended that you follow the first part of this chapter, even if you are going to use centralized management; the information is an excellent introduction, and the exercise will help you understand some of the fundamentals of Samhain.

The Samhain Web site has excellent documentation on building, installing, configuring, and using Samhain. This documentation can be found at *www.la-samhna.de/samhain/s_documentation.html.*

Features and Constraints

This section provides details of the capabilities and limitations of Samhain that are the most relevant to the installation and deployment process To better appreciate each of the steps presented in the following sections, let us first examine what Samhain can do, discuss where it can be deployed, and describe the security features inherent in its design.

The main function of Samhain involves monitoring the integrity of files; however, additional development has features that allow it to monitor other elements of a host, thus qualifying Samhain as an integrity monitoring system, not simply a file integrity checker. Samhain can perform Set User ID (SUID)/Set Group ID (SGID) audits. In addition to being able to single out and keep track of any files with these special privileges, Samhain also provides some quarantine options to mitigate the damage possible by rogue SUID/SGID executables. Samhain can monitor login and logout events and audit the login and logout activity of users for a host. Additionally, Samhain has the ability to monitor the integrity of the kernel and to detect certain rootkits. This functionality is available for limited versions of Linux and FreeBSD kernels. Specifically, Samhain can monitor the integrity of the *syscall* table, *syscall* functions, and the interrupt descriptor table.

Notes from the Underground...

Monitoring Kernel Integrity

Samhain can monitor certain parts of the FreeBSD and Linux kernels by monitoring the integrity of system calls. System calls provide an interface between user applications and privileged kernel space and are the primary target for most rootkits. Most operations eventually translate to a system call (e.g., opening a file or initiating network activity). The handler for each system call is stored in a *system call table*. To deal with a system call, an interrupt is issued, and the handler for that system call is located and executed. It is not uncommon for a rootkit to modify some portion of the chain of events involved in executing a system call. On Linux, Samhain monitors the interrupt handler, the contents of the system call table, parts of the virtual file system layer, and a portion of each system call handler. For FreeBSD, only the system call table and the handlers are monitored. There are other means of compromising the kernel, but monitoring the integrity surrounding the invocation of system calls handlers can be very successful in detecting rootkits.

Samhain can monitor the mount settings for a host's file systems, which can be used to ensure that the policies you have established for mounting your file systems remain intact. For example, if you are mounting a certain file system with the nosuid option to prevent the existence of SUID executables on that file system, Samhain can detect and notify you if it changes. Samhain also has the ability to monitor specific files in certain users' home directories (e.g., a user's .login or .profile files). The idea is that changes to these files can compromise the integrity of that user's environment and be indicative of an attack. All of the aforementioned features have their own configuration sections in the Samhain configuration file and are optional.

The development of Samhain is based on Portable Operating System Interface (POSIX) compliance. As a result, Samhain is limited to UNIX environments, with the biggest disadvantage being that it cannot monitor Windows hosts. Although you can run Samhain on Windows through *Cygwin*, it cannot handle Windows-specific issues (e.g., registry, users, groups, services, drivers, and so on). However, developing with POSIX compliance means that Samhain can be used on a variety of UNIX-based systems, including Mac OS X, Berkeley Software Distribution (BSD), Advanced IBM UNIX (AIX), Hewlett Packard UNIX (HP-UX), Solaris, Unixware, and others. Kernel monitoring capabilities are limited to specific Linux and FreeBSD kernels; other UNIX systems do not benefit from the kernel integrity-monitoring feature.

Intrinsic in Samhain's design are some powerful security features. Although their intentions are good, some of them significantly complicate the deployment and administration of Samhain. Every deployment scenario is different. In some cases, you can choose to ignore the features for the sake of simplicity; in others you cannot. The Samhain agent can be put into stealth mode, which means that the agent executable can be hidden from the process table; additionally, you can encrypt and pack the executable so that it can be easily hidden (such as appending it to a .JPG image file). The Samhain agent executable also contains a compiled-in key used for the verification of signed notifications (e-mail) and log messages. Additionally, each Samhain agent executable has an embedded password that is used to authenticate to the server and establish ephemeral keys for securing their communication. Upon installation, executables are stripped of debug symbols. Furthermore, the installer comes with "sstrip," which is used on systems that support it to further strip the executable of debug symbols to complicate attempts to debug the process. Finally, Samhain can use the GNU Privacy Guide (GnuPG) to sign database and scan configurations.

Deploying Samhain Stand-Alone

Samhain can be installed in a stand-alone fashion, meaning it is installed onto each host that you want to monitor, and all of the functionality and data associated with monitoring each host is contained to that host; no console is involved. The downside to this is that the baseline database is stored on the monitored host and is therefore at risk to tampering. Another problem with this approach is that the more hosts involved, the more administrative burden you incur. Basically, it does not scale. However, if you are a small corporation with only a few servers, this may be your best option, because stand-alone Samhain installations are very easy to install and maintain for a small number of hosts.

This section covers a stand-alone installation of Samhain on a FreeBSD system. You can install Samhain on other UNIX systems by following this example (excluding kernel monitoring). We cover all of the configuration options, but stick to the most simple and practical approaches. Along the way, we point out features and configuration options that are prone to complexity. The point is to end up with an easily administrable integrity monitoring system.

Obtaining and Verifying Samhain

The most current version of Samhain can be found on their main Web site at http://la-samhna.de/samhain. For all releases of Samhain, a Message Digest 5 (MD5) and a Pretty Good Privacy (PGP) signature are provided so that you can verify the authenticity of the source code. The most current version of Samhain can be obtained at http://la-samhna.de/samhain/samhain-current.tar.gz.

Download this file to your system. You can use a Web browser, or if you have *wget*, you can download the source with the following command:

```
$ wget http://la-samhna.de/samhain/samhain-current.tar.gz
```

Alternatively, if you fancy curl, use the following command:

```
$ curl http://la-samhna.de/samhain/samhain-current.tar.gz -O
```

Next, unpack this *tar.gz* file with the following command:

```
$ tar xvfz samhain-current.tar.gz
samhain-2.0.5b.tar.gz
samhain-2.0.5b.tar.gz.asc
```

This leaves you with two files: the actual Samhain source in a *tar.gz* file and the PGP signature for the source file. Burn these two files to read-only media such as a DVD or a CD-ROM. It does not make sense to verify the authenticity and integrity of these files if they can still be modified. Burning them to read-only serves two purposes. First, you only have to conduct the verification once. Later, when you want to deploy the software again, you will not have to go through the verification process because you know that the files on the read-only media cannot be altered. Second, it facilitates and provides for a more controlled deployment. Establishing this as the trusted source for your installation(s) means that all of your hosts use the same release of the trusted software, at least initially.

The next step is to verify the PGP signature. All software should be verified as much as possible, but for software like Samhain, it is especially important because it is common to deploy the software on a large number of your hosts, many of them critical systems. If the source were compromised in some way (such as a backdoor), you would have a real mess on your hands. Do not think that just because you acquire the source code from a known server that you can trust it. Within the last two years, the GNU File Transfer Protocol (FTP) servers were compromised. Always attempt to verify the PGP signatures for software if signatures are available. An informative reference for this practice can be found on the Samhain Web site at www .la-samhna.de/library/PGPSignatures.html.

All Samhain releases are signed with the PGP key that has the following fingerprint:

```
EF6C EF54 701A 0AFD B86A F4C3 1AAD 26C8 0F57 1F6C
```

The KeyID is *0x0F571F6C*, and the owner of the key is *Rainer Wichmann*, the author of Samhain. If you are using GnuPG, you can search for and import this key by doing the following:

```
$ gpg --search-keys 0x0F571F6C
gpg: searching for "0x0F571F6C" from hkp server subkeys.pgp.net
(1)      Rainer Wichmann <rwichmann@la-samhna.de>
         Rainer Wichmann <rwichmann@hs.uni-hamburg.de>
           1024 bit DSA key 0F571F6C, created: 1999-10-31
Enter number(s), N)ext, or Q)uit > 1
gpg: requesting key 0F571F6C from hkp server subkeys.pgp.net
gpg: key 0F571F6C: public key "Rainer Wichmann <rwichmann@la-samhna.de>"
imported
gpg: 3 marginal(s) needed, 1 complete(s) needed, PGP trust model
gpg: depth: 0  valid:   1  signed:   0  trust: 0-, 0q, 0n, 0m, 0f, 1u
gpg: Total number processed: 1
gpg:                    imported: 1
```

Next, verify the fingerprint on the key:

```
$ gpg --fingerprint 0x0F571F6C
pub   1024D/0F571F6C 1999-10-31
      Key fingerprint = EF6C EF54 701A 0AFD B86A  F4C3 1AAD 26C8 0F57 1F6C
uid                    Rainer Wichmann <rwichmann@la-samhna.de>
uid                    Rainer Wichmann <rwichmann@hs.uni-hamburg.de>
sub   1024g/9DACAC30 1999-10-31
```

Once you have the correct key and have verified the signature, set its trust and then verify that the signature file matches the downloaded source. Assuming that the source and signature are in your current directory, use the following commands to trust the signing key and verify the Samhain source:

```
$ gpg --edit-key 0x0F571F6C
gpg (GnuPG) 1.4.1; Copyright (C) 2005 Free Software Foundation, Inc.
This program comes with ABSOLUTELY NO WARRANTY.
This is free software, and you are welcome to redistribute it
under certain conditions. See the file COPYING for details.



pub   1024D/0F571F6C   created: 1999-10-31   expires: never      usage: CSA
                       trust: unknown      validity: unknown
sub   1024g/9DACAC30   created: 1999-10-31   expires: never      usage: E
[ unknown] (1). Rainer Wichmann <rwichmann@la-samhna.de>
[ unknown] (2)  Rainer Wichmann <rwichmann@hs.uni-hamburg.de>


Command> trust
pub   1024D/0F571F6C   created: 1999-10-31   expires: never      usage: CSA
                       trust: unknown      validity: unknown
sub   1024g/9DACAC30   created: 1999-10-31   expires: never      usage: E
[ unknown] (1). Rainer Wichmann <rwichmann@la-samhna.de>
[ unknown] (2)  Rainer Wichmann <rwichmann@hs.uni-hamburg.de>


Please decide how far you trust this user to correctly verify other users'
keys
(by looking at passports, checking fingerprints from different sources,
etc.)


  1 = I don't know or won't say
  2 = I do NOT trust
  3 = I trust marginally
  4 = I trust fully
  5 = I trust ultimately
  m = back to the main menu

Your decision? 5
Do you really want to set this key to ultimate trust? (y/N) y

pub   1024D/0F571F6C   created: 1999-10-31   expires: never      usage: CSA
                       trust: ultimate     validity: unknown
sub   1024g/9DACAC30   created: 1999-10-31   expires: never      usage: E
[ unknown] (1). Rainer Wichmann <rwichmann@la-samhna.de>
```

```
[ unknown] (2)   Rainer Wichmann <rwichmann@hs.uni-hamburg.de>
Please note that the shown key validity is not necessarily correct
unless you restart the program.

Command> quit
$ gpg --verify samhain-2.0.5b.tar.gz.asc
gpg: Signature made Sat Apr  2 08:40:03 2005 MST using DSA key ID 0F571F6C
gpg: checking the trustdb
gpg: 3 marginal(s) needed, 1 complete(s) needed, PGP trust model
gpg: depth: 0  valid:   2  signed:   0  trust: 0-, 0q, 0n, 0m, 0f, 2u
gpg: Good signature from "Rainer Wichmann <rwichmann@la-samhna.de>"
gpg:                   aka "Rainer Wichmann <rwichmann@hs.uni-hamburg.de>"
```

NOTE

In the previous chapter, attention was given to the significance of verifying PGP keys when verifying the PGP signature of the Osiris source code. PGP signatures should not be blindly trusted. If the key you are using to verify a software signature is not trusted, all you are doing is verifying that *some* key was used to sign the software. The goal is to verify that it was signed using a key belonging to someone in particular. Even then, you have to trust that the person who signed it is trustworthy. In this case, the PGP fingerprint for the author of Samhain is printed in this book; however, even that is not completely foolproof. The common way to trust PGP keys is to exchange fingerprints in person, or to rely on the fact that someone you trust has signed the key in question.

Assuming the signature is good, you now have a trusted source on read-only media and are ready to begin setting up your build environment and to build Samhain from a trusted source. You do not have to verify the MD5 if you have verified the PGP signature.

Establishing a Samhain Build Environment

Building Samhain for stand-alone installations is useful because you can become familiar with the software and how to administer it before attempting a complicated client and server installation. When you are ready to start building agents for deployment, you will have to establish a build environment for each unique operating system and architecture type. Here, you are concerned only with a stand–alone installation, so if you are building on a test system, build and install Samhain on the same system. If you want to establish a dedicated build environment, you can make installer packages that can be installed onto your target system. In any case, the main requirements for building Samhain include a:

- POSIX environment
- American National Standards Institute (ANSI) C Compiler
- GnuPG

Samhain was developed with strict POSIX compliance in mind, the benefit being that it will likely run on any POSIX-compliant system ranging from the run-of-the-mill Linux and Solaris to less popular systems such as Minux or AIX. Samhain can be made to run on Windows, but only in an environment such as *Cygwin*. If you have a large Windows base, you may want to consider using Osiris.

Samhain requires an ANSI C Compiler. If you encounter any problems or have questions about building Samhain, you will be able to find help if you are using GCC (most people who use Samhain use GCC). For systems such as Solaris or IRIX, you will probably have other compilers in place; as long as they are ANSI compliant, you should have no problems.

GnuPG must be installed if you want to use the configuration and database file signing features that are part of Samhain. Samhain uses the GPG executable; there-fore, building the source in */usr/local/src* is not sufficient. At the very least, the GPG executable must be installed.

Once you have established a build environment or located the host that you will install Samhain on, copy your verified build source *tar.gz* file onto our system (e.g., */usr/local/src*) and unpack it:

```
$ tar xvfz samhain-2.0.5b.tar.gz
$ cd samhain-2.0.5b
```

Configuring Samhain

There are many configuration options for Samhain. First, run configure without any options:

```
$ ./configure
```

You will see the source configured for your system and a list of the default set-tings that will be used to build Samhain:

```
samhain has been configured as follows:
      System binaries: /usr/local/sbin
  Configuration file: /etc/samhainrc
        Manual pages: /usr/local/man
                Data: /var/lib/samhain
            PID file: /var/run/samhain.pid
            Log file: /var/log/samhain_log
            Base key: 814595996,541491316


  Selected rc file: samhainrc.linux
```

If you do not agree with any of these options, these (and others) can be changed via configure. You can run configure with any options that you want to use to reconfigure the source. Most of these options are fairly straightforward. The **Base** key is the key that will be embedded into the executable. It is actually a 64-bit key, but for programmatic reasons, it is listed as two numbers (two 32-bit integers). You can set the value for this key with a configure option. To see a listing of the available configure options, use the *--help* option:

```
$ ./configure --help
```

This will print standard information common to many configuration scripts, and will then print the information relevant to Samhain under the headings, "Optional Features" and "Optional Packages" (covered in more detail in the Centralized Management section of this chapter). Here, we are concerned with only the configuration options that affect a stand-alone deployment.

General Options

```
--with-rnd=egd|dev|unix
```

This option allows you to configure how the Samhain executable will acquire entropy for use in cryptographic operations. By default, Samhain will use */dev/random* (*dev*). If you want to use the Entropy Gathering Daemon (EGD) or the built-in UNIX entropy gatherer, specify EGD or UNIX here.

```
--with-egd-socket=PATH
```

If you are using EGD, you must specify the path to the EGD socket file (the default is */var/lib/samhain/entryopy*). EGD is a daemon designed specifically to collect entropy from the system. You can read about EGD by downloading it from http://egd.sourceforge.net.

```
--with-sender=EMAIL
```

This option can be used to configure the e-mail address to use as the sender of Samhain e-mail notifications. If only a username is given, the fully qualified domain name of the host is used. If no username is given, the daemon is used.

```
--with-recipient=EMAIL[,EMAIL…]
```

This option allows you to configure e-mail addresses to be sent to all Samhain e-mail notifications. If you specify more than one, separate them with commas or spaces. If you use spaces, make sure to use quotes. You can also specify this in the configuration file.

```
--with-trusted=UID[,UID…]
```

Samhain implements some security checks on the directory where the configuration file is stored. In the case of an agent, if the configuration file is stored in a directory where users other than root can write to, Samhain will not run. If you want to store the configuration file somewhere where other users have write access, you must specify those UIDs here (separate them by commas [e.g., *--with-trusted=501,502*]). You should almost always add "0" to this list of UIDs since the root user is almost always the owner of the path to the configuration file.

NOTE

Keep in mind how you will be running Samhain on your hosts, and what UIDs will need to be set there. This is a compile option and cannot be changed in the configuration file.

```
--with-timeserver=HOST
```

This allows you to specify a time-server to use; the default is to use the system clock. This option can be set in the configuration file.

```
--with-alttimeserver=HOST
```

Use this option to set a backup time-server in the event that the time-server is not responsive.

```
--enable-stealth=XOR
```

Samhain provides the ability to be installed and run in stealth mode. When enabled, it is much harder for an attacker to determine that Samhain is installed or running on the host. Specifically, this option enables the following:

- All of the strings in the Samhain executable are obfuscated with an XOR operation, using the argument specified with this configuration option.

- All log messages are obfuscated with an XOR operation, using the argument specified with this configuration option.

- All strings in the database file are obfuscated with an XOR operation, using the argument specified with this configuration option. In addition, you can append the database file to another file such as an image, to hide its existence.

- The configuration file is hidden in a postscript image file. The image cannot be compressed, and if this configuration option is used with signed configuration files, the configuration file must be signed before it is hidden. This can be accomplished automatically when you perform "make install" to install Samhain.

```
--enable-micro-stealth=XOR
```

This is the same as the aforementioned stealth option, except it does not require the configuration file to be embedded into an image file. In this case, XOR is the value that will be used to obfuscate strings in the executable, log messages, and strings in the database file.

> **WARNING**
>
> Unless you know exactly what you are doing and have justifiable reasons for doing so, do not enable stealth mode. You would complicate your deployment and make administration more of a burden by hiding the existence of Samhain from an attacker.

```
--enable-nocl=PASSWORD
```

This option enables a relatively interesting feature. The password specified as an argument to configure is used to control whether the Samhain executable acknowledges command-line arguments. If the password is given as the first argument, Samhain will read all other arguments from standard input; otherwise, if the password does not match, all other arguments are ignored. This allows the Samhain executable to look like it is running as something other than Samhain.

```
--enable-install-name=NAME
```

The name passed to this configuration option will be used to rename the database file and the executables. For example, if you specified *foo* instead of */var/log/samhain_log*, the file would be called */var/log/foo_log*. Likewise, the executables */usr/local/sbin/samhain* would be */usr/local/sbin/foo*. This is another way to further hide Samhain from being noticeable.

```
--enable-khide=SYSTEM_MAP
```

For x86-based Linux deployments, Samhain can build and install a kernel module that will hide various elements of Samhain from the system. The *SYSTEM_MAP* is the path to the *System.map* file that was created during the compilation of the Linux kernel (usually under the */boot* directory). It hides files containing the string Samhain or the name specified with the *--enable-install-name* configuration option. A second kernel module is then built to hide the *khide* module itself. For 2.6-based kernels, only one module is needed because the *khide* module is self-hiding.

TIP

It is not recommended that you use the configuration option for hiding files and kernel extensions unless you can provide solid justification. This is another feature that will probably be more trouble than it is worth. In this case, it is like a loaded gun under your pillow; it may seem like you are protecting yourself, but it can also be used against you. These modules hide kernel modules and files with a specific string in their name from the system. If this name is discovered, an attacker or malicious user can also hide other files from the system. Read all of the caveats in the Samhain documentation to get a better feel for what you will encounter if you use this option.

```
--enable-base=B1,B2
```

This configuration option allows you to specify the 64-bit key value that will be embedded into the Samhain executable. This is relevant for signing e-mail notifications and for all log messages. You can then use the executable to verify the authenticity of the e-mail or log data. The key is specified as two 32-bit numbers, separated only by a comma (e.g., --enable-base=814595996,541491316).

```
--enable-db-reload
```

When this configuration option is enabled, the agent loads the database file whenever it receives a SIGHUP signal. By default, only the configuration file is reloaded on receipt of this signal.

```
--enable-xml-log
```

This option turns Extensible Markup Language (XML) formatting on for all log messages:

```
--with-database=mysql|postgresql|oracle|odbc
```

Use this configuration option to enable logging to relational databases (only one can be specified). (This will not interest you if you are performing a stand-alone installation.)

```
--with-prelude
```

Prelude is a hybrid Integrated Decision Support (IDS) system that collects and correlates information from various systems into a single interface. This includes everything from Cisco devices to *syslog* daemons, as well as open source monitoring systems such as Samhain and Snort. To use this option, you must have the basic prelude library installed (*libprelude*).

```
--enable-debug
```

You should enable this only if you will be doing testing or troubleshooting an incident. This will slow down Samhain and produce more logging information. In addition, the Samhain agent will be allowed to produce core files.

```
--enable-ptrace
```

This is another Linux-specific option. When enabled, Samhain will periodically check whether a debugger is attached to the process. If a debugger is detected, the process will exit (unless *--enable-debug* is set).

```
--with-cflags=FLAGS
```

If you are a developer or are familiar with the process, you can use this option to pass additional compiler flags to the compilation process.

```
--with-libs=LIBS
```

Like the *cflags* option, this option is used to pass libraries that must be included in the link process.

Module Options

The following options are used to specify which modules the Samhain agent will use:

`--enable-login-watch`

Enabling this option allows you to monitor the login and logout events on the host.

`--enable-mounts-check`

Enabling this option allows you to monitor the various settings that are used when mounting your file systems.

`--enable-userfiles`

When enabled, the agent monitors certain files in users' home directories. The specifics for what files and which users must be configured in the configuration file under this module's settings.

`--enable-suidcheck`

This option enables the agent to perform SUID/SGID audits.

`--with-kcheck=SYSTEM_MAP`

This option allows Samhain to monitor the kernel for Linux and FreeBSD systems. The *SYSTEM_MAP* is the path to the *System.map* file that corresponds to the running kernel.

GnuPG Signing Options

The following options apply to using GnuPG to OpenPGP sign configurations and database files:

`--with-gpg=PATH`

This option turns on GnuPG to sign databases and configuration files. The argument must be the full path to the GPG executable. The GnuPG key used will be the public key of the effective user that the Samhain executable is running as (usually root).

`--with-checksum=CHECKSUM`

This option provides the TIGER checksum of the GPG executable. It embeds the GPG checksum into the Samhain executable so that it can perform a check on the executable before executing it. TIGER is a hash algorithm that produces a 192-bit key. The value specified must be the output from the following command:

```
$ samhain -H /usr/local/bin/gpg
/usr/local/bin/gpg: 166FC24A D16E4661 EC760122  DDB81374 10CB98F8 D323ED2E
```

In this case, you would use the following configuration argument:

```
--with-checksum="166FC24A D16E4661 EC760122 DDB81374 10CB98F8 D323ED2E"
```

If configuring Samhain for the first time, you will not have a Samhain executable. To get around this, use GnuPG to generate the TIGER checksum. (Note that you have to compile GnuPG with the *--enable-tiger=yes* configuration option, because it is not included by default.) Compute the TIGER checksum of the GPG executable as follows:

```
$ gpg --load-extension tiger --print-md TIGER192 /usr/local/bin/gpg
```

In both cases, use the output exactly as it is produced, including spaces.

NOTE

As of GnuPG v.1.2.2, support for the Tiger/192 hash algorithm was disabled by default, and eventually removed from the GnuPG source code. This makes using this configuration option problematic. If you still want to use GnuPG, we recommend not using this option; if you do, you will probably have to build Samhain, use it to compute the Tiger checksum, and reconfigure it accordingly.

```
--with-fp=FINGERPRINT
```

This is an extra safety precaution. If you specify the GnuPG fingerprint for the key with this argument, it will be compiled into the Samhain executable. Samhain will then verify the fingerprint before using the key. It is up to you whether or not you include the spaces in the key fingerprint; it does not make any difference. Here is an example of how to get your GnuPG key fingerprint:

```
$ gpg --fingerprint
/Users/brian/.gnupg/pubring.gpg
-------------------------------
pub    1024D/9674763D 1999-11-10
       Key fingerprint = FBBA B237 EF74 19F1 AC2F  8C0F 0DEC 799E 9674 763D
uid                    Brian Wotring <brian@shmoo.com>
uid                    Brian Wotring <brian@fortnocs.com>
uid                    Brian Wotring <brian@metasecura.com>
uid                    Brian Wotring <brian@hostintegrity.com>
```

Your key value will be different, but as an example, specify the key fingerprint with the following configuration option: *--with-fp= FBBA B237 EF74 19F1 AC2F 8C0F 0DEC 799E 9674 763D*.

You may not need to use many of these configuration options, but it helps to be familiar with them so that you know what Samhain is capable of. Configuration is a big part of Samhain deployment; you should take the time to consider how they match up to what you are attempting to achieve with your Samhain deployment. If you are overwhelmed by these options, you can run configure without any arguments.

For the FreeBSD stand-alone deployment, enable the file system mount check, the SUID auditing, and monitoring the kernel. For FreeBSD systems, you do not have to specify the system map file, just the configure argument. For Linux systems, you have to specify the path to the kernel symbol map file (e.g., *--with-kcheck=/boot/System.map-2.4.20*). For FreeBSD, run configure as follows:

```
$ ./configure --enable-mounts-check --enable-suidcheck --with-kcheck
```

This runs through the configuration process and determines the correct settings for your system. When finished, you should see something similar to the following:

```
samhain has been configured as follows:
          System binaries:  /usr/local/sbin
       Configuration file:  /etc/samhainrc
            Manual pages:   /usr/local/man
                    Data:   /var/lib/samhain
                PID file:   /var/run/samhain.pid
                Log file:   /var/log/samhain_log
                Base key:   275284074,278527851


          Selected rc file:  samhainrc.freebsd
```

Your base key will be different.

Building Samhain

Once you have configured Samhain, you have to build the Samhain agent. The Samhain source is relatively small; therefore, on modern hardware, compiling should take less than one minute:

```
$ make
```

After the agent has been built, you can optionally build an installer package for your system. Unfortunately, there is no package installer for FreeBSD. If you are installing on Linux or Solaris, you can use one of the *make* arguments shown in Table 7.1 to make various package types.

Table 7.1 make arguments for Building Installer Packagers on Linux or Solaris

Package Type	make argument
Debian Package	deb
RPM	rpm
Gentoo (tbz2)	tbz2
Solaris	solaris-pkg

For example, to build a Linux rpm package, do the following:

```
$ make rpm
```

Installing Samhain

The next step is to install the Samhain documentation, agent, configuration file, init scripts, and directories. To do so, you must run *make* with the *install* argument as root:

```
# make install
 /usr/bin/install -c -s -m 700 samhain /usr/local/sbin/samhain
 ./sstrip /usr/local/sbin/samhain
/bin/sh ./mkinstalldirs /usr/local/man/man8
/bin/sh ./mkinstalldirs /usr/local/man/man5
  /usr/bin/install -c -m 644 ./man/samhain.8 /usr/local/man/man8/samhain.8
  /usr/bin/install -c -m 644 ./man/samhainrc.5
/usr/local/man/man5/samhainrc.5
gcc  -DHAVE_CONFIG_H -I. -I./include  -O2 -Wall -W  -fno-strength-reduce -
fno-omit-frame-pointer -DSH_STANDALONE -DSH_IDENT=\"daemon\" -DTRUST_MAIN -
DSL_ALWAYS_TRUSTED=0 -o trustfile ./src/trustfile.c
mkdir /var/lib
mkdir /var/lib/samhain
./samhain-install.sh --destdir= --express --verbose install-data
  cp samhainrc.freebsd samhainrc
  cp samhainrc samhainrc.pre
  mv -f samhainrc.pre samhainrc.install
  ./samhain-install.sh --install-sh  -m 600 samhainrc.install
/etc/samhainrc
  checking whether paths are trustworthy
  configuration file /etc/samhainrc ... OK
  state directory /var/run ... OK
  state directory /var/log ... OK
```

```
data directory /var/lib/samhain ... OK
```

Next, install the init scripts, which will enable Samhain to start when the system is booted. As root, use the following command to install the proper init scripts:

```
# make install-boot
./samhain-install.sh --destdir= --express --verbose install-boot
  FreeBSD system detected
  ./samhain-install.sh --install-sh -m 700  init/samhain.startFreeBSD
/usr/local/etc/rc.d/samhain
  mv /usr/local/etc/rc.d/samhain /usr/local/etc/rc.d/samhain.sh &&  chmod
755 /usr/local/etc/rc.d/samhain.sh
installing init scripts completed
```

This will install an init script in */usr/local/etc/rc.d/*, the preferred location for these files on FreeBSD systems. If you are installing on Linux, it will probably be installed under the */etc/init.d* directory.

Configuring Samhain

After Samhain has been installed, look over the configuration file to see what it is monitoring. For systems including FreeBSD, Linux, AIX, and Solaris, the installation process automatically copies a reasonable default configuration file into */etc/samhainrc*. You can run just this configuration; however, you should at least set up some reasonable defaults for e-mail notification and such. The main items to configure in this file include what should be monitored and how the administrator should be notified.

The Samhain configuration file consists of groups, called *policies*. In addition, there is a section for each module. In this case, we have enabled three modules: SUID/SGID checks, file system mount point checks, and kernel integrity checks. Each module has settings that dictate how often to scan, and what to involve in that part of the scan.

Configuration Policies

One nice attribute of Samhain is its ability to specify what needs to be monitored through security policies. Basically, some files should remain static in all aspects (e.g., executables). On the other hand, log files continually change in their content, size, and time stamps, but they should rarely (if ever) change ownership or permissions. It makes sense to define policies and then add the files you want to monitor under the appropriate policy.

Each policy is noted in the configuration file with square brackets (e.g., [ReadOnly]). To specify files and directories, use the *dir* and *file* directives. Always specify the full path to files. For example:

```
file = /bin/ls
```

Directories require full paths and are specified in a similar manner:

```
dir = /bin
```

By default, directories are not monitored recursively. To specify that a directory be monitored recursively, prepend a recursive depth to the beginning of the path in the form *[N]/path/to/dir*. For example, to scan two directories deep into */usr/local*, use the following directive:

```
dir = 2/usr/local
```

The maximum recursion depth is 99. If you want to scan an entire directory tree recursively, do the following:

```
dir = 99/usr/local
```

Both the *file* and *dir* directives must be absolute paths; however, you can use file *globbing* to specify multiple files or directory paths. For example, to get all files beginning with *rc* under the */etc* directory, you would use the following file directive:

```
file = /etc/rc*
```

Samhain supports the following monitoring policies.

[ReadOnly]

For all files under this policy, all attributes will be monitored, except access time stamps. This is the policy where you want to place your executables and library files.

[LogFiles]

This policy ignores time stamps, file size, and checksums. All other attributes are monitored.

[GrowingLogFiles]

This policy is the same as the LogFiles policy except it generates alerts for files that decrease in size. This is a stricter policy; the basic idea is that log files should not decrease in size, only increase. A decrease in size could indicate a compromise or that an attacker is attempting to cover their tracks by removing the log messages. However, logs files are rotated and sometimes do legitimately decrease in size; that is why there are two policies. If you have the ability to be mindful of your log rotations and correlate these two events, use this policy; otherwise, it is best to avoid false positives and use the LogFiles policy.

[Attributes]

Under this policy modifications of user and group ownership and file permissions are monitored for files.

[IgnoreAll]

This policy ignores all changes to files. However, it generates reports when files are added or go missing.

[IgnoreNone]

This policy monitors all of the attributes of the file (including access time) except for the change time stamp. It is difficult to monitor both the access time and the change time, because monitoring the file attributes resets the access time and resetting the access time involves modifying the time. This is similar to the ReadOnly policy except that instead of access time, the change time is ignored. Use this only where you want to specifically monitor the access time stamp of the file.

[User0] and [User1]

These are user-defined policies. By default, they are configured to monitor all modifications to files under this policy. You can change the meanings of these and other policies (described later in this chapter). There are only two user-specified policies.

[Prelink]

This policy exists solely for monitoring prelinked files on Linux systems. This policy ignores modifications to time stamps, file size, and inodes (all of the attributes that can change as a result of a prelinking update). In addition, the checksums of files are computed by using the prelink executable to perform the verify operation (described in detail in Chapter 9, "Advanced Strategies").

Understanding the Configuration Sections

The following is a brief description of each of the sections you will encounter in a Samhain configuration file.

[Misc]

The Misc section contains various configuration options for Samhain. One thing to note is that this section allows you to redefine some of the default policy meanings. To be effective, you must first specify these redefinitions in the configuration file. The redefinition involves providing a list of attributes to add or remove from the monitoring process (Use the "+"to add monitoring for specific attributes and use the "-"to remove monitoring for specific attributes.) Table 7.2 lists the valid codes to use when specifying a policy modification rule:

Table 7.2 Valid Codes to Use when Specifying Policy Modification Rules

CODE	Attribute
CHK	Checksum
LNK	Symbolic Link
HLN	Hard Link
INO	Inode
USR	User
GRP	Group
MTM	mtime
ATM	atime
CTM	ctime
SIZ	File Size
RDEV	Device Number
MOD	File Permissions (mode)

For example, to modify the ReadOnly policy to not include checks to exclude monitoring device numbers, use the following rule in the Misc section of the Samhain configuration file:

```
RedefReadOnly=-RDEV
```

To remove monitoring of *ctime* from the User0 policy use:

```
RedefUser0=-CTM
```

The next sections of the configuration file are typically the policy sections. Basically, you add files that make sense to each section (e.g., log files to the LogFiles policy, executables and libraries to the ReadOnly policy, and so on). The defaults are helpful, so start with those and then adjust them as needed to satisfy your monitoring requirements.

[EventSeverity]

This configuration section allows you to configure severities to policy violations (e.g., if an executable in the ReadOnly section is modified and the checksum changes, you can decide how severe of an event it is). This becomes powerful when you consider that you can provide thresholds for certain logging facilities so that only severities of a certain level generate alerts. Thus, you can essentially eliminate noise and redirect the most critical of events to the appropriate logging outlets. Table 7.3 (taken from the Samhain documentation) shows the list of event severities.

Table 7.3 Event Severities

Level	Significance
None	Not logged
Debug	Debugging-level messages
Info	Informational message
Notice	Normal conditions
Warn	Warning conditions
Mark	Time stamps
Err	Error conditions
Crit	Critical conditions
Alert	Program startup/normal exit, or fatal error, causing abnormal program termination
Inet	Incoming messages from clients (server only)

For example, to set the ReadOnly violations to only be warnings, add the following line under the EventSeverity section of the Samhain configuration file:

```
SeverityReadOnly=warn
```

Basically, just prepend the word "Severity" to the policy name and assign it a value. The order of these severities is not important. In addition to policy violations, you can assign event severities to the following events:

- File access errors (*SeverityFiles*)

- Directory access errors (*SeverityDirs*)

- Obscure file names (*SeverityNames*)

You can also set severity levels for login and logout events; however, that must be done in that module's configuration section.

[Log]

This section of the configuration file allows you to specify the various logging outlets and their severity thresholds. If an event is equal to or above a logging facility's threshold, that event is logged to that logging facility. To turn off a logging facility, set it to **none**. For example, the following configuration has mail logging turned off, will log all events to the console, and will log events to *syslog* if they are at least warnings:

```
MailSeverity=none
PrintSeverity=*
SyslogSeverity=warn
```

Table 7.4 lists the available logging outlets.

Table 7.4 Logging Outlets

Log Outlet	Description
MailSeverity	E-mail notifications
LogSeverity	Log files.
PrintSeverity	Console
SyslogSeverity	Syslog
PreludeSeverity	Prelude IDS system
ExportSeverity	Logs sent to the Log Server
ExternalSeverity	External program
DatabaseSeverity	External Relational Database Server

In addition, you can specify that certain system calls be logged. The only outlets available include *syslog* and the console. Specify which system calls you want logged with the following:

```
LogCalls=<calls>
```

Calls should be a comma-separated list of system calls on your system that you want to monitor. For example:

```
LogCalls=open,kill
```

Most of these logging outlets are disabled by default. Valid system calls include *execve, utime, unlink, dup (+ dup2), chdir, open, kill, exit (+ _exit), fork, setuid, setgid,* and *pipe.* Be careful when specifying these calls, and mindful of the impact a rule like this can have on disk space and, more importantly, processor usage.

[Misc]

Next, the configuration file contains various sections specific to logging outlets and modules. At the very end of the configuartion file, you will see a large number of miscellanious configuration settings. Some of the most important ones are as follows:

```
Daemon=yes
```

This tells Samhain to fork into the background and run as a daemon unless explicitly told otherwise by the *--forground* command-line option. The only time this is ignored is during the creation of the baseline database (initialization). Set this to **no** if you do not want Samhain to run as a daemon.

```
ChecksumTest=check
```

This option dictates whether or not Samhain will update, check, or initialize a database. This option is best kept to "check" for stand-alone deployments. Setting to none requires the user to specify what they want to happen on the command line.

```
SetFileCheckTime = 7200
```

This is the time period in seconds between file monitoring checks. Setting it to 7200 means that the Samhain agent will wake up every 2 hours and check the file system.

```
ReportOnlyOnce = True
```

Samhain maintains a copy of violations in memory so that subsequent scans do no report on the same violations. If you set this to **false**, all violations will be reported on each check. This is not recommended, as it will produce a great deal of noise.

Stand-Alone Configuration

The Samhain configuration file can be complicated, so it is important to strive towards simplicity; otherwise, you could end up with a great deal of false positives and false negatives. In our case, we are concerned with a basic stand-alone deployment, so the default configuration is created during installation and then adjusted to turn on and configure the modules to reasonable values. Open the configuration file in an editor such as *vi* (as root):

```
# vi /etc/samhainrc
```

First, comment out the directories that do not exist on your system. Take a look through the policies and verify that each directory and file exists. In the case of a typical FreeBSD 5.3 installation, you will have to comment out the following lines:

```
#dir=/stand/modules
#dir=/var/spool/lp/tmp
#file=/kernel
#dir=/modules
#dir=/usr/X11R6/man
#file=/usr/compat/linux/etc
#file=/usr/compat/linux/etc/ld.so.cache
```

Next, locate the [SuidCheck] module section. Using the following configuration, adjust the configuration so that it is active, it monitors the SUID/SGID files every Sunday at 4:00 P.M., and it warns about SUID/SGID files:

```
[SuidCheck]
SuidCheckActive = yes
SuidCheckSchedule = 0 16 * * Sun
SeveritySuidCheck = crit
SuidCheckQuarantineFiles = no
```

Next, find the [Kern] section of the configuration file and activate it to run every 5 minutes with the following configuration:

```
[Kernel]
KernelCheckActive = True
KernelCheckInterval = 300
SeverityKernel = info
```

The default FreeBSD configuration does not have a *mounts* section; therefore, add one after the [Kern] section. First, find out what file systems are being mounted. You can easily find this by printing the contents of the *fstab* file:

```
#   cat   /etc/fstab
#   Device       Mountpoint     FStype     Options      Dump     Pass#
/dev/ad0s1b      none           swap       sw           0        0
/dev/ad0s1a      /              ufs        rw           1        1
/dev/acd0        /cdrom         cd9660     ro,noauto     0        0
```

In this case, there is only a "/" single file system If you have more, add those options as well. In this case, add the following to the Samhain configuration file:

```
[Mounts]
MountCheckActive=1
MountCheckInterval=7200
SeverityMountMissing=warn
SeverityOptionMissing=warn
checkmount=/
```

Once all of the aforementioned elements have been added to the configuration file, save it.

Creating a Baseline with Samhain

Now that Samhain is installed and the configuration file is set up, initialize the baseline database. Ideally, you will do this offline, before the host is ever connected to a network. However, this is not always possible. Create the baseline database with the following command:

```
# /usr/local/sbin/samhain -t init
```

The *-t* flag specifies the type of scan, which can be either initialization, check, or update. Since you are creating the baseline, use the initialization type. At any time, you can run a check against the database and the current system state by using the *check* test. The *update* command updates the database with the current system state. The **preceding** command prints a great deal of information to the console as it creates the baseline database. You will see a final message about Samhain exiting:

```
ALERT   :  [2005-04-23T14:36:13-0600] msg=<EXIT>, program=<Samhain>,
status=<None>
```

Although this seems alarming, it is normal; it means that Samhain has exited. After this command, the baseline is created and stored in the */var/lib/samhain/samhain_file* by default. You should never run Samhain in initialization mode again. Doing so will append the created baseline to this file and it will be ignored by subsequent checks. If you ever want to recreate the baseline, remove the */var/lib/samhain/samhain_file* file (or rename it) and run the preceding command again to create the new baseline.

Tuning Samhain

Now that the baseline is established, run a check on the system to see if there are any configuration problems. Run a check against the database with the following command:

```
# /usr/local/sbin/samhain -t check -p warn --foreground
```

You must run with *--foreground*, otherwise, Samhain will become a daemon process. You want to see the output to see if there are any errors in your policy. If there are errors, they should be labeled as *policy warnings* and provide meaningful output of what the problem is (e.g., missing files or directories). In cases where you do not see any problems, the check should look something like the following:

```
# /usr/local/sbin/samhain -t check -p warn --foreground
ALERT   :   [2005-04-23T14:56:08-0600] msg=<START>, program=<Samhain>,
userid=<0>, path=</etc/samhainrc>,
hash=<D35F502AA0E9264DBD4A4021DCB58550E4A2B61DE7E28AE5>,
path=</var/lib/samhain/samhain_file>,
hash=<6236062364D2F76F3551B241F55F817AB36220216492D1DD>
ALERT   :   [2005-04-23T14:56:09-0600] msg=<EXIT>, program=<Samhain>,
status=<None>
```

The *-p* flag takes an argument for the console severity threshold. In this case, you do not care about informative messages; you only want to see anything above or equal to warnings.

Configuring Notifications

Now it is time to set up e-mail notifications regarding changes. Our policy is pretty simple; we can safely enable e-mail notifications with just a few tweaks to the configuration file. With Samhain, you have to be careful because, by default, e-mail notifications are problematic; each alert is sent in its own e-mail message.

The first thing to do is open the configuration file and enable the mail log severity. In this case, we set the threshold severity to warn; by default, it is disabled:

```
MailSeverity=warn
```

Next, set the e-mail address target. You can comma-separate them (maximum of eight) by putting each additional address on a separate line. Initially, set it to a single administrator until the system is known to be stable and working as expected:

```
SetMailAddress=admin@example.com
```

If you have to use a mail relay, set the following field to be your mail server; otherwise, Samhain will use the built-in Mail Transport Agent (MTA):

```
SetMailRelay = mail.example.com
```

Run another check to see if your notifications are working:

```
# /usr/local/sbin/samhain -t check -p warn –foreground
```

Samhain detects a change in the checksum of the configuration file and reports on it (*/etc/samhainrc* was updated with mail settings, which is a legitimate change). You should receive a notification that looks something like the following:

```
From: <daemon@example.com>
To: <admin@example.com>
Date: Sat, 23 Apr 2005 15:11:16 MDT
Subject: [2005-04-23T15:11:15-0600] localhost
```

```
-----BEGIN MESSAGE-----
[2005-04-23T15:11:15-0600] localhost
CRIT    :   [2005-04-23T15:11:15-0600] msg=<POLICY [ReadOnly] C-------TS>,
path=</etc/samhainrc>, size_old=<13012>, size_new=<13024>, ctime_old=<[2005-
04-23T20:55:39]>, ctime_new=<[2005-04-23T21:10:48]>, mtime_old=<[2005-04-
23T20:54:46]>, mtime_new=<[2005-04-23T21:10:48]>,
chksum_old=<D35F502AA0E9264DBD4A4021DCB58550E4A2B61DE7E28AE5>,
chksum_new=<B59CEE1499D9C6D99915B52B27232AB58CD413D8C7C2744D>,
-----BEGIN SIGNATURE-----
7EDFC17FFA75F70EA7825158D3913BC80DCF486EE4911847
000002 1114290673::localhost
-----END MESSAGE-----
```

Responding to Change

The point of monitoring the integrity of your host is to detect changes. At some point, you will inevitably have to deal with updating your baseline database(s).

For your stand-alone installation, you want to run Samhain in "update" mode. In the previous example, changes were made to the Samhain configuration file, which resulted in the baseline having a different checksum for that file. Those changes were made; therefore, it was a legitimate change and it makes sense to update the database with the current information about that file. To do this, run Samhain with the following arguments:

```
$ /usr/local/sbin/samhain -t update --interactive
```

This will force an interactive update session to the database. You should do this so that you can make sure that it is the only change going into the database. You do not have to specify foreground; Samhain never does updates in the background. You will be prompted to accept the change:

```
CRIT    :   [2005-04-23T15:28:08-0600] msg=<POLICY [ReadOnly] C-------TS>,
path=</etc/samhainrc>, size_old=<13012>, size_new=<13019>, ctime_old=<[2005-
04-23T20:55:39]>, ctime_new=<[2005-04-23T21:20:02]>, mtime_old=<[2005-04-
23T20:54:46]>, mtime_new=<[2005-04-23T21:20:02]>,
chksum_old=<D35F502AA0E9264DBD4A4021DCB58550E4A2B61DE7E28AE5>,
chksum_new=<48141D8599C46914C98A1AEDF363E33911459CF471A8DC63>,
Update /etc/samhainrc [Y/n] ?
```

The database is updated. Verify this by running another check:

```
# /usr/local/sbin/samhain -t check -p warn --foreground
```

```
ALERT   :   [2005-04-23T15:31:00-0600] msg=<START>, program=<Samhain>,
userid=<0>, path=</etc/samhainrc>,
hash=<48141D8599C46914C98A1AEDF363E33911459CF471A8DC63>,
path=</var/lib/samhain/samhain_file>,
hash=<DE472D90B7B20939939A8123593C5D6A8919AA5D052BADE2>
ALERT   :   [2005-04-23T15:31:02-0600] msg=<EXIT>, program=<Samhain>,
status=<None>
```

The baseline is now in sync with the state of the system. You are ready to start Samhain as a daemon and let it do what it does best: monitor the integrity of your system.

Running Samhain

When Samhain was installed, the init scripts were also installed. If you rebooted your system, Samhain would automatically start up as a daemon and periodically monitor your system. However, rebooting is not a practical option; therefore, Samhain can be started as a daemon using the init script with the *start* argument:

```
# /usr/local/etc/rc.d/samhain.sh start
 samhain#
```

You should see "samhain#." Verify that Samhain is running as a daemon by doing the following on FreeBSD (this command varies for each system):

```
# ps -A | grep samhain
35852   ??   S        0:01.22 /usr/local/sbin/samhain -D
```

How do you know that Samhain is running? Tail the Samhain log file:

```
# tail -f /var/log/samhain_log
```

According to the previous configuration, files will be monitored every two hours; however, Samhain is also monitoring the state of the kernel every 5 minutes. The kernel check will show up in this log file within a few minutes.

At this point, Samhain is installed in a stand-alone configuration. All logs and scan data are stored on the host that is being monitored. Administration requires that you login to that host and perform database updates whenever changes are detected. Samhain will not report on the same changes twice; however, if the system is rebooted or the agent restarted, you will be inundated with all of the differences between the system and the baseline. It is best to keep your baseline database updated.

Uninstalling Samhain

When building from source, not many open source software applications provide the ability to easily uninstall. Samhain does. You can uninstall Samhain by changing to the original source directory and typing (as root):

```
# make uninstall
```

This command removes everything except the Samhain configuration file and log files. If you want to remove the configuration file, use the following:

```
# make purge
```

This runs the *make uninstall* process and removes the Samhain configuration file (usually */etc/samhainrc*). Finally, to uninstall the init scripts, do the following:

```
# make uninstall-boot
```

If you have removed the source or installed it via a package, Samhain can be uninstalled using the supplied uninstall script, *samhain-install.sh*. For example, to uninstall do:

```
# ./samhain-install.sh purge
```

To uninstall the init scripts:

```
# ./samhain-install.sh uninstall-boot
```

Deploying Samhain
with Centralized Management

Samhain provides a server known as "Yule," that provides for the centralized management of logs, scan data, and configuration files. Stand-alone deployments versus centrally managed deployments require that you configure, build, and install Samhain differently. That is, even if you already have some stand-alone deployments of Samhain, you must rebuild the agents and reinstall Samhain in order for them to use the Yule server. In the same way that you can over-complicate your stand-alone deployment, you can do the same with Yule and centrally managed Samhain agents.

This section discusses how to establish a simple and effective centralized Samhain deployment. We will install Yule on a FreeBSD system and use Postgresql as a database server that will store all of the log data collected from the Samhain agents. To keep the commands from becoming confusing, prompts have been established: the monitored host will be *agent#* and the prompts on the Yule server will be *yule#*.

Overview of Yule

Yule is a server that is responsible for maintaining trusted communications with Samhain agents by storing their configuration files, scan data, and logs. Yule requires that the Samhain agents authenticate with a key embedded in the agent executables. This means that if you establish a Yule server and then install Samhain from a binary package or some type of ports tree, they will not be compatible without performing additional steps to reset the key. This makes for more of a deployment effort, but also forces you to deploy a more secured system.

Notes from the Underground...

Centralized Management of Configuration and Scan Data

If you want Yule to act as a centralized store for your host's scan configuration files and baseline database, you will have to compile the Samhain agents yourself. These options cannot be specified in the configuration file. Samhain can be compiled to use a local path for the configuration file as a backup, but if you want the agent to request the configuration file and scan data from the server, you must use special configure options to hard-code this functionality into the agent.

Yule is first and foremost a log server. You can choose not to have configuration files and scan databases stored by Yule, in which case, Yule would just be used as a centralized log server. Yule can log to all of the same logging outlets that Samhain can, only it manages streams of logs coming from remote Samhain agents, verifies them, and signs them. Yule is not much different than Samhain in the sense that it is built from the same source and does not monitor the host. The locations for configuration files, database files, logs, and the format of the configuration file are all the same.

Yule can also act as a minimal console for Samhain agents by writing Hypertext Markup Language (HTML) files locally for administrators to view the status of each agent and some statistics about connections for managed agents. For more information about monitored hosts, use Beltane, the Web-based console (covered in the next section).

Yule can also be used to send messages to agents in a limited fashion. Since the agent always initiates communication to the Yule server, agents do not listen on a network port. Thus, it is not possible to send messages to the agents in real time. However, messages can be queued so that the next time the agent connects to the server, it is given the message. Yule can send two kinds of messages: RELOAD and STOP. The RELOAD message tells the agent to reload its configuration file. The STOP message tells the agent to shut down. The only way to send these messages to the agent is through a separate command-line application called *yulectl*. The *yulectl* executable is built as part of the Yule compilation process.

Figure 7.1 illustrates the functionality provided by the Yule log server in a centrally managed Samhain deployment.

Figure 7.1 Functionality Provided by the Yule Log Server

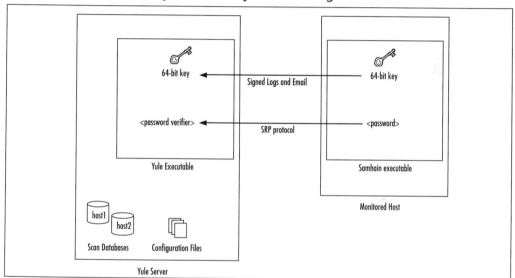

Build Environments

It is recommended that you establish a separate build and test environment, and that you establish a Yule server and some test hosts to become familiar with how the process works and how to administer Samhain in a centralized deployment scenario. Once you understand how things work, you will be better prepared to establish a solid centrally managed Samhain deployment in your production environment. Plan to dedicate a host specifically to the Yule server. Ideally, this host will run nothing but Yule, and possibly a relational database server. If you want to use the Beltane console, you have to run a Web server; however, there are obvious risks involved. You need to determine if the benefits associated with the Web-based console outweigh the risks.

The build requirements for Yule are the same as with the Samhain agents. Specifically, you need a:

- POSIX Environment
- ANSI C Compiler
- Gnu Privacy Guard (GnuPG)
- Database Server (Postgresql, MySQL, Oracle, or Open Database Connectivity (ODBC) Compliant)

GnuGP is a requirement only if you have to have your configuration files and database files cryptographically signed. The database server is only a requirement if you want to store your logs in a database. If you are monitoring many hosts, it makes sense to put them into a database. Configuring Samhain to do this is easy and makes sense for large-scale deployments. If you do not want to do this, you can skip the related steps; the configuration options that are only used for the database will also be explained.

You can build your Yule server and your Samhain agents on the same host and from the same source tree. If you need to build Samhain agents for multiple operating systems, you must build an environment for each unique operating system and architecture type.

Installing and Configuring Postgresql

Postgresql is the chosen database server to store all of the received log data; however, MySQL or some other database can also be used. The general idea is the same: install the database environment, create a database for Samhain, and establish the schema from the template provided in the Samhain source. (If you are not interested in storing logs in a database, feel free to skip this section.)

Installing Postgresql on FreeBSD is simple if ports are installed. Otherwise, it is relatively easy to build from source. Change to the ports directory and, as root, run *make install* to install the Postgresql port:

```
yule# cd /usr/ports/databases/postgresql73
yule# make install
```

This will take a few minutes, depending on your hardware configuration and how many dependencies you already have installed. Alternatively, if you are on a Linux system and you use the *yum* system, you can install Postgresql by doing something like the following (as root):

```
yule# yum install postgresql
```

If you do not have a ports system, of if you are not using yum on Linux, it is suggested that you build Postgresql from source. Once you have downloaded and unpacked the source, the well-known process is:

```
yule# ./configure
yule# make
yule# make install
```

Once you have installed Postgresql, make sure it is initialized. Each port may vary in how Postgresql is installed. You will probably be informed of what you need to do to start the database; it may already be initialized. To see if Postgresql is running, use the init script. On FreeBSD, do this with the following command:

```
yule# /usr/local/etc/rc.d/010.pgsql.sh status
pg_ctl: postmaster or postgres is not running
```

To see if Postgresql has been initialized as part of your installation, look in the *pgsql* directory for a directory called *data*. On FreeBSD, verify this by doing:

```
yule# ls /usr/local/pgsql
dot.cshrc.dist          dot.profile.dist          post-install-notes
```

In this case, it has not been initialized; therefore, it is initialized (as root) with the following command:

```
yule# su -l pgsql -c initdb
The files belonging to this database system will be owned by user "pgsql".
This user must also own the server process.

The database cluster will be initialized with locale C.

creating directory /usr/local/pgsql/data... ok
creating directory /usr/local/pgsql/data/base... ok
creating directory /usr/local/pgsql/data/global... ok
creating directory /usr/local/pgsql/data/pg_xlog... ok
creating directory /usr/local/pgsql/data/pg_clog... ok
creating template1 database in /usr/local/pgsql/data/base/1... ok
creating configuration files... ok
initializing pg_shadow... ok
enabling unlimited row size for system tables... ok
initializing pg_depend... ok
creating system views... ok
loading pg_description... ok
```

```
creating conversions... ok
setting privileges on built-in objects... ok
vacuuming database template1... ok
copying template1 to template0... ok


Success. You can now start the database server using:

    /usr/local/bin/postmaster -D /usr/local/pgsql/data
or
    /usr/local/bin/pg_ctl -D /usr/local/pgsql/data -l logfile start
```

The commands suggested by the port can be used, but you might as well start Postgresql with the installed init script:

```
yule# /usr/local/etc/rc.d/010.pgsql.sh start
 pgsql
yule#
```

Now, verify that it is running:

```
yule# /usr/local/etc/rc.d/010.pgsql.sh status
pg_ctl: postmaster is running (pid: 745)
Command line was:
/usr/local/bin/postmaster
```

Next, create a database and populate some tables using a schema that Yule will expect and use. First, create the Samhain database using the Postgresql command *createdb*; call it "samhain":

```
yule# sudo -u pgsql /usr/local/bin/createdb samhain
CREATE DATABASE
```

Now, create a user for this database called "samhain":

```
yule# sudo -u pgsql /usr/local/bin/createuser samhain
Shall the new user be allowed to create databases? (y/n) n
Shall the new user be allowed to create more new users? (y/n) n
CREATE USER
```

> **NOTE**
>
> The user created here is a Postgresql user, not a system user. This is generally done to limit users who connect to the database, to certain databases, or to parts of databases. In this case, we are creating a database for Samhain, and only the Samhain user created will have access to this database. Locking down a database such as Postgresql is not a simple task. Read the "Security" section of the Postgresql manual for tips on how to harden the security of your database.

Finally, create the tables within the Samhain database. Fortunately, the Samhain source contains a script specific for Postgresql that can be used to populate the database. By default, the Samhain user does not have access to the log table, so it must be added to the script. Assuming that you have unpacked the Samhain source in */usr/local/src*, navigate to the source and, using the *psql* command, redirect the contents of the *samhain.postgres.init* file:

```
yule$ cd /usr/local/src/samhain-2.0.5b
yule$ cd sql_init/
yule$ echo "GRANT SELECT ON log TO samhain;" >> ./samhain.postgres.init
yule$ sudo -u pgsql /usr/local/bin/psql -d samhain <
./samhain.postgres.init
CREATE SEQUENCE
CREATE TABLE
CREATE INDEX
CREATE INDEX
CREATE INDEX
CREATE INDEX
GRANT
GRANT
GRANT
```

The database is set up and Yule can send data to it. This database could be established on another host, but it is not recommended. Samhain has no native way to protect the information once it leaves the host that the Yule server is running on. If it must be sent to another host, steps must be taken to secure the privacy of the log data. Technically, the integrity of the log data can be verified because the Samhain agents and the Yule server sign them; however, that does not prevent an attacker or eavesdropper from monitoring that data.

Configuring Yule

Configuring Yule source code is the same process as for configuring a Samhain agent. The major difference is that you must use configure the argument *--enable-network=server* to tell the build system that you will be building Yule, not Samhain. Likewise, you need to configure all Samhain agents with *--enable-network=client* to tell Samhain that it will be communicating with a Yule server, and not in stand-alone mode. All of the configuration options listed in the previous section except for the enabling of modules, are applicable to Yule. There are additional configuration options specifically for centralized deployment:

```
--enable-network=client|server
```

This option is used to specify that a network-aware executable will be built, and specifically, whether or not it will be a Yule server or a Samhain agent.

```
--disable-encrypt
```

This option allows you to disable encrypted communications between Yule and the Samhain agents. By default, all communications are encrypted using AES. The main reason this configuration option exists is to allow the use of Samhain in environments where strong cryptographic algorithms are prohibited. Never use this option in a production environment.

```
--enable-encrypt=1
```

Starting with version 1.8.x of Samhain, a new enhanced version of client/server encryption was implemented (i.e., version 2). By default, Yule can communicate with agents that use either implementation of client/server encryption. However, to explicitly set Yule to only communicate with agents that use version 1, use this option, which will produce a Yule server that is unable to communicate with version 2 agents.

```
--disable-srp
```

As detailed in Chapter 5, Samhain uses the zero-knowledge protocol known as the Secure Remote Password (SRP) protocol. If you wish, you can disable SRP using this option. However, SRP is behind the scenes and best left on. If you use this option, you must be consistent and use it on all of your Samhain agents.

```
--with-libwrap=PATH
```

This configuration option allows you to specify the location for the *libwrap* file in order to force Yule to use Transmission Control Protocol (TCP) wrappers.

```
--with-port=PORT
```

You can specify the port that the Yule server listens on with this configuration option. By default, Yule listens on port 49777. Although Yule will always drop root privileges, it will do so only after this port is bound to, so that you can specify a privileged port (privileged ports are ports less than 1024). If you use this option, you must be consistent and use it on all of your Samhain agents so that they know which port the Yule server is listening on.

In this case, you will establish a basic Yule server on a FreeBSD system and use Postgresql as storage for all of the log data. To use the database server, you must enable XML-formatted log messages. Also, you have to use the *--with-database* configuration option. Configure the Yule server with the following configuration options:

```
yule# ./configure --enable-network=server --with-database=postgresql --
enable-xml-log
```

NOTE

If you do not want to use a database server with Yule, do not use the —*enable-xml-log* or the —*with-database* configuration options. Instead, run configure as follows: *yule# ./configure —enable-network=server*

The configure will run through a series of tests and configure the source for a Yule build, and eventually print out the configuration settings that were established:

```
samhain has been configured as follows:
       System binaries: /usr/local/sbin
    Configuration file: /etc/yulerc
          Manual pages: /usr/local/man
                  Data: /var/lib/yule
              PID file: /var/run/yule.pid
              Log file: /var/log/yule/yule_log
              Base key: 816971544,813154367


       Selected rc file: yulerc
```

Note how the configuration file is */etc/yulerc* and that the other configuration options all make sense for a Yule build and installation, as opposed to the Samhain agent. Save the base key used to build Yule, because you will need it when building agents. This key should be the same for all agents so that the Yule server can verify the authenticity of the agent's log messages.

Building Yule

It is now necessary to build the Yule server executable and relevant utilities (e.g., *yulectl*). With modern hardware, the build process should take less than a minute:

```
yule# make
```

Next, install Yule:

```
yule# make install
```

This will install all of the binaries relevant to the Yule server, man pages, default configuration file, and all of the needed paths. To have the Yule server start upon boot, install the init scripts relevant for the platform you are running:

```
yule# make install-boot
./samhain-install.sh --destdir= --express --verbose install-boot
  FreeBSD system detected
  ./samhain-install.sh --install-sh -m 700  init/samhain.startFreeBSD
/usr/local/etc/rc.d/yule
  mv /usr/local/etc/rc.d/yule /usr/local/etc/rc.d/yule.sh &&  chmod 755
/usr/local/etc/rc.d/yule.sh
installing init scripts completed
```

Yule is now installed and will start upon boot. The default configuration file is installed in */etc/yulerc*, the database file(s) will be kept in */var/lib/yule*, and all logs related to the Yule server will be in the */var/log/yule/* directory.

Configuring Yule

The Yule configuration file is relatively simple compared to a typical Samhain agent configuration file. The format for a Yule configuration file has the following main sections:

- [Log]
- [Database]
- [External]
- [Misc]
- [Clients]

The following section establishes a reasonable starting point for your Yule server configuration. The file is located in */etc/yulerc*. Open this file (as root) with *vi* or your preferred editor:

```
yule# vi /etc/yulerc
```

Put the severity thresholds for the various logging outlets in the [Log] section. This will have a direct impact on the amount of data that is sent to your database server. The first time you deploy Samhain in your test environment, be mindful of the effects that certain settings will have on your database server. It is always a good idea to log to *syslog*. Since this is a dedicated Yule server, the console can be used; however, remember that if something happens, you may have to start dodging console messages while performing administrative tasks, which can be annoying. Locate the [Log] section of your configuration file and use the following settings:

```
[Log]
MailSeverity=none

## Console
##
PrintSeverity=info

## Logfile
##
# LogSeverity=none

## Syslog
##
SyslogSeverity=info

## External script or program
##
# ExternalSeverity = none

## Logging to a database
##
DatabaseSeverity=info
```

NOTE

If you are not using Postgresql to store your logs, you should set the *DatabaseSeverity* setting to **none**.

Next, you will configure Yule to use your Postgresql database server. This will be set up so that it uses the defaults you created (specifically, the database named "samhain" as the "samhain" pgsql user on the local server):

NOTE

If you are not using Postgresql to store your logs, you should leave the default values established for this section, which is disabled.

```
[Database]
##
## --- Logging to a relational database
##

## Database name
#
SetDBName = samhain

## Database table
#
SetDBTable = log

## Database user
#
SetDBUser = samhain

## Database password
#
# SetDBPassword = (default: none)
```

For the *external* section, you can safely leave the defaults, which means not using any external logging outlets. If you want to set up additional logging outlets, establish a base configuration, get it to work according to your requirements, and then go back and add external logging. This reduces the number of variables involved and allows you to easily build upon a working configuration one step at a time.

The next section is the *miscellaneous* section where you can set a number of things related to the runtime and behavior of the Yule server. The important setting is the daemon setting, which is set to **yes** so that Yule can start in the background. The *SetClientFromAccpet* setting specifies whether or not Yule should use the address provided by the client or from the socket communications layer. Locate the [Misc] section and configure it as follows:

```
[Misc]
Daemon=yes

## Interval between time stamp messages
SetLoopTime = 600
# SetClientTimeLimit = 86400

SetClientFromAccept = False
SeverityLookup = crit

# SetConsole = /dev/console
UseSeparateLogs = False

#SetUDPActive = False
#MessageQueueActive = False

SetReverseLookup = False

SetUseSocket = False
SetSocketAllowUid = 0

## --- E-Mail ---

SetMailTime = 86400
## Maximum number of mails to queue
SetMailNum = 10
# SetMailAddress=root@localhost
# SetMailRelay = NULL
# MailSubject = NULL
```

```
## --- end E-Mail ---

SamhainPath=/usr/local/sbin/yule

# SetTimeServer = (default: compiled-in)

# TrustedUser = (no default; this adds to the compiled-in list)
HideSetup = False
SyslogFacility = LOG_AUTHPRIV
# MACType = HMAC-TIGER
```

The e-mail settings are left disabled. Once you have verified that the system is working, attempt to establish some e-mail notifications. Again, this is to keep things simple and establish the functionality of the server one part at a time.

Save this configuration file. The clients have not been configured yet; it will be done after verifying that the configuration is valid. On FreeBSD, start the Yule server with the following command:

```
yule# /usr/local/etc/rc.d/yule.sh start
<log sev="INFO" tstamp="2005-04-24T12:20:00-0600" msg="/usr/local/sbin/yule
has checksum: 15EA067554C512429052DD8E641318B5BE06C267D629E42F"
subroutine="sh_unix_self_hash" />
```

If there are any errors in the configuration file, they will be printed as error messages to the console, along with their line numbers. Configuration errors some-times occur if you mistype a configuration setting, or if an option is enabled that was not included as part of the configuration process. If there are no errors, you should see something similar to what is listed in the preceding command snippet. To verify that Yule is running, do the following on FreeBSD:

```
yule# ps -A | grep yule
20630   ??  S      0:00.05 /usr/local/sbin/yule -D
```

You should see Yule start with the daemon option (*-D*). Now you need to build and configure clients. Stop the Yule server and verify that it is stopped with the following commands:

```
yule# /usr/local/etc/rc.d/yule.sh stop
 yule
yule# ps -A | grep yule
yule#
```

Building Network-Aware Samhain Agents

Building Samhain agents that talk to a Yule server requires special configuration options, and also requires you to compile in the Internet Protocol (IP) address (or hostname) of the Yule server. If you plan on storing the configuration file and base-line database file on the Yule server, you have to use additional configuration options to tell the build system. For Yule to verify log data, the base key built into the Yule server must be the same one that is built into the Samhain agent. You will use a configuration option to set the base key that will be embedded into the agent; otherwise, the configuration script will generate a random key that will not work with your Yule server.

This section builds agents similar to the ones in the stand-alone section, except that now they are built to talk to the newly established Yule server. The agent will use a similar configuration to monitor the file system mount points, will be capable of performing SUID/SGID audits, and will monitor the integrity of the kernel.

The first step is to establish a build environment. You can use the same source tree as you used to build the Yule server for FreeBSD agents (with different configuration options), but you have to use a different source tree for other operating systems.

Assuming that you have the source code downloaded and verified on a host that satisfies the build requirements, unpack the source:

```
agent# cd /usr/local/src
agent# tar xvfz samhain-2.0.5b.tar.gz
```

Enter the source directory and configure the source. Use the same options for modules as were used before. To build a network-aware Samhain agent, use the *--enable-network=client* configuration option. In addition, use configuration option *--with-logserver* to specify the hostname or IP address of the Yule log server. Use the *--with-config-file* option to tell the agent to request the configuration file from the Yule server. Finally, use the *--with-data-file* option to tell the agent to request the database file from the Yule server. Configure the source with the following command:

```
agent# cd samhain-2.0.5b
agent# ./configure --enable-network=client --enable-mounts-check --enable-
suidcheck --with-kcheck --with-logserver=10.10.0.5 --enable-xml-log --with-
config-file=REQ_FROM_SERVER/etc/samhainrc --with-data-
file=REQ_FROM_SERVER/var/lib/samhain/samhain_file --enable-
base=816971544,813154367
```

For the *--with-logserver* argument, you must specify the IP address of your Yule server. Likewise, the base key specified should match the key printed at the end of your Yule configuration. The path at the end of the *--with-data-file* and *--with-config-file* arguments is the path to these files on the monitored host. Although you will be storing them on the Yule server, they are still needed during the initialization process. Thereafter, the database and configuration files are stored on the Yule server and downloaded for checking, when necessary. When completed, the configuration process will configure the Samhain source for a network-aware agent and produce output that looks something like this:

```
samhain has been configured as follows:
      System binaries: /usr/local/sbin
   Configuration file: REQ_FROM_SERVER/etc/samhainrc
         Manual pages: /usr/local/man
                 Data: /var/lib/samhain
             PID file: /var/run/samhain.pid
             Log file: /var/log/samhain_log
             Base key: 816971544,813154367


      Selected rc file: samhainrc.freebsd
```

Make sure that the base key is the same key generated by the configuration of the Yule source code. These keys must match for log message verification. Make sure you keep this key in a safe place.

Next, build the agent:

```
agent# make
```

Next, install the Samhain agent:

```
agent# make install
  mkdir /var/lib
  mkdir /var/lib/samhain
  ./samhain-install.sh --destdir= --express --verbose install-data
  cp samhainrc.freebsd samhainrc
  cp samhainrc samhainrc.pre
  mv -f samhainrc.pre samhainrc.install
  ./samhain-install.sh --install-sh  -m 600 samhainrc.install
/etc/samhainrc
  checking whether paths are trustworthy
  configuration file /etc/samhainrc ... OK
  state directory /var/run ... OK
  state directory /var/log ... OK
  data directory /var/lib/samhain ... OK
```

```
You can use 'samhain-install.sh uninstall' for uninstalling
i.e. you might consider saving that script for future use

Use 'make install-boot' if you want samhain to start on system boot
```

Alternatively, if you have packaged Samhain using one of the *package-make* targets, install the package accordingly. If you are installing from source, install the init scripts with the following command:

```
agent# make install-boot
  ./samhain-install.sh --destdir= --express --verbose install-boot
  FreeBSD system detected
  ./samhain-install.sh --install-sh -m 700  init/samhain.startFreeBSD
/usr/local/etc/rc.d/samhain
  mv /usr/local/etc/rc.d/samhain /usr/local/etc/rc.d/samhain.sh &&  chmod
755 /usr/local/etc/rc.d/samhain.sh
installing init scripts completed
```

Pairing Agents with the Yule Server

Now that you have built a network-aware Samhain agent, you need to establish trust between that Samhain agent and the Yule server. To accomplish this, embed a shared key (password) into the agent executable, and then register that key with the Yule server. The *yule* executable is used to generate new passwords, and then a utility named *samhain_setpwd* embeds that password into the Samhain agent executable. Finally, the Yule configuration file is updated with a string that contains the generated password so that it can be used to authenticate communications with that particular agent. This process must be done for every host communicating with the Yule server.

On the Yule server, generate a random password:

```
yule# /usr/local/sbin/yule -G
9819459AC26B3AD3
```

Your password should be different. Next, generate a configuration file entry for this agent, using the generated password as input (again, your output should vary):

```
yule# /usr/local/sbin/yule -P 9819459AC26B3AD3
Client=HOSTNAME@6463C338BED5B77B@45D32B98039A9A50B8817DB7BF828CCE70C5EBE4679
6C00967BED3E9D0A017064439EB201EDE39D0BA6D3F94C4AEFD7D53C850FE3DFFFCD67CA3F65
4BC1B82C3DB5085432F188F8AC53EC0E788B423A50B77744D559BFE5DE63DAD031A5CA9C98F2
6D733060B25B805103C7DBB93C3832DF4FFA808B2C875EB5077DF31871854
```

This output must be placed into the configuration file with *HOSTNAME* replaced by the hostname for this agent. You can add this to the configuration file directly, or you can generate the password, replace the hostname, and add this data to the configuration file automatically with the following command:

```
yule# /usr/local/sbin/yule -P 9819459AC26B3AD3 | sed
s%HOSTNAME%host.example.com% >> /etc/yulerc
```

You have to replace *example.com* with a hostname or IP address for the agent you are configuring. Verify that the correct information was added to the *yulerc* file:

```
yule# tail -1 /etc/yulerc

Client=host.example.com@6463C338BED5B77B@45D32B98039A9A50B8817DB7BF828CCE70C
5EBE46796C00967BED3E9D0A017064439EB201EDE39D0BA6D3F94C4AEFD7D53C850FE3DFFFCD
67CA3F654BC1B82C3DB5085432F188F8AC53EC0E788B423A50B77744D559BFE5DE63DAD031A5
CA9C98F26D733060B25B805103C7DBB93C3832DF4FFA808B2C875EB5077DF31871854
```

Now, you need to update the Samhain agent executable. On the host where you just installed the Samhain agent, navigate to the Samhain source code; the samhain_setpwd executable should be in the root of the source tree. This executable takes a "samhain" executable and a password as input and then outputs that same executable with the password replaced. By default, the password is arbitrary. The password must be generated in the preceding Yule server, as shown previously. Reset the password with the following commands:

```
agent# cd /usr/local/src/samhain-2.0.5b

agent# ./samhain_setpwd /usr/local/sbin/samhain new 9819459AC26B3AD3

INFO    old password found

INFO    replaced:  f7c312aaaa12c3f7  by:  9819459ac26b3ad3

INFO    finished
```

This command leaves */usr/local/sbin/samhain* unmodified and creates */usr/local/sbin/samhain.new*. Your output will vary with respect to the password, but the results should be similar. Now, replace the old *samhain* executable with the new one:

```
agent# mv /usr/local/sbin/samhain.new /usr/local/sbin/samhain
```

Configuring the Agent

The final step in establishing an agent that can successfully trust and communicate with the Yule server is to make changes to the configuration file. Since the agent you built is basically the same as the one you built in the beginning of this chapter, you need only to make slight modifications to the configuration file before creating the baseline database. Specifically, you must tell it to redirect log messages to the Yule server.

Copy the configuration file that was established on the agent host in the beginning of this chapter, and edit it using *vi* or your preferred editor:

```
agent# vi /etc/samhainrc
```

For simplicity, disable the e-mail settings established in this configuration file. You will make Yule handle all of the e-mail notifications, which will make administration much simpler. Make sure the e-mail configurations are commented out as follows:

```
# SetMailTime = 30


## Maximum number of mails to queue
#
#SetMailNum = 30


## Recipient (max. 8)
#
#SetMailAddress=admin@example.com


## Mail relay (IP address)
#
#SetMailRelay = mail.example.com


## Custom subject format
#
# MailSubject = NULL
```

Next, locate the [Log] section of the configuration file and make sure the mail severity threshold is set to **none** (to disable it); the export severity will send all alerts of severity errors and greater to the Yule log server.

```
MailSeverity=none
## Remote server (yule)
##
ExportSeverity=err
```

Save the configuration file after making these changes.

Creating an Agent Baseline

Now that the agent is configured to successfully communicate with the Yule server, you have to establish a baseline database for this host. The result will be a configuration file and database that will be stored on the Yule server. If your Yule server is not running, start it now with the following command (FreeBSD):

```
yule# /usr/local/etc/rc.d/yule.sh start
<log sev="INFO" tstamp="2005-04-24T13:50:49-0600" msg="/usr/local/sbin/yule
has  checksum:  15EA067554C512429052DD8E641318B5BE06C267D629E42F"
subroutine="sh_unix_self_hash" />
```

If Yule is already running, make sure that it has reloaded its configuration since you lasted updated with the client password information. On FreeBSD, do this with the following command:

```
yule# /usr/local/etc/rc.d/yule reload
```

On the agent host, run Samhain in the foreground in *init* mode to create the baseline database:

```
agent# /usr/local/sbin/samhain -t init -p warn
```

This establishes the baseline database. To keep these on the server, you must copy them. Use the secure copy command to copy both the local Samhain configuration file and the baseline database to the Yule server. By default, the Yule server stores the configuration files and database files in */var/lib/yule* with the fully qualified domain name or IP address as part of the file. The database names are in the: *file.<hostname>*form and the configuration files are in the *rc.<hostname>* form. Assuming your Yule server is 10.0.0.5 and the hostname is foo, copy the files to the Yule server with the following command:

```
agent# scp /var/lib/samhain/samhain_file admin@10.0.0.5:/var/lib/yule/file.foo
agent# scp /etc/samhainrc admin@10.0.0.5:/var/lib/yule/rc.foo
```

Subsequent scans will download both the configuration file and the database from the Yule server and run checks. This can be verified by doing a scan by hand:

```
agent# /usr/local/sbin/samhain -t check -p info --foreground
INFO    :  [2005-04-25T14:58:19+0000] msg=<Session key negotiated>
INFO    :  [2005-04-25T14:58:20+0000] msg=<File download completed>
INFO    :  [2005-04-25T14:58:20+0000] msg=<Downloading database file>
INFO    :  [2005-04-25T14:58:21+0000] msg=<File download completed>
...
```

You can now safely start the Samhain agent to run as a daemon using the installed init scripts. On FreeBSD this command is:

```
agent# /usr/local/etc/rc.d/samhain.sh start
```

Dealing with Detected Changes

Eventually, you will have to deal with the fact that your monitored systems are getting out of sync with your baseline databases. There are two options for updating your Samhain agent databases. First, you can login to the monitored host and run Samhain manually with the *update* option. The second option is to use the Beltane Web-based interface (explored in the next section).

To update the database from the agent host, login to the host and disable the agent so that there is no chance of concurrent access to the Yule server. Do this by sending a *SIGUSR2* signal. For example, on FreeBSD, do the following:

```
agent# ps -A | grep samhain
21423  ??  S       0:00.10 /usr/local/sbin/samhain -D
agent# kill -USR2 21423
```

The Process ID (PID) you encounter will likely be different than what is shown in the previous example. Next, on the Yule server, use SCP to transfer this host's Samhain database file to the agent host. Agent database files are kept (by default) in */var/lib/yule/* and are named in the *file.name* format where name is the hostname where the agent is running. For example, to update the database for the host foo logging in as the user "admin" (assuming the correct privileges):

```
yule# cd /var/lib/yule/
yule# scp file.foo admin@foo:/var/lib/samhain/samhain_file
```

Then, on the agent host, run Samhain in update mode in the foreground to update the */var/log/samhain/samhain_file* database:

```
agent# samhain -t update --foreground --interactive
```

This will produce a series of questions and ask you to update the database for each one. When finished, bring the database file back down to the Yule server with the following command:

```
yule# scp admin@foo:/var/lib/samhain/samhain_file file.foo
```

Finally, wake up the Samhain agent so that it can continue monitoring. Do that by sending another SIGUSR2 signal to the same agent process:

```
agent# kill -USR2 21423
```

The database file for this agent is now updated. To manage large numbers of hosts, use Beltane to update databases and monitor the status of your agents.

Yule Server Status

Yule exports an HTML status page by default, which is located in the same location as the *yule_log* file (*/var/log/yule/yule.html* by default,). If you have a Web server enabled on this host, you can view the basic status of the agents being managed by the Yule server (see Figure 7.2).

Figure 7.2 Viewing the Basic Status of the Agents Managed by the Yule Server

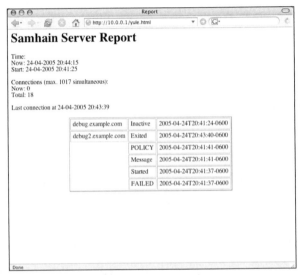

To gain more control over managed agents, you will need to use the Beltane Web-based console interface as described in the next section.

Using Beltane: The Web-Based Console

Beltane allows you to administer Samhain agents and update their databases through a Web browser interface. It is based on PHP and requires that you install both PHP and Apache on your Yule server. The true benefits of Beltane can be realized when Samhain is deployed in a client/server setup, and making use of a relational database such as Postgresql. This section covers the basic setup and use of Beltane to make the administration of Samhain more enjoyable.

This section covers using Beltane version1, not v.2, which requires payment to Samhain Labs. Go to *http://www.la-samhna.de/beltane* to see the list of Beltane version 2 features. If you are investing a great deal in a Samhain deployment, you will probably want to get Beltane v.2.

Beltane Requirements

To run Beltane, you have to install both Apache and PHP. On FreeBSD, if you have ports installed, you should be able to do this with the following commands:

```
yule# cd /usr/ports/databases/postgres7
yule# make install
yule# cd /usr/ports/textproc/expat2
yule# make install
yule# cd /usr/ports/www/apache2
yule# make install
yule# cd /usr/ports/lang/php4
yule# make install --enable-pgsql
yule# cd /usr/ports/textproc/php4-xml
yule# make install
```

Using Beltane requires the installation of Apache and PHP. Installing these on your Yule server can be a security risk. Securing Apache and attempting to secure a PHP installation (if that is even possible) is beyond the scope of this book. If you do deploy Beltane, be sure to consider the risks involved and establish a plan for how you will protect the data stored on the Yule server. A common tactic is to configure Apache to listen only on localhost and use SSH to tunnel your Web session to Beltane. This allows only local shell users the ability to access Beltane remotely.

Before continuing, verify that you have a working Apache configuration that allows you to execute the PHP parser for files that end in *.php*. You can usually do this by creating a test PHP file that looks like the following:

```
<html>
<head>
<title> PHP Test Script </title>
</head>
<body>
<?php
phpinfo();
?>
</body>
</html>
```

Basically, you want to make sure that the PHP library is being loaded by Apache, and that you have a type handler for PHP scripts defined in your Apache configuration file (*httpd.conf*). Once you can successfully execute PHP scripts, you are ready to install Beltane. Additionally, the Beltane source provides help in various formats (including HTML) in the *beltane_help* directory of the source code. If this fails, you should revisit your Apache configuration and your PHP installation. Additionally, check your Apache error log for hints as to why you are not seeing the PHP script execute correctly.

Preparing to Install Beltane

The installation of Beltane is problematic with respect to permissions. Every system installs Apache differently, with different locations on the file system, and with different file permissions. It is likely that you will run into problems getting Beltane to work correctly the first time; this is usually due to file permissions in some way. The following steps are not necessary, but may help you set up a Beltane/Yule server configuration that works. These steps were performed on a FreeBSD system:

```
yule# mkdir /usr/local/www/data/beltane
yule# chown www /usr/local/www/data/beltane
```

Building and Installing Beltane

After you have downloaded the source for Beltane and verified the PGP signature, copy the source file to a logical place on your system (e.g., */usr/local/src*). Next, unpack the source *tar.gz* file:

```
yule# tar xvfz beltane-1.0.7.tar.gz
```

Enter the Beltane source directory and run configure. You must provide configuration options that are dependent on your Apache and PHP installation. For FreeBSD, if you have used the ports to install Apache and PHP, you must run configure with the following options:

```
yule# ./configure --enable-mod-php --with-php-dir=/usr/local/www/data/beltane
--with-php-extension=php --with-user=www --with-user-
home=/usr/local/www/data/beltane
```

This configures the Beltane source for your system and enables the PHP module as opposed to the PHP Common Gateway Interface (CGI). It will install the Beltane configuration file (*.beltanerc*) in */usr/local/www/beltane* and run as the Apache user (WWW). Since we are using the PHP module, this must be the user that Apache runs as. If you are on Linux, your Apache user and *home-dir* location will probably be different. At the end of the configuration, you will see a configuration summary that looks something like the following:

```
beltane has been configured as follows:
            PHP files: /usr/local/www/data/beltane
      System binaries: /usr/local/bin
   Configuration file: /usr/local/www/data/beltane/.beltanerc
             Log file: /var/log/beltane_update_log
                 Data: /var/lib/yule
             PHP user: www
            PHP group: www
       Home directory: /usr/local/www/data/beltane
    PHP file extension: php
         PHP is module: yes
            XOR value: 0
```

Next, build the Beltane system; this will take only a few seconds:

```
yule# make
gcc  -DHAVE_CONFIG_H -I. -I.   -O2 -Wall -W  -fno-strength-reduce -fno-
omit-frame-pointer  -o encode ./encode.c
encode 0 config.h
```

```
./encode 0 beltane_update.c  -->  x_beltane_update.c
gcc  -DHAVE_CONFIG_H -I. -I.   -O2 -Wall -W  -fno-strength-reduce -fno-
omit-frame-pointer -c x_beltane_update.c
gcc  -O  -o beltane_update  beltane_update.o
./encode 0 beltane_cp.c  -->  x_beltane_cp.c
gcc  -DHAVE_CONFIG_H -I. -I.   -O2 -Wall -W  -fno-strength-reduce -fno-
omit-frame-pointer -c x_beltane_cp.c
gcc  -O  -o beltane_cp  beltane_cp.o
```

Next, install Beltane:

```
yule# make install
```

This installs the utilities needed by Beltane, as well as the PHP code, images, and some configuration files. Now, you need to adjust some file permissions so that the Beltane console will be able to read databases, logs, and other related files.

```
yule# chgrp www /var/log/yule/yule.html
```

Configuring Beltane

The first thing to do once Beltane is installed is reset the Administrator password. Using a Web browser, type in the IP address or hostname for your Yule server and the path to Beltane. If you configured Beltane with the aforementioned options on FreeBSD, it would be in the format:

```
http://<yule_hostname>/beltane
```

You should see a login screen that looks something like the one shown in Figure 7.3.

Figure 7.3 Beltane's Login Screen

Next, log in as user *rainer* with the password *wichmann*. You will be presented with a console interface that looks similar to one shown in Figure 7.4.

Figure 7.4 Beltane's Console Interface

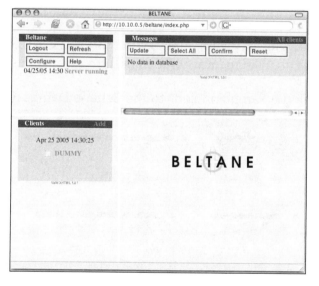

You will now be asked to set your password. In the upper right-hand corner of the browser is a button named **Configure** (see Figure 7.5). Click on that to be presented with the configuration screen. The bottom right frame of the browser should reveal many fields for configuring Beltane, including the admin username and password. Enter your admin user name and choose a password. While this configuration settings pane is open, make sure that the Postgres radio button is set to **TRUE** and that the Yule HTML file path is */var/log/yule/yule.html*. When finished, click the **OK** button at the bottom of the frame.

Figure 7.5 Setting a Password on Beltane

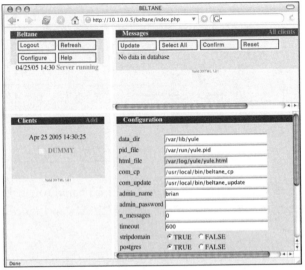

Next, add your Samhain client to the Beltane database. Click on the **Add** link in the **Clients** pane. This will produce a dialog similar to the one shown in Figure 7.6.

Figure 7.6 Adding a Samhain Client to the Beltane Database

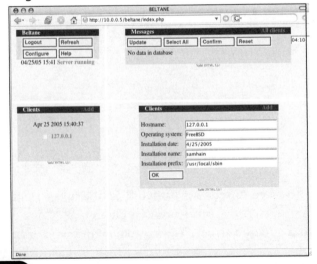

This will prompt you for some generic fields such as the hostname, the operating system, and the init date. The installation name is the name of the Samhain executable on the remote host. The installation prefix is the path to the Samhain executable. Fill those in according to the settings for your Samhain host and click **OK** to save.

At any time, you can view the latest status of the Yule server by clicking on the **Server Status** link in the upper-left frame (see Figure 7.7). This pull the data out of the *yule.html* file generated by the Yule daemon.

Figure 7.7 Viewing the Latest Status of the Yule Server

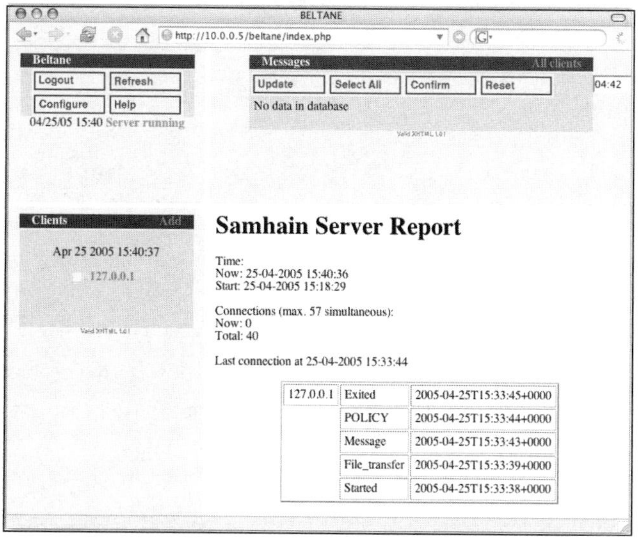

Using Beltane

Beltane is really useful for managing a number of clients, and for updating their databases when changes are detected. To see how this process works, you will create a change by modifying the time stamp of an executable, note that Beltane reports this, and then update that host's database.

On the agent host, open the */bin/ls* file to modify the *ctime* value:

```
agent# touch /bin/ls
```

Next, run Samhain in the foreground to download the database and check the current system. Normally, the agent would be running in the background and detect this on its normal schedule; however, we want to see the results immediately:

```
agent# /usr/local/sbin/samhain -t check --foreground
```

You should see the last scan trail, including a critical alert shown in red for the time-stamp modification just created (see Figure 7.8).

Figure 7.8 Viewing Beltane's Last Scan Trail

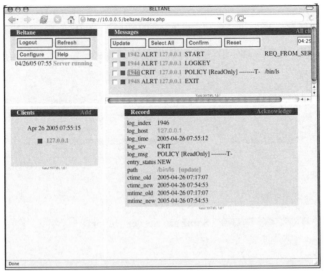

To update the database, select the checkbox to the left of the critical record (in this case, record 1946) and click **Update**. After the database is updated, you will see the message shown in Figure 7.9.

Figure 7.9 Updating the Beltane Database

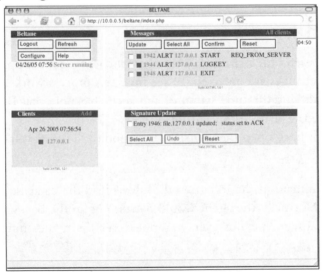

Next, to confirm the noncritical alerts regarding the scan, select them and click **Confirm**. You should see an acknowledgment. Click **Refresh** and the console will return to its normal state (see Figure 7.10).

Figure 7.10 Confirming Noncritical Alerts from a Beltane Scan

Using Beltane can ease the administrative burden associated with monitoring the changes on a large number of hosts. Although it requires installing a Web server, a database, and PHP, these may be worthwhile risks considering the benefits associated with being able to quickly acknowledge changes on your host through a Web browser.

Summary

Samhain provides a very efficient way to monitor the integrity of your UNIX and UNIX- like host environments. It can be installed as a stand-alone system such that each host has a self-sufficient installation that requires its own administration. In cases where there are only a few hosts, it is recommended that you take this approach. Alternatively, for monitoring a large number of hosts, you can deploy Samhain to be centrally managed using the log server Yule and a Web-based console named Beltane.

Samhain can monitor file attributes as well as user login and logout events, file system mount options, SUID and SGID executables, sensitive files in user home directories, and various attributes surrounding the integrity of the kernel. Samhain can monitor these elements of a host environment and report on changes to a number of logging outlets including files, *syslog*, external applications, the console, and relational databases. When configured correctly, Samhain can be an effective HIMS. However, its configuration can be problematic due to the design of the client/server architecture it implements and the security features that are available as an administrator. Throughout your planning and deployment of Samhain, be mindful of the ongoing efforts that will be needed to administer and maintain the system, and how receptive it will be to common administrative changes.

Solutions Fast Track

Features and Constraints

☑ Samhain provides solid support for monitoring various elements of the host environment, including kernel integrity, login/logout events, and file system mount options.

☑ Samhain is UNIX-based and supports many disparate UNIX-based systems such as AIX and HP-UX. Consequently, Samhain is not designed to monitor the integrity of Windows systems.

☑ Samhain has many attractive security features as part of its design, including the ability to hide itself inside an image file, hide itself from the process table, and GnuPG signed configuration and database files.

Deploying Samhain Stand-Alone

☑ Samhain can be deployed in a stand-alone fashion meaning that all configurations, scan data, and logs are kept on the monitored host as opposed to being managed centrally by a server or a console.

☑ Stand-alone deployments of Samhain are much easier to install and administer.

☑ Stand-alone deployments of Samhain do not scale. If you are monitoring a large number of hosts, you must deploy Samhain using Yule.

Deploying Samhain with Centralized Management

☑ Yule is a log server that provides a secure trusted system for managing logs, scan configuration files, and scan databases for all Samhain agents.

☑ Samhain agents must be registered with the Yule server by embedding a shared password into the Samhain agent and then keeping that shared key in the configuration file for the Yule server.

☑ The Yule server requires strict security and pairing between the Samhain agent and the server, which can be problematic for complex deployments or changes in your deployment scenario.

Using Beltane: The Web-Based Console

☑ Beltane v.1 is an open source PHP Web-based console for managing Samhain agents, which allows you to perform updates to your agent databases.

☑ Beltane requires the installation of Apache and PHP on your Yule server, which may present a problem for the security of your Yule server system.

Frequently Asked Questions

The following Frequently Asked Questions, answered by the authors of this book, are designed to both measure your understanding of the concepts presented in this chapter and to assist you with real-life implementation of these concepts. To have your questions about this chapter answered by the author, browse to **www.syngress.com/solutions** and click on the **"Ask the Author"** form. You will also gain access to thousands of other FAQs at ITFAQnet.com.

Q: I receive the error, "Untrusted Path" when running Samhain. What does this mean?

A: This will occur if your Yule or Samhain paths are group writable and the group contains members that are not considered "trusted." By default, only the effective user and the root are trusted users. To specify additional trusted users, use the configuration option —*with-trusted* (e.g., trust users with UID 501 and UID 502, using configuration argument —*with-trusted=501,502*).

Q: Can Samhain be used to monitor prelinked files?

A: Yes, there is a specific policy for monitoring files that are prelinked. This policy (by default), ignores modifications to the inode, change time, and file size. To verify the contents of the file, the *verify* option to the prelink application is used to undo and perform a cryptographic checksum on the file contents.

Q: What are my options for mass deployment of Samhain agents?

A: The source for Samhain has a system for mass deployment that uses a shell script and Secure Shell (SSH). This deployment system is capable of installing and automatically initializing (or updating) the database. Information on the deployment system can be found in the Samhain manual at www.la-samhna.com/samhain/manual/ under the "Deployment" section.

Q: Can I install and run Samhain on the Yule server?

A: Yes, and it is a good idea to do so. Monitoring the integrity of your Yule server is critical. If the Yule server is compromised, your entire deployment is meaningless. This Samhain agent is handled just like any other Samhain host.

Q: Can Samhain be integrated with hybrid IDS systems or other integrity monitoring solutions?

A: Yes. Samhain can be used with host monitoring system Nagios (*http://www.nagios.org*) and with Prelude (*http://www.prelude-ids.org*), a hybrid intrusion detection framework that can serve as a centralized reporting station for host and network security tools.

## Chapter 8

Log Monitoring and Response

Solutions in this chapter:

- **Log Monitoring**
- **Incident Response**

☑ **Summary**

☑ **Solutions Fast Track**

☑ **Frequently Asked Questions**

Introduction

At this point, you have successfully deployed either Osiris or Samhain and are now generating log data and alerts that detail changes to your host environments. The next step is monitoring and responding to events. Many security administrators that install Osiris and Samhain do not take advantage of the information provided (i.e., do not monitor the logs, configure a solution to monitor the logs, or establish a plan for incident response). At some point, changes will happen that initiate some kind of response. Even though hosts are secured, eventually they will be subject to attacks or some type of misuse. To be prepared, you must first establish a means of detecting the important change and then have a plan for responding to that change. This chapter discusses practical ways to establish log monitoring for Osiris and Samhain, and explores issues related to incident response.

Log Monitoring

Logs are essential. For your host integrity monitoring system (HIMS) deployment to be useful, you must configure, maintain, and analyze the logs that it produces. Both Osiris and Samhain have the ability to send notifications regarding detected changes to various outlets such as applications, databases, and e-mail addresses. However, the most effective way to analyze the information is to use an additional application to analyze and respond to logs.

Osiris and Samhain were not designed to be log analyzers, even though each can be configured to single out and report on certain types of change. These features were added for convenience; it makes sense to have Osiris and Samhain report on all types of changes, use a specific application to monitor changes, and use the appropriate notification vectors for changes concerning your enterprise. This allows you to configure Osiris and Samhain to log and archive everything, and to use a configurable log-monitoring engine with more capabilities than the ones integrated into Osiris and Samhain.

Another reason to use a separate log-monitoring system is for the correlation of logging data. Osiris and Samhain are still in their infancy with respect to host correlation (i.e., they focus on each host as a separate entity and cannot perform any high-level analysis on the overall changes that are occurring in your host landscapes). Log-monitoring systems that can report and provide collective information and statistics are useful for troubleshooting, optimizing performance, and detecting weak areas in networks.

Having a separate log-monitoring engine is convenient because it can be used to monitor and correlate logs for a number of applications, not just your HIMS. Several attacks and anomalies can be prevented if the logs are read and analyzed regularly. With a separate log-monitoring system, you can correlate log data for all of the hosts you are monitoring and the applications and services (e.g., Web, mail, Secure Shell [SSH], Domain Name System [DNS], and so forth), intrusion detection, and network security measures such as NIDS and firewalls. Collecting and analyzing data from all of these areas helps highlight and confirm where you should focus your attention as a security administrator. The following section covers the installation and deployment of Swatch (Simple WATCHer) to monitor logs and alerts generated by Osiris and Samhain. For more information about tools and techniques associated with log analysis see www.loganalysis.org.

Log Monitoring Using Swatch

Swatch is an open source active log-monitoring application, which is written in Perl. The official site for Swatch source code, mailing lists, and documentation is http://swatch.sourceforge.net. Swatch can monitor and respond to log events in real time and can be run as a UNIX daemon or on the command line. Swatch has many different notification methods that can be used for specific events; essentially, you provide regular expressions for it to match against log data and a list of notification methods. This feature is useful because you can establish different notification methods based on the severity of the event (e.g., you may want to be paged when Osiris or Samhain produce log events about changes to system executables, whereas changes involving user home directories may only generate e-mail). There are many open source log-monitoring tools and hybrid log-monitoring solutions available. The reason Swatch is highlighted is because it is simple to install, configure, and use. There are two distinct versions of Swatch. This section uses the most recent implementation, which is hosted at *sourceforge*.

Swatch is available only for UNIX and UNIX-like platforms, which works fine for Samhain; however, if you are using Osiris and have already established your management console on Windows, there are a handful of log-monitoring and log-parsing tools available for Windows listed in the "Library" section at www.loganalysis.org.

Installing Swatch

The source code for Swatch can be downloaded from the SourceForge project site at http://swatch.sourceforge.net. Unfortunately, there is no Message Digest 5 (MD5) or Pretty Good Privacy (PGP) signature provided, therefore, it is not possible to verify that you are working with the correct source. At the time of this writing, Swatch is at Release 3.1.1 and the MD5 source is:

```
$ openssl md5 swatch-3.1.1.tar.gz
MD5(swatch-3.1.1.tar.gz)= fe38cc8d073e692a7426693837c3749d
```

> **NOTE**
>
> It is best to install Swatch on the host being used as your management console. However, if you are uncomfortable because of the set up required for the various notification methods (e.g., mail or paging), a reasonable solution is to establish a dedicated log-monitoring system. You can have all of the logs that are sent to *syslog* or the Event Viewer directed to a dedicated log host using Osiris or Samhain.

First, verify that you have the proper dependencies for Swatch. Specifically, you need Perl 5 and the following Perl modules:

- Time::HiRes
- Date::Calc
- Date::Parse
- Date::Format
- File::Tail

Verify the version of Perl by doing:

```
$ perl --version
This is perl, v5.8.1-RC3 built for darwin-thread-multi-2level
(with 1 registered patch, see perl -V for more detail)
...
```

List and verify that you have the required modules with the following command:

```
$ perl -MCPAN -e autobundle
```

Install any missing modules that use Comprehensive Perl Archive Network (CPAN) by typing the following command:

```
# cpan install <module_name>
```

Unpack the Swatch source file. Your filename may be different if a newer release is available; all of the information in this section assumes Version 3.1.1:

```
$ tar xvfz swatch-3.1.1.tar.gz
```

Enter the created directory and read the README file looking for any important information related to the specific release that you downloaded. Use Perl to create the makefile:

```
$ cd swatch-3.1.1
$ perl Makefile.pl
Writing Makefile for swatch
```

Build Swatch by typing **make**:

```
$ make
cp lib/Swatch/Actions.pm blib/lib/Swatch/Actions.pm
AutoSplitting blib/lib/Swatch/Actions.pm (blib/lib/auto/Swatch/Actions)
cp lib/Swatch/Throttle.pm blib/lib/Swatch/Throttle.pm
cp swatch blib/script/swatch
/usr/bin/perl "-MExtUtils::MY" -e "MY->fixin(shift)" blib/script/swatch
Manifying blib/man1/swatch.1
Manifying blib/man3/Swatch::Throttle.3pm
Manifying blib/man3/Swatch::Actions.3pm
```

Next, test the build:

```
$ make test
PERL_DL_NONLAZY=1 /usr/bin/perl "-MExtUtils::Command::MM" "-e"
"test_harness(0, 'blib/lib', 'blib/arch')" t/*.t
t/01cpan_modules....ok
All tests successful.
Files=1, Tests=1,  0 wallclock secs ( 0.25 cusr +  0.04 csys =  0.29 CPU)
```

Finally, as root, install Swatch:

```
# make install
Installing /Library/Perl/5.8.1/auto/swatch/Actions/autosplit.ix
Installing /Library/Perl/5.8.1/Swatch/Actions.pm
Installing /Library/Perl/5.8.1/Swatch/Throttle.pm
Installing /man/man1/swatch.1
```

```
Installing /man/man3/Swatch::Actions.3pm
Installing /man/man3/Swatch::Throttle.3pm
Installing /usr/bin/swatch
Writing ///Library/Perl/5.8.1/darwin-thread-multi-
2level/auto/swatch/.packlist
Appending installation info to ///System/Library/Perl/5.8.1/darwin-thread-
multi-2level/perllocal.pod
```

At this point, you should have the Swatch executable installed in */usr/bin/swatch* or */usr/local/bin/swatch.*You may want to modify the default permissions so that all users can read and execute the Swatch application. For example:

```
# chmod a+rx /usr/bin/swatch
```

Configuring and Using Swatch

Although Swatch can be run on the command line, you should run it as daemon so that it continually monitors log events generated by Osiris or Samhain. Swatch works by monitoring what is appended to a log file, which is similar to the UNIX *tail* command. When started, Swatch reads a configuration file that contains a list of regular expressions to be matched against each log message, and an action to perform when a match occurs. Swatch can only monitor one log file at a time; if your Osiris or Samhain logs are being sent to multiple files, you must run an instance of Swatch for each file. By default, Osiris sends log messages to the main *syslog* file (usually */var/log/messages*), and Samhain sends them to */var/log/samhain_log*. Ideally, you want all of your events going to a single file specific to Osiris or Samhain.

We recommend that you establish a configuration file and add a few basic rules to understand how Swatch works. To view the main page for Swatch, use the following command:

```
$ perldoc swatch
```

As you become comfortable with its features, add the rules for Osiris or Samhain. It will not take long for you see how powerful this simple log-monitoring tool is.

The Basics

Swatch is run when it is provided a file containing log data and a configuration file that specifies all of the patterns and actions to perform when a match is found. Swatch can read log data that is input in three ways:

- Read the file and wait for more input (tailing)
- Read the file and exit
- Read the output from a command

You should use the tail method for Osiris and Samhain. By default, Swatch automatically uses this method on the *syslog* file; however, you should always specify the file you want to monitor. For example:

```
$ swatch --tail-file=/var/log/messages
```

The next step is to establish a configuration file. This file should be stored somewhere reasonable, such as */etc/swatchrc*. Then, run Swatch as follows:

```
$ swatch --tail-file=/var/log/messages --config-file=/etc/swatchrc --daemon
```

The daemon option causes Swatch to fork as a background process. In this case, Swatch uses the */etc/swatchrc* file to continue monitoring the *syslog* file. You must specify whether Osiris or Samhain are logging to a different file instead of to */var/log/messages*. If your system has locked-down file permissions on *syslog* files, you should run *syslog* with the required privileges. This should also be configured to start monitoring upon boot. All that is left to do is to create the configuration file that will match and report on changes that are important to you.

Swatch Configuration

The Swatch configuration file contains a list of rules, which can be specified on a single line or on multiple lines. These rules have one of the following formats:

```
watchfor /regex/,[/regex/,...] action,[action,...]
ignore /regex/,[/regex/,...]
```

The *watchfor* rule performs a list of actions for every log entry that matches any of the specified regular expressions. In all cases, the resultant action causes the matching log entry to be used (e.g., e-mail causes the matching line to be sent in an e-mail message.

The *ignore* rule causes Swatch to explicitly ignore every log entry that matches the specified regular expressions. This is useful when you have additional rules catching all remaining log messages or messages of a certain type; you want to explicitly exclude certain log entries from those rules.

Swatch rules are best explained with examples. The following is a rule that catches failed pseudo attempts, prints the error to the console in red, and sends e-mail to an administrator:

```
watchfor /sudo.*incorrect password/
```

```
echo=red
mail=admin@example.com,subject=--[ sudo: denied access ]----
```

Suppose you want to receive mail about these failed pseudo attempts if they occur after hours (e.g., between 5 P.M. and 7 A.M). The modified rule would be:

```
watchfor /sudo.*incorrect password/
   echo=red
   mail=admin@example.com,subject=--[ sudo: denied access ]----
   when=1-7:17-7
```

The "when" option has the format *day_of_week:hour_of_day*. In this case, all days between 5 P.M. and 7 A.M. are the only times when the actions are performed. The complete list of supported options is as follows:

- **echo [mode]** Print the log message to the console. The mode is used to specify the type of text to print including highlighting, bolding, blinking, and various colors. The following modes are valid: normal, bold, underscore, blink, inverse, black, red, green, yellow, blue, magenta, cyan, white, black_h, red_h, green_h, yellow_h, blue_h, magenta_h, cyan_h, and/or white_h The _h modes are highlighted text; the default is normal.

- **bell[[N]** Issue a system bell N number of times.

- **exec** Execute the specified application.

- **mail** Send the log message via e-mail.

- **pipe command[,keep_open]** Pipe matching a log entry to a command. If *keep_open* is specified, the pipe to the command remains open until another pipe match occurs.

- **write [user:user:...]** Send the matching log entry to a user(s) using the "write" command.

- **throttle hours:minutes:seconds,[use=message|regex|<regex]>** Limit the number of times the actions will be performed in a specified period of time.

- **threshold events:seconds,[repeat=no|yes]** Limit the number of times the actions will be performed based on how many times a match has already occurred in a given time frame.

- **continue** Continue to apply the other rules in the configuration after a match.

The following is an example of an e-mail regarding Osiris detecting a time-stamp change on an executable:

```
To: brian@example.com
Subject: [ osiris log: executables changed ]
Date: Sun, 17 Apr 2005 15:34:13 -0600 (MDT)
From: brian@example.local (Brian Wotring)


Apr 17 15:34:12 localhost osirismd[22357]:
[211][local][cmp][/usr/bin/as][mtime][Fri Apr 15 21:12:56 2005][Sun Apr 17
15:34:05 2005]
```

For details on using any of the Swatch options, see the *perldoc* main page.

Swatch Rules for Osiris and Samhain

There is no perfect Swatch configuration file for Osiris and Samhain. The rules that you specify in your Swatch configuration file will be based on your goals, your existing notification infrastructure, and your available resources. It may be that sending e-mail about critical alerts works best for you. Or, your organization may have an alert database that you will have Swatch send critical alerts to. In any case, what you consider critical and how you deal with those critical alerts is something that you must decide as early as the planning phase of your HIMS deployment. This section provides some useful Swatch configurations that will catch critical events. Rules for both Osiris and Samhain are provided. These configurations work well as a starting point for your own custom Swatch configurations.

Example Swatch Configuration for Osiris

The following is an example Swatch configuration file for Osiris, which captures the most important Osiris log messages:

```
# swatch configuration template for Osiris
# monitors for the following changes:


# email, bell, and red echo for changes to bin and libs.

watchfor /\[cmp\].*(bin|lib)/
    echo=red
    bell 1
    mail=admin@example.com,subject=[ osiris log: executables changed ]
    continue # for SUID/SGID changes.
```

```
# yellow echo for attempts to login to console from unauthorized host.
# logging code 15.

watchfor /\[15\]\[\*\]/
    echo=yellow


# yellow echo for failed login attempts.

watchfor /\[102\]\[\*\]/
    echo=yellow


# green echo for console logins.

watchfor /\[101\]\[\*\]/
    echo=green


# green echo for scan started

watchfor /\[504\]\[\*\]/
    echo=green


# red echo for scan failures.

watchfor /\[503\]\[\*\]/
    echo=red
    mail=admin@example.com,subject=[osiris scan failure]


# red echo and email for SUID/SGID related changes.

watchfor /\[perm\].*\[-r.*s/
    echo=red
    mail=admin@example.com,subject=[osiris SUID/SGID changes]


# yellow echo and email for lost/invalid/missing session keys for agents.

watchfor /\[(603|604|605)\]/
    echo=yellow
    mail=admin@example.com,subject=[osiris agent rekey]
```

```
# white echo for all other osiris logs.

watchfor /osirismd/
    echo=white
```

> **NOTE**
>
> You must customize this configuration to your environment. Upgrades to many system executables or libraries could generate a great deal of mail.

Example Swatch Configuration for Samhain

Unlike Osiris, which only has informational, warning, and error messages, Samhain has thresholds for alerts and a number of severity levels that can be assigned to certain types of log messages in the Samhain configurations. The following Swatch configuration takes advantage of those severities.

```
# swatch configuration template for Samhain
# monitors for the following changes:

# email, bell, and red echo for changes to bin and libs.

watchfor /\[ReadOnly\]/
    echo=red
    bell 1
    mail=admin@example.com,subject=[ samhain log: executables changed ]

# debug messages

watchfor /^DEBUG/
    echo=blue

# info messages

watchfor /^INFO/
    echo=cyan

# notice messages
```

```
watchfor /^NOTICE/
     echo=magenta

# Warning messages
watchfor /^WARN/
     echo=yellow

# timestamps

watchfor /^MARK/
     echo=green

# error conditions

watchfor /^ERR/
     echo=red_h

# critical alerts

watchfor /^CRIT/
     echo=red

# program startup/normal exits.

watchfor /^ALERT/
     echo=green

# all other messages.

watchfor /.*/
     echo=white
```

Running Swatch

After establishing a *config* file, you can begin testing it by running it on the console. One you have it to the point where you are comfortable, you can set up your system to automatically daemonize the Swatch process on boot. To run Swatch on the console, do something like the following for Osiris:

```
$ swatch --config-file=/etc/swatchrc.osiris --tail-file=/var/log/osiris.log
```

or, the following for Samhain:

```
# swatch --config-file=/etc/swatchrc.samhain --tail-file=/var/log/samhain_log
```

To run Swatch as a daemon process, use the following argument:

```
--daemon
```

Incident Response

The majority of host integrity monitoring is planning and configuring software to be able to successfully detect change. However, a critical final step to being successful in establishing a HIMS is "response." You have taken steps to lock down and secure your networks and hosts, but eventually you will be attacked and will have to deal with breaches in your security. You must plan for responding to alerts. It is not uncommon for companies to establish complicated schemes for integrity monitoring (at the host or network level) to detect attacks within seconds, only to fumble with procedure because they do not know how to respond or who to direct the information to.

This section provides some fundamental information regarding incident response in general, as well as how it applies to your HIMS deployment. Incident response is not a simple topic; there are entire books written about it (see Appendix C). There is no simple set of answers. How you choose to respond and the policy you define regarding incident responses, will depend on the nature of your business and your available security administration resources. This section sticks to the main points of incident response, including the incident response cycle and where you can get more information on the topic. The following books contain more information on incident response:

- *Incident Response* by Ken van Wyk and Richard Forno A concise guide to all of the ins and outs of incident response. Additional information is available at www.oreilly.com/catalog/incidentres/index.html.

- *Investigating Computer-Related Crime* by Peter Stephenson A resource tailored to the corporate security specialist who needs detailed information on investigating attacks. This book provides thorough coverage of the technical and legal aspects of computer crime.

General Overview of Incident Response

How involved your incident response deployment is depends on your goals and an analysis of risk. If you are a home user installing Osiris or Samhain on a couple of systems, you do not need a large incident response policy. However, if you are a large enterprise with thousands of monitored hosts, you need an official policy and an entire coordinated response team that is ready to respond to incidents generated by your HIMS and other security measures.

Incident response is not entirely an internal effort. There are a number of external incident response teams that collect information, provide tips, and help coordinate mitigation efforts for large-scale attacks. The most widely known external incident response team is the Computer Emergency Response Team Coordination Center (CERT/CC). CERT/CC was formed in 1988 (funded by the government) after the Morris worm infected large portions of the Internet. CERT/CC releases information about vulnerabilities, worms, viruses, and spyware. The information released by CERT/CC can be very helpful for security administrators. For example, consider that a new worm is making its way around the globe, infecting and compromising the security of the hosts it infects. Armed with information from an external incident response team, you may be able to mitigate the damage by modifying your HIMS configuration to look for known signs of infection, or by keeping your eye out for HIMS notifications that seem related to the information provided in the external alerts. More information about CERT/CC and the information it provides can be obtained from the main Web site at www.cert.org.

Operating system vendors usually have regular security announcements regarding patches, vulnerabilities, and known software exploits. As with CERT, this information can be valuable when monitoring the alerts generated by your HIMS. Establish a way to regularly receive this information so that your security administration staff can incorporate it into the log analysis and incident response process.

If you are deploying a HIMS in a small to mid-size company or organization, the rest of this chapter will be helpful. If you are a large organization with thousands of monitored hosts, you will need to find a more in-depth discussion of incident response.

The Incident Response Cycle

Developing an incident response cycle is a constantly improving process. Expect to learn something from each incident, and use that knowledge to improve your response procedures and fine-tune your response capabilities. There is no such thing as perfect security; however, you can greatly improve the overall security of your hosts if you use your HIMS to detect incidents, you learn from those incidents, and you use that information to harden your defenses against another attack.

In the same way that there are many software development methods, there are many different incident response cycles. However, the goal is the same: to define procedures for dealing with security incidents, detecting incidents, responding to incidents, and then applying the knowledge to improve future security and response (see Figure 8.1). The basic sequence is as follows:

- **Planning** Create policy and procedures for anticipated incidents.

- **Detection** Isolate and determine the severity of the incident.

- **Response** Deal with the incident and fix any of the problems that it created.

- **Feedback** Study the incident and feed the learned knowledge back into the response process.

Figure 8.1 The Incident Response Cycle

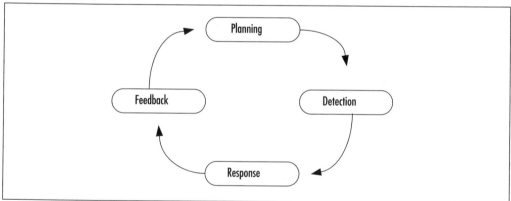

Planning

Planning for incident response is critical. Collecting as much information regarding what to expect, how it will impact your hosts or networks, and how you will handle it can be very helpful. The last thing you want to do is make rash decisions about how to mitigate the effects of an attack, when you are trying to put out fires from all directions including management, users, and the effects of the attack itself.

The first step in planning is to identify the systems involved, which may be firewalls, workstations and other endpoints, network sensors, intrusion detection systems, or servers. In addition to collecting a list of these systems, you should note any significant resources they have and services they run, which will provide an overall map of what is being monitored. (This information may already be assembled from when you planned your HIMS deployment.) In addition to resources, collect contact information for those technically responsible for the systems, as well as management or business contacts that can be consulted when determining the most appropriate course of action from the business perspective.

NOTE

As part of the planning process, make sure that you keep all of the information about monitored systems, resources and services, and contact information in a secured, accessible location. In the event of an incident, you do not want to be scrambling to locate this information. If it is stored on the monitored hosts, keep in mind that you may not have access to it in the event that the host becomes unavailable.

Next, establish an "escalation" procedure, which is essentially a list of contacts that must be notified with the details of an incident. You will probably need to establish separate lists for each host or group of hosts, from management to technical staff such as information technology to system and security administrators, and to anyone who could be impacted from a business perspective.

As part of the planning process, you should establish a "chain of custody" procedure for information related to the detection and analysis of the incident. This can be very important for forensics; there may be requirements for handling log data, scan data, alerts, or e-mail notifications. If you are going to use this in a legal setting, you should determine what the requirements are for of this information. You must have available procedures for creating the chain of custody documents that are kept with the data at all times. This document should provide a detailed listing of who had access to the data, where it was stored, and how it was secured. Your incident response plan should state the procedures for how this will be accomplished in your organization.

Detection

A successfully deployed HIMS can provide the detection share of the incident response cycle; however, there is no such thing as a perfect system. You still have to deal with false positives and false negatives.

Sometimes, detected change is legitimate. Even with the fine-tuning of configurations and filtering and prioritizing log messages, eventually a legitimate change slips through the cracks and drums up the attention of your response team despite the fact that there is no incident to deal with. In some cases, it may not be an attack at all. This part of the incident response cycle should define steps to follow to intelligently determine the nature of the incident, how severe it is, and how to avoid overreacting. The most important part about detection is to maintain a balance between the facts and the security administrator's experience. In some cases, you have to rely on the facts to prevent jumping to conclusions. Consider what you know for sure, and what the possibilities are. It may not be an attack. On the other hand, there are cases where the experience of the system administrator combined with what you know at the time will help direct your attention towards certain explanations for the incident. For example, an increase in traffic on port 22 combined with recent advisories about an SSH vulnerability may cause you to investigate some suspicious changes detected on systems running SSH servers.

Response

This is where the response cycle gets tricky. Your responses to certain incidents may be simple, or they may involve a complex sequence of procedures. The important thing to remember is that your goal is to protect the integrity of your monitored environments. How you choose to respond to certain incidents may jeopardize that goal. Secondly, you need to collect as much information about the incident as possible. The thing to be mindful of is that your response could destroy valuable evidence that would short circuit the response cycle by not allowing you to continue to respond to the event (legally or technically), and then prevent you from learning from the incident and utilizing that information for the betterment of the process.

Common procedure for response is to quarantine and make a copy of the system. The first part of this process is to determine which hosts were affected. If a host shows signs that it was compromised, the first thing to consider is that other hosts of a similar configuration may also have been compromised. Using your HIMS, you should be able to quickly verify if this has occurred.

Part of response is restoration. If you have the resources, you may already have offline builds of a system waiting to be deployed (it is not uncommon for companies to maintain backups of critical hosts to minimize the effect of a security incident). In that case, you need to fix the vulnerability in your backup system before placing it online. If you do not have a backup system, you need to dedicate resources to restoring a new system after you have determined the source of the incident and made any appropriate changes to prevent it from happening in the future.

Feedback

Once the incident has been responded to and any side effects dealt with, you need to define a set of procedures for incorporating what was learned during the process, which includes everything from the security details surrounding the incident to the overall function of the incident response cycle itself. It may be that you underestimated the amount of technical resources you need. You may have gaps in your contact points or escalation chains. The most important thing you can do is document everything surrounding the incident so that you can review it afterwards and find ways to improve the overall incident response procedures.

At the very least, all of the security administrators involved should be assembled to review the incident or incidents. The two main issues of concern are deciding why the incident happened and how you can prevent it from happening in the future. Remember to focus on improvement, not blame. This process is heavily based on the interactions and successful communication between people. If your goal is to improve the security of your hosts, pointing fingers will accomplish little towards this goal. Also, in your review of the incident, keep the big picture in mind; it is easy to focus on the details of an exploit or vulnerability and miss a bigger problem. For example, if a server is continually being compromised because new vulnerabilities are being discovered with a certain piece of software, it may be time to consider options for migrating to a new solution, or finding ways to harden or protect that software. Finally, decide which parts of the HIMS were effective for this incident, and which were not. Document your analysis and use that to inject changes into your HIMS configuration.

Summary

Reading and analyzing logs on a regular basis is the most effective way to use HIMS output. Without analyzing your log data, you will not have a high-level correlation of events and will eventually be ignorant of critical events occurring on your hosts. Swatch is a very simple yet effective way to make sense of all of the log data generated by Osiris and Samhain. If you do not use Swatch, at least make use of some kind of log-monitoring system in order to effectively maintain visibility into the most important changes occurring in your host environments.

No matter how well you have secured your hosts and networks, you will eventually encounter the need to respond to an attack or some type of security violation. Having an established set of procedures in place for dealing with incidents before they occur enables you to effectively handle the incident and learn from it so that you can use that incident for the bettering of host integrity. Incident response is a cycle; it is not a static set of procedures. Each incident should improve your response capabilities and harden your defenses.

Solutions Fast Track

Log Monitoring

☑ When using Osiris or Samhain, you will need to use some kind of log-monitoring tool to prioritize and send notification for detected critical events.

☑ Swatch is a very useful tool for Osiris and Samhain because it is very simple to use, very configurable, and easy to deploy.

☑ Swatch can also be used to monitor events other than Osiris and Samhain; it can be used to help correlate other events surrounding the integrity of your hosts.

Incident Response

☑ Incident response is a continually improving cycle for responding to security events, not a set of static procedures that are defined once.

☑ Incident response involves planning for incidents, detection and analysis, responding tactfully, and learning from the incident to better the response cycle and prevent the incident from occurring in the future.

Frequently Asked Questions

The following Frequently Asked Questions, answered by the authors of this book, are designed to both measure your understanding of the concepts presented in this chapter and to assist you with real-life implementation of these concepts. To have your questions about this chapter answered by the author, browse to **www.syngress.com/solutions** and click on the **"Ask the Author"** form. You will also gain access to thousands of other FAQs at ITFAQnet.com.

Q: I already have existing Swatch configurations. Should I add rules for Osiris or Samhain to them, or create a separate configuration?

A: The obvious advantage of having a single configuration is that you only have to administer one configuration. However, having a separate Swatch configuration for Osiris or Samhain is likely to be more effective. You have less risk of clobbering or interfering with your other monitoring rules. Additionally, it is best to isolate the logs from Osiris and Samhain into their own log file; therefore, if you are using Swatch, you have to use a separate configuration. Plan on having a custom configuration and Swatch instance specifically for monitoring Osiris and Samhain logs.

Q: With Swatch, how can I apply more than one pattern and action set to a certain log event?

A: Use the "continue" option. This option takes no arguments and will cause Swatch to continue down the list of patterns and apply any additional rules to be applied to that log event. Otherwise, it will stop applying rules after the first match.

Q: How does active response play into the development of an incident response plan for a HIMS?

A: Generally, it does not. Osiris and Samhain are not active. Technically, Samhain has a couple of features that are arguably active, but both of them are essentially passive in function. Unlike host intrusion protection systems or certain host intrusion detection systems deployments, you do not have to worry about issues related to active response with Osiris and Samhain.

Q: Should public disclosure of an attack or a compromise be addressed by my incident response plan?

A: Yes. This falls under the business side of response. generally, a response should consider everything from how the incident affects the technical side of the business to the business impact the incident will have.

## Chapter 9

Advanced Strategies

Solutions in this chapter:

- **Performing SUID/SGID Security Audits**
- **Conducting Unscheduled Scans**
- **Looking for Rogue Executables**
- **Testing and Verification**
- **Prebinding and Prelinking**

☑ **Summary**

☑ **Solutions Fast Track**

☑ **Frequently Asked Questions**

Introduction

This chapter contains strategies for the successful deployment of Osiris and Samhain. You do not have to utilize all of this material to be successful; however, it is helpful because it was gathered from personal experience, and from feedback from both Osiris and Samhain users. Both of these systems are very effective at monitoring the integrity of host environments, and each has their own strong points. The following sections use some of those strong points to explore Set User ID (SUID) and Set Group ID (SGID) audits, and to look for rogue executables, perform checks on a deployment, and handle the cumbersome effects of prebinding and prelinking of executables.

Performing SUID/SGID Security Audits

SUID and SGID executables require a great deal of scrutiny and caution. Poorly written software is dangerous to host integrity; poorly written software with elevated privileges is worse. Do not trust that the developers of SUID executables took steps to protect the application from being exploited (including the applications that ship with the operating system). Also, do not trust that the default file permissions limit access to these types of executables. Staying on top of SUID and SGID executables is an administrative effort that requires research and careful inspection of the systems being managed. Osiris and Samhain can help with only part of that effort. Specifically, they can look for and report on changes that involve SUID and SGID executables. You can obtain a quick listing of the SUID and SGID executables by running the following command on every applicable file system:

```
# find / –perm –4000 –o –perm –2000 –type f –ls > /tmp/suid.txt
```

To narrow things down, you may want to only look for SUID or SGID root applications:

```
# find / –perm –4000 –o –perm –2000 –type f –ls –user root > /tmp/suid.txt
```

These commands save all of the found file paths to the */tmp/suid.txt* file. This is important. It does not make sense to monitor changes to SUID or SGID executables if you start with a system that already has vulnerable or suspect SUID or SGID executables. Before you start to monitor these executables, research every application on the list. Consider the following helpful set of questions:

- Is the executable running as the root?
- Does this host need the executable to function?

- Do the permissions follow the principle of least privilege?

- Does it have any vulnerability, or is there an updated version?

You may be able to purge many of the executables, or at least prevent non-privileged users from accessing them. You should not conduct regular SUID and SGID audits with Osiris or Samhain until you have conducted an audit of every executable, made any appropriate changes (e.g., changing the permissions or removing the executable), and are comfortable with your system.

You should periodically generate a new list of SUID executables and review the resultant output for any changes. This is where Osiris and Samhain are helpful; you do not have to do it manually, and you can perform this type of audit on thousands of machines as often as you like and with little effort, and be notified of the results via e-mail. If you do not have the "find" command on your system, or the command does not support all of the arguments used in the aforementioned examples, you will have to either use a more complicated script or have Osiris or Samhain develop the list for you.

For Samhain, conducting an SUID or SGID audit is as simple as configuring your build to include the SUID module, and enabling the SUID check in the Samhain configuration file. The SUID/SGID check supported by Samhain scans the entire file system, skipping all NFS, ISO9660, Virtual File Allocation Table (VFAT), Microsoft Disk Operating System (MSDOS), and proc file systems. It also skips any file system with the *nosuid* mount option specified (for systems that support it). To enable the SUID check, add the following to your configuration file:

```
[SuidCheck]
SuidCheckActive = 1
```

Use the *SuidCheckExclude* directive to exclude a specific directory. For example, to exclude the */dev* directory, add the following to your configuration:

```
SuidCheckExclude = /dev
```

Scheduling can specify a cron-like format or an interval (in seconds). For example, to have the system scanned every day at 3 A.M., add the following to your configuration:

```
SuidCheckSchedule = 0 3 * * *
```

Because this is an input/output (I/O)-intensive operation, this module supports a means of restraining the Samhain agent so that it does not bring the system down when looking for SUID/SGID executables. To limit the number of files per second that the agent processes, use the *SuidCheckFps* directive:

```
SuidCheckFps = 100
```

The quarantine feature of the Samhain SUID/SGID module allows you to do more than report on changes to the list of SUID and SGID executables on a host. When Samhain encounters an SUID or SGID executable, it can be configured to do one of three things:

- Delete the file.

- Remove the SUID or SGID bit(s).

- Move the file into quarantine.

Adding the following directive to your configuration file turns this feature on:

```
SuidCheckQuarantineFiles = yes
```

The action you take when you encounter an SUID or SGID file is determined by the value of the *SuidCheckQuarantineMethod* directive. Specifying "0" means delete, "1" means remove the suspect permissions from the file, and "2" means quarantine the file. When a file is deleted, it is truncated; it is not removed from the file system. This means that the file is left empty with no SUID or SGID permissions set. When quarantined, the file is moved to the Samhain root directory, into a directory named *.quarantine*. If you want Samhain to remove any discovered SUID or SGID files instead of truncating, add the following to your configuration file:

```
SuidCheckQuarantineDelete = yes
```

Having an application like Samhain remove the files it encounters is not a good idea. Although there may be occasional circumstances where this feature is useful, for most deployments it is not. However, the other available quarantine options are useful. Although they cross the line of monitoring, they may be able to mitigate further damage without having an irreversible effect on the system. In some cases, you will not be able to justify a full SUID/SGID scan every hour, or every day. The scheduling will vary significantly. As for dealing with the SUID/SGID executable, you should reset the permissions; you want to do the least amount of modifications to the system to render the SUID/SGID executable powerless. In a case where the Samhain agent encounters a rogue SUID/SGID executable, resetting the permissions will render it powerless, much like moving it to a quarantine directory. Do not move or delete files from arbitrary locations. The resultant Samhain configuration for monitoring SUID and SGID executables once per day at 3 A.M and resetting the permissions on any discovered, is as follows:

```
[SuidCheck]

# activate (0 for switching off).
```

```
SuidCheckActive = 1


# scheduled check every morning at 3am.
SuidCheckSchedule = 0 3 * * *


# logging severity.
SeveritySuidCheck = crit


# throttle files per second.
SuidCheckFps = 100


# quarantine detected SUID/SGID files
SuidCheckQuarantineFiles = yes


# remove SUID/SGID permissions on detected files.
SuidCheckQuarantineMethod = 1


# in case this is gets enabled, set it to only truncation.
SuidCheckQuarantineDelete = no
```

Unfortunately, performing regular SUID/SGID scans using Osiris must be done manually. To do this, you have to temporarily suspend normal scans, perform the audit, and then reset the host so that the scheduler continues normal monitoring activities. To conduct an SUID/SGID scan of a host using Osiris, create a new scan configuration that looks like the following:

```
Recursive yes
Hash md5


<Directory />


    Recursive yes
    FollowLinks no

    NoEntry dev
    NoEntry .vol
    NoEntry Network
    NoEntry automount
    NoEntry Volumes
```

```
     Include suid
     Include guid
```

```
</Directory>
```

The *NoEntry* directives are there to prevent the scan agent from entering directories that will cause it to hang onto device files. The configuration in the preceding example is specific to Mac OS X; the *NoEntry* directives you need to add will vary depending on the operating system. Next, disable and unset the baseline database for that host (remember what the baseline is; you will be resetting it after the scan):

```
osiris-4.1.6-release: host local
local is alive.
osiris-4.1.7-dev[local]: baseline
Base DB: 10
osiris-4.1.6-release[local]: disable
 >>> host local is now disabled.
osiris-4.1.6-release[local]: unset-baseline
 >>> there is  now NO baseline db for host: local
```

The host should be disabled so that the scheduler does not interfere with the audit. The baseline is unset so that the scan will not be compared against the baseline database for this host. When done, you can set the baseline back so that normal monitoring for this host continues. Next, push the new configuration to the host and start a scan:

```
osiris-4.1.6-release[local]: push-config suid-cfg
 >>> the configuration: (suid) has been pushed to host:  local
osiris-4.1.6-release[local]: scan
 >>> scanning process was started on host: local
```

Scanning the entire file system takes time. When the scan is complete, note the name of the created database, set the baseline for this host back to what it was before the scan started, and enable it again so that the normal scan procedures for that host continue:

```
osiris-4.1.6-release[local]: set-baseline 10
 >>> database: 10 is now the baseline for host: local
osiris-4.1.6-release[local]: enable
 >>> host local is now enabled.
```

You now have a database that contains only SUID or SGID files, which can be printed using the *print-db* command through the Osiris command-line interface.

Whenever you want to conduct an SUID or SGID audit, set the baseline database to be the database that was created during the initial audit, push the SUID configuration to the host, and start scanning. Next, set the baseline database back. Any detected changes will be logged or e-mailed to you, depending on your notification settings.

The alternative method is to trick the management console by adding the same host twice so that the second entry can be used specifically for SUID audits. The advantage is that you can set up a separate schedule and maintain separate databases without disrupting normal scans. Make sure that the schedules do not conflict; otherwise, both scans will fail.

Samhain is equipped to conduct SUID and SGID audits as part of its regular functionality. It was developed with more emphasis on monitoring hosts for bad as opposed to general monitoring. It is only natural that SUID and SGID audits are part of its native functionality. However, both Osiris and Samhain are capable of monitoring hosts for these types of executables; these checks should be performed on a regular basis.

Conducting Unscheduled Scans

One of the advantages of centralized monitoring is that you can automatically establish regular scanning of many hosts. The downside is that an attacker can possibly avoid detection if the scan schedule is known. This is attractive to attackers because they would not have to tamper with the monitoring system; as long as the system is restored before the next scheduled scan, the agent reports no changes since the last scan.

Both Osiris and Samhain lack built-in features to deviate from their normal scheduled scans. However, scans can be run manually on a few select hosts. For Osiris, it is as easy as logging into the console, pushing the host's configuration, and telling it to scan. In most cases, the agent already has its configuration loaded so you can tell the hosts to scan without entering a host context:

```
$ osiris
Osiris Shell Interface - version 4.1.6-release
 >>> authenticating to (localhost)

User: admin
Password:

connected to management console, code version (4.1.6-release).
hello.
```

```
osiris-4.1.6-release: scan local
 >>> scanning process was started on host: local
osiris-4.1.6-release: scan freebsd1
 >>> scanning process was started on host: freebsd1
osiris-4.1.6-release: scan freebsd2
 >>> scanning process was started on host: freebsd2
osiris-4.1.6-release: scan freebsd3
 >>> scanning process was started on host: freebsd3
...
```

If you are using Samhain, conducting a random scan is as simple as logging into the remote host and running a check session. If Samhain is already running as a daemon or daemon mode is specified in your configuration file, you should force Samhain to run in the foreground. For example:

```
# samhain -t check --foreground
ALERT   :   [2005-04-02T08:43:16-0700] msg=<START>, program=<Samhain>,
userid=<0>, path=</etc/samhainrc>,
hash=<289A179EF36AE3AC928A0845B41C4A918D9DF635A8A26CF4>,
path=</var/lib/samhain/samhain_file>,
hash=<3893C153614FEF7B440FA622D2FEE3B0253DF64509CF60B3>
CRIT    :   [2005-04-02T08:43:18-0700] msg=<POLICY [ReadOnly] --------T->,
path=</bin/ls>, ctime_old=<[2005-03-30T14:45:58]>, ctime_new=<[2005-04-
02T15:39:04]>, mtime_old=<[2005-03-30T14:45:58]>, mtime_new=<[2005-04-
02T15:39:04]>,
ALERT   :   [2005-04-02T08:43:18-0700] msg=<EXIT>, program=<Samhain>,
status=<None>
```

Keep in mind that this will reveal all of the differences between your host and the database for that host. Any Samhain daemon that is running will have already reported these alerts and are keeping them resident so that they are not reported with each scan. Since you are already logged into the host to run a random scan, you may also want to update the database interactively. If you have a running daemon and are running Samhain in client/server mode, you must suspend it to prevent concurrent access to the log server. To do that, send a SIGUSR2 signal to the currently running daemon, run the update, and resume the daemon by issuing another SIGUSR2 signal:

```
$ ps -auxw | grep samhain | grep root
root    4171    0.0   0.0     75676     612   ??   S      8:35AM    0:24.94
samhain -t check
# kill -SIGUSR2 4171
```

```
MARK    :  [2005-04-02T08:50:30-0700] msg=<SUSPEND> program=<Samhain>
3E694FAFF8EA223A8EE84E31712492B5CDE4B8FE290673D8


# samhain -t update --foreground --interactive
ALERT   :  [2005-04-02T08:51:20-0700] msg=<START>, program=<Samhain>,
userid=<0>, path=</etc/samhainrc>,
hash=<289A179EF36AE3AC928A0845B41C4A918D9DF635A8A26CF4>
CRIT    :  [2005-04-02T08:51:22-0700] msg=<POLICY [ReadOnly] --------T->,
path=</bin/ls>, ctime_old=<[2005-03-30T14:45:58]>, ctime_new=<[2005-04-
02T15:39:04]>, mtime_old=<[2005-03-30T14:45:58]>, mtime_new=<[2005-04-
02T15:39:04]>,
Update /bin/ls [Y/n] ? y
ALERT   :  [2005-04-02T08:51:27-0700] msg=<EXIT>, program=<Samhain>,
status=<None>
# kill -SIGUSR2 4171
```

Looking for Rogue Executables

Operating systems have general guidelines for where certain types of files are kept. For example, configuration files are commonly stored under */etc*, growing and changing files such as logs or Packet Identifier (PID) files are stored under */var*, and executables are stored in bin directories such as */bin /usr/bin, /usr/local/bin*, and the like. On Windows, executables are stored under *%SystemRoot%\Program Files* or under the *%WindowsRoot%* directory. There are exceptions to all of these, but this is generally the case.

Almost all scan configurations are created to monitor the standard locations for executables, because they are relatively free from noise. These files should change only when system updates are performed; therefore, monitoring them frequently is generally not an administrative burden. For example, the following Osiris report reveals that *nmap* has been installed on some kind of UNIX host:

```
compare time: Sat Apr  2 09:25:39 2005
         host: local
   scan config: default.darwin (f02587b9)
      log file: no log file generated, see system log.
 base database: 15
compare database: 18


[211][local][cmp][/usr/local/bin][mtime][Mon Mar 21 08:36:32 2005][Sat Apr
2 09:25:33 2005]
```

```
[213][local][cmp][/usr/local/bin][ctime][Mon Mar 21 08:36:32 2005][Sat Apr
2 09:25:33 2005]

[206][local][cmp][/usr/local/bin/nmap][inode][952675][1192113]

[211][local][cmp][/usr/local/bin/nmap][mtime][Tue Mar  1 06:31:43 2005][Sat
Apr  2 09:25:33 2005]

[213][local][cmp][/usr/local/bin/nmap][ctime][Tue Mar  1 06:31:43 2005][Sat
Apr  2 09:25:33 2005]


Change Statistics:

--------------------------------


          checksums: 0

         SUID files: 0

   root-owned files: 2

   file permissions: 0

                new: 0

            missing: 0


total differences: 5
```

For certain types of systems, you should keep a detailed list of which executables reside on the system and where they are located. For hosts that do not have a compiler and do not allow many user logins, there is no reason to look for executables stored in different directories; executables will be installed with the operating system.

There are two parts to maintaining the integrity of the executable base of a host. First, you need to determine what executables exist on your system. Once you have compiled this baseline, you can begin to monitor for changes involving executables. An executable may mean binaries or it could include executable scripts. Again, what may be acceptable for one host may not be for another. Generally, this type of monitoring is the most effective on server environments where you know without doubt that an executable should never reside outside certain locations on the file system. This section examines how to use Osiris to monitor the state of a host focusing exclusively on executable files or scripts. Osiris has an *executable file filter* and a *script filter*, which examine the contents of files that look like native executables or scripts. The advantage is that even if the permissions, the locations, or the file names are not usually indicative of an executable, it will still be seen as an executable by the agent. These filters are based on the UNIX file command. Samhain has the ability to monitor for rogue SUID and SGID applications, but is not as well suited for this type of monitoring.

The following example explains how to set up and configure rogue executable monitoring on a host running Mac OS X (note that the steps are the same for all systems). Because you will be doing this for only select hosts, you can use the strategy of adding a host to the console a second time. In this case, you will create a scan configuration specifically to look for executables and to monitor them whenever you choose; in other words, this will not be a regularly scheduled scan for the host.

> **NOTE**
>
> When setting up and configuring rogue executable monitoring that uses the *executable* and *script* filters implemented by Osiris, the *executable* filter is only supported for Linux, FreeBSD, OpenBSD, NetBSD, Mac OS X, Solaris, and Microsoft Windows. This filter is not supported on other platforms.

First, add a new host entry to the console. In this case, the name of the host is *local*, so this host is named *local-rogue*. Do not enable or initialize this host. Your configuration should look something like the following:

```
host                   => local-rogue
hostname/IP address    => 127.0.0.1
description            => local scanner, rogue executable configuration
agent port             => 2265
host type              => generic
log enabled            => no
archive scans          => no
auto accept            => yes
purge databases        => yes
notifications enabled  => yes
notifications always   => no
notify on rekey        => no
notify on scan fail    => no
notify email           => (management config)
scans starting on      => (not configured)
scan frequency         => daily (every 1440 minutes).
enabled                => no


Is this correct (y/n)? y
```

```
>>> new host (local-rogue) has been created.
Initialize this host? (yes/no): no
```

Next, create a scan configuration for this host. If you plan on doing this for a handful of different hosts, you may want to make the scan configurations local to that host so that they do not clutter the shared configuration store. Name the configuration something obvious and add the following to it:

```
Recursive yes
Hash md5


<Directory />

        Recursive yes
        FollowLinks no

        NoEntry dev
        NoEntry .vol
        NoEntry Network
        NoEntry automount
        NoEntry Volumes

        Include executable
        Include script


</Directory>
```

Notice that the *NoEntry* directives are the same ones you used when scanning for rogue SUID and SGID executables. This is to prevent the agent from getting into infinitely recursive peril with file descriptors or proc-like file systems. Because this scan will take time, you should disable the host so that your scan does not interfere with regularly scheduled scans. Make sure the host is idle and then disable it:

```
osiris-4.1.6-release: status local

[ current status of host: local ]

      current time: Sat Apr  2 09:59:02 2005
         up since: Fri Apr  1 19:58:53 2005


   last config push: Sat Apr  2 09:22:14 2005
```

```
configuration id: f02587b9


    agent status: idle.
    config status: current config is valid.
  osiris version: 4.1.6-dev
            OS: Darwin 7.8.0


osiris-4.1.6-release: disable local
 >>> host local is now disabled.
```

Next, initialize this host with your newly created configuration:

```
osiris-4.1.6-release: init local-rogue

Initializing a host will push over a configuration, start
a scan, and set the created database to be the
trusted database.

Are you sure you want to initialize this host (yes/no): y

OS Name: Darwin
OS Version: 7.8.0

use the default configuration for this OS? (yes/no): no

[shared configs]

  [ name ]                [ id ]

  default.aix             6d2857b0
  default.bsdos           99a38a8c
  default.darwin          f02587b9
  default.freebsd         c3dcf455
  default.irix            ed6c0108
  default.linux           c8ce9c09
  default.netbsd          0cf39a70
  default.openbsd         91a7a6a1
  default.sunos           5c4aef88
  default.unix-generic    e088d50b
```

```
default.windows2000    951cbd4e
default.windowsnt      69a22176
default.windowsserve   63f6bd00
default.windowsxp      974cd899
default.wrt54g          cd2c17fa
local-rogue            7c0052c0
suid                   6fc8fcd3


total: 20


-no local configurations-


Specify a configuration: local-rogue
 >>> configuration (local-rogue) has been pushed.
 >>> scanning process was started on host: local-rogue
```

This scan will take time, depending on your hardware and how much disk memory the agent has to go through. When the scan is complete, you will be left with a baseline database for this host that contains all of the found executable files and scripts. As soon as the scan is complete, enable the regular host entry so that scheduled scans can continue:

```
osiris-4.1.6-release: enable local
 >>> host local is now enabled.
```

To see the scan results, print the database header for this baseline:

```
osiris-4.1.6-dev[local-rogue]: print-db-header 1


   DATABASE:  1


  status: complete
  errors: 0
 records: 1320
   config: local-rogue (7c0052c0)


  SCAN RESULTS:


        record type: UNIX1
```

```
                files encountered: 447538
                   files scanned: 1320


             symlinks encountered: 9504
              symlinks followed: 0


                 files unreadable: 0
         directories unreadable: 0
           symlinks unreadable: 0


                 scan started: Sat Apr  2 10:00:13 2005
                 scan finished: Sat Apr  2 10:20:52 2005
```

You can see that the agent scanned almost a half-million files and found more than one thousand executables and scripts. The scan also took 20 minutes to complete. This is something to consider when determining how often you will conduct a rogue executable scan.

You can view the list of files by printing a file listing from the database using the *print-db* command:

```
osiris-4.1.6-release[local-rogue]: print-db 1
This may take a while...


100% [=======================================>] 891289 bytes

    h) show database header.
    r) list file records.
    d) list file record details.
    m) list module records.
    x) list errors.
    q) quit


[local-rogue:database: 1]: r


[/bin/\133]
[/bin/bash]
[/bin/cat]
[/bin/chmod]
[/bin/cp]
[/bin/csh]
```

```
[/bin/date]
[/bin/dd]
[/bin/df]
[/bin/domainname]
[/bin/echo]
[/bin/ed]
[/bin/expr]
[/bin/hostname]
[/bin/kill]
[/bin/ln]
[/bin/ls]
[/bin/mkdir]
...
```

Now that you have an established baseline, you can conduct subsequent scans of this host for rogue executables by disabling scheduled scans, pushing the rogue configuration, scanning the host, and then enabling normal scans. The procedure will look something like the following:

```
osiris-4.1.6-dev: disable local
 >>> host local is now disabled.
osiris-4.1.6-dev: host local-rogue
local-rogue is alive.
osiris-4.1.6-dev[local-rogue]: push-config
 >>> the configuration: (local-rogue) has been pushed to host:  local-rogue
osiris-4.1.6-dev[local-rogue]: scan
 >>> scanning process was started on host: local-rogue

<wait until scan completes...>

osiris-4.1.6-dev[local-rogue]: q
osiris-4.1.6-dev: enable local
 >>> host local is now enabled.
```

You must remember to push the rogue scan configuration because, by default, the agent hangs on to its configuration after a scheduled scan. When you start the scan, it will scan with the normal configuration for that host. When you enable the host again, the scheduler will make sure the proper configuration is pushed before resuming normal scans.

Testing and Verification

If you use default scan configurations for deployments, you are less likely to have to test beyond the initial deployment. However, once you start to develop your own custom scan configurations and deployments, you should verify that the system is working according to your expectations and intentions. It is also a good idea to conduct spot checks (fire drills) on your host integrity monitoring system so that you have reasonable assurance that it will respond when needed. Systems change, host configurations change, and security administrators come and go. Therefore, you should take steps to ensure that your HIMS is up and running as it should be. In the unfortunate case of a compromise, the last thing you want is for your HIMS to fail because of an administrative error. The frequency in which you conduct fire drills on your HIMS is up to you and your security policy. The following section shows you how to conduct some simple tests, including verifying scan configurations against real change, and verifying alerts thresholds and filters.

Is It Working?

The easiest test to perform is to verify that the files you are monitoring are actually being monitored, and that any changes are being reported correctly. Generally, you can make specific changes and then verify that they are reported on correctly. If your file-scanning schedule is not frequent, you may be tempted to conduct manual scans; however, it is best if you let the system find the changes, to keep the tests more realistic. If you start scans manually, make sure you take the proper care to disable or suspend the scan agent so that you do not disrupt the normal scan cycle.

A good set of tests to perform for file-related monitoring include:

- Creating a new file
- Deleting a file
- Changing time stamps (*mtime* and *ctime*)
- Changing permissions
- Changing user and group ownership
- Changing the contents of a file

This can be done manually, or you can establish a script that does it for you. A script may be more helpful if you plan to regularly monitor multiple locations on your file system. Creating files is easy; however, making changes to system files is not always possible. As a workaround, plant specific files into the location to be used for test cases; the changes to these dummy files will have no impact on the system.

The following shell script can create files to add to your baseline, and can make changes to them to verify that the proper alerts are being generated:

```
$ cat ./firedrill.sh
#!/bin/sh

LOC="/bin"

start()
{
    # create files to modify or be deleted.
    touch ${LOC}/hitest.deleted
    touch ${LOC}/hitest.timestamps
    touch ${LOC}/hitest.perms
    chmod g-rwx ${LOC}/hitest.perms
    touch ${LOC}/hitest.owner
    touch ${LOC}/hitest.contents
    echo "init" > ${LOC}/hitest.contents
}

change()
{
    # test creating a new file
    touch ${LOC}/hitest.new
    echo "  >> created new file: ${LOC}/hitest.new"

    # test deleting a file
    rm ${LOC}/hitest.deleted
    echo "  >> deleted file: ${LOC}/hitest.deleted"

    # test changing mtime and ctime
    touch ${LOC}/hitest.timestamps
    echo "  >> changing timestamps for: ${LOC}/hitest.timestamps"

    # test changing permissions
    chmod g+rwx ${LOC}/hitest.perms
    echo "  >> changing permissions for file: ${LOC}/hitest.perms"

    # test changing
```

```
        chown nobody ${LOC}/hitest.owner
        echo "  >> changing owner for file: ${LOC}/hitest.owner"


        # test changing file contents
        echo "garbage" >> ${LOC}/hitest.contents
        echo "  >> changing checksum for file: ${LOC}/hitest.contents"
}


restore()
{
        rm ${LOC}/hitest.*
}


if [ "$1" = "init" ] ; then
        start
elif [ "$1" = "restore" ] ; then
        restore
else
        change
fi


exit 0
```

The variable *LOC* at the top of this script is the location where all of the dummy files will be kept. Change this value to whatever directory you want to test in your scan configuration. To run this script for the first time, run it with the argument *init* as root:

```
# ./firedrill.sh init
```

This will create all of the necessary files, but will not produce any output. Next, run another scan on your system to incorporate these files into your baseline. To test what your agent is able to detect, run the *firedrill* script with no arguments. This will perform some changes to the system on the dummy files:

```
$ sudo ./firedrill.sh
  >> created new file: /bin/hitest.new
  >> deleted file: /bin/hitest.deleted
  >> changing timestamps for: /bin/hitest.timestamps
  >> changing permissions for file: /bin/hitest.perms
  >> changing owner for file: /bin/hitest.owner
  >> changing checksum for file: /bin/hitest.contents
```

Finally, run another scan of the system to detect the changes; Osiris will produce the following report. As you can see, it is relatively easy to find the changes that have occurred, and whether or not they were expected. The contents file has a new checksum as well as bytes and time stamps (since the file was modified). The files that were changed in ownership and permissions also show *ctime* changes because their *inodes* were updated. The time stamps for files were changed and are indicated in the logs. Finally, a new file alert was generated for the created file, and a missing file alert was generated for the file that was deleted. All of the changes were detected.

```
compare time: Sat Apr  2 13:22:49 2005
         host: local
   scan config: default.darwin (5dc9978e)
      log file: no log file generated, see system log.
  base database: 31
 compare database: 33


[211][local][cmp][/bin][mtime][Sat Apr  2 13:22:11 2005][Sat Apr  2
13:22:45 2005]

[213][local][cmp][/bin][ctime][Sat Apr  2 13:22:11 2005][Sat Apr  2
13:22:45 2005]

[204][local][cmp][/bin/hitest.contents][checksum][a8ba672d936979971031015181d
7008c3][6e7af3ca66b56a0cf58439d903c6f8ef]

[211][local][cmp][/bin/hitest.contents][mtime][Sat Apr  2 13:22:11
2005][Sat Apr  2 13:22:45 2005]

[213][local][cmp][/bin/hitest.contents][ctime][Sat Apr  2 13:22:11
2005][Sat Apr  2 13:22:45 2005]

[215][local][cmp][/bin/hitest.contents][bytes][5][13]

[202][local][missing][/bin/hitest.deleted]

[209][local][cmp][/bin/hitest.owner][uid][0][4294967294]

[213][local][cmp][/bin/hitest.owner][ctime][Sat Apr  2 13:22:11 2005][Sat
Apr  2 13:22:49 2005]

[207][local][cmp][/bin/hitest.perms][perm][-rw----r--][-rw-rw-r--]

[213][local][cmp][/bin/hitest.perms][ctime][Sat Apr  2 13:22:17 2005][Sat
Apr  2 13:22:49 2005]

[211][local][cmp][/bin/hitest.timestamps][mtime][Sat Apr  2 13:22:11
2005][Sat Apr  2 13:22:45 2005]

[213][local][cmp][/bin/hitest.timestamps][ctime][Sat Apr  2 13:22:11
2005][Sat Apr  2 13:22:45 2005]

[203][local][new][/bin/hitest.new]
```

```
Change Statistics:

---------------------------------


           checksums: 1
          SUID files: 0
    root-owned files: 5
    file permissions: 1
                 new: 1
             missing: 1


total differences: 14
```

As you can see in the following example, Samhain detects the same changes after a foreground check is performed:

```
# samhain -t check --foreground
ALERT   : [2005-04-02T13:22:59-0700] msg=<START>, program=<Samhain>,
userid=<0>, path=</etc/samhainrc>,
hash=<289A179EF36AE3AC928A0845B41C4A918D9DF635A8A26CF4>,
path=</var/lib/samhain/samhain_file>,
hash=<A41FE8148338E95D3E64B0E7F5CD181CD4AE834630521A44>
CRIT    : [2005-04-02T13:23:00-0700] msg=<POLICY [ReadOnly] --------T->,
path=</bin>, ctime_old=<[2005-04-02T20:22:11]>, ctime_new=<[2005-04-
02T20:22:45]>, mtime_old=<[2005-04-02T20:22:11]>, mtime_new=<[2005-04-
02T20:22:45]>,
CRIT    : [2005-04-02T13:23:01-0700] msg=<POLICY [ReadOnly] --------T->,
path=</bin/hitest.timestamps>, ctime_old=<[2005-04-02T20:22:11]>,
ctime_new=<[2005-04-02T20:22:45]>, mtime_old=<[2005-04-02T20:22:11]>,
mtime_new=<[2005-04-02T20:22:45]>,
CRIT    : [2005-04-02T13:23:01-0700] msg=<POLICY [ReadOnly] -----M--T->,
path=</bin/hitest.perms>, mode_old=<-rw----r-->, mode_new=<-rw-rwxr-->,
ctime_old=<[2005-04-02T20:22:17]>, ctime_new=<[2005-04-02T20:22:49]>,
CRIT    : [2005-04-02T13:23:01-0700] msg=<POLICY [ReadOnly] ------U-T->,
path=</bin/hitest.owner>, owner_old=<root>, owner_new=<nobody>,
ctime_old=<[2005-04-02T20:22:11]>, ctime_new=<[2005-04-02T20:22:49]>,
CRIT    : [2005-04-02T13:23:01-0700] msg=<POLICY ADDED>,
path=</bin/hitest.new>, mode_new=<-rw-r--r-->, imode_new=<33188>,
hardlinks_new=<1>, idevice_new=<0>, inode_new=<1194522>, owner_new=<root>,
iowner_new=<0>, group_new=<wheel>, igroup_new=<0>, size_old=<0>,
size_new=<0>, ctime_new=<[2005-04-02T20:22:45]>, atime_new=<[2005-04-
02T20:22:45]>, mtime_new=<[2005-04-02T20:22:45]>,
chksum_new=<24F0130C63AC933216166E76B1BB925FF373DE2D49584E7A>
```

```
CRIT   :  [2005-04-02T13:23:01-0700] msg=<POLICY [ReadOnly] C-------TS>,
path=</bin/hitest.contents>, size_old=<5>, size_new=<13>, ctime_old=<[2005-
04-02T20:22:11]>, ctime_new=<[2005-04-02T20:22:45]>, mtime_old=<[2005-04-
02T20:22:11]>, mtime_new=<[2005-04-02T20:22:45]>,
chksum_old=<714E1C6E96547CFC17F18D418F0E2EF32855C3ACCE7CB4C0>,
chksum_new=<DD57DE6C0F6A3750EAAC362BFB85AB28309E48AD2D2B571E>,
CRIT   :  [2005-04-02T13:23:01-0700] msg=<POLICY MISSING>,
path=</bin/hitest.deleted>, mode_old=<-rw-r--r-->, imode_old=<33188>,
hardlinks_old=<1>, idevice_old=<0>, inode_old=<1194515>, owner_old=<root>,
iowner_old=<0>, group_old=<wheel>, igroup_old=<0>, size_old=<0>,
size_new=<0>, ctime_old=<[2005-04-02T20:22:11]>, atime_old=<[2005-04-
02T20:22:11]>, mtime_old=<[2005-04-02T20:22:11]>,
chksum_old=<24F0130C63AC933216166E76B1BB925FF373DE2D49584E7A>
ALERT  :  [2005-04-02T13:23:01-0700] msg=<EXIT>, program=<Samhain>,
status=<None>
```

To restore the dummy files to their original states (minus time stamps), run the *firedrill* script again, this time with the *restore* argument:

```
# ./firedrill.sh restore
```

Testing Filters

The next test to perform is on alert filtering. It is obvious if you can reduce noise by adding a filter or adjusting your scan configuration; however, it is not obvious if your filter has blocked more than you intended. Improper filter or alert settings can introduce false negatives. The best way to handle this is to simulate your production system as much as possible. Ideally, you will clone a production system to try new configurations and filters on before pushing those changes into your production HIMS. This is undoubtedly better than conducting tests on a production host. For example, suppose you have a directory */usr/local/web-app* that contains executables and log files under */usr/local/web-app/bin* and */usr/local/web-app/logs*, respectively. Assuming you want to block changes to anything under the *logs* directory, you can easily test a filter by making changes to files under both directories and verifying that only the changes to the *bin* directory generate alerts.

Another way to test Osiris filters is to use the *test-filter* command with the Command Line Interface (CLI). This can be useful in many cases, but if you are going to test a lot of log messages against a filter, it will end up being a clumsy, time-consuming solution. To get around this, run your log messages through the global regular expression parser (grep) to test the effects your regular expressions will have on real log files. Suppose you encounter the following log messages on a daily basis:

```
compare time: Sun Apr  3 20:28:33 2005
```

```
            host: local
      scan config: default.darwin (67f3c6b4)
         log file: no log file generated, see system log.
    base database: 41
 compare database: 42
```

[204][local][cmp][/var/log/lastlog][checksum][49b7c4d9db6a5d3f19b94ac50083cd dd][f925180264138bd61e0d50f95d145978]

[211][local][cmp][/var/log/lastlog][mtime][Sun Apr 3 20:25:31 2005][Sun Apr 3 20:28:03 2005]

[213][local][cmp][/var/log/lastlog][ctime][Sun Apr 3 20:25:31 2005][Sun Apr 3 20:28:03 2005]

[204][local][cmp][/var/log/system.log][checksum][bb56a6a7352fa5688e411d4a315 c8a3f][ce4fc2a39e1f5d83d87b53a26c8bf4aa]

[211][local][cmp][/var/log/system.log][mtime][Sun Apr 3 20:27:50 2005][Sun Apr 3 20:28:33 2005]

[213][local][cmp][/var/log/system.log][ctime][Sun Apr 3 20:27:50 2005][Sun Apr 3 20:28:33 2005]

[215][local][cmp][/var/log/system.log][bytes][2803124][2910649]

[216][local][cmp][/var/log/system.log][blocks][5480][5688]

[204][local][cmp][/var/log/wtmp][checksum][e5b1bda706ab602d697e27596a877bbd] [4e6e4314ad5ca0ccb2fe94b6aee99324]

[211][local][cmp][/var/log/wtmp][mtime][Sun Apr 3 20:25:31 2005][Sun Apr 3 20:28:03 2005]

[213][local][cmp][/var/log/wtmp][ctime][Sun Apr 3 20:25:31 2005][Sun Apr 3 20:28:03 2005]

[215][local][cmp][/var/log/wtmp][bytes][166932][167004]

```
Change Statistics:
----------------------------------

           checksums: 3
           SUID files: 0
    root-owned files: 3
    file permissions: 0
                 new: 0
             missing: 0


total differences: 12
```

The main problem is that you want to monitor these files, but not all of its attributes. With Samhain, this is easy because you can simply drop this directory into the *LogFiles* or *GrowingLogFiles* policy section. For Osiris, you need to create a filter to weed out the attributes that are expected to change. In this case, you are not concerned with time stamps, size, or checksums. All of the aforementioned log entries apply to files under */var/log*, so we limit the filter to that directory. First, copy the log file somewhere where you can safely work on it. If you are not saving log files, the last log is always called *log.temp*. Otherwise, it will be specified in the notification:

```
# cp /usr/local/osiris/hosts/local/logs/log.temp /tmp
```

Next, test a regular expression using cat and grep. Capture just the log entries by catching all lines that start with an open square bracket:

```
# cat /tmp/log.temp | grep -E "^\["
[204][local][cmp][/var/log/lastlog][checksum][49b7c4d9db6a5d3f19b94ac50083cd
dd][f925180264138bd61e0d50f95d145978]

[211][local][cmp][/var/log/lastlog][mtime][Sun Apr  3 20:25:31 2005][Sun
Apr  3 20:28:03 2005]

[213][local][cmp][/var/log/lastlog][ctime][Sun Apr  3 20:25:31 2005][Sun
Apr  3 20:28:03 2005]

[204][local][cmp][/var/log/system.log][checksum][bb56a6a7352fa5688e411d4a315
c8a3f][ce4fc2a39e1f5d83d87b53a26c8bf4aa]

[211][local][cmp][/var/log/system.log][mtime][Sun Apr  3 20:27:50 2005][Sun
Apr  3 20:28:33 2005]

[213][local][cmp][/var/log/system.log][ctime][Sun Apr  3 20:27:50 2005][Sun
Apr  3 20:28:33 2005]

[215][local][cmp][/var/log/system.log][bytes][2803124][2910649]

[216][local][cmp][/var/log/system.log][blocks][5480][5688]

[204][local][cmp][/var/log/wtmp][checksum][e5b1bda706ab602d697e27596a877bbd]
[4e6e4314ad5ca0ccb2fe94b6aee99324]

[211][local][cmp][/var/log/wtmp][mtime][Sun Apr  3 20:25:31 2005][Sun Apr
3 20:28:03 2005]

[213][local][cmp][/var/log/wtmp][ctime][Sun Apr  3 20:25:31 2005][Sun Apr
3 20:28:03 2005]

[215][local][cmp][/var/log/wtmp][bytes][166932][167004]
```

Next, add another grep call to test the regular expression:

```
# cat /tmp/log.temp | grep -E "^\[" | grep -E
"\[cmp\]\[/var/log.*\].*\[(mtime|ctime|bytes|blocks|checksum)\]"
[204][local][cmp][/var/log/lastlog][checksum][49b7c4d9db6a5d3f19b94ac50083cd
dd][f925180264138bd61e0d50f95d145978]
```

```
[211][local][cmp][/var/log/lastlog][mtime][Sun Apr   3 20:25:31 2005][Sun
Apr   3 20:28:03 2005]

[213][local][cmp][/var/log/lastlog][ctime][Sun Apr   3 20:25:31 2005][Sun
Apr   3 20:28:03 2005]

[204][local][cmp][/var/log/system.log][checksum][bb56a6a7352fa5688e411d4a315
c8a3f][ce4fc2a39e1f5d83d87b53a26c8bf4aa]

[211][local][cmp][/var/log/system.log][mtime][Sun Apr   3 20:27:50 2005][Sun
Apr   3 20:28:33 2005]

[213][local][cmp][/var/log/system.log][ctime][Sun Apr   3 20:27:50 2005][Sun
Apr   3 20:28:33 2005]

[215][local][cmp][/var/log/system.log][bytes][2803124][2910649]

[216][local][cmp][/var/log/system.log][blocks][5480][5688]

[204][local][cmp][/var/log/wtmp][checksum][e5b1bda706ab602d697e27596a877bbd]
[4e6e4314ad5ca0ccb2fe94b6aee99324]

[211][local][cmp][/var/log/wtmp][mtime][Sun Apr   3 20:25:31 2005][Sun Apr
3 20:28:03 2005]

[213][local][cmp][/var/log/wtmp][ctime][Sun Apr   3 20:25:31 2005][Sun Apr
3 20:28:03 2005]

[215][local][cmp][/var/log/wtmp][bytes][166932][167004]
```

Keep in mind that grep is matching all of the log entries that are filtered out. Therefore, make sure that each of the log messages that are printed using this command are log messages that you want filtered into subsequent scans. Feel free to experiment with this regular expression to make sure that it matches the correct log messages. To see which log entries are *not* being filtered out, use the -*v* option of grep to invert the regular expression. (A good reference for regular expressions is *Mastering Regular Expressions* by Jeffrey E. F. Friedel [O'Reilly and Associates]).

Testing Notifications

Another item to test for is notifications. If you are relying on Samhain or Osiris directly regarding notifications about detected changes to your hosts, you should regularly verify that these notification vectors are working correctly. For Osiris, there is a notification test command in the CLI. To verify that the management console can successfully send you e-mail, login to the management console and do the following:

```
osiris-4.1.7-dev: test-notify
>>> connecting...
>>> notification test message(s) sent.
```

If unsuccessful, an error is printed indicating the reason why the test message was not sent. The standard Osiris test message is a plaintext e-mail that looks something like the following:

```
To: bob@example.com

From: "Osiris Host Integrity System" <osirismd@example.com>

Date: Sun,  3 Apr 2005 16:14:37 -0600

Subject: [osiris test][notification system test]


This is a test notification message sent by the Osiris management console.
```

Prebinding and Prelinking

With Mac OS X and some Linux systems, executables (and libraries) may contain information about their dependencies on other libraries. Specifically, when an executable that is linked against shared libraries is loaded, any referenced symbols must be resolved at runtime. In order to speed this up, some systems have ways of embedding this information into the executable so that the necessary runtime resolution is reduced; therefore, the application starts quicker. This is called *prebinding* on Mac OS X and *prelinking* on Linux. Whenever prebinding or prelinking information is updated, it changes the contents of the executable, and as a result, the checksum for the file. This makes it very difficult to monitor the integrity of these files.

Prebinding: Mac OS X File Integrity

With Mac OS X, both Samhain and Osiris generate false positives when prebinding information is updated. This is problematic because prebinding information is updated not only whenever new software is installed (including all software updates), but also when applications are launched and the prebinding information is discovered to be out of date. This means that at any point (not just when installing software), prebinding information for executables or libraries may be updated. To make this problem even more overwhelming, prebinding information is specific to the host, so in theory, 100 Mac OS X systems could each produce a different set of checksums for the same executable.

Although Osiris and Samhain cannot deal with this problem on Mac OS X, there is a small command-line application called ctool that will produce the Message Digest 5 (MD5) and Secure Hashing Algorithm 1 (SHA-1) values for prebound files, minus their prebinding information. Ctool is available from www.hostintegrity.com/tools/ctool and falls under a Berkeley Software Distribution (BSD)–style license. The options for ctool are as follows:

```
$ ctool

usage: ctool [options...] <file> | <directory> ...

   options:

     -a, --alg <alg>    one of {md5,sha1} default is md5.
     -d, --debug        verbose; display verbose debugging information.
     -r, --recursive    recursively process a directory.
     -s, --stat         show all stat information for specified file.
     -v, --version      display program version information.
     -h, --help         display this usage statement.
```

To compute a checksum minus prebinding information, provide the path to the executable as a single argument:

```
$ ctool /bin/ls
ctool-MD5(/bin/ls)= 3f678c69a72464f8a84287cb110d48d5
```

Remember, this is not the MD5 of the complete file contents, but the file contents *minus* prebinding information. Any Mac OS X system with the same version of */bin/ls* will render this same checksum using ctool. The downside is that an attacker could tamper with just the prebinding information. Since that information is not included with the checksum, it is technically possible for a compromised executable to appear sound when compared against a legitimate one using ctool. However, the alternative is that you have no way of knowing that an executable was modified because of prebinding or because the executable is compromised. While prebinding information is sensitive, it is more likely that the entire executable has been compromised. This being the case, ctool is useful in distinguishing prebinding changes from a Trojan. Furthermore, attacks that take advantage of prebinding will likely manifest themselves in other places. Any changes made to a library will cause ripples of changes in all of the executables that use that library.

To see the details of what was excluded in the computation of the checksum, run ctool in debug mode. For example:

```
$ ctool --debug /bin/ls
====[ file: (/bin/ls) ]====
file type: executable
number of load commands: (15)
...read section __TEXT,__text (offset=3404,size=17344).
...read section __TEXT,__cstring (offset=22796,size=1620).
```

```
...read section __TEXT,__literal8 (offset=24416,size=48).
file size: (32464) bytes.
excluded a total of 13452 bytes from checksum.
ctool-MD5(/bin/ls)= 3f678c69a72464f8a84287cb110d48d5
```

If you provide a directory, all of the files in that directory will be processed. If you specify —*recursive* as an option, all of the subdirectories will also be processed. For example, if you want to take a snapshot of your */bin* directory on a host, assign it a directory and it will automatically compute the contents:

```
$ ctool /bin
ctool-MD5(/bin/[)= 91f366fc40dc513bb98b1e732828e771
ctool-MD5(/bin/bash)= b10d9f6a19144dcb26844ed967f03853
ctool-MD5(/bin/cat)= e2c23a3a794e69d2d8ae2eb3f1bd4941
ctool-MD5(/bin/chmod)= a60aae9d2b863f4cbb049c9b265f1d5e
ctool-MD5(/bin/cp)= e1574422a105e0024bf0c723f47b4408
ctool-MD5(/bin/csh)= c2b372ee986a471b45337c762aed9a07
ctool-MD5(/bin/date)= 10aa150426017f195cdfa90b090e447e
ctool-MD5(/bin/dd)= 37b489d99a2d752de72b10317500660b
ctool-MD5(/bin/df)= 3f6fa1ae859fd16a04a09d42092645ca
ctool-MD5(/bin/domainname)= 3ea582c293c12969527652dffb09fd49
ctool-MD5(/bin/echo)= de4bfe4f8879fbca8b1fcddb62f05d32
ctool-MD5(/bin/ed)= 3c4db2aeef0ab0a7719a6db0303c126b
ctool-MD5(/bin/expr)= 2e83f9ec3d1549cce02f144762b5f634
MD5(/bin/hitest.contents)= 6e7af3ca66b56a0cf58439d903c6f8ef
...skipping zero length file.
...skipping zero length file.
...skipping zero length file.
...skipping zero length file.
ctool-MD5(/bin/hostname)= 157759db15edfbea7f63ac38e6a068f2
ctool-MD5(/bin/kill)= 3c4948a8bd94839c36e9a21065c124c4
ctool-MD5(/bin/ln)= 02e403e7ba0260b863bb40f3d298f9dd
ctool-MD5(/bin/ls)= 3f678c69a72464f8a84287cb110d48d5
ctool-MD5(/bin/mkdir)= a5aab25da37646158665c00e90beb7f3
ctool-MD5(/bin/mv)= 2a0de8e885a2f7a999a18956920974b5
ctool-MD5(/bin/pax)= 2bebd0dc665096faafd0a1181a7d9d26
ctool-MD5(/bin/ps)= bbc3cc36a12891cc9a159d1415e0425f
ctool-MD5(/bin/pwd)= cec65d53323bec319724b14191d70aa5
ctool-MD5(/bin/rcp)= 26aba7bd06163b8252e56160ce4ec95b
ctool-MD5(/bin/rm)= 6addb8226e6288b3d321f5674aaf29f5
```

```
ctool-MD5(/bin/rmdir)= c049c4100bb68e98786021baa160e958
ctool-MD5(/bin/sh)= b10d9f6a19144dcb26844ed967f03853
ctool-MD5(/bin/sleep)= c38e6bc7139bdf0af593be9775607d27
ctool-MD5(/bin/stty)= 4e78d0e2a00a6b7c89b23bed62269ce5
ctool-MD5(/bin/sync)= 618b91dd04f4951f4aa40d090d17aef9
ctool-MD5(/bin/tcsh)= c2b372ee986a471b45337c762aed9a07
ctool-MD5(/bin/test)= 91f366fc40dc513bb98b1e732828e771
ctool-MD5(/bin/zsh)= 5075dc40cf5386412e16bfea074a32e3
ctool-MD5(/bin/zsh-4.1.1)= 5075dc40cf5386412e16bfea074a32e3
```

Finally, ctool can produce the *stat* record for a file (similar to the **stat** command on Linux systems). Mac OS X does not have an easy way to view the contents of the stat record for a file; therefore, ctool is used to do so:

```
$ ctool --stat /bin/ls
ctool-MD5(/bin/ls)= 3f678c69a72464f8a84287cb110d48d5

stats for (/bin/ls):

      device: 234881026
       inode: 860280
        mode: -r-xr-xr-x (33133)
       links: 1
         uid: 0 root
         gid: 0 wheel
        rdev: 0
       mtime: Sat Apr  2 08:39:04 2005 (1112456344)
       atime: Sun Apr  3 08:46:22 2005 (1112539582)
       ctime: Sat Apr  2 08:39:04 2005 (1112456344)
       bytes: 32464
      blocks: 64
  block size: 4096
       flags: 0
  gen number: 0
```

One way to take advantage of ctool is to maintain an offline Mac OS X host to use exclusively as a store for known good file checksums computed with ctool. The known good system is then updated with software updates via read-only media that have been verified; the system is never hooked up to a network. A current listing of known good ctool checksums can be maintained and used to verify suspect files on your systems. To create a listing of ctool-based checksums on your known good system, run the following command after every update:

```
# find / -type f -xdev  -exec ctool '{}' \; > /tmp/ctool.txt
```

After taking some time to run, this command will produce a checksum for every file on the system and store the list in */tmp/ctool.txt*. That data can then be used to perform spot checks on your systems. Keep in mind, that if you have reason to believe that an executable is compromised, the only true way to do this is to perform an offline analysis of the suspect files.

Using ctool is not a perfect solution. The only reason it is useful is because the alternative is nothing. The reason that ctool functionality is not built into Osiris is that it is not viewed as a long-term solution. Prebinding has plagued file integrity on Mac OS X systems for years. The real solution is to build a verification process into the prebinding system itself so that the tree of dependencies can be verified external to the host. In the meantime, ctool is better than nothing.

Prelinking: Linux File Integrity

Some Linux systems implement the concept of *prelinking*, which is basically the same concept as with Mac OS X where the launch time is reduced by resolving symbols beforehand and storing the information in the executable itself. The problem is that it will generate false positives for the HIMS being used. When you think about it, it is not really a false positive when the contents of an executable change. If this executable were updated to a new or patched version, the result would be the same. The difference with prelinking is that it can happen so much that it becomes noise to most of us. For the few of you that enjoy being bombarded with each prelinking alert, carry on. For the rest of us, there are steps to take to ignore them.

With Osiris, the only real option is to disable the prelinking system altogether. Unlike Mac OS X, prelinking on Linux is something you have to seek out. With Mac OS X, prebinding is on, it cannot simply be turned off, and every system has to deal with it. If the decision to use prelinking on your Linux system(s) is not your decision, then Samhain provides some ways to mitigate the noise problem.

Prelinking on Linux systems is handled by an application appropriately named *prelink*, which is usually in */usr/sbin/prelink*, but not always. All prelinking information is handled by the */etc/prelink.conf* configuration file. Specifically, this file contains a listing of directories that contain files to be prelinked. Only files specified in this configuration file or on the command line are altered by the prelink application. This will help you configure Samhain correctly for your system.

The prelink application can be used to interact with and modify prelinked files. For example, to prelink a specific executable, you would do:

```
$ /usr/sbin/prelink --verbose /bin/ls
Assigned virtual address space slots for libraries:
/lib/ld-linux.so.2                                          41000000-
410126b8
/lib/libc.so.6                                              41015000-
4110f644
/lib/libpthread.so.0                                        41112000-
41161e64
/lib/libncurses.so.5                                        41164000-
4119cb2c
/lib/librt.so.1                                             4119f000-
411b09b8
dhcp-64-101-69-194 root #
```

This will update the prelink information for *bin/ls* and any libraries it depends on (assuming that the prelink information needs updating). To undo prelinking for a file, use the —*undo* option:

```
$ /usr/sbin/prelink --undo --verbose /bin/ls
```

This restores the file to its original state. Verify that this has a reverse operation by computing the MD5 or some other checksum before and after the undo operation:

```
$ openssl md5 /bin/ls
MD5(/bin/ls)= 53002c24dc40d2cb33d8c3d51e666d11
# /usr/sbin/prelink /bin/ls
$ openssl md5 /bin/ls
MD5(/bin/ls)= 64efb2aec7647e992f8c2a904a631faf
# /usr/sbin/prelink --undo --verbose /bin/ls
$ openssl md5 /bin/ls
MD5(/bin/ls)= 53002c24dc40d2cb33d8c3d51e666d11
```

This part of the Linux prelink system is very useful; similar functionality would also be very useful on Mac OS X systems. This system also features an option to pre-link called *verify* that will undo and then redo prelink information and verify that the resultant executable is the same as before. If an executable is corrupted or maliciously tampered with, undoing the prelinking and redoing it will reveal the difference. However, if the entire prelink system is compromised, the *verify* feature has little value. And if the prelink system is corrupted, there are much bigger problems to worry about. The *verify* option also outputs the contents of the unprelinked executable, making it easy to pass to another application for checksumming:

```
# /usr/sbin/prelink --verbose --verify /bin/ls | openssl
 md5
53002c24dc40d2cb33d8c3d51e666d11
$ openssl md5 /bin/ls
MD5(/bin/ls)= 64efb2aec7647e992f8c2a904a631faf
```

This will verify the prelink information, and the resultant file will still be prelinked. The only exception to this is if the prelink information does not match. In that case, an error is printed. To demonstrate this, make a copy of */bin/ls*, modify it, and attempt to verify it. It must be kept in the */bin* directory so that it falls under one of the directories specified in the */etc/prelink.conf* file. Note that the modified version of *ls* still seems to be functioning correctly. However, since the file was modified and the prebinding information does not match anymore, the verify option will display an error as opposed to outputting the contents of the file.

```
# cp /bin/ls /bin/ls.copy
# /usr/sbin/prelink --verbose /bin/ls.copy
Assigned virtual address space slots for libraries:
/lib/ld-linux.so.2                                          41000000-
410126b8
/lib/libc.so.6                                              41015000-
4110f644
/lib/libpthread.so.0                                        41112000-
41161e64
/lib/libncurses.so.5                                        41164000-
4119cb2c
/lib/librt.so.1                                             4119f000-
411b09b8
# echo "smargs" >> /bin/ls.copy
# /bin/ls.copy /
bin    dev   home   lost+found   opt                    proc  sbin  tmp
var
boot   etc   lib    mnt          portage-20050326.tar.bz2  root  sys   usr

# /usr/sbin/prelink --verbose --verify /bin/ls.copy
/usr/sbin/prelink: /bin/ls.copy: prelinked file size differs
# rm /bin/ls.copy
```

Finally, to make this even easier, prelink has the option to verify and print the resultant MD5 checksum or SHA-1 checksum to standard output. Basically, this is the —*verify* option, but instead of printing the file, it prints the checksum value. This has obvious application; it is clear that the developers had integrity verification in mind when designing this system:

```
# /usr/sbin/prelink --verbose --verify --md5 /bin/ls
53002c24dc40d2cb33d8c3d51e666d11   /bin/ls
```

As of Version 2.0, Samhain addresses the prelink problem head on by defining a specific policy for executables and files that are affected by prelinking. Usually, executables fall under the *ReadOnly* policy. Files that are subject to prelinking fall under the *Prelink* policy. Specifically, this means that changes to the time stamps, size, and inode are ignored during file checks for files under this policy. Samhain uses the prelink executable to verify prelinked files using */usr/sbin/prelink* —*verify* on each file under the *Prelink* policy (i.e., the output of the verify option is used as input for computing the checksum.

The good thing about prelinking is that prelinked files are specified by the prelink configuration file */etc/prelink.conf*. Generally, anything being monitored under this policy should be specified in the *Prelink* section of the Samhain configuration file. For example, the following is a default *prelink.conf* file for a Gentoo Linux system:

```
# prelink.conf autogenerated by env-update; make all changes to
# contents of /etc/env.d directory
-l /bin
-l /sbin
-l /usr/bin
-l /usr/sbin
-l /lib
-l /usr/lib
-h /usr/local/lib
-h /usr/lib/gcc-lib/i386-pc-linux-gnu/3.3.4
-h /usr/local/bin
-h /opt/bin
-h /usr/i386-pc-linux-gnu/gcc-bin/3.3
-b /usr/lib/wine
-b /usr/lib/valgrind
```

Assuming you are monitoring most of these directories, add them to the Samhain configuration file under the Prelink policy. ***Make sure you remove them*** *from your ReadOnly policy section.* The policy will look something like the following:

```
[Prelink]
##
## Use for prelinked files or directories holding them
##

dir=/bin
dir=/sbin
dir=/usr/bin
dir=/usr/sbin
dir=/lib
dir=/usr/lib
dir=/opt/bin
```

Next, set up the Prelink options under the *Misc* section of the configuration file. There are two different options: *SetPrelinkPath* and *SetPrelinkChecksum*. The *SetPrelinkPath* is the full path to the prelink executable. The *SetPrelinkChecksum* option is used to perform verification of the prelink executable. Because Samhain will be launching the prelink executable to use the output of the verify option, it makes sense to perform some sanity checks on the prelink executable itself. If you do not specify the path, */usr/sbin/prelink* is assumed. If you do not specify a checksum for prelink executable, no checks are performed before executing it. Find out where your executable is, and produce a TIGER–192 checksum:

```
# which prelink
/usr/sbin/prelink

# samhain -H /usr/sbin/prelink
/usr/sbin/prelink: 4A2B8C37 BA9CF227 C73E32C8  AF0A844B 26D9A660 BF4E8D0C
```

Next, add the proper path and checksum to the Samhain configuration file under the Misc section. Make sure to remove the whitespace from the checksum (your checksum and path may vary):

```
SetPrelinkPath = /usr/sbin/prelink
SetPrelinkChecksum = 4A2B8C37BA9CF227C73E32C8AF0A844B26D9A660BF4E8D0C
```

To test this, undo the prebinding information in */bin/ls* and run another scan. Because Samhain will be using the prelink —*verify* output, no alerts about changes to this file are generated:

```
# openssl md5 /bin/ls
MD5(/bin/ls)= 64efb2aec7647e992f8c2a904a631faf
# prelink --undo /bin/ls
# samhain -t check
ALERT  :   [2005-04-03T06:12:11-0700] msg=<START>, prog
ram=<Samhain>, userid=<0>, path=</etc/samhainrc>,
hash=<5052F560713D1016CF10CAD7
B54EC36A728272070FCC6DA3>, path=</var/lib/samhain/samhain_file>,
hash=<98468F58F
4301B45D7F582826D3F2FEB318F64F3159BFBE6>
#
```

To verify, add a bogus application for */bin/ls* and verify that Samhain picks up on it. The following example makes a backup copy of */bin/ls* in */tmp*, then copy */bin/mv* to */bin/ls*. The next scan reveals a violation in the Prelink policy. Specifically, the checksum for */bin/ls* no longer matches. However, notice what happens after */bin/ls* is restored:

```
# cp /bin/ls /tmp
# cp /bin/mv /bin/ls
# samhain -t check
ALERT  :   [2005-04-03T06:16:52-0700] msg=<START>, prog
ram=<Samhain>, userid=<0>, path=</etc/samhainrc>,
hash=<5052F560713D1016CF10CAD7
B54EC36A728272070FCC6DA3>, path=</var/lib/samhain/samhain_file>,
hash=<98468F58F
4301B45D7F582826D3F2FEB318F64F3159BFBE6>
CRIT   :   [2005-04-03T06:17:02-0700] msg=<POLICY [Prel
ink] C--------->, path=</bin/ls>,
chksum_old=<9BF12969CF1EF0117B7A092F0AC9F542CF
F37E5BAFD1765B>,
chksum_new=<F1B8C3C66CDC214ABF7A0132F7C3E6CE3375C82CFE8D432A>,
# cp /tmp/ls /bin/ls
# samhain -t check
ALERT  :   [2005-04-03T06:20:33-0700] msg=<START>, prog
ram=<Samhain>, userid=<0>, path=</etc/samhainrc>,
hash=<5052F560713D1016CF10CAD7
B54EC36A728272070FCC6DA3>, path=</var/lib/samhain/samhain_file>,
hash=<98468F58F
4301B45D7F582826D3F2FEB318F64F3159BFBE6>
```

The alert regarding the */bin/ls* file checksum not matching disappeared after being restored it its original value. Because Samhain ignores time stamps, size, and inode changes, it is possible to load new executables for files under the prelink policy and remain undetected as long as the file is restored whenever Samhain conducts a scan. This is the best argument for the importance of conducting random integrity scans on your hosts.

Summary

Both Osiris and Samhain are beneficial out of the box. However, every deployment has its own requirements and needs. In this chapter you learned how to use some of the selling points for both of these applications and put them to use to make a good deployment even better.

Solutions Fast Track

Performing SUID/SGID Security Audits

☑ SUID and SGID root executables can prove deadly to the integrity of a host and should be monitored.

☑ You can take advantage of Osiris and Samhain's abilities to monitor, only after conducting a full audit of your existing SUID/SGID executables.

☑ SUID and SGID audits are I/O-intensive and should be weighed against the risk and needs of the host.

Conducting Unscheduled Scans

☑ Unscheduled scans are useful for spotting check hosts so that they are not always scanned with the same frequency. In the event that an attacker has learned your scan frequency, you can prevent them from evading detection.

☑ Unscheduled scans with Osiris and Samhain must be performed manually, because neither of them has the ability to deviate from its schedule.

Looking for Rogue Executables

☑ Osiris has special filters that enable it to look inside the contents of files looking specifically for native executables or scripts. These filters can be used to locate rogue executables on a host.

☑ Rogue executable scans are very I/O-intensive and, like SUID/SGID audits, consider the impact on the system before conducting them.

☑ Not all systems are good candidates for rogue executable scans because there is too much noise. Generally, systems that are mostly static (e.g., servers) take to these scans the best.

Testing and Verification

- ☑ Performing spot checks on your integrity monitoring deployments is easy and well worth the effort to ensure that your systems have not fallen into a useless state.

- ☑ Filters can be used to reduce false positives, but they can also introduce false negatives if not configured correctly.

Prebinding and Prelinking

- ☑ Prebinding and prelinking executables have the unfortunate side effect of altering the contents and therefore the checksum of a lt to verify the integrity of the file over time.

- ☑ Samhain has the ability to monitor the integrity of prelinked files on Linux systems.

- ☑ Mac OS X has prebound executables that make monitoring the integrity of executables very difficult for Osiris and for Samhain. Use ctool for spot checks of executables on Mac OS X.

Frequently Asked Questions

The following Frequently Asked Questions, answered by the authors of this book, are designed to both measure your understanding of the concepts presented in this chapter and to assist you with real-life implementation of these concepts. To have your questions about this chapter answered by the author, browse to **www.syngress.com/solutions** and click on the **"Ask the Author"** form. You will also gain access to thousands of other FAQs at ITFAQnet.com.

Q: Are SUID and SGID executables not owned by root worth noticing?

A: Yes. The SUID and SGID root executables are going to be the ones that you scrutinize and can justify their existence; however, non-root owned SUID and SGID executables must not to be overlooked. Often, applications create users specifically to handle daemons or configurations or files containing sensitive data. Some applications run with privileged groups such as kmem to read kernel memory. All SUID and SGID applications that justify their existence and the appearance of new applications with these bits set should not be taken lightly. Conducting regular SUID and SGID audits of a host using Osiris or Samhain is worth the effort.

Q: SUID and SGID checks are very I/O-intensive. How often should I run these scans?

A: There are many variables at play: the kind of host it is (e.g., server, vs. workstation); network exposure; and running services (e.g., e-mail, Web, File Transfer Protocol [FTP]). SUID- and SGID-based exploits are not going to be at the top of the list, so do not constantly scan for SUID root applications. Instead, concentrate on the more important areas such as scanning for new open network ports and kernel modules. Make a decision based on your configuration and facts. Often, SUID and SGID applications are targeted for buffer overflows. A great deal can be accomplished in this area by doing an audit on existing SUID/SGID applications. As far as scheduling goes, Samhain provides excellent support for this; you can specify a scan interval specifically for the SUID/SGID check. For some systems, once per day may not be unrealistic. For others, spot checks might be sufficient.

Q: Despite testing my deployment, I still require proof that scans have taken place. How is that accomplished with Osiris and Samhain?

A: For Osiris, you can turn on notifications regardless of scan results. For Samhain, you can set the threshold severity to alert so that you will receive e-mail even if no changes are detected. In both cases, receipt of e-mail confirms that the scan is complete.

Q: Are unscheduled scans really helpful?

A: It depends. It is particularly important on systems with prebound executables such as Linux and Mac OS X, as some tricks against prebounding are likely to slip past administrators and integrity monitoring systems that conduct only periodic scans. By introducing unscheduled scans, you increase your chances of uncovering attacks based on knowledge of the monitoring schedule.

Q: How can I tell if I have prelinking installed on my Linux system?

A: Look for /etc/prelink.conf and an executable called prelink. The prelink executable is usually located in /usr/sbin/prelink. Most Linux distributions have prelink packages or ports of some type. It takes a conscious effort to install prelinking; avoid installing it if possible. However, many administrators opt to install it because the speed increase is significant.

Monitoring Linksys Devices

Solutions in this chapter

- Using Prebuilt Firmware
- Building Custom Firmware
- Configuration and Administration

Introduction

The Linksys WRT54G and WRT54GS wireless broadband routers are clever devices that run Linux. Because of a licensing issue with the General Public License (GPL), Linksys released the source code for its firmware. As a result, many open source projects began, which provided application ports, toolsets, and complete firmware images packed with additional applications and features. This appendix explores the options for monitoring the environment of a Linksys WRT54G(S) with Osiris. This device is normally found on home or (very) small business networks. Additionally, they are often positioned as border devices and, therefore, are exposed to many types of threats. Given that their environment must remain fairly static, using a HIMS such as Osiris is a very important.

These devices do not have disks, only nonvolatile random access memory (NVRAM). The first models had just over 4MB, but recent models (starting with Version 2.2) have twice as much memory. One of the biggest problems you will encounter when building software for the WRT54G is the size of the executables. The Osiris scan agent depends on OpenSSL, which is not a small library. As a result, it may be challenging to run an Osiris scan agent and all of your favorite tools in one firmware image. However, running the scan agent in addition to the stock functionality of the device is easily accomplished. Most of the significant settings are stored in NVRAM; thus, monitoring the environment necessitates monitoring these settings. To monitor the contents of NVRAM, an Osiris module (*mod_nvram*) was developed.

There are two options for running Osiris on the Linksys WRT54G. The first option is to use a prebuilt firmware image based on code that was released by a company called Sveasoft. The second option is to build the image from source. One big advantage with building from source is that you can add additional tools to the image, including the scan agent's root certificate; otherwise, the root certificate is susceptible to tampering.

> **WARNING**
>
> Some of the steps outlined in this appendix may render your access point a doorstop and void your warranty. Although I have gone to great lengths to make sure the information is accurate, new versions of the software and hardware may become available. Consequently, it is possible that your access point may wind up in an unusable state.

Using Prebuilt Firmware

Using a prebuilt image is the easiest option. The biggest disadvantage is that you have to trust that the image was built correctly and that it is not going to compromise your security or harm your network. The biggest advantage is that you can be up and running in a couple of minutes, without compiling any code.

A prebuilt image based on the Sveasoft firmware distribution is available from the Osiris Web site at http://hostintegrity.com/osiris/linksys.html. Basically, it is the Sveasoft image altered by the addition of the Osiris scan agent software. After downloading the image file, from the Administration tab select **Firmware Upgrade** and use the provided form to upload the new image (see Figure A.1)

Figure A.1 Uploading a New Firmware Image

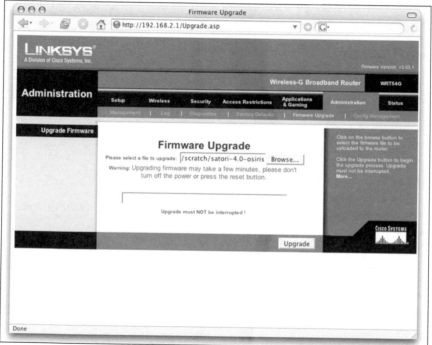

WARNING

Do not attempt to upload custom firmware images via Trivial File Transfer Protocol (TFTP); use only the Web interface. I have noticed that using TFTP for images that are approaching the NVRAM size limit will fail to upload correctly.

If you have Version 2.2 or later of the Linksys WRT54G(S), you will not be able to use certain older Sveasoft firmware images. Attempting to upload older firmware on a new device will fail soon after the upload process begins. The Osiris Web site provides details about which images work with which devices. The version is printed under the Linksys logo on the underside of each device.

After the firmware is uploaded, it will automatically reboot off of the new image. At this point, you should have an Osiris scan agent running and listening on port 2265. All that is necessary is to add this host to your Osiris management console. The root certificate is stored in */tmp/osiris_root.pem* and is lost upon reboot. It is created automatically the first time the management console connects to the agent. Because this file is writable and not part of the firmware image, it is susceptible to tampering. To prevent this, you must build a custom image and build the certificate into the firmware image.

Building Custom Firmware

In order to build a custom firmware image for the WRT54G, you will need:

- Access to a Linux system with a fair amount of disk space (~800MB)
- The Linksys GPL source code
- The modified Sveasoft source code

The Linksys source code can be found on the Web at www.linksys.com/support/gpl.asp. There are source packages for many different Linksys devices; make sure you get the firmware for the WRT54G. The modified Sveasoft source that contains the Osiris scan agent code is also located at the Osiris Linksys Web site at http://hostintegrity.com/osiris/linksys.html.

First, unpack the Linksys source code. You do not have to use the Linksys source, but you do have to install the development toolset:

```
$ tar xvfz wrt54g.2.04.4.tgz
$ tar xvfz wrt54g.2.04.4.tgz
WRT54G/
WRT54G/tools/
WRT54G/tools/README.TXT
WRT54G/tools/brcm/
...
```

This is a large *tar.gz* file, so it will take some time to unpack. Inside the *WRT54G* directory is a *tools* directory. Follow the instructions specified in the README.TXT to install the Linksys development tools. Recent releases of the tools may have different instructions, so use the following only as a guide:

```
$ cd WRT54G/tools
# cp -rf brcm /opt
$ export LINKSYS_PATH="/opt/brcm/hndtools-mipsel-
linux/bin:/opt/brcm/hndtools-mipsel-uclibc/bin"
$ export PATH="$LINKSYS_PATH:$PATH"
```

At this point, the Linksys source code that was unpacked is useless; feel free to delete it. Next, unpack the modified Sveasoft source:

```
$ tar xvfz satori-4.0-osiris.tar.gz
WRT54G/
WRT54G/src/
WRT54G/src/et/
WRT54G/src/et/cfe/
...
```

This will take some time to unpack. If you want to update the osirisd source code with the latest version or if you want to add modules, do so now (the *mod_nvram* module is included). The osirisd source is located within the source tree at *WRT54G/src/router/osiris/src/osirisd/*. You can drop in the osirisd source from any Osiris source distribution and add modules to the source as you would for any build.

By default, the scan agent's root certificate is stored in */tmp* and will be lost upon power cycling the device. If you want to avoid this and protect the certificate from tampering, you can build it into the firmware image. The disadvantage of this is that if you ever need to change this certificate, you will have to rebuild the firmware image. To add a root certificate to the image, copy the file into *WRT54G/src/router/osiris/osiris_root.pem*. It is important that the filename be *osiris_root.pem*; otherwise, the scan agent will not use it.

Next, to build the source, enter the top-level directory and type:

```
$ cd WRT54G
$ make
```

The build time will vary depending on your hardware, but it will generally take at least a half hour to compile. Once finished, the image is *WRT54G/image/code.bin* or *WRT54G/image/code_gs.bin*, depending on your device type. At this point, you can attempt to upload the image to your device.

Configuration and Administration

There are a few differences between monitoring a Linksys WRT54G and monitoring the average Linux system. The biggest difference is with monitoring the contents of NVRAM. The prebuilt images and the modified source code both include *mod_nvram*. In addition, the normal built-in Osiris modules are also used to monitor users, groups, network ports, and kernel extensions. Because of the nature of this device, the network port module is arguably the most important.

Secure Shell (SSH) access may prove useful. The Sveasoft code has an SSH server running by default; however, you will have to configure it in order to allow logins. Having SSH access to the router makes it easy to troubleshoot problems and conduct additional configuration changes. Although not necessary, if you are going to monitor your host for changes, it is recommended that you also establish SSH so that you are not rushing to set it up when you need it. With the Sveasoft images, you must provide an SSH key to make SSH connections (at the time of this writing). The Web-based interface provides instructions for how to set this up.

Included with the Osiris source is a default scan configuration file for the WRT54G:

SYNGRESS
syngress.com

```
Hash md5
FollowLinks no


<System>
      Include mod_users
      Include mod_groups
      Include mod_kmods
      Include mod_nvram
</System>


<Directory />
      Recursive yes
```

```
    NoEntry dev
    NoEntry proc
    NoEntry tmp
    NoEntry var
    IncludeAll
</Directory>
```

This configuration is simple. The four modules, including *mod_nvram*, are used to monitor various elements of the environment. Also, a recursive scan is done on most of the root file system. This makes sense because the file system is read-only. The mount points that are not monitored are *dev*, *proc*, *tmp*, and *var*. Because the file system is read-only, many of these mount points are used to store volatile data while the system is operating.

Although the WRT54G is a Linux environment, there are a few peculiarities to be aware of:

- Make sure that the date is set correctly. After loading images, the clock is set to 1970 and it does not sync to a timeserver, which presents a problem for certificate validation. As a result, any attempt to talk to the scan agent fails, because the agent assumes that the certificate is not valid. To set the time on the default image or the Sveasoft image, navigate to the **Setup | Basic Setup** menu, scroll down to the bottom, and select **automatic** to have the time automatically synced to an NTP server.

- Set the *boot_wait* NVRAM parameter to **on**. This will cause the device to wait at boot and give you the opportunity to use TFTP to upload a good image in the event that the firmware upload did not work. If not set, the router will rush into loading the bad image and then you will have no choice but to open up the case and perform some odd hardware pin-shorting tricks to recover it.

- The Squash file system that comes with the Sveasoft image triggers false positives for blocks and *block_size* changes to files. To ignore these, add the following Osiris filter to prevent these changes from triggering alerts:

```
\[<hostname>\].*\[(blocks|block_size)\]
```

Monitoring the integrity of devices such as the Linksys WRT54G is not only simple, but also very useful. Because these devices are often used as the border to many home and small business networks, they are exposed to a great deal of threats. Generally, these devices are configured once and left alone. Whenever possible, you should add these devices to your HIMS.

Extending Osiris and Samhain with Modules

Solutions in this chapter:

- Osiris Modules
- Samhain Modules

Introduction

Both Osiris and Samhain sport a modular interface that allows you to extend the functionality of their scan agents. This interface is useful for a number of reasons. First, it allows for a number of developers to contribute to improving the functionality of the software. Second, it keeps the agent code small and manageable. As an administrator, you can add modules to your agents to satisfy the various needs of your deployment; you only have to add the modules that make sense for your environment.

The word "module" can be used to describe many things in software. With some applications (e.g., Apache) you can write modules that can by dynamically linked into the application. Both Osiris and Samhain only allow for static modules, which means that if you want to add or remove the functionality of a module from the agent, you must recompile. This appendix examines ways to customize Osiris and Samhain to extend the monitoring capabilities of their agents. Each section walks through the creation of a simple module and shows you how to test it. The goal here is to teach you the basic procedures so that you can develop your own modules.

Both Osiris and Samhain and their modules are written in C; therefore, it is assumed that you have some familiarity with C programming. You must have a system with a C compiler as well as the latest Osiris and/or Samhain source. Do not attempt to follow these examples on a production system. It is recommended that you establish a dedicated test environment just to be safe.

Osiris Modules

Osiris Interface Release 4.0 allows you to extend the functionality of the scan agent by writing your own code for collecting information from the host environment. Aside from monitoring files, all of the Osiris monitoring features (including the monitoring of users, groups, kernel extensions, and open network ports) are implemented as modules.

With each scan, the Osiris agent runs through its list of enabled modules and passes execution to them by calling the module's handler function. With most modules, the handler function involves collecting pieces of information (called records) and sending them back to the console to be stored in the scan database. Each record is a 1K buffer, and requires a unique identifier. When the management console compares two scan databases, their unique IDs are used to iterate through the list of records in each database. A string comparison is done on the text payload of the two records, and if the payloads differ, an alert is generated. The console does not know anything about the content of the modules; the details of what was monitored and the significance of the collected data is contained in the agent code.

An Example Module: *mod_hostname*

The best way to understand how Osiris modules are implemented is to build one. This section goes through the process of implementing a module to monitor hostnames. If the hostname for the host is changed, an alert is generated.

The first step in making an Osiris module is creating a directory and setting up the build environment. Since modules are just extensions to scan agent code, they are kept in a modules directory under the osirisd directory of the Osiris source (*/src/osirisd/modules*). Each module is in its own directory. All you need to do is create the directory, the Makefile, and a *.c* file; the Osiris build environment does the rest. First, make the directory:

```
$ cd src/osirisd/modules
$ mkdir mod_hostname
```

Next, create a Makefile; do this by copying another module's Makefile and modify it accordingly:

```
$ cd mod_hostname
$ cp ../mod_users/Makefile .
```

Edit the Makefile and change the SRCS line so that it reads:

```
SRCS=mod_hostname.c
```

Next, create your source file:

```
$ touch mod_hostname.c
```

All that is left is to implement the module's handler function. Since this module is very simple, all of the work can be done in a single function. Before doing that, however, you need to include the module's header files and define the module's name. Using your editor of choice, add the following to the *mod_hostname.c* file:

```
#include "libosiris.h"
#include "libfileapi.h"
#include "rootpriv.h"
#include "common.h"
#include "version.h"
#include "scanner.h"
#include "logging.h"
```

Now define the module's name:

```
static char *MODULE_NAME = "mod_hostname";
```

Next, define the handler function. The name of the handler function must match the name of the module's directory and the name set in the *MODULE_NAME* character in the preceding example:

```
1 void mod_hostname( SCANNER *scanner )
2 {
3     char name[255];
4     SCAN_RECORD_TEXT_1 record;
5
6     if ( scanner == NULL )
7     {
8         return;
9     }
10
11    if ( gethostname( name, sizeof( name ) ) < 0 )
12    {
13        log_error( "module: %s, error getting hostname.",
           MODULE_NAME );
14        return;
15    }
16
17    initialize_scan_record( (SCAN_RECORD *)&record,
       SCAN_RECORD_TYPE_TEXT_1 );
18
19    /* copy module name into record. */
20    osi_strlcpy( record.module_name, MODULE_NAME,
       sizeof(record.module_name) );
21
22    /* copy a unique record name into the record's  name field. */
23    osi_strlcpy( record.name, "hostname", sizeof( record.name ) );
24
25    /* copy value for this record. */
26    osi_strlcpy( record.data, name, sizeof( record.data ) );
27
28    /* send data. */
29    send_scan_data( scanner, (SCAN_RECORD *)&record );
30 }
```

The first thing to notice is line 11, where you acquire the hostname value into a buffer. Line 17 uses the *initialize_scan_record* function to set the record type and zero-out the payload. At the time of this writing, the *TEXT_1* record type is the only type supported by modules; therefore, all modules use this function to initialize each record.

Line 20 copies the name of the module into the scan record. Not all scan records have a name; however, module records do so that records for each module can be easily distinguished from other records in the database. This is a simple string copy; however, note that function *osi_strlcpy()* is used instead of *strcpy()* or *strncpy()*. Osiris defines a number of safe string-handling functions in */src/libosiris/utilities.h*. For security reasons, you should always use one of these functions in place of the typical C string functions.

Line 23 copies a unique identifier for this record. Since you only have one record, this value is arbitrary. For clarity, copy in the string hostname. In line 30, the value of the hostname acquired from line 13 was copied into the record payload. Finally, the record is sent back to the console in line 34 using the *send_scan_data()* function.

This module generates only one record. If you need to generate multiple records, the code is not much different. The pseudo-code is something like the following:

```
For each record:

    initialize_scan_record()
    set record.module_name
    set record.name
    set record.data
    send_scan_data()
```

There are no module initialization or shutdown routines. To generate a log message, you can use three types of log messages including the *log_error()*, *log_warning()*, and *log_info()* functions. These functions follow a *printf()* style format for arguments.

Now that you have implemented the *mod_hostname*, you must build and verify that it compiles. To build the scan agent, cd into the osirisd directory and type **make**. The Makefile should automatically find all modules and link them into the scan agent executable. You should see something like the following:

```
Making all in modules
./genmods.sh
======================================
Found Scan Agent Modules:

     ==> mod_groups
     ==> mod_hostname
     ==> mod_kmods
     ==> mod_ports
     ==> mod_users
======================================
```

This module is simple; therefore, barring any syntax errors, you should see the Osiris agent build. This newly compiled agent executable has the capability to monitor the hostname for changes.

Testing Your Module

Testing modules is very important; a misbehaving module can seriously impact the overall functionality of a scan agent. To test the basic functionality of a module, verify that the records are received and stored in the database, and verify that the changes are properly detected. In this case, make sure that the database contains a single record containing the value of the hostname. You will then change the hostname and verify that the change triggers an alert.

The best way to test modules is to install a console and a scan agent on a system dedicated for testing. Do not test modules on a production system. After you have implemented and compiled your module and the new agent is running, log in to the management console and create a test scan configuration using *new-config*:

```
osiris-4.1.3: new-config test
```

Add the following code to the test configuration file:

```
<Modules>
Include mod_hostname
</Modules>
```

In this case, you are going to run only the hostname module that you just created. Next, push that configuration to the local agent. Assuming the agent is called local and the configuration is called test:

```
osiris-4.1.3[local]: push-config test
  >>> the configuration: (test) has been pushed to host:  local
```

Next, start the scan using the *scan* command; this should take less than a second. Once complete, look at the database records to see if the hostname record is there:

```
osiris-4.1.3[local]: print-db 1
This may take a while...


100% [=======================================>] 114688 bytes


    h) show database header.
    r) list file records.
    d) list file record details.
    m) list module records.
    x) list errors.
    q) quit


[local:database: 1]: m


[ mod_hostname ]


[hostname][myhost.example.com]
```

In this case, there is the single record sent by the *mod_hostname* module. Next, change the hostname from *myhost* to *myhost2* and run another scan. To view the result of the scan, print out the latest log file. You should see something like the following:

```
osiris-4.1.3[local]: print-log log.temp


-------- begin log file --------


    compare time: Mon Feb 21 15:37:17 2005
            host: local
      scan config: test (aba0a173)
         log file: no log file generated, see system log.
     base database: 1
  compare database: 2


[223][local][cmp][mod_hostname][hostname][myhost.example.com][myhost2.exampl
e.com]
```

```
Change Statistics:
---------------------------------

         checksums: 0
        SUID files: 0
  root-owned files: 0
  file permissions: 0
               new: 0
           missing: 0


total differences: 1


--------  end log file  --------
```

In this case, the testing is simple. If your module is more complicated, you must perform additional tests to make sure that your code is functioning properly. Modules are extensions of the scan agent code, and thus, it is very important that your implementation be well tested. Redistributing scan agents because of a minor bug in a module is not fun. Also, agents are daemons, so problems such as memory leaks will eventually take their toll.

Packaging Your Module

If you are going to distribute your module for public use, make sure you include a README file that explains the functionality of the module, any parameters, and the supported platforms. All that is needed is to tar up the module directory. Make sure you clean the directory of object files first:

```
$ cd src/osirisd/modules/mod_hostname
$ rm *.o
$ cd ..
$ tar cvfz mod_hostname.tar.gz mod_hostname
mod_hostname/
mod_hostname/Makefile
mod_hostname/mod_hostname.c
```

You can also submit Osiris modules to the Osiris developers list (*osiris-devel@lists.shmoo.com*) to be included on the modules download page (http://hostintegrity.com/osiris/modules.html).

General Considerations

There are some limitations with the Osiris module interface. First, the records are basically text records of limited size; thus, any information that you gather from the environment has to be translated into textual form. Second, only the agent functionality is capable of being extended, not the management console. Since the console performs all of the analysis, you are left only with string comparisons of the record data.

Another module issue to consider is that they do not have to generate records. The point of producing records is to store them on the console so that previous states of the host environment can be compared against the current state of the host environment. It may be that you want to write a module to look at some element of the environment for signs of malicious behavior. If nothing is detected, your module does nothing. If you detect something worth noting, however, you can construct a record and make the payload an alert message with the details of what was detected. This would trigger a new record alert, but would also still serve its purpose: to alert the administrator.

Samhain Modules

Like Osiris, some of the functionality of Samhain is implemented as modules. The code is organized in such a way that you can copy an existing module and modify it to suit your purposes. Some examples of this are the code for the kern, the Set User ID (SUID) check, and the UTMP modules.

Developing a module for Samhain is more complicated than developing one for Osiris, the main reason being that writing a Samhain module involves altering many parts of the source tree. The benefit over Osiris is that in addition to being able to extend what gets monitored, you can also control how your module interprets the differences in the collected data. When you develop a module for Samhain, you can also extend the syntax of the *samhainrc* file and add whatever options you want to apply to your module. Writing a module involves four steps:

1. Defining and integrating a function pointer table.
2. Defining a header and implementation file.
3. Defining log message types.
4. Modifying the build system.

All modules are kept in the *src* directory. The log messages are defined in the *include/sh_cat.h* and *src/sh_cat.c* files. Modifying the build system involves modifying *Makefile.in*. It is recommended that you develop your Samhain modules on a test system using a local database file. This makes it easier to verify the contents and discard the database file, if necessary. It is also faster to test your module on a localized setup.

An Example Module: hostname

As with the previous section, you are going to develop a very simple module to monitor a host's hostname. You will use a single parameter, *HostnameCheckInterval*, which will specify the frequency at which the Samhain agent checks the hostname value.

First, define and extend the list of function tables defined in *src/sh_module.c*. Every Samhain module has a function table. The structure for this is *sh_mtype* and is defined in the *include/sh_module.h* file. An array of *sh_mtype* structures is initialized in the *src/sh_module.c* file. The easiest way to define your module's function table is to copy and paste and modify an existing entry in the *modList* array. Your module name is "hostname," therefore, add the following as an entry to *modList* in *src/sh_module.c*:

```
#ifdef SH_USE_HOSTNAME
{
    N_("HOSTNAME"),
    0,
    sh_hostname_init,
    sh_hostname_timer,
    sh_hostname_check,
    sh_hostname_end,
    sh_hostname_null,

    N_("[Hostname]"),
    sh_hostname_table,
},
#endif
```

The first item is the name of the module. The next five items are the names of the functions you are required to define in your module implementation file. Samhain will call these functions as part of the scan cycle. The last two items in the structure are the name of the configuration file heading, and a function table (defined later) for methods to handle any configuration directives you create for this module.

Next, you create a header and implementation file for your module:

```
$ touch src/sh_hostname.c include/sh_hostname.h
```

The header file contains prototypes and the declaration for the configuration table:

```
#ifndef SH_HOSTNAME_H
#define SH_HOSTNAME_H

#include "sh_modules.h"


int sh_hostname_init   (void);
int sh_hostname_timer (time_t tcurrent);
int sh_hostname_check (void);
int sh_hostname_end    (void);
int sh_hostname_null   (void);
int sh_hostname_set_timer (char * c);
int sh_hostname_check_internal();
extern sh_rconf sh_hostname_table[];


#endif
```

The module implementation file is more involved. All of the functions specified in the header file of the preceding example, and some helper functions for storing the hostname in the database are defined. Samhain records are geared toward storing files, so you must be creative. Use the *filepath* element of a record to store the string *K_hostname* as a unique identifier for your hostname record. "K" is specified as the first character of the file path to signal to Samhain that it is not actually a record about a file. Use the *linkpath* field of the record to store the value of the hostname.

The main function here is *sh_hostname_check_internal()*, which is called when the timer for this module fires or whenever a check request is issued. Normally, the *init* and *end* functions are used to initialize and free memory and other created resources; however, this module is so simple, that these functions are basically empty. The two functions used to obtain and store information into the database are *sh_hash_get_it()* and *sh_hash_pushdata()*. The final implementation of *sh_hostname.c* is:

```
#include "config_xor.h"

#include <stdio.h>
#include <stdlib.h>
#include <string.h>
#include <sys/types.h>
#include <sys/stat.h>
#include <fcntl.h>
```

```c
#include <unistd.h>
#include <errno.h>
#include <limits.h>
#include <sys/wait.h>
#include <signal.h>

#undef  FIL__
#define FIL__  _("sh_hostname.c")

#if defined (SH_WITH_CLIENT) || defined (SH_STANDALONE)

#if TIME_WITH_SYS_TIME
#include <sys/time.h>
#include <time.h>
#else
#if HAVE_SYS_TIME_H
#include <sys/time.h>
#else
#include <time.h>
#endif
#endif


#include "samhain.h"
#include "sh_utils.h"
#include "sh_error.h"
#include "sh_modules.h"
#include "sh_hostname.h"
#include "sh_ks_xor.h"

#include "sh_unix.h"
#include "sh_hash.h"
#include "sh_cat.h"

#define HOSTNAME_KEY "K_hostname_0000"
static unsigned char db_hostname[256] = "";

sh_rconf sh_hostname_table[] = {
  {
```

```
    N_("hostnamecheckinterval"),
    sh_hostname_set_timer
  },
  {
    NULL,
    NULL
  },
};


static time_t   lastcheck;
static int      ShHostnameActive   = S_TRUE;
static int      ShHostnameInterval = 300;

int sh_hostname_null()
{
  return 0;
}


int sh_hostname_init ()
{
  SL_ENTER(_("sh_hostname_init"));
  if (ShHostnameActive == S_FALSE)
    SL_RETURN( (-1), _("sh_hostname_init"));

  lastcheck  = time (NULL);
  sh_hostname_check_internal ();
  SL_RETURN( (0), _("sh_hostname_init"));
}


int sh_hostname_end ()
{
  return (0);
}


int sh_hostname_timer (time_t tcurrent)
{
  if ((int) (tcurrent - lastcheck) >= ShHostnameInterval)
    {
      lastcheck  = tcurrent;
```

```
      return (-1);
    }
  return 0;
}


int sh_hostname_check ()
{
        sh_error_handle (-1, FIL__, __LINE__, 0, MSG_HN_CHECK, "checking
hostname" );
  return (sh_hostname_check_internal ());
}


int sh_hostname_set_timer (char * c)
{
  long val;

  SL_ENTER(_("sh_hostname_set_timer"));

  val = strtol (c, (char **)NULL, 10);
  if (val <= 0)
    sh_error_handle ((-1), FIL__, __LINE__, EINVAL, MSG_EINVALS,
                         _("hostname_timer"), c);

  val = (val <= 0 ? 60 : val);

  ShHostnameInterval = (time_t) val;
  SL_RETURN( 0, _("sh_hostnmae_set_timer"));
}


int get_hostname_from_db()
{
    file_type    tmpFile;
    int result = 0;

    result = sh_hash_get_it( HOSTNAME_KEY, &tmpFile);

    if ( result == 0 )
    {
        strcpy( db_hostname, tmpFile.linkpath );
```

```
    }

    else
    {
        db_hostname[0] = '\0';
    }

    return result;
}

void set_hostname_in_db( const char *hostname )
{
    file_type    tmpFile;

    if ( hostname == NULL )
    {
        return;
    }

    strcpy( tmpFile.fullpath, HOSTNAME_KEY );
    strcpy( tmpFile.linkpath, hostname );

    tmpFile.size  = 0;
    tmpFile.mtime = 0;
    tmpFile.ctime = 0;

    tmpFile.atime = 0;
    tmpFile.mode  = 0;
    tmpFile.owner = 0;
    tmpFile.group = 0;
    sl_strlcpy(tmpFile.c_owner, _("root"), 5);
    sl_strlcpy(tmpFile.c_group, _("root"), 5);

      tmpFile.c_mode[0] = 'l';
      tmpFile.c_mode[1] = 'r'; tmpFile.c_mode[2]  = 'w';
      tmpFile.c_mode[3] = 'x'; tmpFile.c_mode[4]  = 'r';
      tmpFile.c_mode[5] = 'w'; tmpFile.c_mode[6]  = 'x';
      tmpFile.c_mode[7] = 'r'; tmpFile.c_mode[8]  = 'w';
      tmpFile.c_mode[9] = 'x'; tmpFile.c_mode[10] = '\0';
```

```
        sh_hash_pushdata( &tmpFile,

_("0000000000000000000000000000000000000000000000000000"));
}

int sh_hostname_check_internal()
{
    char name[255];

    SL_ENTER(_("sh_hostname_check_internal"));

    if ( gethostname( name, sizeof( name ) ) < 0 )
    {
        sh_error_handle (-1, FIL__, __LINE__, 0, MSG_E_SUBGEN,
                _("unable to retrieve system hostname!!")," " );

        return 0;
    }

    if ( sh.flag.update == S_TRUE )
    {
        set_hostname_in_db( name );
        return 0;
    }

    /* get the hostname in the database. */

    if ( get_hostname_from_db() != 0 )
    {
        sh_error_handle (-1, FIL__, __LINE__, 0, MSG_E_SUBGEN,
                _("unable to retrieve hostname from database")," " );

        return 0;
    }

    /* compare here with current. */

    if ( strcmp( name, db_hostname) != 0 )
```

```
        {
            sh_error_handle (-1, FIL__, __LINE__, 0, MSG_HN_DIFF, db_hostname,
    name );
        }


        SL_RETURN( (0), _("sh_hostname_check_internal"));
    }
#endif
```

Next, establish logging identifiers and format strings for your module. Because this is an example, define only two: one for announcing the module execution and one for reporting on detected changes. Most modules have more than two log message types; the log ID is defined in *include/sh_cat.h,* and the actual formats are defined in *src/sh_cat.c.* Add the following to the large enum structure in *include/sh_cat.h*:

```
#ifdef SH_USE_HOSTNAME
  MSG_HN_CHECK,
  MSG_HN_DIFF,
#endif
```

The *src/sh_cat.c* file contains the actual format strings for log messages. There are two large enumerations in this file; one is Extensible Markup Language (XML) formatted, and the other is not. You should add your log messages to both of these enumerations. For the hostname module, add the following to the XML enumeration:

```
#ifdef SH_USE_HOSTNAME
{ MSG_HN_CHECK,      SH_ERR_INFO,      RUN,     N_("msg=<Checking hostname>")},
{ MSG_HN_DIFF,       SH_ERR_WARN,      EVENT, N_("msg=<Hostname>, prev=<%s>,
now=<%s>")},
#endif
```

Then, to the non–XML enumeration, add the following:

```
#ifdef SH_USE_HOSTNAME
{ MSG_HN_CHECK,      SH_ERR_INFO,      RUN,     N_("msg=\"Checking hostname\"")},
{ MSG_HN_DIFF,       SH_ERR_WARN,      EVENT, N_("msg=Hostname
previously=\"%s\" currently=\"%s\"")},
#endif
```

Finally, you have to adjust the build system so that your module is included and compiled into the Samhain executable. To do that, you must (at minimum) edit the *Makefile.in* file and follow these steps:

1. Add *sh_hostname.h* to the HEADERS directive.

2. Add *$(srcsrc)/sh_hostname.c* to the SOURCES directive.

3. Add *sh_hostname.o* to the OBJECTS directive.

4. Add *$(srcinc)/sh_hostname.h* to the dependency list for *sh_modules.o*.

5. Add the following target:

```
sh_hostname.o: $(srcsrc)/sh_hostname.c Makefile config_xor.h
$(srcinc)/samhain.h $(srcinc)/sh_utils.h $(srcinc)/sh_error.h
$(srcinc)/sh_modules.h $(srcinc)/sh_hostname.h sh_ks_xor.h
$(srcinc)/sh_unix.h $(srcinc)/sh_hash.h $(srcinc)/sh_cat.h
```

Issuing a make from the top-level directory should recompile and build your module. It is recommended that you turn off executable checksum verification on Samhain while developing your module, as it can be cumbersome to deal with. Do that by running the configure script again using the **with-checksum** configure option:

```
$ ./configure --with-checksum=no
```

Testing Your Module

Testing Samhain modules is a little easier than testing Osiris modules. It is very important that you do as much testing as possible on your module, no matter what your distribution plans are. Modules are compiled into the Samhain agents; therefore, fixing a development mistake has an unavoidable administrative overhead.

Install and test on a single dedicated testing environment as much as possible (e.g., hostname module). After building and installing the Samhain agent that supports the hostname checking, modify the *samhainrc* configuration file and add the following:

```
[Hostname]
HostnameCheckInterval = 30
```

This will cause the agent to check the hostname every 30 seconds. First, set the hostname to something you can recognize and then perform a database update:

```
# hostname foobar
# samhain -t update
```

This will update the database with the current hostname record. You can verify this by looking at the local Samhain database file:

```
# strings /var/lib/samhain/samhain_file | grep -A 3 "K_hostname"
```

```
K_hostname_0000
foobar
root
wheel
```

You can clearly see that the hostname has been saved in the database *linkpath* entry of the file record. Next, run Samhain again to make sure that the check worked as intended. You should see only the hostname module get initialized:

```
INFO    :  [2005-02-25T14:46:32-0700] msg=<Module initialized>,
module=<HOSTNAME>
```

Next, change the hostname to *smarg*, and run another check. The hostname module will detect this and print out an alert that looks something like:

```
WARN    :  [2005-02-25T14:47:47-0700] msg=<Hostname>, prev=<foobar>,
now=<smarg>
```

Finally, to ensure that the agent properly conducts the hostname check at the interval specified, run it in daemon mode and watch for this same alert to appear a few times at 30-second intervals:

```
NOTICE :   [2005-02-25T14:48:56-0700] msg=<File check completed.>, time=<2>,
           kBps=<21733.504000>
INFO    :  [2005-02-25T14:49:24-0700] msg=<Checking hostname>
WARN    :  [2005-02-25T14:49:24-0700] msg=<Hostname>, prev=<foobar>,
           now=<smarg>
INFO    :  [2005-02-25T14:49:54-0700] msg=<Checking hostname>
WARN    :  [2005-02-25T14:49:54-0700] msg=<Hostname>, prev=<foobar>,
           now=<smarg>
INFO    :  [2005-02-25T14:50:24-0700] msg=<Checking hostname>
WARN    :  [2005-02-25T14:50:24-0700] msg=<Hostname>, prev=<foobar>,
           now=<smarg>
```

Packaging Your Module

Modules for Samhain are not contained in a directory. Packaging the module means packaging the entire modified source tree for custom agent building and distribution. You can modify the source and hard-code your module into Samhain, or you can adjust the proper configure files so that you can turn the module on and off. This adjustment is useful if you ever need to build the agent without the module and do not want to hack source files. To add a configure option, modify *acconfig.h, aclocal.m4,* and *configure.ac*. Add the following to *configure.ac* in the enable features section:

```
AC_ARG_ENABLE(hostname-check,
        [  --enable-hostname-check              check for hostname changes[[no]
]],
        [
        if test "x${enable_hostname_check}" = xyes; then
                AC_DEFINE(SH_USE_HOSTNAME)
        fi
        ]
)
```

This allows you to specify —*enable-hostname-check* a value of either **yes** or **no** to enable or disable the hostname module. For this to work, you must set up its macro that is used throughout the source code. Add the following string to the *SH_ENABLE_OPTS* variable in *aclocal.m4*:

```
hostname-check
```

Finally, add the following to *acconfig.h*:

```
#undef SH_USE_HOSTNAME
```

To rebuild the configure script, do:

```
$ autoheader
$ autoconf
```

If you run the new configure script with the —*help* option, you will see a line that looks like:

```
--enable-hostname-check          check for hostname changes[no]
```

The **--enable-hostname-check** option can now be used to toggle the module from being included in the building of the Samhain agent. More information about Samhain modules can be found online at http://la-samhna.de/samhain/HOWTO-write-modules.html.

Appendix C

Additional Resources

Introduction

Host integrity monitoring intersects many areas of security, including intrusion detection, change management, security administration, and intrusion prevention. To effectively monitor the integrity of your hosts, you must understand them and how they interact with each other. This appendix provides various resources and organizations related to host integrity and computer security in general.

Online Documentation

Osiris
http://hostintegrity.com/osiris/docs/documentation.html

Samhain
www.la-samhna.de/samhain/manual/

Online Publications

Dunston, Duane. "Mass Deploying Osiris"
www.linuxsecurity.com/content/view/101884/49/

Lesko, Matt. "Host-based Intrusion Detection with Samhain"
www.newsforge.com/article.pl?sid=03/07/29/1727249

Wichmann, Rainer. "A Comparison of Host/File Integrity Checkers"
www.la-samhna.de/library/scanners.html

Wichmann, Rainer. "PGP Signatures on Open Source Software and why You Should Check Them"
www.la-samhna.de/library/PGPSignatures.html

Wotring, Brian. "Host Integrity Monitoring: Best Practices for Deployment"
www.securityfocus.com/infocus/1771

Books

Proctor, Paul E. *Practical Intrusion Detection Handbook*. Prentice Hall, 2001

Rash, Michael, Angela Orebaugh, Graham Clark, Becky Pinkard, and Jake Babbin. *Intrusion Detection and Active Response: Deploying Network and Host IPS.* Syngress, 2005
Northcutt, Stephen and Judy Novak. *Network Intrusion Detection*, New Riders, 2002

Beale, Jay, Brian Caswell et al. *Snort 2.1 Intrusion Detection, Second Edition.* Syngress, 2004

Anderson, Ross. *Security Engineering: A Guide to Building Dependable Distributed Systems.* Wiley, 2001

Viega, John, Matt Messier, and Pravir Chandra. *Network Security with OpenSSL.* O'Reilly and Associates, 2002

Korff, Yanek, Paco Hope, and Bruce Potter. *Mastering FreeBSD and OpenBSD Security.* O'Reilly and Associates, 2005

Hoglund, Greg and Gary McGraw. *Exploiting Software How to Break Code.* Addison Wesley, 2004

Krusse, Warren G. II, and Jay G. Heiser. *Computer Forensics Incident Response Essentials*, Addison Wesley, 2002

Farmer, Dan and Wietse Venema. *Forensic Discovery.* Addison Wesley, 2004

Friedl, Jeffrey E. F. *Mastering Regular Expressions.* O'Reilly and Associates, 2002

System Security Resources

FreeBSD Security Information
www.freebsd.org/security/

Mac OS X Security Information
www.apple.com/macosx/features/security/

Microsoft Windows Security Information
www.microsoft.com/security/

NetBSD Security Information
www.netbsd.org/Security/

OpenBSD Security Information
www.openbsd.org/security.html

Sun Security Coordination Team
http://sunsolve.sun.com/pub-cgi/show.pl?target=security/sec

Organizations

CERT Coordination Center
www.cert.org

Forum of Incident Response and Security Teams (FIRST)
www.first.org

Samhain Labs
www.la-samhna.com

Useful Web Sites

Common Vulnerabilities and Exposures
http://cve.mitre.org

Known Goods Database
www.knowngoods.org

Log Analysis Information
www.loganalysis.org

RootKit: The Online RootKit Magazine
www.rootkit.com

Software

Academic Release of Tripwire
http://sourceforge.net/projects/tripwire

Bastille Project
www.bastille-linux.org

Ctool
www.hostintegrity.com/tools/ctool
GnuPG
www.gnupg.org

SWATCH (Simple WATCHer)
http://swatch.sourceforge.net

Mailing Lists

Bugtraq (Security Focus)
www.securityfocus.com/archive/1

Forensics (Security Focus)
www.securityfocus.com/archive/104

Full Disclosure
http://lists.netsys.com/mailman/listinfo/full-disclosure

US–CERT Advisories
majordomo@us–cert.gov

Companies

Host Integrity, Inc.
www.hostintegrity.com

Immunix, Inc.
www.immunix.com

PGP, Inc.
www.pgp.com

Tripwire, Inc.
www.tripwire.com

Index

A

access
   local access attacks, 84–85
   login of users/groups on UNIX, 30–32
   to logs, 113
   to management console, 117–118
   physical access, 117
   UNIX file permissions, 38–41
Access Control Entries (ACE)
   of ACL, 46
   order of in ACL, 47–48
access control lists (ACLs)
   ACE order in, 47–48
   NTFS, 45–47
   registry and, 48
access time (atime) time stamp, 43
access tokens, 67
ACE. See Access Control Entries
ACLs. See access control lists
Active Directory, 33–35
Active Perl, 147, 148
admin password, 176
administration, 110
   See also Osiris, administration of
administrative abuse, 86
administrative negligence, 85–86
administrative overhead
   with HIM system, 12–13
   of Osiris, 131
administrator account, 34
administrator group, 34
administrator password, Beltane, 296–298
administrators
   multiple users on Osiris management
      console and, 232
   SUDO and SU commands for, 32
advanced strategies
   prebinding/prelinking, 352–362
   rogue executables, looking for, 335–342
   scans, unscheduled, 333–335
   SUID/SGID security audits, 328–333
   testing/verification, 343–352
agent executable, 96
agent-based deployment scenario, 7
agents, 15–16
alert filtering, 348–351

alerts
   administrative overhead of HIM system, 13
   Beltane, 301
   from HIM system, auditing, 12
   host environment and, 28
   notifications, planning, 112–113
   See also notifications
alias, 43
allow=<IP>|<HOSTNAME>, 174
Alternate Data Streams, 51–52
American National Standards Institute
      (ANSI) C Compiler, 249, 274
antitampering defenses, Samhain, 136
antivirus software, 81
Apache
   for Beltane, 292, 293–294
   Beltane build/installation and, 295
architecture types
   HIMS deployment planning and, 110–111
   Osiris installer package and, 155
archives
   Osiris scan data, 128
   of scan data, 121
   scan databases, archiving, 202
atime (access time) time stamp, 43
attacks
   internal attack detection with HIM, 19–20
   on nonvolatile memory, 72–73
   subversion of HIM, 14–17
   user/group files and, 30
   See also threats
attributes
   NTFS Alternate Data Streams, 51–52
   of NTFS files, 45
[Attributes] policy, 261
auditing
   advantage of HIM, 18
   host security with, 86
audits
   security audits with Samhain, 243
   SUID/SGID security audits, 328–333, 363
authentication
   Osiris CLI, 179–181
   Osiris components, 126–127
   Osiris management console, 164
   Samhain components, 133–134
   scan agents, 204

401

D

X

Y

Syngress: *The Definition of a Serious Security Library*

Syn·gress (sin-gres): *noun, sing.* Freedom from risk or danger; safety. See *security*.

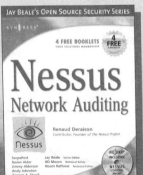